# Singapore

**World Cities Series**

Edited by
Professor R. J. Johnston and Professor P. Knox

Published titles in the series:

Forthcoming titles in the series:

Other titles are in preparation

# Singapore

## A Developmental City State

**Martin Perry**
**Lily Kong**
and
**Brenda Yeoh**
*National University of Singapore*

## JOHN WILEY & SONS

Chichester · New York · Weinheim · Brisbane · Singapore · Toronto

Copyright © 1997 by John Wiley & Sons Ltd,
Baffins Lane, Chichester,
West Sussex PO19 1UD, England

National          01243 779777
International      (+44) 1243 779777
e-mail (for orders and customer service enquiries):
cs-book@wiley.co.uk
Visit our Home Page on http://www.wiley.co.uk
or http://www.wiley.com

*Other Wiley Editorial Offices*

John Wiley & Sons, Inc., 605 Third Avenue,
New York, NY 10158-0012, USA

VCH Verlagsgesellschaft mbH, Pappelallee 3,
D-69469 Weinheim, Germany

Jacaranda Wiley Ltd, 33 Park Road, Milton,
Queensland 4064, Australia

John Wiley & Sons (Canada) Ltd, 22 Worcester Road,
Rexdale, Ontario M9W 1L1, Canada

John Wiley & Sons (Asia) Pte Ltd, 2 Clementi Loop #02-01,
Jin Xing Distripark, Singapore 129809

*Library of Congress Cataloging-in-Publication Data*

Perry, Martin, 1956–
      Singapore : a developmental city state / Martin Perry, Lily Kong and Brenda Yeoh.
         p.   cm. – (World cities series)
      Includes bibliographical references and index.
      ISBN 0-471-97190-1
      1.   Singapore.   I.   Kong, Lily.   II.   Yeoh, Brenda, S. A.
      III.   Title.   IV.   Series.
      DS609.P47   1997
      915.957–dc21                                                                     96-50141
                                                                                              CIP

*British Library Cataloguing in Publication Data*

A catalogue record for this book is available from the British Library

ISBN 0-471-97190-1

Typeset in 10/12pt Palatino from author's disks by Poole Typesetting Ltd, Bournemouth
Printed and bound in Great Britain from PostScript files by Biddles Ltd, Guildford and King's Lynn

This book is printed on acid-free paper responsibly manufactured from sustainable forestation, for which at least two trees are planted for each one used for paper production.

# Contents

# List of figures

# List of tables

# List of plates

# Preface

The purpose of the World Cities Series is to provide an inter-disciplinary introduction to cities of major international significance. As the intended readership of the series is wide, including students and scholars pursuing academic research, consultants compiling in-depth background reports and the serious-minded traveller, the style of the series is to minimise jargon and narrow theoretical debates. As well as through style, consistency is given to the series through attention to a common set of themes related to the city's historical development and changing role in national and international urban systems, demographic patterns, political management of the city and the planning of urban facilities.

In keeping with the spirit of the World Cities Series, we have done more than simply provide an encyclopedia of facts and figures. The book is also concerned to provide a sense of place and give something of an 'insider's' view of the city. Two of the authors have lived most of their lives in Singapore and witnessed some of the enormous changes that have transformed the island during its still comparatively young existence as an independent nation. The third author owes his understanding of Singapore to two periods of employment as an expatriate lecturer in the Department of Geography, National University of Singapore.

The writing of this book has been made simpler by the large amount of attention that researchers have given Singapore particularly over the last two decades. While there are notable exceptions, there is a tendency for some of this literature to be either glowingly congratulatory in its account of the city-state's achievements or excessively critical. This divergence is perhaps understandable in terms of the extent of the change that has overtaken Singapore and the peculiarities of its political management.

Our interpretation attempts to balance the contrasting points of view. We stress the importance of understanding the constraints and vulnerabilities operating on a small city-state that had to build a national identity where none had previously existed. We are also sympathetic to the challenges of adjusting to sudden change in economic and political fortunes, building a standard of living out of all proportion to its regional neighbours. But we recognise that Singapore's transformation is part of the changing structure of the world economy. Its achievements are not simply the product of its leaders' and people's efforts, important though these contributions have been. Finally, we also stress how the development ambition is changing as Singapore enters its so-called *Next Lap*. New priorities have emerged that are intended to promise a technologically sophisticated and gracious urban lifestyle.

As well as the references listed in the bibliography, a number of Singapore government publications and annual reports have provided information for the book. For these sources, where there is no specific author, we have generally cited the publication title in the text as an alternative to duplicating the reference in the bibliography. Two publications that readers may wish to consult to update information are *Singapore*, an annual publication of the Ministry of Information and the Arts and the *Yearbook of Statistics*, published annually by the Department of Statistics. Singapore's main English language daily newspaper *The Straits Times* is frequently cited as a source, reflecting how this newspaper is the main outlet for official news. Government departments tend not to issue their own reports where they can rely on *The Straits Times* for this purpose, which explains our reliance on this source. Unless otherwise stated, all currency figures refer to Singapore dollars (see statistical summary for exchange rate in 1996).

While the book is jointly authored, individual authors have taken primary responsibility for individual chapters. Martin Perry is responsible for Chapters 1, 3, 5 and 6; Lily Kong for Chapters 4, 8 and 10 and Brenda Yeoh for Chapters 2, 7 and 9. We gratefully acknowledge Warwick Neville (Figures 6.1, 6.4–6.6), Michael Hilton and Sarah Manning (Figure 6.3) for access to their original drawings of figures which we have included in Chapter 6. We are also indebted to the Department of Geography cartographers, Mrs Lee Li Kheng and Mrs Chong Mui Gek, for their assistance in drawing the figures for this volume.

Martin Perry, Lily Kong and Brenda Yeoh
*Singapore, September 1996*

# Abbreviations

| | |
|---|---|
| APU | Anti-pollution Unit |
| ARF | Additional registration fee |
| ASEAN | Association of Southeast Asian Nations |
| CAAS | Civil Aviation Authority of Singapore |
| CC | Community Centre |
| CCC | Citizens Consultative Committee |
| COE | Certificate of entitlement |
| CPF | Central Provident Fund |
| CPTE | Council for Professional and Technical Education |
| DGP | Development Guide Plan |
| EDB | Economic Development Board |
| EIA | Environmental impact assessment |
| ENV | Ministry of Environment |
| FDI | Foreign direct investment |
| GIC | Government of Singapore Investment Corporation |
| GLC | Government linked corporation |
| GPC | Government Parliamentary Committee |
| GRC | Group Representation Constituency |
| GRR | Gross reproduction rate |
| HDB | Housing and Development Board |
| HUDC | Housing and Urban Development Corporation |
| JTC | Jurong Town Corporation |
| LTA | Land Transport Authority |
| MAS | Monetary Authority of Singapore |
| MENDAKI | Council for the Development of Muslims in Singapore |
| MIA | Ministry of Information and the Arts |

| | |
|---|---|
| MTI | Ministry of Trade and Industry |
| MRT | Mass rapid transit |
| NCB | National Computer Board |
| NCMP | Non-constituency Member of Parliament |
| NGO | Non-government organisation |
| NHB | National Heritage Board |
| NMP | Nominated Member of Parliament |
| NPB | National Productivity Board |
| NSS | Nature Society of Singapore |
| NSTB | National Science and Technology Board |
| NTP | National Technology Plan |
| NTUC | National Trades Union Congress |
| NWC | National Wages Council |
| OHQ | Operational headquarters |
| PA | People's Association |
| PAP | People's Action Party |
| PARF | Preferential additional registration fee |
| PCD | Pollution Controls Department |
| PMB | Preservation of Monuments Board |
| PSA | Port of Singapore Authority |
| PSB | Productivity and Standards Board |
| PWD | Public Works Department |
| PUB | Public Utilities Board |
| RC | Residents' Committee |
| SDF | Skills Development Fund |
| SDU | Social Development Unit |
| SERS | Selective *En Bloc* Redevelopment Scheme |
| SFPPB | Singapore Family Planning and Population Board |
| SISIR | Singapore Institute of Standards and Industrial Research |
| SIT | Singapore Improvement Trust |
| SME | Small and medium-sized enterprise |
| STDB | Singapore Trade Development Board |
| STPB | Singapore Tourist Promotion Board |
| SMRT | Singapore Mass Rapid Transport |
| TAS | Telecommunication Authority of Singapore |
| TEU | Twenty-foot equivalent unit |
| TNC | Transnational corporation |
| URA | Urban Redevelopment Authority |

# Statistical summary

*General*

| | |
|---|---|
| Land area (1995) | 646.1 – km$^2$ |
| Population (mid-1994) | 2 930 200 |
| share of Chinese | 77.4% |
| share of Malays | 14.2% |
| share of Indians | 7.1% |
| Annual resident population increase | 2.0% |
| Share of population 60 years and over | 9.7% |
| Labour force in employment (1994) | 1 649 296 |
| Women's share of labour force | 36% |
| Labour force participation rate (1994) | 64.9% |
| male participation rate | 79.6% |
| female participation rate | 50.9% |
| Unemployment rate (1994) | 2.6% |

*Economy*

| | |
|---|---|
| Exchange rate (mid-1996) | US$1.41 |
| GDP (1994) | $105 313 million |
| share of agriculture | 0.2% |
| share of manufacturing | 26.9% |
| share of construction | 7.5% |
| share of commerce | 17.0% |
| share of transport and communications | 12.0% |
| share of financial and business services | 29.5% |
| Resident foreigners' and resident foreign companies' contribution to GDP (1994) | $31 624 million |

| | |
|---|---|
| Indigenous GDP (1994) | $73 624 million |
| GNP (1994) | $104 879 million |
| Indigenous GNP (1994) | $84 448 million |
| Per capita indigenous GNP (1994) | $28 820 million |
| Real GDP annual growth rate 1986-1994 | 8.2% |
| Gross domestic savings (% of GDP) 1994 | 51.3% |
| Scientists and technicians per 1000 people 1988–1992 | 1.8 |
| R&D expenditure (% of GDP) 1994 | 1.12 |

*Quality of life*

| | |
|---|---|
| Earnings per employee annual growth rate 1980–1991 | 5.0% |
| Male life expectancy (1994) | 74.4 years |
| Female life expectancy (1994) | 78.4 years |
| Persons per doctor (1994) | 666 |
| Persons per public bus (1994) | 285 |
| Persons per car (private and company owned) (1994) | 9.1 |
| Persons per residential telephone line (1994) | 3.5 |
| Daily newspapers, copies per 100 people (1992) | 34 |
| Population (%) living in HDB flats | 86% |
| Population living in owner-occupied public flats | 80% |
| Adult literacy rate (1992) | 89.9% |
| Income distribution | |
| lowest 40% of households 1981–1992 | 15.0% |
| ratio of highest 20% to lowest 20% 1981–1992 | 9.6 |
| Public expenditure on | |
| education as % of 1990 GNP | 3.4% |
| health as % of 1990 GNP | 1.1% |
| Military expenditure as % of combined education and health expenditure 1990–91 | 129% |

*Sources:*
Department of Statistics, *Yearbook of Statistics 1994*, Singapore.
Ministry of Information and the Arts, *Singapore 1995*, Singapore.
United Nations Development Programme, *Human Development Report 1995*, Oxford University Press, New York.

# 1

# Global processes and a developmental city state

Singapore as an independent city-state is a young country. It acquired self-governing status from Britain in 1959 and became an independent republic in 1965, having spent the intermediate years under transitional control or as part of the Malaysian Federation. While the modern development of Singapore can be traced back to the early part of the nineteenth century, when British interests acquired the island as a trading outlet for the Malay peninsula, its post-independence economic growth has been built on new roles. Singapore is now a world city whose fate is dependent on events in New York, London, Tokyo and connected nodes in the international economy. Its trading, investment and information links to distant countries are far more important than those to its immediate regional neighbours. This global orientation is strikingly illustrated by the contrasting international gateways to Singapore. As a small island state lying at the southern end of the Malay Peninsula (Figure 1.1), international visitors arrive through one of three routes, each of which provides a different lens on Singapore.

The business traveller and international tourist is most likely to arrive through Changi Airtropolis, as local officials style their international airport. The airport is regularly chosen in business traveller polls as the best worldwide. With the aid of modern technology and efficient organisation, arriving passengers can be in a taxi within half an hour of landing and, because of stringent controls on private car ownership, within an hour of landing, the business executive can be checking into a downtown hotel. In 1994, Singapore was linked by 66 airlines to 124 cities in 56 countries

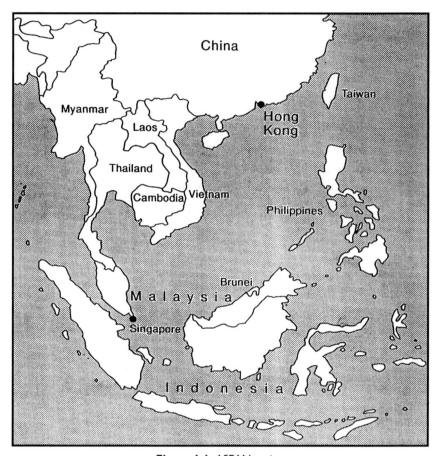

**Figure 1.1** ASEAN region

with more than 2800 weekly scheduled flights. This linkage continues to grow. Plans are in place to expand passenger handling capacity by a third in the early years of the next century. Efficiency and the web of linkages around the globe have been key components in Singapore's modern economic success.

In comparison with the smooth organization of international air travel, the causeway crossing to the southern Malaysian state of Johor is often chaotic. Around 50 000 persons a day use this crossing, as well as it being a major artery for freight transport. At peak times traffic commonly backs up for several kilometres as traffic queues to squeeze over the single crossing which was constructed originally in 1923. The failure of the causeway capacity to keep pace with demand, and the slowness in commencing a second crossing (construction of a road bridge linking Tuas in the west of Singapore with Johor started in 1995, 25 years after Singapore had proposed its need to Malaysia (Regnier, 1991, p. 152)), can mainly be explained by the suspicion with which Malaysian authorities have viewed their smaller but wealthier neighbour. The constraints on closer integration result in a sharp economic disjunction along the border zone. Singapore has a standard of living that is the third highest in Asia, after Japan and Brunei, while per capita incomes in Malaysia are 75% lower (Asian Development Bank, 1994). The difference in economic well being is heightened by Singapore's role as the control and communication centre for Southeast Asia, resulting in a sharp contrast in the availability and quality of modern communication technologies and other aspects of urban infrastructure.

The third crossing point to Singapore is via ferry from the nearby Riau islands of Indonesia (Figure 1.2). While the closest island is within 30 minutes by ferry, travel and linkages across this border zone are minimal in comparison with other entry routes to Singapore. Since the 1970s, Indonesian planners have thought that the Riau islands of Batam and Bintan, as the nearest to Singapore, could provide land and labour for uses linked to the city state. The Indonesian Minister for Research and Technology, Dr D. J. Habibie, developed his 'balloon theory' to support this case, arguing that Singapore's economy had limited capacity and would burst if it did not have safety valves to draw off some of the excess growth (Grundy-Warr and Perry, 1996). Until the 1990s, despite sustained economic expansion, Singapore showed little need to make use of this safety valve. Despite some greater economic integration with Johor, generally investment has dispersed widely reflecting the location capability of the multinational corporations that dominate Singapore's economic space. It is only in the 1990s that connections between Singapore and the Riau islands have grown. In a project which became known as the 'growth triangle' (see Chapter 7), Singaporean investment is building industrial estates and leisure facilities on several islands. Other island sites are being developed to meet additional needs of land-scarce Singapore, including an island devoted to pig and other animal rearing and another to heavy marine industry and oil storage, and there is a long-term project to pipe water from mainland Sumatra via the Riau.

A ferry journey from the Riau terminates in the world's second busiest port (measured by shipping tonnage) and close to a petrochemical complex that fills several small islands and part of the adjoining southwest corner of Singapore. While the airport symbolises the modern economy of international business executives and mobile professionals, this routeway links Singapore to its historic importance as a major maritime crossroads for international trade. In the nineteenth century, Singapore developed as

**Figure 1.2** Singapore's border zone

a free port under British control. After the opening of the Suez canal in 1869, Singapore became the premier staging post in Southeast Asia and the intermediary between European traders and the indigenous population of the region. The wealth generated from this role faded with the gradual demise of Britain's economic power during the twentieth century. The reinvigoration of its trading function commenced in the 1960s with the development of Southeast Asia as a major centre of manufacturing activity supplying markets around the globe. The old trade in raw materials has been taken over by the trade in processed and manufactured goods, much of it comprising components and partly assembled items being distributed within the production networks of multinational corporations. It has also broadened geographical linkages to include North America, Japan, Germany, Korea and Taiwan as major trading partners. Singapore is now the world's twelfth biggest exporter and thirteenth largest importer. The historic role as Southeast Asia's entrepôt remains important, but in 1994 re-exports (a classification used within Singapore's trade statistics giving an approximate measure of entrepôt activity) accounted for less than 20% of Singapore's total external trade (*Yearbook of Statistics 1994*), a fall of over half from 1960 (Regnier, 1991, p. 37).

Singapore has shared an economic transformation from developing country, to newly industrializing economy, to its present status of 'advanced industrializing nation' with the other 'Asian tiger' economies of Hong Kong, South Korea and Taiwan. For over a quarter of a century from the 1960s, the 'tiger economies' maintained the highest rate of GNP growth in the world, in the process winning substantial shares of the world market economy and substantially transforming their economic and social conditions. The coincidental emergence of these economies is partly explained by their similar developmental experiences and the historical context in which their growth took off (Henderson and Appelbaum, 1992). A colonial legacy left an inheritance that proved supportive of future growth, through its impact in developing efficient systems of government administration, establishing trade networks and building industrial capacity and infrastructure.

The initial industrialization of the East Asian growth economies further benefited from the unprecedented expansion in world trade in the late 1950s and through the 1960s. The sustained 'long boom' in the industrial world provided space for newcomers that did not previously exist and, some suggest, has never subsequently existed to the same degree. When that boom was followed by the general economic slowdown during the 1970s, the newly industrializing economies obtained a further boost. This was the period when a new international division of labour took shape as assembly capacity in industries such as textiles, garments and electronics, that were able to take advantage of comparatively low cost, plentiful and unorganised labour, shifted to the newly industrializing economies (Frobel *et al.*, 1980). Since this common beginning, the 'tiger economies' have tended to pursue divergent paths with Singapore increasingly carving its niche as a regional control and service centre, rather than as a manufacturing powerhouse.

## Singapore as a developmental state

Whatever the economic success attained, the political style of Singapore's leadership is to cultivate a continual sense of crisis and urgency amongst the population. While much fragility has surrounded Singapore's rapid transformation, maintaining a permanent state of insecurity has helped keep the state free from the challenge of alternative agendas, minimizing the impediments to economic development. Such an approach to political management is another characteristic shared with the newly industrialized Asian economies. For South Korea a threat is perceived from the north, for Taiwan and Hong Kong it is the uncertainty of the relationship with the People's Republic of China, while in Singapore the most frequently cited insecurity derives from it being a Chinese city in a Malay-dominated region (Grice and Drakakis-Smith, 1985, p. 357). As regional relations have improved and affluence has grown, so the state has stressed the continued importance of upgrading the economy and the dangers of complacently settling for present levels of prosperity (Birch, 1993).

As part of its sacrifice for Singapore's economic achievements the population has accepted extensive curbs on the individual freedoms western society tends to emphasize. In the workplace, union activity is government-controlled through the need for affiliation to the National Trade Union Congress, which is headed by a government minister and run by government-linked officials. In the home, citizens are instructed on family size, the timing of household formation and child birth, the language they ought to speak, are compulsorily required to save a fifth of their income and, since 1996, to financially support their parents in old age. Choice of residential location and tenure are controlled by state regulations and for most of the population there is no possibility of owning freehold property (owner-occupiers of new public housing buy a 99-year lease). In the public arena, the access to a free press is constrained by the controls on the circulation of foreign news publications and the government's control of local media. Political debate is expected to be channelled through government-controlled agencies or officially-registered political parties that are not offered the same opportunities as the ruling People's Action Party (PAP) (Chan, 1987, p. 147). In addition to these and many other controls on individual freedom, citizens are frequently admonished on how to behave through government campaigns on issues such as littering, courtesy and public and personal hygiene.

The ability of the government to exercise such tight control of society, and the basis on which the population accepts this direction, have been central to Singapore's economic success. The description of Singapore as a 'developmental state' provides perhaps the most widely accepted interpretation of how these conditions have been obtained and sustained. According to Castells (1992, p. 56) a state is developmental when:

> . . . it establishes as its principle of legitimacy its ability to promote and sustain development, understanding by development the combination of steady high rates of economic growth and structural change in the productive system, both domestically and in its relationship to the international economy.

Two important ideas are linked to the application of such developmental status to Singapore. First, that the state gives much greater priority to transforming economic conditions than it does to changing aspects of the social order. Respect of the broad parameters of the inherited social structure helps retain popular acceptance of the state's economic programmes. Second, economic development attains high status because it is both a means to larger goals, as well as being an end in itself. These greater objectives in Singapore, as in the other Asian growth economies, have been to ensure the survival of the country and to break away from their previous dependency on former colonial authorities. The developmental state is thus engaged in a two-stage project. The first is to marshall resources and societal cohesion around the pursuit of survival. The second is to gradually assert its own cultural and political identity, so as to confirm its break from dependency and to reaffirm national confidence in its political direction.

While Castells may exaggerate when describing Singapore as a 'nonentity' on its independence in 1965 (see Huff, 1994), it undoubtedly faced challenges to the survival of the state as a viable social, economic and political entity. Three major challenges provided the conditions out of which Singapore's developmental state emerged:

1. *Regional isolation:* the PAP, which has ruled Singapore since independence, had invested considerable effort in obtaining popular support for their strategy of joining the Federation of Malaysia. Only as part of this larger territory was it thought that the island had a viable economic future. Singapore however was treated with great suspicion and perceived as a threat by the governments of Malaysia, Indonesia and Thailand. In each of these countries, the urban economy was dominated by minority overseas Chinese groups with well-established links to Singapore's trading houses (Grice and Drakakis-Smith, 1985, p. 351). In

the case of Malaysia, fear about economic subordination was accentuated by the PAP's successful participation in Malaysian elections after the Federation came into being. The PAP's campaign for a 'Malaysian Malaysia' stood opposed to the wish of Malaysia's leadership to build a new state around a Malay culture and language (Hill and Lian, 1995, p. 92). Singapore's ejection from the Federation in 1965 as a result of this conflict of interest, and the so-called confrontation between Singapore, Malaysia and Indonesia from 1963–1966, ended any immediate prospects for regional economic cooperation. The isolation of the new state was further underlined by the closure of Britain's military bases on the island over the period 1968–1971. As well as the loss of security, this was also a serious economic blow as the bases accounted for around 20% of GDP and 6% of employment.

2. *National identity:* prior to 1965 Singapore citizenship, first introduced in 1957, had limited meaning as aliens were free to work and own businesses and property in Singapore. Singapore's population included large numbers of immigrants with little attachment to the island and only a few longer-settled residents had contemplated the possibility of an independent Singapore. Immigration and custom controls at the causeway did not exist prior to 1965 from when the urgent task of nation building began. To create a society collectively focused on development two challenges had to be overcome. First, developing a shared commitment amongst the three major ethnic communities – Malay, Indian (mainly Tamil) and Chinese – under the majority rule of the Chinese who comprised around three quarters of the population. Second, redirecting the loyalty of the Chinese population away from dialect, clan and family associations, linked to an individual's ties to China and reinforced within Singapore by the activities of business and social organizations and the territorial separation of communities with different affinities (Cheng, 1985).

3. *Political division:* the PAP had originally risen to power as a socialist party, but with its dominant elements, led by Lee Kuan Yew, comprising a more conservative element, they had used the socialist banner as a way of maximizing their support and uniting the population in the pursuit of independence from Britain (Bellows, 1970; Hill and Lian, 1995). Once in power, the PAP had to assert the supremacy of their political vision against its former socialist allies. When the latter defected, to form a separate party, the PAP saw a serious threat of communist insurrection. The systematic anticommunist repression it saw as necessary was sometimes extended to other opponents. While Singapore had been part of a Federation with Malaysia, the Federation was the jurisdiction responsible for detaining left-wing leaders. After

independence the PAP government took charge which meant taking action against some Chinese-controlled institutions linked to socialist infiltration.

To tackle these challenges the PAP constructed a strong state apparatus and put it to work through the implementation of a new policy agenda, in which economic development was given highest priority. This has been referred to as the 'ideology of survival' in which economic and political survival were seen as inseparable with all other considerations secondary (Chan, 1971).

The emphasis on building a strong state and delivering rapid economic growth are consistent with the model of a developmental state. In the case of Singapore, a strong state was brought about through several mechanisms. Political control was concentrated within a single tier of parliament, eliminating municipal administration, and within the ruling PAP there was a further centralization of power upon 200 most trusted party members. The public service was politicized and drawn into close alliance with the PAP, both by exposing senior administrators to party ideology and by establishing a network of community-based organizations under the control of the Prime Minister's office (Hill and Lian, 1995, p. 23). During its initial rise to power, the PAP liquidated all serious political opposition, making use of special emergency measures in 1961–63, and subsequently took control of the trade union movement. Although there is no longer a serious threat of communal insurrection or communist infiltration, the state has retained authority to detain indefinitely individuals suspected of 'subversive activity' and continues to restrain the freedom of the press. Vigilance in attacking every sign of opposition, on the grounds of it risking the city state's prosperity and stability, is relentlessly employed, helped by the fragmentation of opposition parties.

The economic programme launched by the PAP brought immediate results compared with the limited development that had occurred in the last years of the former colonial administration. This was helped by the existence of a development plan completed in 1961, which, although designed under the expectation that Singapore would be part of the Malaysian Federation, had recognised the necessity of developing an independent economic role (Rodan, 1989, p. 64). The plan had been based on a United Nations Industrial Survey Mission, headed by Albert Winsemius, which had developed a set of proposals for industrialization out of the recognition that entrepôt trade and banking, the traditional mainstays of the economy, would not provide adequate employment for the growing population. Key elements of the industrialization strategy recommended by Winsemius included: control of wage costs and workforce behaviour;

provision of serviced industrial estates in close proximity to sources of labour; the upgrading of technical education; taxation incentives and the free remittance of capital. After separation, with some realignment of taxation incentives to focus on export-orientated manufacturing and legislation to control trade union activity, Singapore proved to be spectacularly successful in bringing in foreign investment. In 1968 the first electronics companies opened and as others followed over the next four years the manufacturing sector doubled in size. Subsequent adjustments in economic strategy have taken place, to match changing opportunities and priorities, but the key role of the state in supporting and directing economic activity remains.

Economic development, of course, is a priority in all types of country. The developmental state is distinguished through the absolute prioritizing of economic growth and its use as a prime indicator of government performance. In the case of Singapore, some indicators of the status of economic development, which are explained more fully in later chapters, are: the reallocation of land use in ways that have given maximum flexibility to economic development; the absence, or at least minimization of development controls whether, for example, in the form of performance requirements on foreign investors or the preparation of environment impact statements; the status of state economic agencies and administrators and the coordination of planning at the highest levels of government; the privileging of national economic performance over issues of income distribution; the continuous fine tuning and multiplication of incentives and economic programmes, based partly on the detailed monitoring of industry needs and development intentions.

Rapid economic growth and attendant social transformation added substantially to the prestige of the PAP and ensured popular acceptance of its political programme. This was further encouraged by the PAP's tendency to 'keep up an atmosphere of psychosis, in direct relation to the perpetual challenges of shaky external events' (Regnier, 1991, p. 230). Retention of the developmental state has also depended on various initiatives designed to build the cohesion of society, of which three important components have been:

1. A public housing programme which resulted in the proportion of the population occupying public housing growing from 9.1% to 34.6% 1960–1970 and then to over 80% in the 1990s. The public housing programme delivered an improved living environment for those moved out of the more derelict and congested parts of the city. It also provided a means of encouraging home ownership, an important priority to reduce the sense of transiency which continued after independence

(Ong, 1989, p. 937). House purchase is the main pre-retirement use that can be made of the Central Provident Fund (CPF) account that each employed person is required to build up from compulsory savings contributions taken out of wages. Through the use of CPF, the rate of home ownership in the public sector has grown to around 80% of households, and in so doing has given individuals assets 'one would stand to defend' (Wong and Yeh, 1985, p. 231).

2. A network of 'parapolitical' institutions (Hill and Lian, 1995), funded by government but linked to the PAP, provide community-based facilities and participation forums. These are managed by 'grassroots' leaders, appointed by the Prime Minister's Office, whose role is also to capture local political debate and channel community views back to government.

3. Public campaigns and programmes designed to change behaviour in respect of issues which at particular points of time have been viewed as important to national development. From 1958 to 1982, 66 campaigns were launched on themes including productivity, courtesy, public transport, public hygiene, personal health, speaking Mandarin, moral values, family planning, energy use and looking after elderly parents (Regnier, 1991, p. 241). One of the most recent and ambitious campaigns has tried to promote acceptance of five 'shared values' to form the basis of a national ideology transcending ethnic, religious and political affinities.

Collectively these three forms of intervention blend elements of control, reform and reward in support of the goal of replacing attitudes or practices by a more disciplined and uniform society.

An unanswered question about the developmental state is its capacity for survival. The attempt to control wide aspects of social activity is having to confront a new generation of Singaporeans, born into relative material wealth and for whom national survival does not have the same meaning as for those who directly lived through the uncertainty of early nationhood. It must also confront a widening economic gulf between those on low incomes who remain dependent on public services and an affluent middle class who live outside the managed environment of a public housing estate, the majority in self-contained condominiums walled-off from the neighbouring community. Any cracks in the developmental state however remained hard to detect in the mid-1990s. Although the PAP's share of the national vote has declined since the election of the first post-independence opposition MP in 1981, its hold on political power is not threatened. Moreover, in the early 1990s political control was passed successfully to a 'new guard' of leaders in the PAP, without the prestige of being responsible for independence. Partly to smooth this transition, careful adjustments to the political system and mechanisms of social control have been made and new campaigns launched to consolidate the developmental state. These innovations are given fuller consideration in our review of government and politics (Chapter 3).

## World city formation

World cities are generally envisaged as sites primarily for the development, production and supply of financial and business services to global markets, rather than being service centres for their domestic or regional hinterland (Friedmann, 1986). A global hierarchy to the formation of world cities is recognized according to the extent to which the city is orientated to global rather than regional financial and business service markets. At the apex of the world city formation, London and New York have the greatest concentration of international banks and related services and control the most important financial markets. At the lowest tier in the hierarchy, third-ranked cities are linked to global markets, but act mainly as regional financial centres.

Within the world city hierarchy, Singapore is ranked in the second tier, amongst those aspiring for 'superleague' status. Collectively the 25 international centres within the world city hierarchy effectively control almost all the world's financial transactions, as well as being the principal control points for a high proportion of the world's largest multinational corporations (Dicken, 1992). Reflecting their role in servicing international transactions, the distribution of world cities is seen to be shaped by their ability to integrate overlapping time zones to enable continuous round-the-clock trading in financial markets (Daly, 1984; Langdale, 1985). True 24-hour trading is currently limited to only a few types of financial trading, but the expectation is that it will become standard in 'virtually all kinds of financial service' (Dicken, 1992).

Reflecting these characteristics, the emergence of world cities has been connected to three developments in the international economy: (i) the greater size and velocity of world capital flows; (ii) the increased need for centralized command and control posts within a decentralized world economy; (iii) the extensive technical infrastructure needed by the finance and business service industries (Fainstein, 1994, p. 27). These processes provide the context for Singapore's capture of world city status.

Up to the 1950s, the major international transactions were related to trade, concentrated in raw materials, other primary products and resource-based manufacturing. In the 1980s, the gap between the growth rate of exports and that of financial flows widened sharply through the greater acceleration of the latter. This growth arises from the expansion of foreign direct investment (FDI), foreign currency and other forms of financial and service transaction (Sassen, 1991; Hirst and Thompson, 1996). For instance, from 1983 to 1990 FDI flows expanded at an average annual rate of 34% compared with an annual rate of 9% for global merchandise trade (OECD, 1992, p. 12). Many factors have fuelled the growth of FDI: several developed countries became major capital exporters, most substantially Japan; the number of cross-border mergers and acquisitions increased as the impetus to construct transnational business organizations has grown; services emerged as a new source of substantial FDI, doubling their share of the total stock of FDI from the early 1970s to the end of the 1980s. FDI has had a multiplier impact on financial transactions through the development of intrafirm trade, which now accounts for a third of the United States international trade (UNCTC, 1991), and the financial flows generated by their activity.

The emergence of new financial instruments such as 'swaps' (exchanges of debt), 'junk bonds' (high interest bearing notes issued by companies), 'index futures' (agreements to purchase stocks at a future date) and 'debt securitization' (the bundling of loans into tradeable investments) provided a second stimulus to the acceleration of international transactions. Much of this innovation was made possible by the deregulation of financial markets which allowed new innovative organizations into the previously controlled world of international banking.

Corporate head offices and business services have swelled to finance and service the growth of FDI. Rather than becoming obsolete because of the dispersal made possible by information technologies, cities are strengthened by the need for spatial concentration amongst command and business service activities (Sassen, 1991). Only a few places offer a pool of sophisticated personnel, technological capabilities and consultant services sufficient to enable the direction and integration of decentralized business organizations. Places with these capabilities benefit from the growing service intensity in the organization of industry. Whether in manufacturing or distribution, firms are using more legal, financial, advertising, consulting and financial services, in proportion to the growing concentration of industrial activity in fewer, larger organizations (Marshall *et al.*, 1988). These services can operate at a distance from their customers, but the nature of their production process is such that proximity between service suppliers remains important. The production of a financial instrument, for example, requires inputs from accounting, advertising, legal services, economic consulting, public relations, design and printing. Moreover, the lifestyle needs and expectations of the people likely to be employed in skilled professional work tends to require the amenities of a large city, which further encourages the concentration of service production.

Technology is a contributor to global city formation through the way it has tended to reinforce the concentration of business service functions. The expansion in financial and advanced business services depended on the development of technology adequate to handle the soaring volume of transactions. As only a few centres generate a sufficient density of transactions to support the technology infrastructure that has developed, a spiralling process of concentration has tended to ensue (Fainstein, 1994, p. 32). Businesses reliant on information retrieval and processing require a heavily backed-up communications grid and a pool of technical personnel to operate and maintain equipment, as well as modern office accommodation to facilitate information technology usage (Daniels and Bobe, 1993). Air transport facilities are also critical to the functioning of the world city network to the extent that they have been considered the 'most visible manifestation of world city interaction' (Keeling, 1995, p. 118). This reflects how air transport is the necessary mode of intercity travel for business managers as well as for an increasing proportion of high value, low bulk freight.

As well as these shared influences on their growth, world cities can be distinguished by a distinctive employment structure. The rapid growth of the financial industry and of highly specialized services has generated highly-remunerated technical and managerial employment as well as a dependence on low-paid unskilled jobs (Sassen, 1991). Thus, to go back to the example of the production of a financial instrument, this calls on a variety of occupations, including secretaries, office maintenance workers, cleaners and fast food sellers. In addition, the consumption preferences of high-income professionals can multiply the generation of low paid work through demands for leisure and entertainment, household services and customized goods, for example, fashion clothes and furnishings produced by small firms through subcontracting and possibly homework. Gentrification of inner city housing areas, combined with redevelopment for commercial space, can add to the marginalization of low income groups. It can push them out of central residential areas, requiring greater travel to work and problems gaining access to services such as child care (Rose and Chicoine, 1991). Immigration into the city, especially illegal foreign migration, and the loss of a former manufacturing base to the urban economy are two factors which tend to accentuate the polarization of lifestyles by increasing the competition for low paid work.

Singapore as a world city

The processes encouraging world city formation are abundantly evident in Singapore, although its urban experience also retains an individual identity. The distinctiveness can in part be traced to Singapore's existence as a city state under the tight control of a developmental regime. These particular patterns and processes form much of the content of subsequent chapters. This introductory section continues by briefly reviewing some indicators of the island's world city status and some of its individual character.

Singapore's economy has grown through it becoming a major recipient of FDI. It is a small island of less than three million citizens and permanent residents, but throughout the 1980s and into the early 1990s, Singapore attracted over 10% of all FDI received by destinations outside the OECD (UNCTAD, 1994, pp. 13–15). Measured by the number of affiliates of foreign transnational corporations present, Singapore is now a major world site of international business (Table 1.1). Indeed as measured by share of GDP, Singapore is amongst the most internationalized economies in the world (Table 1.2). In 1989, almost 95% of the stock of FDI originated from industrialized nations, almost equally divided between North American, Japanese and European owners (UNCTC, 1992, p. 19). This was a marked change from the 1970s when investment from neighbouring countries had been a much larger share of its foreign-owned sector. In total, branches and affiliates of foreign multinationals accounted directly for 70% of Singapore's exports and 40% of its employment in the early 1990s.

One factor assisting Singapore's predominance in FDI statistics is the attraction of highly capital intensive petrochemical activities: these accounted for almost a third of cumulative FDI in 1989 (Low *et al.*, 1993, p. 449). The continuous upgrading of foreign operations has also been important. Recent years have seen a qualitative shift in the nature of FDI as the island has grown from an offshore manufacturing base to a regional control and coordination centre.

Two influences lie behind the transformation in activity. The first of these processes was the emergence of a 'regional focus' in the corporate strategy of many multinational corporations. This resulted in the decentralization of an extended range of business functions to enable fuller exploitation of the regional market than had previously been attempted. The original focus for investment – low production costs – has not disappeared as a consequence of this strategic change, rather it has changed the use made of different locations. The second and related process is the regional decentralization of foreign investment to nearby countries in

**Table 1.1**  Number of parent transnational corporations and foreign affiliated area and country (variable years)

| | Parent corporations resident | Foreign affiliates resident | Year |
|---|---|---|---|
| All developed countries | 34 353 | 93 331 | |
| *Select countries* | | | |
| Australia | 732 | 2450 | 1994 |
| Canada | 1447 | 4475 | 1993 |
| France | 2216 | 7097 | 1993 |
| Germany | 7003 | 11 396 | 1993 |
| Italy | 445 | 1474 | 1993 |
| Japan | 3650 | 3433 | 1993 |
| Netherlands | 1608 | 2259 | 1993 |
| New Zealand | 247 | 1717 | 1993 |
| Sweden | 3700 | 6150 | 1993 |
| Switzerland | 3000 | 4000 | 1985 |
| United Kingdom | 1443 | 3376 | 1992 |
| United States | 2966 | 16 491 | 1992 |
| All developing countries | 3788 | 101 139 | |
| *Select countries* | | | |
| China | 379 | 45 000 | 1993 |
| Hong Kong | 500 | 2828 | 1991 |
| Indonesia | 313 | 3472 | 1995 |
| Mexico | – | 8420 | 1993 |
| Philippines | – | 1952 | 1987 |
| South Korea | 1049 | 3671 | 1991 |
| Singapore | – | 10 709 | 1986 |
| Taiwan | – | 5733 | 1990 |
| World | 38 541 | 251 450 | |

*Source:* UNCTAD (1995, p. 8)

pursuit of less constrained manufacturing environments than are now found in Singapore, particularly in terms of labour and land availability. Under these twin processes, an ASEAN division of labour has emerged in which Singapore has assumed importance as a distribution, testing, design and administrative centre for production that is dispersed amongst a new 'periphery' of low wage countries (Indonesia, Malaysia, Thailand, Philippines). The Economic Development Board (EDB), Singapore's premier economic promotion agency (see Chapter 5), estimates that around

**Table 1.2** Share of inward foreign direct investment of GDP, by selected area and country (variable years)

|  | FDI share of GDP (%) | Year |
|---|---|---|
| *Select developed countries* | | |
| Australia | 26.0 | 1991 |
| Canada | 18.7 | 1990 |
| France | 4.9 | 1989 |
| Germany | 5.5 | 1989 |
| Italy | 5.3 | 1989 |
| Japan | 0.6 | 1990 |
| Netherlands | 27.2 | 1989 |
| New Zealand | 7.8 | 1989 |
| Sweden | 4.1 | 1988 |
| Switzerland | 13.8 | 1989 |
| United Kingdom | 19.4 | 1990 |
| United States | 7.4 | 1990 |
| *Select developing countries* | | |
| China | 0.8 | 1987 |
| Hong Kong | 17.0 | 1987 |
| Indonesia | 43.4 | 1987 |
| Malaysia | 24.0 | 1987 |
| Philippines | 4.0 | 1987 |
| South Korea | 2.3 | 1987 |
| Singapore | 89.5 | 1987 |
| Taiwan | 5.3 | 1987 |
| Thailand | 5.8 | 1987 |

*Source:* UNCTAD (1993) *World Investment Directory*, Volume 1 Asia and Pacific and Volume 3 Developed Countries

2000 organisations have a regional office in the city state (*The Straits Times*, 31 January 1996).

Singapore's comparatively low population growth (Table 1.3) relieves the city state of the urban management problems encountered in neighbouring cities. Selection of Singapore as the staging post for transnational business also reflects its superiority in world city facilities over other capital cities in Southeast Asia. One survey of regional office managers found that few gave any serious consideration of alternative locations as their main base in Southeast Asia (Perry, 1995). Excellent financial services and international communications were high on the list of attributes in Singapore's favour as an international business centre. A separate survey of regional head offices found similar high regard, concluding:

> It is not simply Singapore's geographical location *per se* that is important; other parts of Southeast Asia are also well-located. Rather it is the fact that Singapore has added value to its intrinsic locational attributes by investing heavily in transport and communications infrastructure and by creating an amenable business environment for foreign companies. (Dicken and Kirkpatrick, 1991, p. 181)

The infrastructure is not just being judged against that offered in other Southeast Asian countries, but in comparison with that available in other centres of international business. Singapore has been identified as amongst eight top-ranking international business centres (along with London, New York, New Jersey, Chicago, Los Angeles, Paris and Tokyo) with respect to their technological base for international business (Fainstein, 1994, p. 33). In a survey of international business centres, *Fortune* magazine has judged Singapore the best location for international business in the world, referring to it as a place which 'seems as if it were conceived entirely for business' (Barlyn, 1995, p. 68). The *Fortune* ranking was derived from business executive opinions and data related to market potential, infrastructure facilities and costs, cultural acceptance, personal risk and labour recruitment and retention. A more restricted survey of Asia–Pacific business centres gives Singapore the highest executive quality of life rating (a composite indicator covering housing, consumer, recreation, education, health and general conditions) although its cost of living is judged comparatively high (Table 1.3). Office accommodation costs, in particular, now exceed that of some European and North American cities (Table 1.4). However as the executive surveys indicate, for ease of business and expatriate living, Singapore is perceived as the only viable business centre in the region.

The supporting finance and business community to the regional business hub further illustrates the way Singapore has developed as a major servicing centre for international business. Table 1.5 gives an indication of the scale and variety of Singapore's business and financial services sector in the early 1990s. The high involvement of foreign business is illustrative of the cumulative processes in world city formation: regional offices of transnational corporations attract their home-based service providers, whose presence acts to attract new investors. The concentrations of business in certain activities identify markets for which Singapore has developed particular prominence, notably foreign exchange dealing and commodity trading. Daily turnover in foreign exchange has exceeded US$100 billion (*Singapore 1995*) placing Singapore in the top five centres for foreign exchange dealing with London, New York, Tokyo and Zurich. Singapore continues as a commodity trading centre for regional produce such as rubber and palm oil, but this is now less important than trading in oil and financial futures (Perry, 1994).

**Table 1.3**  Comparison of Southeast Asian capital cities

| | Singapore | Bangkok | Jakarta | Kuala Lumpur | Manila | Seoul | Taipei |
|---|---|---|---|---|---|---|---|
| Population 1995[a] (,000) | 2853 | 8454 | 11 236 | 2103 | 10 694 | 12 372 | 3435 |
| Average annual population growth rate 1990–1995[a] | 1.03 | 3.53 | 3.98 | 4.45 | 3.25 | 2.39 | 3.40 |
| Number of cities with direct flight connection[b]: | | | | | | | |
| – in North America | 7 | 8 | 2 | 1 | 7 | 15 | 13 |
| – in Europe | 19 | 19 | 8 | 11 | 6 | 7 | 5 |
| – in Japan | 5 | 2 | 8 | 4 | 3 | 9 | 4 |
| Number of foreign banks (excluding representative offices)[c] | 181 | 19 | 32 | 26 | 25 | 16 | 48 |
| Expatriate cost of living[d] | 100 | 83 | 85 | 82 | 75 | 105 | 105 |
| Expatriate quality of life[d] | 100 | 74 | 76 | 93 | 75 | 82 | 77 |

*Source:*   [a]UN (1993) *World Urbanisation Prospects: the 1992 Revision*, UN, New York.
[b]World Airways Guide December 1994
[c]Asia Law & Practice Ltd (1994) *The Asian Bank Directory*, Euromoney, Hong Kong.
[d]Corporate Resources Group (1995) Asia Human Resource Atlas, CRG, Singapore.

**Table 1.4** Comparison of CBD office costs in selected world cities, January 1996

| City | US$ per sq.m. per year | |
| | Rent | Total cost including taxes & service charge |
| --- | --- | --- |
| Tokyo–Inner central | 1188 | 1408 |
| Hong Kong | 1185 | 1340 |
| London–West End | 704 | 1169 |
| London–City | 580 | 1096 |
| Singapore | 681 | 875 |
| Paris | 650 | 795 |
| Tokyo–Outer central | 561 | 716 |
| Geneva | 602 | 645 |
| New York–Mid-town | 414 | 636 |
| Frankfurt | 514 | 595 |
| Zurich | 516 | 559 |
| Berlin | 403 | 477 |
| Sydney | 365 | 476 |
| Brussels | 327 | 415 |
| Stockholm | 380 | 408 |
| New York–Downtown | 219 | 404 |
| Rome | 310 | 392 |
| San Francisco | 222 | 380 |
| Vienna | 296 | 355 |
| Toronto | 156 | 333 |
| Amsterdam | 279 | 326 |
| Kuala Lumpur | 219 | 289 |
| Jakarta | 175 | 262 |
| Auckland | 201 | 261 |
| Bangkok | 207 | 250 |

*Source:* Richard Ellis, cited in *Property Link* (1996), Vol. 2, 14

Singapore's economic transformation as part of the phenomenon of world city formation intersects with local development ambition and political management. While income equality in Singapore is at the high end of the range for OECD countries (Rao, 1990), the bifurcation of urban population between an affluent professional class and an impoverished service class is being held in check through several influences. Unemployment has practically ceased to exist since the early 1970s and the first flush of inward investment. This has allowed much of the local workforce to opt out of low paid service employment, assisted by the expansion of education and technical training. State regulation, partly designed to raise service productivity and release labour for priority sectors, has also been important, notably in the relocation of hawkers into food centres. It is the case as well that Singapore's economic planners

**Table 1.5** Major business service activities in Singapore, 1994

| | Number of companies | | |
|---|---|---|---|
| Business activity | 1988 | 1994 | Share foreign 1994(%) |
| Management services | 47 | 42 | 40.4 |
| Electronic data processing | 125 | 198 | 41.4 |
| Software packages | 57 | 84 | 45.1 |
| Management consultants | 144 | 159 | 38.3 |
| Accountants | 98 | 107 | 28.0 |
| Lawyers and solicitors | 109 | 108 | 19.4 |
| Market research | 31 | 41 | 46.3 |
| Advertising and public relations | 99 | 100 | 33.0 |
| Regional representative offices | 357 | 440 | – |
| Banks (full service) | 38 | 49 | 85.7 |
| Banks (restricted service) | 16 | 17 | 88.2 |
| Merchant banks | 59 | 63 | 98.4 |
| Offshore banks | 85 | 70 | – |
| Foreign bank representative offices | 32 | 32 | – |
| Foreign exchange dealers | 24 | 23 | 82.6 |
| Commodity and futures broking | 19 | 39 | 97.4 |
| General insurance | 64 | 75 | 76.0 |
| Re-insurance | 21 | 43 | 83.7 |
| Foreign insurance service offices | 11 | 2 | – |
| Property development & management | 236 | 263 | 12.1 |

*Source:* Based on entries in *Kompass Singapore 1994* and Dicken and Kirkpatrick (1991, p. 181)

have never embraced entirely a post-industrial future for the island. Although the island's manufacturing sector has shed much of the factory-based assembly work attracted in the 1960s and 1970s, it has built expertise in selected electronics technologies which continue to attract investment. Under its 'Manufacturing 2000' strategy, the target is to retain at least a quarter of national output from manufacturing (it accounted for 27% in 1994 compared with 12% in 1960).

As well as high labour demand, it has been possible to exert an unusual degree of control over labour supply. Being a city state without a rural hinterland, Singapore has been able to impose tight controls on immigration. Low paid jobs have increasingly become the domain of foreign workers, particularly in construction, domestic service, cleaning and assembly-line work (Chew and Chew, 1995). Some of these are daily commuters from Johor but the majority are employed on temporary work permits giving close regulation of their presence. As an alternative to importing low cost labour, as noted above, integration of the Riau and Johor into Singapore's space economy has gained momentum. This initiative envisages the control of outlying factories from Singapore although, as we explore in Chapter 6, this is not necessarily in keeping with the development aspirations of its neighbours.

For senior managerial and professional jobs in international business organizations, foreign workers also account for a large share of employment. Whilst living in relatively high class residential districts, their expatriate status reduces the local accumulation of wealth. A local affluent class asserting their consumption preferences has also been constrained by the state's tight control of housing and private transport as well as the absence, until recently, of inner city environments serving this market. State campaigning against the adoption of western lifestyles has been a further constraint on the convergence with other world cities, although as we discuss in later chapters, greater interest in the promotion of arts and 'cosmopolitan creativity' did enter the political agenda in the 1990s.

The distinctive experience of urbanization in Singapore is linked to the nation building programme and its central concern to promote multiculturalism. This abiding belief in according equal status to Chinese, Malays and Indians, as the founding races of Singapore, has produced a concern to avoid the creation of an ethnic underclass. The PAP has remained opposed to welfare support or positive discrimination, believing these create a 'crutch mentality', but has expended considerable energy in other ways to instill a national consciousness. As well as self-help initiatives and campaigns, the built environment has been refashioned in the interests of multiculturalism. This is reflected in the dispersal of ethnic groups amongst housing estates and the construction of living environments which have made little or no concession to ethnic customs or religious practice. The imperative to create a new Singapore also justified the destruction of much of the inherited landscape that reflected the identity of individual ethnic groups. Conservation has been a late addition to the urban management agenda and even now, as Chapter 9 shows, often seems to give primacy to commercial interests in promoting tourism and business opportunities over historical faithfulness.


**Structure of the book**

This book offers a broad review of Singapore's economic, social, physical and political characteristics. It seeks to give an introductory understanding of the city state's recent growth, current development strategies and dilemmas. The preliminary chapters examine the legacy of Singapore's origins and historical development for the management of the city; government and politics; population structure and management; economic growth and strategy. Subsequent chapters examine key components of the contemporary city environment: land use patterns and communications; planning policy; residential structure and environment; culture, conservation and tourism. The final chapter summarizes the government's plan for the 'next lap' in the island's growth and comments on current development dilemmas and strategies, including the means of accommodating the aspirations of an increasingly affluent population and overcoming the physical constraints of a small island state.

# 2

# History and legacy

This chapter traces the historical development of Singapore as a city, from its colonial foundations in the early nineteenth century to independence in the late 1950s. Among the major developments in the urban environment over almost one and a half centuries, this review focuses on the colonial state's plans and visions for the city and the strategies employed to resolve urban problems. Three broad periods will be considered: first, the establishment and growth of the colonial town in the early to mid-nineteenth century; secondly, rapid expansion of the colonial city accompanied by increasingly complex problems and concerted planning responses in the late nineteenth and early twentieth centuries; and thirdly, the postwar era leading up to the attainment of self-rule in 1959 characterised by the urgent need for social and economic reconstruction in the city. The overall aim is to examine the makings of a colonial city in terms of economic, demographic and spatial growth, its social and ethnic composition, housing and health conditions, and the question of urban governance in a colonial city, as well as to assess, in a final section, the urban legacy of colonialism.

## Colonial foundations

While Singapore can trace its origins back to antiquity (Colless, 1969; Sheppard, 1982), the form of the modern city is mainly derived from European colonial influence. In the early nineteenth-century world of mercantile capitalism, European imperial powers were engaged in a race to secure control of important sea routes to further their trading interests in the Far East. In order to counter Dutch ambitions to dominate the Strait of Malacca and the Sunda Straits, British officials attempted to secure a strategic foothold at the southern end of the Strait of Malacca from where to control the trade routes to China and the Malay Archipelago for British trade (Wong, 1991a). On 30 January 1819, a British expedition led by Stamford Raffles, Lieutenant-Governor of Bencoolen and an agent of the English East India Company, signed a preliminary agreement with the local Malay chief, Temenggong Abdul Rahman, to protect the island in return for permission to establish a British trading post on the island. This agreement was ratified on 6 February 1819, when Raffles concluded a treaty of alliance with Sultan Hussein of the Johor Empire centred at Riau. In return for exclusive treaty rights to secure Singapore as a British trading base, the British pledged to pay the Sultan 5000 Spanish dollars per annum and to aid him against any external attack (Chew, 1991a). While Raffles planted the British flag on Singapore soil, it was not until 1824 after the conclusion of the Anglo-Dutch Treaty (which had the effect of officially recognising the hitherto disputed British position at Singapore) and under the Residency of John Crawfurd that the British acquired the cession of full sovereignty over the entire island. Singapore's status as a British territory underwent several administrative changes in the nineteenth century. In 1826, the East India Company united Singapore with Penang and Malacca to form the Presidency of the Straits Settlements under a Governor, subsequently downgraded to a Residency dependent on the Presidency of Bengal four years later. After a period under Indian administration, the Straits Settlements became a Crown Colony in 1867 under the direct control of the Colonial Office in London.

The original blueprint for the development of the town of Singapore was conceived by Raffles prior to the full cession of the island and concerned that portion of land which came under the British Resident's jurisdiction. Raffles' ideas were formally crystallized in his instructions of 4 November 1822 to the then newly appointed town committee, and later committed to cartographic representation by Lieutenant Phillip Jackson in his *Plan of the Town of Singapore*. Within a few years the island's population grew to between 5000 and 10 000, having previously been an undeveloped island inhabited by about 150 Malay fishermen living on the river banks and a number of Chinese engaged in agricultural development in the interior. The first census taken in January 1824 identified 10 683 residents (Braddell, 1861). The rapid growth of the island accorded with the purpose of drawing up the town plan and Raffles' vision that the new trading settlement would rise to fulfil its promise of becoming 'the emporium and pride of the East' and 'a place of considerable magnitude and importance' (Buckley, 1984, pp. 67, 81). To regulate the appropriation of land for specific purposes, Raffles' instructions to the town committee focused on remodelling the town according to principles which would facilitate public administration and maximize mercantile interest, inscribe public order in space, and also cater for the accommodation of the principal races in separate quarters.

Central to Raffles' plan (Figure 2.1) was an expansive central space on the north bank of the Singapore River devoted solely to public purposes and dominated by grand edifices such as a church, government offices and a court house opening out to a central square. These colonial structures which epitomised the ideals of British governance were flanked on the east by an equally expansive 'European Town', carved out as a residential area for the European administrative and mercantile community. Raffles also ordered that the swampy south bank of the Singapore River, hitherto occupied by Chinese traders and raft houses, be drained to make way for a line of wharfs and warehouses along the bank. In time, this became the principal commercial heart of the town. In planning his new town, Raffles stressed that the mercantile community should have first priority in claiming advantageous sites:

> At present a considerable portion of the sea and river face, which may hereafter become important for mercantile purposes, is occupied by the lower classes of Chinese, and as might be expected many of the early settlers have occupied positions and extent of ground which are now urgently demanded by a higher and more respectable class. A line must be drawn between the classes engaged in mercantile speculation and those gaining their livelihood by handicrafts and personal labour; the former, and particularly the principle merchants, will require the first attention, and there does not appear any reason why the latter should in any instance be allowed to occupy those situations which are likely at any time to be required by the commercial community (Buckley, 1984, p. 82).

Securing to the mercantile community 'all the facilities which the natural advantages of the port afford[ed]' (Buckley, 1984, p. 82) fitted Raffles' objective of making commerce the main rationale for Singapore's existence and future (Wurtzburg, 1954).

In the laying out of public spaces, Raffles emphasized the importance of open, orderly arrangement, uniformity and regularity. The siting of public buildings in 'a central and open situation' with 'considerable space to be kept clear in the vicinity' was stressed (Buckley, 1984, pp. 84–85). Public streets and highways were to run at right angles as far as practicable and conform to a predetermined width according to class and relative position. In response to the haphazard arrangement of houses 'scattered without any attention to order or convenience', Raffles specified that the minimum space occupied by each house along the street was to be predetermined so as to 'fix the exact number of houses' contained in each street.

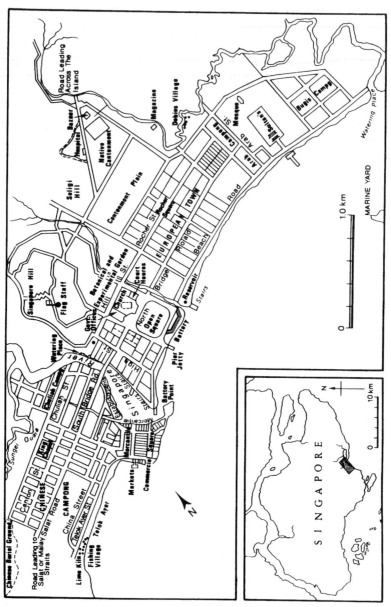

**Figure 2.1** Raffles' Town Plan of 1822

In essence, a gridiron system of streets with separating rectangular plots formed the basis of Raffles' plan.

The use of the standard gridiron plan was both an efficient and an expedient measure in the laying-out of a new colonial town. Not only did the gridiron provide an equitable method of dividing the land in a new city formed by colonization, for the colonist unfamiliar with the lay of the land, it was a means of simplifying spatial order in order to provide for a swift and rough division of territory (Mumford, 1961, p. 224). The grid structure also fostered growth and expansion of the city for by 'setting out the whole town at once, creating in a sense an artificial scarcity, and by parcelling out urban lots in standard rectangular blocks that could easily be surveyed, described and transferred on standard legal documents, the grid favoured speculation and rising urban land prices' (Statham, 1989, p. 19). Raffles was keenly conscious that careful allocation of land was crucial to the orderly growth and prosperity of his new city.

Not only did Raffles' plan inscribe spatial order in terms of the laying out of streets and houses, he was also concerned to ensure the orderly use of public spaces. Each house, for example, was to have a veranda of a certain depth, open at all times to provide a continued and covered walkway for pedestrians on each side of the street. A proclamation was issued in November 1822 prohibiting the 'lower classes of Chulias' (south Indians) from living in the verandas of houses in the northern (European) part of the town and a Chulia *kampung* was specifically marked out on the upper banks of the Singapore River on the south side (Braddell, 1855, p. 459; Buckley, 1984, p. 85). By the mid-1820s, hawkers of food and other merchandise were also prohibited from setting up stalls or sheds in the open streets as this was considered 'a nuisance, prejudicial to the health and comfort of the inhabitants' (Crawfurd, 1828, p. 556). Hawkers were only allowed within the confines of the two public, government-owned markets, one within Chinatown and the other at Kampong Glam.

In planning for the accommodation of the increasing numbers of Asian immigrants, Raffles demarcated the town into 'divisions' or '*kampungs*' for particular racial and occupational groups. The residential spaces of different racial groups were to be as far as possible segregated: the European town was allotted the expanse to the east of the government reserved area, while the Chinese, Bugis, Arabs, Chulias and Malays were relegated to more peripheral locations in well-demarcated *kampungs*. Each *kampung* was placed under the immediate superintendence of its own chiefs or *kapitans*. These chiefs were then made responsible to the Resident for policing their respective jurisdictions (Buckley, 1984, p. 57).

In effect, Raffles' town plan both specified the spatial configuration of the town's urban development (Savage, 1992) and served to address vital

*Conclusion*

questions underlying the founding of a colonial city such as those of establishing public administration and order, strengthening the economic base, and accommodating a rapidly expanding and highly diverse population. While the plan did not materialize in its entirety, it etched into the fabric of the colonial town a structure which continued to influence future developments. — *important*

Singapore continued to grow steadily over the next six decades, attracting traders and labour migrants from China, India and the surrounding Southeast Asian countries. This consolidated Singapore's position as a viable commercial port for different types of trades: the sailing vessels from the Malay Archipelago, the Chinese junks which carried trade between China and Southeast Asia, square-rigged vessels which plied the sea routes connecting Europe and India in the west and Thailand, Indo-China and China in the east. As a free port, it served both Asian and Western private enterprise without the burden of monopolies, duties and other forms of trade restrictions, a concept which was virtually unknown in the East at that time. In 1824, Singapore already controlled international trade valued at $11.6 million; by 1883, this had increased more than twelve-fold to $147.4 million (Wong, 1991b, p. 51).

With commercial success, the colonial town of Singapore continued to grow, both in demographic and spatial terms. From a total of over 10 000 returned in January 1824, the population of the settlement increased almost thirteen-fold by the 1881 census to 137 722 (Table 2.1), of which 68.5% resided within municipal limits (Saw, 1969, pp. 38–39; Dunlop, 1881). The population grew mainly by migrational surplus. As the Chinese and Indian immigrants were mainly male unlike the Malays – the sex ratio was highly skewed, with about three men to every one woman among the migrant classes – continued migration had the effect of depressing the contribution of indigenous population growth (Table 2.2).

Migration gave the settlement a distinctively plural character. The local Malay population was soon augmented by immigrants from Malacca, Sumatra, Java, the Riau archipelago and other eastern islands and they became boatmen, fishermen, wood cutters, carpenters, policemen, watchmen, office 'boys', drivers and house-servants (Turnbull, 1977, p. 37; Roff, 1964, p. 77). Their main residential area was in Kampong Glam near the Kallang and Rochor rivers, comprising an aggregation of Malay-style wooden houses and shops surrounding a mosque and the *istana* (palace) occupied by descendants of Sultan Hussein. On the fringe of Kampong Glam on the tidal swamps near the river mouth were the stilt houses of the Bugis, Boyanese, Javanese and other Malay-Muslim immigrants. Other Malay settlements included Telok Blangah where the followers of the Temenggong of Johore settled and Kampong Malacca, inhabited ini-

**Table 2.1** Distribution of population by race, 1824–1957

| Year | Chinese No. | Chinese % | Malays No. | Malays % | Indians No. | Indians % | Other Races No. | Other Races % | Total No. | Total % |
|---|---|---|---|---|---|---|---|---|---|---|
| 1824 | 3317 | 31.0 | 6431 | 60.2 | 756 | 7.1 | 179 | 1.7 | 10 683 | 100.0 |
| 1830 | 6555 | 39.4 | 7640 | 45.9 | 1913 | 11.5 | 526 | 3.2 | 16 634 | 100.0 |
| 1836 | 13 749 | 45.9 | 12 538 | 41.7 | 2932 | 9.9 | 765 | 2.6 | 29 984 | 100.0 |
| 1840 | 17 704 | 50.0 | 13 200 | 37.3 | 3375 | 9.5 | 1110 | 3.1 | 35 389 | 100.0 |
| 1849 | 27 988 | 52.9 | 17 039 | 32.3 | 6284 | 11.9 | 1580 | 3.0 | 52 891 | 100.0 |
| 1860 | 50 043 | 61.2 | 16 202 | 19.8 | 12 973 | 15.9 | 2516 | 3.1 | 81 734 | 100.0 |
| 1871 | 54 572 | 56.8 | 26 141 | 27.1 | 10 313 | 11.9 | 3790 | 4.0 | 94 816 | 100.0 |
| 1881 | 86 766 | 63.0 | 33 012 | 24.0 | 12 086 | 8.8 | 5858 | 4.3 | 137 722 | 100.0 |
| 1891 | 121 908 | 67.1 | 35 956 | 19.7 | 16 009 | 8.8 | 7727 | 4.3 | 181 602 | 100.0 |
| 1901 | 164 041 | 72.1 | 35 986 | 15.8 | 17 047 | 7.8 | 9768 | 4.3 | 226 842 | 100.0 |
| 1911 | 219 577 | 72.4 | 41 806 | 13.8 | 27 755 | 9.2 | 14 183 | 4.7 | 303 321 | 100.0 |
| 1921 | 315 151 | 75.3 | 53 595 | 12.8 | 32 314 | 7.7 | 17 298 | 4.2 | 418 358 | 100.0 |
| 1931 | 418 640 | 75.1 | 65 014 | 11.7 | 50 811 | 9.1 | 23 280 | 4.2 | 557 745 | 100.0 |
| 1947 | 729 473 | 77.8 | 113 803 | 12.1 | 68 967 | 7.4 | 25 901 | 2.8 | 938 144 | 100.0 |
| 1957 | 1 090 595 | 75.4 | 197 060 | 13.6 | 124 084 | 8.6 | 34 190 | 2.4 | 1 445 929 | 100.0 |

*Source: Saw, 1964*

**Table 2.2** Sex ratio by race (males per thousand females), 1824–1957

| Year | Chinese | Malays | Indians | All Races |
|------|---------|--------|---------|-----------|
| 1824 | 8188    | 1058   | 5873    | 1987      |
| 1830 | 11 275  | 1141   | 10 387  | 2762      |
| 1836 | 14 642  | 1168   | 9580    | 3148      |
| 1849 | 11 500  | 1421   | 6499    | 3905      |
| 1860 | 14 407  | 1672   | 8504    | 6039      |
| 1871 | 6174    | 1267   | 4294    | 3189      |
| 1881 | 5112    | 1281   | 3943    | 3089      |
| 1891 | 4680    | 1383   | 4216    | 3209      |
| 1901 | 3871    | 1279   | 4129    | 2951      |
| 1911 | 2790    | 1172   | 4914    | 2453      |
| 1921 | 2123    | 1230   | 5021    | 2044      |
| 1931 | 1656    | 1161   | 5372    | 1713      |
| 1947 | 1132    | 1208   | 2998    | 1218      |
| 1957 | 1039    | 1101   | 2257    | 1117      |

*Source:* Saw, 1964

tially for the most part, as the name suggests, by Malays from that settlement.

While the Malays were the dominant ethnic group in 1824, the Chinese soon assumed numerical dominance and accounted for 63% of the total population by 1881 (Table 2.1). The Chinese immigrants hailed mainly from the provinces of Kwangtung and Fukien in Southeast China and comprised five major *bang* or dialect groups: Hokkien, Teochew, Cantonese, Hakka and Hylams (Hainanese). Spanning a wide range of occupational niches including merchants, shopkeepers, agriculturalists, artisans and manual labourers of all sorts, they brought with them an entire array of organizations such as clan and dialect associations, trade guilds, temples dedicated to a panoply of Chinese deities, and secret societies which provided the institutional structures within which social, cultural, religious, and recreational activities were performed (Yen, 1986, p. 317). Through these institutions, Chinese groups had access to a certain range of services which supported immigrant life such as the provision of medical care, job protection, education, entertainment, and facilities which catered to the observance of the rites of passage.

The traditional core area of the Chinese was Chinatown south of the Singapore River in an area originally marked out by Raffles as the Chinese *kampung*, but with rapid growth, the Chinese soon came to dominate the area directly north of the Singapore River, originally designated 'European Town' by Raffles. The port area around Tanjong Pagar also constituted another overspill area adjacent to 'old' Chinatown as well as a convenient location for port workers. The archetypal Chinese dwelling

Singapore. Boat Quay.

**Plate 2.1** Singapore River: trading lifeline in the mid-nineteenth century. Photograph courtesy of the National Archives

Malay Village on the Rochor River, Singapore

**Plate 2.2** The stilt houses of the Malay-Muslim immigrants

was the two-storey shophouse built in rows using brick pillars and clay tiles for the roof and featuring a five-foot way fronting the house (this was the local interpretation of the 'veranda' stipulated in Raffles' 1822 plan).

**Plate 2.3** Shophouses along South Bridge Road. Photograph courtesy of the National Archives

The houses had very narrow frontage but tended to be much deeper, with rooms separated by airwells. While the upper floors were used as a residence, the lower floors were often turned over to commerce, retail trades or cottage industries.

Like the Chinese, Indian immigrants arrived in Singapore mainly as traders and labourers although some came as garrison troops, camp followers and transmarine convicts (Turnbull, 1977, p. 37). They were particularly conspicuous in textile and piece-goods wholesaling and retailing, moneylending as well as working around the port and railway. Most were south Indian Tamils although Sikhs, Punjabis, Gujeratis, Bengalis and Parsis also numbered among them. The Indian population was mainly focused on the Serangoon Road–Kampong Kapur area, although smaller pockets could also be found in various parts of the city such as concentrations of South Indian chettiars, Tamil Muslim traders, moneychangers, petty shopkeepers, boatmen, and quayside workers on the fringe of the central business core in the Kling (later Chulia) Street–Market Street area; Sindhi, Gujerati, and Sikh textile merchants in the High Street area; Gujerati and other Muslim textile and jewellery merchants in the Arab Street region; and Tamil, Telugu, and Malayali dock workers in the harbour area (Sandhu, 1970, pp. 197–98).

Of the smaller minority groups, the European population itself never expanded beyond about one to two per cent of the population although their influence as the governing and mercantile elite was disproportionate to their numbers; while the Eurasians, people of mixed European and Asian parentage, accounted for another similar proportion of the population. Originally allocated land in 'European Town' by Raffles, European settlers had by the second half of the nineteenth century moved to suburban locations, particularly the Tanglin–Claymore–lower Bukit Timah area. In these European enclaves, villas and bungalows with large verandas stood sequestered in large gardens and compounds. Also of note were the Arabs and Jews, many of whom were wealthy merchants and landowners; while the Armenian and Japanese communities, though small, also found a place in Singapore's cosmopolitan landscape.

Spatially, the outward expansion of the town broadly assumed the pattern shown in Figure 2.2. The physical fabric of the town was gradually transformed as jungle and marsh were pushed back, swamps filled in and covered with houses and shops, roads constructed in different directions, some across the island, and wooden houses made way for more substantial brick buildings. While sailing vessels dominated before the 1870s, the Singapore River continued to act as the trading lifeline with the main anchorage located near Boat Quay.

With the early rapid growth and consolidation of the colonial town, a number of urban problems soon had to be addressed. These were resolved into two closely related issues: first, the failure to provide adequate public facilities and services to minister to the needs of the town's inhabitants; and secondly, the question of public representation and participation in the administration of local urban affairs.

In the early years, the town was administered directly by the central government, which appointed *ad hoc* committees as the occasion demanded to attend to drains, street lighting and the regulation of buildings (Hallifax, 1921, pp. 316–17). None of these committees had any continuous life, nor were they in any way representative. The failure of such committees to satisfactorily solve various urban ills such as deteriorating sanitary conditions and inefficient policing of the town was interpreted as government neglect and the failure to accommodate public representation in the running of urban affairs.

The campaign for public representation and participation in municipal government was led primarily by European residents anxious to foster local autonomy and control over urban affairs. In 1839, mounting grievances over the deteriorating sanitary conditions of the town led to much discontent and agitation among European residents which resulted in the establishment of an Assessment Fund to be used for municipal purposes (Singapore Municipality, 1923, p. 11). The Fund was disbursed by executive officers of government and used mainly for the upkeep of a small police force to maintain order in the town. It failed to quell European

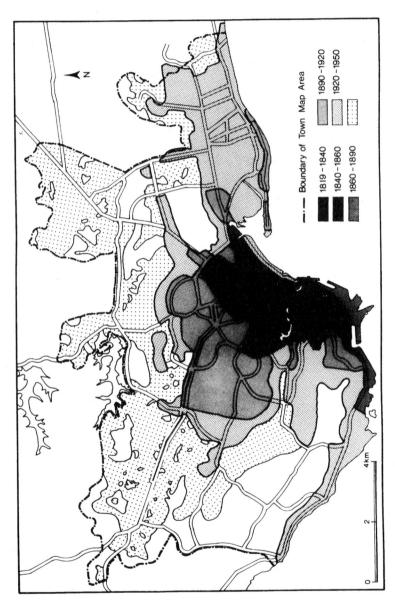

**Figure 2.2** Outward expansion of the town in the nineteenth and twentieth centuries
*Source:* Master Plan, Report of Survey (1955)

demands for representation in local affairs and in January 1845, a motion at a public meeting proposing that the assessment funds be controlled by three persons – one appointed by the government and two elected by ratepayers – was carried by a large majority (Buckley, 1984, p. 423).

Hopes for greater responsibility over municipal affairs through elected representation were frustrated by the introduction of a new assessment bill in June 1846 providing for a municipal committee of five assessors – two official and three non-official – nominated by the Governor to administer the funds. The bill was passed and came into effect in 1848 but this so-called 'first milestone in the development of municipal government' (Turnbull, 1977, p. 67) aroused little public enthusiasm. Instead, the Grand Jury which made presentments on social conditions (apart from carrying out judicial duties), the local English language press and petitions to government continued to highlight urban sanitary ills and offensive nuisances such as the disgraceful state of the jail, the 'ruinous' church and the 'sickening malaria' arising from inefficient and filthy drains in the town, and to urge stronger public representation in the running of municipal affairs. This protest against the neglect of public welfare and the centralization of power in the hands of the executive government did succeed in encouraging steps to extend Indian municipal laws to the Straits Settlements. Act XXVIII of 1856 provided for the establishment of a municipal board comprising five members: the Resident Councillor (and later the Colonial Secretary after the 1867 Transfer) as President, one other official and three representatives chosen by ratepayers paying annual rates over 25 Rupees. Two other complementary Acts defined the powers and functions of the municipal board: Act XXV provided for assessment and collection of municipal taxes; and Act XIV (commonly known as the Conservancy Act) directed municipal commissioners to 'administer the funds applicable to the purpose of conservancy and improvement' and empowered them 'to make, cleanse, light and water streets, to remove filth, and to control erections of new huts, to pull down ruinous houses, . . . to drain the town' as well as to enforce penalties, supply water, regulate slaughter houses and license dangerous trades and burial grounds (Singapore Municipality, 1923, pp. 11–12). A fourth Act, XIII of 1856 or the Police Act, provided for the establishment and organization of a police force in the town.

In the years after the Municipal Acts came into effect, the board attempted to abate some of the longstanding nuisances in the town including raising some of the main streets to prevent flooding, clearing up the filth and stench in public places and replacing dilapidated bridges with iron ones (Turnbull, 1972, pp. 41–42). The town's first municipal engineer, surveyor and architect, J. W. Reeve, was appointed in 1858.

However, the compulsory levy demanded by the government for the upkeep of the police force depleted the annual municipal revenue by more than half, and little was left over for carrying out functions contained in the Conservancy Act.

In sum, while the town of Singapore consolidated its foundations and grew rapidly in the early decades, urban problems such as inefficient policing, sanitary neglect and the lack of funds for various improvement works continued to persist. The search for a solution to these problems centred around the question of the balance of power between central government and local residents in controlling urban affairs. From the perspective of local residents, urban ills were not adequately addressed given the indifference of government to local conditions and the parsimonious and piecemeal nature of solutions. During these decades, while certain concessions were made to local autonomy, they were neither large enough to satisfy the demands of ratepayers nor sufficiently consequential in effecting major improvements in the town.

### The growing colonial city

While the conversion of the Straits Settlements into a Crown Colony in 1867 did not revolutionize the fabric of colonial society overnight, it introduced a new system of rule. The Governor at the helm assumed executive supremacy, subject only to the Colonial Office's ultimate control. He was assisted by the executive council which constituted a type of cabinet which met in private and the legislative council which comprised official members (members of the executive council and the Chief Justice) and non-official members nominated by the Governor. Over the years, the basis of consultation was broadened to increase the number of non-officials and also to include Asians in the legislative council but the Governor retained the casting vote such that the final authority still rested with him and the Colonial Office (Turnbull, 1979, pp. 79–80). This constitutional system remained largely intact until the outbreak of World War II and continued to serve the city as it entered a phase of rapid growth in both economic and demographic terms.

During the last quarter of the nineteenth century, Singapore's status as the premier entrepôt port in the Far East was consolidated. The opening of the Suez Canal in 1869 and the arrival of the steamship from the 1870s soon added to the island's original geographical advantage by making the Malacca Strait rather than the Sunda Strait the favoured route from Europe to the Far East. Singapore became an important transaction point for the east–west trade and a coaling station for steamers. Reduced transport time and greater reliability helped to stimulate an expansion of world trade. The late nineteenth century also heralded the emergence of a world market and a system of trade in which the needs of capitalist interests in the industrializing west were met by a re-orientation in the productive and accumulative activities of the 'periphery' (Sundaram, 1986, p. 138). British commercial capital abroad began responding to attractive possibilities for profitable investment in production in its colonies.

In Malaya, with Singapore functioning as the bridgehead, the extension of British political control over the Malayan hinterland from 1874 (Thio, 1969) went hand in hand with western capitalist penetration of the interior. European capital investments in the Malayan tin industry and plantation agriculture generated large-scale bulk movement of primary products which were channelled for export through the port of Singapore. Singapore also acted as a base for European trading agencies and merchant houses which not only dominated the import-export trade but also handled the financial, commercial, shipping, insurance and other related services connected with the rapidly expanding trade. The rapid expansion of trade soon necessitated a new deep-water harbour (later known as Keppel Harbour) and a line of docks as the shallow waters at Boat Quay could no longer accommodate transoceanic steamships. With the development of Keppel Harbour, western companies, banks and agency houses were concentrated at Raffles Place while Boat Quay continued to serve the Chinese-dominated inter-Asian trade in Straits produce. In actual figures, total trade peaked in 1926 at S$1886.7 million although it tended to decline thereafter, plummeting to S$512.8 million in 1933 in the midst of the Depression before recovering slightly to S$689.9 million in 1938 (Wong, 1991b, p. 54).

Singapore's rapidly expanding economy, coupled with a liberal opendoor policy on immigration, drew large numbers of immigrants in the late nineteenth and early twentieth centuries. Between 1881 and 1931, the annual growth rate of the population of the Settlement ranged from 2.3% to 3.7%, with actual figures increasing from 137 722 persons in 1881 to more than 500 000 in 1931 (Saw 1969, p. 39). As a component of population dynamics, migrational surplus greatly outweighed natural increase which was in fact negative prior to 1921, partly because of the continued imbalance in the sex ratio (and thus low fertility rates) as well as the impact of high mortality rates.

As noted earlier, by 1881, 68.5% of the total population resided within municipal limits, a proportion which was substantially increased to 83.2% in 1891 partly as a result of the expansion of the municipal limits to include eight additional outer census divisions. This redrawing of municipal boundaries was a reflection of the rapid physical expansion of the built-up area in the last quarter of the nineteenth century as demographic pressure on urban land and housing within the central area of the town reached unprecedented levels. Up to the 1870s, the city and its residential suburbs had remained circumscribed within a two to two and a half mile radius from the Singapore River. By the 1880s, however, it began to expand beyond these confines, initially as ribbon developments along main trunk roads such as Tanjong Pagar Road, River Valley Road, Orchard Road, Bukit Timah Road, Thomson Road, Serangoon Road and Kallang Road. New middle-class residential suburbs were established to the west of the city to accommodate wealthier families fleeing the environmental malaise and congestion of the central area. The bulk of the labouring classes, however, remained confined to the highly congested inner districts where accessibility to work could be maximized and transport cost minimized. The population residing within municipal boundaries continued to reflect a highly cosmopolitan flavour which, at the turn of the century, comprised a majority (74%) of Chinese belonging to various dialect groups, but which also included sizeable minorities of 'natives of the Malay Archipelago' (14%), 'natives of India' (8%), Eurasians (2%), Europeans (1%) and 'other nationalities' (1%), principally made up of Arabs, Jews, Sinhalese and Japanese.

By the turn of the century, the principal components of colonial urban morphology were clearly inscribed in the built form of the city. A western-style central business district, Commercial Square (present-day Raffles Place) with its assemblage of principal banks, trading agencies, merchant houses, the post office and the shipping office thrived as the commercial heart of the city. Across the Singapore River from Commercial Square was the government administrative quarter with its collage of government offices, the Supreme Court, the Town Hall, the Anglican and Roman Catholic cathedrals, the chief European hotels and English-language schools. On the seaward fringe of this quarter was the Esplanade. In distinct contrast to these imposing edifices symbolic of British commercial capital and government, the Asian districts were complicated mosaics of specialized trade areas, bazaars, densely packed tenement housing and concentrations of eating-houses, theatres and brothels.

As colonial urban life in Singapore assumed greater complexity in the late nineteenth and early twentieth centuries, a number of problems became increasingly pressing. The first to dominate the urban agenda was the question of maintaining a sanitary environment in the face of the unprecedented strains of urban and demographic growth. Mortality rates in colonial Singapore were indisputably high, even by Asian standards, among the immigrant and indigenous communities: crude death rates within the municipal area averaged over 40 per thousand in the late nine-

**Plate 2.4** Commercial Square (later renamed Raffles Place): the western-style commercial heart of the city. Photograph courtesy of the National Archives

teenth and early twentieth centuries, only falling to below 30 per thousand in the mid-1920s. The diseases which felled the greatest numbers during this period were malarial fevers, tuberculosis and beri beri, although 'dangerous infectious diseases' such as cholera, enteric fever, smallpox and bubonic plague also took their toll on the population. From the perspective of colonial medical science, high morbidity and mortality rates were largely attributable to the insanitary environments inhabited by Asian communities: what defiled the environment and caused disease were the insanitary domestic practices and habits of the Asian population (Yeoh, 1991).

A second issue of concern to those who governed colonial Singapore was that of maintaining public order in the urban environment. In the face of rapid growth and change in the urban landscape, the pressing aim was to produce a public landscape which was orderly, disciplined, easily policed, and amenable to the demands of urban development and efficiency. An urban environment with clearly defined public spaces was essential to the policing and surveillance functions of the colonial state. This involved various issues including improving the legibility of the landscape through naming and signifying places, controlling and canalizing urban traffic, whether pedestrian, motorized, horse- or human-drawn, and segregating different types of land uses by demarcating space along a multiplicity of lines such as private/public, sacred/profane and progressive/offensive. For example, to ensure public order, the authorities championed notions of 'public right of way' and mounted various campaigns to prevent shopkeepers and hawkers from obstructing pedestrian walkways. Legislation was also passed to close or control burial grounds which proliferated in the municipal area so as to release land for urban development and to achieve a more 'rational' use of space (Yeoh, 1996).

A third problem which confronted the authorities during this period was an acute housing shortage. The unremitting pressure of a rapidly growing population on an increasingly short supply of housing stock led to a deepening 'crisis of habitability' (Warren, 1986, p. 194) as the labouring classes resorted to subdivided tenements, makeshift cubicles, back-to-back houses and squatter settlements in and around the central area. During the late nineteenth and early twentieth centuries, neither the colonial state nor private enterprise was willing to shoulder the expense of providing housing for the labouring classes for such investments yielded far lower returns compared to those in rubber, tin and commerce (*PRCAICPHD*, 1918, p. A12). Private and public housing attempts were further hampered by a series of political and economic events: the First World War which led to difficulties in obtaining building materials; the Depression years of the 1930s characterized by severe unemployment and a shortage of capital; and the Japanese Occupation which brought the economy and the construction of housing to a standstill (Teo and Savage, 1991, p. 325). The severe shortage of housing for the masses and the overcrowded and appalling conditions of slum housing were continually reiterated in official reports as detrimental to the health of the people. A report by a sanitary expert Professor W. J. Simpson in 1907, for example, argued that the high incidence of tubercular and respiratory diseases in the city was a result of poor housing conditions where the building of houses back-to-back, the subdivision of each floor into tiny makeshift cubicles and the severe overcrowding (Simpson, 1907).

Two main responses emerged to the urban challenges of colonial Singapore. In the first instance, the colonial government sought to increase the scope of municipal powers in order to enforce stronger measures of environmental control. From time to time, the local English press echoed the opinion that the 'great need here [was] to bring about big conceptions of civic duty and the final abandonment of the infamous policy of *laissez faire* which ha[d] made Singapore the pigsty that it [was]' (*The Straits Times*, 21 November 1919). On 2 May 1887, a draft bill was introduced into the Legislative Council to amend and consolidate existing municipal laws. As with Victorian cities in Britain, municipal reform was closely identified with the improvement of public health, morality and order through a commitment to environmental control (Fraser, 1979, pp. 167–69). More specifically, large sections of the ordinance were devoted to investing the municipality with surveillance powers to control insanitary buildings, overcrowding, the disposal of rubbish and nightsoil, the supply of water, the reporting of infectious diseases, the control of street traffic, the use of burial and burning grounds, and the running of public places such as markets and slaughter-houses. The 1887 Municipal Ordinance formed the nucleus of all subsequent amendments in the next half-century and although it underwent considerable elaboration as municipal government steadily enlarged its spheres of influence, imposed new duties and assumed new obligations, the basic pattern of municipal affairs set out by this ordinance continued to persist.

Enlarging municipal legislative and surveillance powers alone, however, was not sufficient to change behaviour as the transient urban population owed little allegiance to the colonial state. In 1910, a report by a commission into municipal affairs concluded that larger scale measures which were more automatic in operation were necessary if any improvement in urban conditions was to be realized (Yeoh, 1991). To this end, one of the measures adopted in the early twentieth century was the spatial re-arrangement of building blocks through back lane and area reconstruction schemes. In 1907, a bill was introduced to demolish unhealthy slum dwellings, drive back lanes between blocks of back-to-back houses and reconstruct entire unhealthy areas through improvement schemes. However, the lack of finance, ineffective legislation and legal tussles over compensation meant that these schemes made little headway in alleviating overcrowding and urban congestion. In 1918, a report submitted by the housing commission recommended that if town improvement were to be conceived in broader terms, it could no longer be entrusted to the municipal authorities which, apart from being already overburdened with multifarious day-to-day functions, did not possess the technical expertise to plan and lay out the city according to modern planning principles. The report recommended the creation of new machinery in the form of an Improvement Trust and this finally bore fruit with the passing of the Singapore Improvement Ordinance in 1927 which instituted the setting up of the Singapore Improvement Trust (SIT) to supervise urban improvement and development in Singapore. The 1920s therefore witnessed a move from dependence on sanitarianism and municipal bye-law control to solve urban problems, to landuse planning and urban management on a more ambitious scale (Yeoh, 1996).

In effect, however, the SIT was empowered only to prepare schemes laying out roads, open spaces, and building lines but had no zoning power to dictate the type of buildings or land use suitable for a particular area. As such, instead of dictating future land use in a rational and systematic fashion, the General Improvement Plan was assessed in *Homes for the People* (published by the HDB after independence) to be 'in no sense a complete development plan, but merely a record, built up in piecemeal fashion, of existing development, together with layouts for proposed future development which had received statutory approval'.

The SIT also inherited from the municipality the responsibilities for condemning 'houses unfit for human habitation' and the eradication of slum property in the city. Again, progress was slow and piecemeal as improvement schemes requiring the buying up of large blocks of slums for demolition and reconstruction proved far too expensive as compensation had to be paid not simply for the houses affected but also for the site value. In the long term, while a back lane programme proved a more feasible way of opening up insanitary blocks, its actual value in solving the slum problem was rather doubtful. First, renewing the rear portions of old and dilapidated houses gave a new lease of life to property which was obsolete and overdue for demolition and rebuilding, thereby perpetuating rather than ameliorating the slum problem. Second, by reconstructing the rear portion of a house for back lane purposes, living accommodation was cut down by almost half in many cases, thus creating rehousing problems and aggravating overcrowding (Fraser, 1948, p. 10). During its early years, the Trust had no power to build except where expressly laid down in an improvement scheme and was under no obligation to provide housing except for persons made homeless as a result of the execution of an improvement scheme. As such, the lack of public provision of working-class housing to ameliorate the unremitting pressure on the existing housing stock caused by rapid demographic increase as well as the reduction of living space resulting from back lane improvements meant that the SIT, as in the case of its predecessor (the municipality), fought a rapidly losing battle against the problems of overcrowding, congestion and the proliferation of slum properties.

The provision of public housing progressed slowly. It was in the 1930s that the SIT finally ventured into public housing in recognition of the shortage of housing for the lower income groups (*SIT Report*, 1953, p. 7). A site at Tiong Bahru which had originally been acquired for an improvement scheme provided the ideal site which could serve as a test case for the development of a public housing estate. From 1936 to 1941, the Trust built 784 flats housed in two- or three-storey blocks, 54 tenements and 33 shops in Tiong Bahru (Fraser, 1948, p. 11). The estate was largely planned on the basis of principles used for postwar British New Towns such as Harlow, Stevenage, Crawley and others where the empha-

**Plate 2.5** Singapore Improvement Trust flats in Tiong Bahru, a popular residential location in 1996

sis was on small neighbourhoods, maximum privacy between individual homes and the provision of open spaces for recreation and playgrounds (*Homes for the People*, n.d., p. 40). Apart from British planning principles, local influence was also evident, as seen in the design of the flat layout based on a modified shophouse plan including airwells and back lanes. An attempt to put up the Tiong Bahru flats for sale failed and the flats were ultimately rented out to tenants instead (*SIT Report*, 1953, p. 7). By 1941, the new estate accommodated over 6000 people including Europeans from the middle income groups who could not afford to pay more than a certain limited amount in rents. The SIT's efforts in building a model estate were soon, however, interrupted by the outbreak of war. Thus, while public housing finally made some headway under the SIT, its achievements were small in comparison with the magnitude of the problem.

In sum, up to the eve of the Second World War, both municipal bye-law control to effect environmental improvement and the creation of new machinery in the form of a Trust to oversee urban planning and housing problems were ineffective in solving Singapore's urban problems. The onset of the war and the Japanese Occupation (1942–1945) was to further worsen Singapore's urban dilemmas.

### Reconstructing the post-war city

The Syonan years, as the Japanese Occupation has been called, represented a period of considerable confusion and suffering for the people of Singapore. In the city, while life settled down to some semblance of the old order (one where local concerns were subordinated to those of the imperial power) but under new masters after the initial chaos of the battle for Singapore, there were major fundamental changes (Thio, 1991). The city was essentially still run by the same machinery, the Municipality or *tokubetsu-si*, but this time, the Military Administration or *gunseikan-bu* had precedence and the *kempetai* (military police) controlled the city. As such, transport and housing conditions worsened as stocks which suffered wartime damage were not restored and infrastructure degenerated through lack of maintenance and general neglect; monopolistic systems replaced the British *laissez-faire* policy in the control of industries and food supplies; and discipline, surveillance and the fear of arbitrary punishment came to dictate the rhythm of everyday life in the city. By the end of the Occupation, while the physical fabric of the city – its buildings, streets, public works and harbour – survived largely intact, the population was 'undernourished, disease-ridden, poorly housed, and had inadequate educational, health and welfare facilities' (Cheng, 1991, p. 182).

Arguably too, the Occupation was not only a painful interlude but marked a significant turning point in Singapore's history. When the British reoccupied Singapore on 5 September 1945, they encountered a city which had not only suffered severe social and economic disruptions but a population 'that had undergone fundamental changes in political attitudes and aspirations' (Yeo and Lau, 1991, p. 117; Chou, 1995, pp. 33–39). The myth of British superiority and invincibility which had long prevailed in the colonial era was undermined and Britain's right to reimpose colonial rule called into question. Earlier in December 1943, the British government had pledged that after the war it would prepare Singapore (and Malaya) for eventual self-government within the British Empire. The constitutional struggle and party politics which marked this period from colonial rule to independence have been detailed elsewhere (Drysdale, 1984; Cheah, 1983; Yeo and Lau, 1991); suffice to say that progress towards the various milestones such as becoming a distinct British colony separate from the Malayan mainland in 1946, the attainment of internal self-government in 1959, the merger with Malaya in 1963 and the achievement of independence in 1965 were slow and uneven. Our focus here will be to trace the urban plans and policies aimed at reconstructing the social, economic and demographic fabric of the city in the years leading up to independence so as to provide some baselines from which to mount a more in-depth analysis of urban development in the post-independence years in subsequent chapters.

In the 1950s, the state embarked on surveying the land and planning for a city of the future. According to the government publication *Master Plan, Report of Survey* (1955, p. 15), 'the feature which overshadow[ed] all others . . . [was] the rapid increase in population and its relationship to the limited area of land'. As a result of the imminent onset of the Second World War, the volume of in-migration had dwindled considerably in 1941, and, in the post-war era, while there was a net flow of migrants from Malaysia to Singapore, migrant numbers had been greatly reduced compared to the pre-war situation. According to the *Census of Population* (1970) published by the Department of Statistics, this was a result of the uncertain socio-economic conditions in Singapore such as a high unemployment rate and limitations imposed by a 1953 legislation permitting entry of persons from countries other than West Malaysia on economic or compassionate grounds only. Natural increase replaced migrational surplus as the principal component of population growth and this was in turn due to high fertility rates – indeed, the period constitutes the postwar baby boom period – and declining mortality rates. Between 1947 and 1957, population increased from 938 144 to 1 445 929, representing an intercensal increase of 54.1% (Cheng, 1989, p. 163).

Various factors contributed to the high fertility rates. First, attitudes still favoured large families, a carry-over from an era when children were favoured for they contributed to free labour on the farms and in workshops. Secondly, although a Family Planning Association was set up in 1949, it was a voluntary association, receiving input from the government only insofar as it provided some grants and shared its maternal and child-health facilities. The association was largely ineffective and failed to disseminate knowledge of family planning methods and techniques effectively. Thirdly, while the nineteenth and early twentieth century was characterized by an imbalanced sex ratio (Table 2.2), the situation had started to change after 1933 when the Aliens Ordinance (which regulated the admission of aliens) raised the price of passage for male migrants. This led to an influx of females until the late 1930s when restrictions were imposed on female immigration (Lebra and Paulson, 1980, p. 7), but by then, a more balanced sex ratio had already been achieved, with effects on reproductive patterns in the 1940s and 1950s, during which many of these women were in the child-bearing age group.

At the same time that fertility rates were increasing, mortality rates were declining. Between 1947 and 1957, the crude mortality rate declined from 13.3 per thousand to 7.3 per thousand. This was largely due to the youthfulness of the population as well as a fall in infant mortality rates because of rapidly improving medical conditions. Specifically, between 1947 and 1957, infant mortality rates fell by more than half from 87.3 per thousand to 41.4 per thousand (*Report of the Registration of Births, Deaths, Marriages and Persons*, 1965).

The high population growth rate placed certain demands on the country. First, the young dependency ratio, that is, the number of young that each economically active person has to support, was high. This was a strain on the struggling economy. Secondly, there was a need to increase the quantity of schools to meet the increasing numbers of school-age children. As a consequence, the quality of education could not be given very much attention, and this had further implications on the quality of the future labour force. Thirdly, as infants aged, there was a high demand on public utilities and public housing, placing fairly high demands on an economy just recovering after the Japanese Occupation. Fourthly, greater sex parity also presaged a more stable, settled community, and this opened up the need for more community services (*Master Plan, Report of Survey*, 1955, p. 18).

Against this background of rapid demographic growth and the pressures it created, one of the first priorities was to remedy the city's economic difficulties and create means of livelihood for its people. In 1957, unemployment was estimated at 24 000 or 5% of the labour force and expected to rise significantly in the next few years (Cheng, 1991, p. 188). The immediate post-war economy was heavily dependent on entrepôt trade. Compared with the pre-war composition of entrepôt trade, the main change was the relative decline of Straits produce (except rubber) and a substantial increase in the volume of trade in manufactured goods such as textiles, machinery, processed foodstuffs and petroleum products. In the post-war era of increasing national and international trade restrictions and widely fluctuating prices and volume in commodity trading, it was feared that entrepôt trade could no longer sustain economic growth and provide adequate employment for the rapidly growing population in the long term. Furthermore, unlike in pre-war days when migration ebbed and flowed in response to the prosperity of the economy, the more settled and relatively young population in the post-war era provided a permanent and growing population base. As entrepôt trade could no longer be relied upon to generate the requisite volume of employment and income, attention was focused on developing other sectors of the economy, particularly manufacturing (Cheng, 1991, p. 185).

The stress on the importance of an industrialization strategy as a means of absorbing the rapidly increasing labour force was reiterated by a number of reports commissioned in the late 1950s and early 1960s. These included the 1955 report of a mission organized by the International Bank for Reconstruction and Development at the request of the government; a 1959 report by Canadian industrial development specialist, F. J. Lyle, requested under the Colombo Plan; and a 1961 report submitted by a United Nations mission headed by A. Winsemius. The Lyle report, for example, resulted in the Pioneer Industries Ordinance of 1959 which exempted pioneer product manufacturers from the prevailing 40% company tax for five years and the Industrial Expansion Ordinance of 1959 by which existing firms enjoyed income tax relief for five years on a sliding scale adjusted according to the amount of new capital invested in the approved expansion. The Winsemius Report provided much of the content of the first (and only) State Development Plan (1961–64) that provided the machinery to further the industrial ambition (Chapter 5).

In tandem with the need to generate employment for a rapidly growing population, 'a problem of equal severity' in the late 1940s and 1950s was the existence of slum and squatter properties on valuable land in the city centre. The municipal population of about 520 000 in 1938 had increased to just under 700 000 by 1947 with more than 100 000 living in squalid shacks according to the report of the government-appointed *Housing Committee of Singapore* (1948, p. 4). Areas such as Chinatown and Kampong Glam were 'occupied by acre after grim acre of ramshackle shophouses in which gross overcrowding was common' (*Homes for the People*, n.d., p. 30). Tuberculosis which accounted for one sixth of deaths in Singapore was rife and attributed to the dark and unventilated living conditions tolerated by the large numbers living in cubicles and tenements. A Housing Committee appointed in 1947 described housing conditions in Singapore as 'a disgrace to a civilised community' (*Report of the Housing Committee of Singapore*, 1948, p. 16) while several years later, Kaye (1960, p. 5) who documented the living conditions of a typical street in Chinatown in 1954 described it as 'among the most primitive in the urban areas of the world'. In a similar study on housing and poverty conducted in 1953–54, Goh Keng Swee (then director of Social Welfare and later Deputy Prime Minister) reported that 73% of surveyed households lived in badly overcrowded conditions (Goh, 1956). Chang (1970), in turn, observed that there was a growing blight of squatter settlements around the city fringes which housed an estimated quarter of a million people in 1962. These squatters occupied substandard shacks of attap, planks, corrugated zinc and other scrap material. In another estimate, it was suggested that one quarter of a million people lived in badly degenerated slums in the city centre and another one-third of a million lived in squatter areas on the city fringe in 1960 (Teh, 1975, p. 5).

Severe residential overcrowding was further conflated with other problems associated with slum areas in rapidly burgeoning and modernizing cities: dilapidated and insanitary buildings; high land values and irregular plot sizes which set a high premium on redevelopment; the lack of public open spaces and community services; a complicated mix of residential, industrial and commercial land use in close proximity; and road congestion and inadequate car parking facilities (*Master Plan, Report of Survey*, 1955, p. 12). To address these problems and to pave the way for 'comprehensive redevelopment', a Master Plan Committee was commissioned in 1951 and completed and published its report in 1955 although the plan was only approved by the government in 1958 and formally adopted as a statutory document in 1959. The plan gave emphasis to physical planning, that is, the control of land use through zoning mechanisms and density controls.

More specifically, the plan proposed a redistribution of the population living in the city centre by the construction of new suburbs close to the city such as Queenstown; new towns located further away incorporating places of work and community services for self-sufficiency; expanded villages as centres of rural life; and agricultural settlements to accommodate farmers and market gardeners (*Master Plan, Report of Survey*, 1955, p. 47). In sum, the main concept was 'the containment of the built-up area [in the city] by a green belt, the expansion of existing villages and rural centres and the construction of new towns to accommodate new growth (*Revised Master Plan, Report of Survey*, 1980, p. 1). Such a redistribution of people was predicated on public authorities undertaking a comprehensive housing policy to produce a peak rate of 11 000 permanent and 3000 temporary houses per annum by 1960 if the housing problem were to be conquered by 1972. In turn, this was an essential corollary if a programme of redevelopment were to be instituted for the Central Area to demolish derelict and insanitary buildings and to redevelop the cleared sites for 'the principal business, shopping and civic centres' (*Master Plan, Report of Survey*, 1955, p. 48). The plan also proposed reservation of sites for schools, community centres, health facilities and open spaces, as well as improvements to transport and communications.

While the need to redevelop the Central Area and provide alternative housing on a large scale was identified as the crux of the urban dilemma as early as the *Housing Committee Report of 1947* and reiterated again in greater detail in the master plan of 1958, little was achieved in terms of concrete results in the 1940s and 1950s. When the SIT resumed building activity after the war, some 20 907 units were constructed between 1947 and 1959, mainly in the Alexandra/Queenstown area as well as at Kallang Airport, St Michael's and Farrer Park. The Trust had become the *de facto* public housing agency in the post-war years although the enormity of the task at hand was not matched by increased statutory powers. Overall, it is estimated that the Trust provided housing for about 100 000 out of a population of a million and a half which was increasing in size at a rate of about 60 000 a year (Gamer, 1972, p. 43). Among the many reasons for its unremarkable record, the presence of squatters on land already purchased for public housing, financial stringency and the lack of political commitment on the part of the colonial government in backing its schemes were the most important (Lee, 1991, pp. 18–19; Teo and Savage, 1991, p. 328). While the master plan of 1958 contained various ideas which were later taken up by subsequent plans after independence, little was put into effect before the end of the colonial period given the time-lag between research and preparation of the plans, publication and official adoption as well as the uncertainty of the future of local government during a time of political change (Bristow, 1992). There was also a certain lack of dynamism about the plan for it assumed a slow and steady rate of social change, an assumption which collapsed in the face of the rapid social and economic changes which seized Singapore with the onset of independence (Teo, 1992).

## The colonial legacy

Like other colonial cities of the nineteenth and twentieth centuries, the distinctiveness of the social, morphological and functional features of colonial Singapore reflects its role in establishing, systemizing and maintaining colonial rule (King, 1985). The colonial process bequeathed to the new republic created in 1965 certain key features which were either affirmed, rejected or reworked by the post-independence government. Some of these features will be reviewed here.

### *From ethnic pluralism to the multiracial ideology*

Colonial societies with their complex matrix of indigenous, immigrant and colonialist groups were not only characterized by racial, cultural, social and religious pluralism but also a social stratification system which privileged *race* as the key mode of reference group ascription. In colonial Singapore, the planning of separate quarters for different 'races', the ranking and stereotyping of different communities on the basis of supposedly inherent racial attributes, and the general subordination of the 'natives' to white superiority in political and social spheres was a durable feature of life in the colonial city. The stark asymmetry of power between the colonized and the colonizers (Simon, 1984, p. 499) is also etched into the dualistic structure of the colonial urban landscape, symbolized by segregated European and indigenous quarters with their own distinct type of economic activities, land use patterns and architectural styles.

On the eve of independence, the colonial legacy was evident in the plural nature of society, comprising different fractions, each with its own trades, traditions and institutionalized practices. Singapore's population consisted primarily of immigrants hailing from different 'homelands' (e.g. China, India and the Malay world) and where even the local-born 'had to anchor their political [and cultural] orientation through myths of the ancestor homes' (Chua and Kuo, 1990, p. 2). While Maurice Freedman (1965) claimed that in the longer term immigrant minority communities in the Southeast Asian context will be assimilated into the majority population, Demaine (1984, p. 48) has more convincingly argued that, at least for Singapore and Malaysia, 'plurality created in the colonial period must be recognized and a national culture built upon it' in the post-independence period. In Singapore, plurality is further compounded by the wide social and economic gulf between the working classes comprising port workers, hawkers, trishaw riders, shop assistants, manual and casual labourers and the ruling elite; and a poverty profile with 19–21% of households below the poverty line in a thriving city (Lee, 1989, p. 37). In the words of one commentator, 'in spite of its wealth and strategic importance' Singapore was 'in many respects a sociologically immature city where racial, tribal and economic divisions are still quite sharp' (Hodder, 1953, p. 25).

For Singapore's political leaders, the question of national integration in a multi-ethnic society loomed large. Prior to the merger with Malaya in 1963, the People's Action Party (PAP) had consistently campaigned for 'independence through merger', as it was never believed at the time that Singapore could survive economically or politically without its hinterland, the Federation of Malaysia (Yeo and Lau, 1991, p. 148). 'National identity' as conceived then was thus directed towards Malaya. However, with the merger, the anti-communalist leadership of the city-state 'was increasingly at odds with the more conservative, Malay-dominated leadership of the Central Government' (Chew, 1991b, p. 363). Within the new polity, the PAP's vision of a non-communal multiracial 'Malaysian Malaysia' rekindled fears within the Federation that Malay privileges would be withdrawn and that the 'racial arithmetic' might be turned against the Malays if the PAP should gain ascendency (Yeo and Lau, 1991, p. 147). Merger soon 'exploded the myth that Singapore and Malaysia were naturally complementary and compatible' (Chan, 1991, p. 159). This propelled Singapore's exit from Malaysia and with the union peremptorily and, ironically, severed in August 1965, the PAP found itself having to disprove its original contention that an independent Singapore was not viable.

The political uncertainty and racial tensions which surrounded the birth of the new republic were reflected in Goh Keng Swee's (then Minister of the Interior and Defence) description of Singapore as 'a complex, multiracial community with little sense of common history, with a group purpose which is yet to be properly articulated, . . . in the process of rapid transition towards a destiny which we do not know yet' (quoted in Chew, 1991b, p. 363). National survival became the dominant preoccupation of Singapore's political leaders, who lost no time in urging the local population to 'buckle down to the job of 'nation-building' (Benjamin, 1988, p. 20). As a means of integrating the disparate fractions of society and forging a single identity out of the heterogeneous population riven by racial, religious, language and cultural lines, the PAP espoused the ideology of multiracialism (along with non-communism, non-alignment and democracy). In theory, this formulation assumes that each of the major races – Chinese, Malays, Indians and 'Others' – is 'separate but equal' and encourages acceptance of the co-existence of different religious practices, customs and traditions of the various communities 'without discrimination for any particular community' (Chan and Evers, 1978, p. 123). This abiding belief in the multiracial ideal based on the separate ethnic identities that had developed under British colonialism and further reinforced by political developments leading to independence (Hill and Lian, 1995, p. 91) played a major part in shaping public policy in many spheres of life in the post-independence years as subsequent chapters will show.

*The entrepôt inheritance and manufacturing development*

Entrepôt trade, in which the island functioned as the commercial heart of a Malay hinterland, was the essential feature of Singapore's economic development during its colonial status. During the 1950s, this function had been further consolidated despite the frequency with which the imminent decline of the entrepôt trade was predicted. While the price of rubber continued to regulate the overall prosperity of trade (in 1960 Singapore accounted for over a third of world production), by the mid-1950s petroleum exports had expanded to four times their pre-war volumes. The Royal Dutch Shell group stationed its Far Eastern headquarters of its tanker fleet in Singapore and Caltex began marketing operations in 1959. By the time oil refining operations had commenced in 1960, the port was already the biggest oil storage, blending, packing and bunkering base in Southeast Asia (Huff, 1994, p. 279). Despite the diversification of the commodity base, as late as the mid-1960s, 40% of external commerce was still tied to Malaysia and Indonesia and 70% of employment and 75% of revenue depended on services (Regnier, 1991, p. 36).

The initial underdevelopment of the manufacturing sector was a challenge to achieving industrialization and full employment in the newly independent republic. Excluding processing and servicing, the output of manufacturing accounted for only 14% of GDP in 1960. Out of the total manufacturing labour force of 43 000 in 1960, three quarters worked in establishments of fewer than 10 workers while the manufacture of goods for international markets engaged around a quarter of the industrial workforce. Moreover, during 1957–1960, a United Nations Industrial Survey Mission reported that most branches of manufacturing had been in decline, resulting in a 20% drop in the workforce (UNISM, 1961).

The entrepôt inheritance offered advantages and disadvantages to the post-independence industrialization programme. The trading function had encouraged a good infrastructure, augmented in 1955 by the opening of Paya Lebar airport and ongoing improvements in port facilities to accommodate the increased tonnage and size of ships. Another important benefit obtained was in encouraging the adoption of an export-orientated manufacturing strategy. At the time, the conditions for manufacturing development tended to be viewed as antithetical to the needs of international trade. Whereas the virtually unrestricted movement of goods and credit assured the viability of trade and commerce, the conventional wisdom was that the development of manufacturing depended on import protection. As this form of industry promotion was not an option in Singapore, it left little choice but to embark on the development of export manufacturing which, as it later was to discover, suited the changing structure of the world economy. It should also be noted that while entrepôt had helped produce a comparatively wealthy society, it had also helped establish a consumer preference for well-known foreign products. This again tended to give little opportunity for local production, further supporting the shift to export manufacturing (UNISM, 1963, p. 22).

Less in Singapore's favour, the Survey Mission saw Singapore's entrepreneurs as being largely immobilized from participation in industrialization, although they were judged 'amongst the best in the world'. Trading was based on short-term investment with a quick turnaround. Manufacturing demanded a longer-term outlook as well as new management skills. The banking sector, comprising both local Singapore Chinese banks and European banks, constituted the basis of a modern financial sector. The lack of a central bank in Singapore and the regional status of Chinese banks, which tied them to cyclical commodity markets, necessitated the retention of high reserve ratios which limited local lending. Recognition of the need for capital and skills was suggested in the government's Industrial Survey 1958–59 which reported that around a fifth of manufacturing firms were interested in cooperation with foreign firms (UNISM, 1963, p. 74). It may be argued, however, that the financial constraints, while in one sense a weakness, did tend to make the option of attracting international capital a relatively problem-free choice.

In considering the viability of attracting international capital, relative wage costs and the state of industrial relations were given much attention by the UN survey team. While Singapore's population growth provided an elastic supply of labour, the average wage in larger manufacturing establishments was judged to be 20–30% too high to compete with the main exporters of manufactured goods of similar types in Southeast Asia. Labour legislation which provided for a 44 hour working week, 7 days paid annual leave, 11 public holidays, 28 days paid sick leave, 2 months paid maternity leave and an overtime rate of 150% (200% for Sunday and public holidays) was seen to be inflating labour costs above international market levels. To support such conditions, greater use of shift working was recommended – at the time only six manufacturing establishments worked shifts – as a means of raising overall workplace productivity. In the shipyards, for example, it was found that working weeks of 76 hours were not uncommon, one third paid as overtime.

As well as saving wage costs and making more use of fixed capital, shift working offered a way of maintaining present conditions with least risk of bringing industrial unrest. While it was noted that the industrial relations had improved during the 1950s, the UN felt that the general environment was still too confrontational and already a barrier to accelerated economic expansion. Industrial unrest was however intertwined with the broader political change affecting the island, with all political parties using trade union agitation to promote their interests (Huff, 1994, p. 296). The UN investigation team concluded that considerable common ground existed between management and union attitudes but it was clearly pessimistic about this occurring. More positively, the UN reported that the quality of labour was high and the Singaporean worker industrious with 'considerable aptitude to work in manufacturing industries' (UNISM, 1961, p. v). It did however caution that Singaporeans tended to have a preference for white-collar jobs, locally called 'mental work', a characteristic which has helped accommodate the large numbers of foreign workers who today supply much of the construction, labouring and factory assembly workforce.

### From laissez faire to state-directed planning

Colonial Singapore thrived not simply on trade but on *free* trade. According to Lee (1989, p. 4), the 'logic of free trade' was not only 'the lifeblood' of colonial Singapore but also 'the ideology behind its governance' because free trade 'presupposes a *laissez-faire* style of government: no tax on imports and exports, no tax on income or company profits, and no "welfarism" either'. Private enterprise was seen as the engine of growth and the ideology of *laissez-faire* invaded other spheres of life. It was typical of colonial sentiments and policy that industrial, commercial, residential and community developments should be left as far as possible in the hands of the private sector and that there should be minimum state involvement.

Until the master plan of 1958, planning was limited to what could be achieved through the control of private development by regulations governing building and land subdivisions, a strategy which was woefully inadequate to regulate the city's growth. The abdication of social responsibility to the private sector in areas such as housing for the masses spelled massive shortages and dismal housing conditions from as early as the late nineteenth century and reached crisis proportions in the 1950s. Before the war, where the colonial state had intervened to alleviate overcrowding, it had often done so with inadequate financial commitment and over-zealous attention to reforming the people's habits and customs. When the SIT finally embarked on housing programmes, it was never of a scale large enough to bring about real improvement. The one innovation of note during the final years of colonial administration was the establishment of the Central Provident Fund (CPF) in 1955. This was a social security system later adopted by the PAP government. By allowing CPF members to utilize substantial portions of their accounts to purchase public flats, this scheme provides a 'regulatory link between housing provision, savings, investments and economic growth' (Hill and Lian, 1995, p. 117). In general, it took a radical change of the socio-political context heralded by independence and stronger advocacy for planning to lift the development of the city to a fundamentally different plane as subsequent chapters on housing and the built environment will show.

Similarly, in the field of education, the colonial government adopted a largely hands-off attitude. It only became substantively involved in the provision of educational facilities in 1902 when the Education Code provided for the establishment of a limited number of English-medium primary schools (Gopinathan, 1991, p. 269). Where vernacular education was concerned, the colonial government was prepared to be responsible for Malay schools but not for schools in the other vernacular languages, Chinese and Tamil, preferring to leave these in the hands of community-based organizations. Edwin Lee (1989, p. 22) records that in the period before the Second World War, there were 27 000 pupils in English schools, 38 000 pupils in Chinese schools, 5800 pupils in Malay schools, and 1000 pupils in Tamil schools. In his assessment of British education policy, he notes that 'in so far as the British had a policy, it was conceived in economy, not to say parsimony, executed with expedience, and its outcome was separatism. The schools were allowed to exist in separate linguistic and communal compartments' (Lee, 1989, p. 22). Mary Turnbull (1977, p. 121) provides a similar evaluation: British education policy was 'socially divisive, separating the English- and the vernacular-educated, widening the gap between the different communities except at the highest level, accentuating racial, cultural, and linguistic differences and stressing the rift between rich and poor'. It was not until 1946 that a ten-year programme containing the principle of free primary education was introduced and a decade later that Chinese schools were incorporated into an integrated national school system with a common syllabus and a mandatory bilingual policy (Lee, 1989, p. 24; Hill and Lian, 1995, p. 76).

State intervention in the provision of medical and health services during the colonial era was similarly limited, the official view being that the population was largely transitory and 'people who drifted in and out did so at their own risk' (Lee, 1989, p. 31). While the colonial government ran several hospitals offering a range of services to the people, some of these such as the Tan Tock Seng Hospital would not have been established without the philanthropic contributions from private individuals. Given the inadequacies of a municipal system of health care, vernacular medical delivery systems filled a much felt void in the lives of the people. The Chinese community, for example, ran its own medical institutions, medical halls and clan-based recuperation centres based on the tenets of Chinese medicine (Yeoh, 1996). As in the case of education, it was only after the return to civil rule in 1947 that the first ever Medical Plan for the colony was introduced 'to provide essential health services for the community as a whole and to furnish individuals with medical care at prices within the reach of all its subjects' (Tan, 1991, p. 346).

In sum, the *laissez-faire* style adopted by the colonial government facilitated a free trading system but contributed little to the socio-economic development of the city. In the words of Edwin Lee (1989, p. 40):

> It was a city solidly built to facilitate the functions of trading houses, banks, and government offices. Grace, elegance, and beauty were not altogether absent, but the emphasis of the builders was on the utilitarian and modern rather than the aesthetic and the antiquarian. So the chief glories of British rule, as far as the urban landscape was concerned, must be looked for in such things as piped sewers, ventilating backlanes, impounding reservoirs, power stations, metalled roads, mechanized public transport, and civil airports and airline services. The British understood the need to invest in infrastructure and Singapore was their show-piece, an artefact of colonial design and engineering skill. . . . [In contrast,] schools, hospitals, and homes for the people were either not enough or not up to standard.

The move towards the creation of a new nation-state warranted a reassessment of the free reign of *laissez-faire* principles in the various spheres of life. As Benjamin (1988, p. 3) has argued, the formation of a new nation-state represents a radical discontinuity, 'an increasing separation from its own past' rather than a smooth progression from the previous polity. This discontinuity is associated with the view that a new nation-state must necessarily be the product of 'conscious goal-directed planning' (Benjamin, 1988, p. 3). Such consciousness was already evident in the last years of colonial rule during the run-up to independence as can be seen in the proliferation of grand plans such as the ten-year education plan, the ten-year medical plan, the 1958 Master Plan and the 1961-64 State Development Plan intended to spearhead industrialization (Cheng, 1991, p. 189). In the first flush of independence, strategies were mounted to tackle major socio-economic problems which threatened the fragile fabric of the newly created 'nation' including racial tensions, economic backwardness and unemployment, housing shortages and slum problems as well as health concerns. These policies and plans were not only intended to improve living conditions for the people but were also intimately linked to the government's bid to secure political legitimacy, to build ideological consensus and to transform the population into a disciplined industrial workforce (Chua, 1991). As will be seen in subsequent chapters, beyond meeting the immediate and more long-term material needs of the people, state-directed planning in the various areas of housing, the environment, demography and heritage was also aimed at forging common consciousness of a sense of identity with the nation-state.

## The legacy of governance

Apart from the more tangible aspects of colonial legacy outlined above, commentators such as Edwin Lee (1989, p. 41) contend that one of the most important legacies bequeathed to the republic by the British is 'the ideal of good clean government' with high standards of justice, efficiency and incorruptibility. He elaborates:

> One hundred and forty years or so of British rule have etched on the Singapore consciousness certain principles and values which have become part of the national ethos. Singapore today is a country where the responsibility of government is assumed as a sacred trust, where the prime minister sets the tone of public life as the colonial governor once did, where the rule of law prevails, where corruption and graft are serious offences, where Commissions of Enquiry are appointed when matters of national importance are at stake, where civic-mindedness is a living reality, and where the public loves justice and fair play (Lee, 1989, p. 42).

While Lee's enthusiastic description must almost definitely refer to the ideal state rather than reality, it is clear that some of the principles underlying the machinery of government in post-independence Singapore trace their roots back to British colonial administration. It is generally accepted that parliamentary democracy in Singapore is a legacy of British colonial rule, with the first legislative council to include elected members dating back to 1948 (Chan, 1987). Characterized by a dominant single party, the Singapore system, however, has deviated significantly from the British model which is predicated on the existence of an opposition in the legislature to bring the government to account for its performance and policies (see Chapter 3). The civil service, the bureaucratic layer which translates the decisions of the political leadership into tangible programmes, is the longest surviving institution in Singapore from colonial times. Precisely because of the long interlude between the outbreak of the Second World War and Singapore's independence a quarter of a century later, the ocal population which had largely been excluded from the civil service before the war had time and opportunities to gain much experience during the extended process of decolonization (Huff, 1994). With independence, Singapore inherited a well-seasoned civil service of high quality. While it once represented the writ of colonial powers, it continues today to work closely with the political leadership to wield 'fused political–administrative powers' in widening arenas of decision-making (Seah, 1985, p. 98).

British colonial influence is also apparent in Singapore's legal system. As a local lawyer and academic has argued, not only does English law provide the foundation of modern Singapore's legal system, its principles are so widely accepted and legitimated that there is little interest to develop an autochthonous Singaporean legal system more consistent with local needs, mores and aspirations (Phang, 1990). The independence of the judiciary, a fundamental assumption underlying the Singapore legal system, is also part of the colonial inheritance. Judges are expected to decide on cases according to the law without being answerable to either the executive or the legislature in order to ensure the integrity and impartiality of the courts (Chan, 1995, p. 45). Until recently, the final appellate court in Singapore's judicial system was the Privy Council comprising British judges. The process of phasing out the Privy Council was only started in 1989 and eventually replaced by a local Court of Appeal, a reflection of Singapore's growing confidence in itself as a sovereign nation.

# 3

# Government and politics

Singapore has a single tier of government comprising a unicameral parliament of 83 elected representatives. This single tier of government has been under the continuous political control of the People's Action Party (PAP) since 1959 when a general election was held for the first fully elected legislative assembly. A system of elected local government was introduced in 1951 but within a few weeks of taking office the PAP government pushed through the merger of local and central government to 'streamline the machinery of government' (Turnbull, 1989, p. 269). Further centralization of power was obtained by the concentration of authority in government departments and statutory bodies amongst a small group of individuals closely aligned to the PAP. Political stability has been further entrenched by the low turnover of personnel amongst senior cabinet members during the first 25 years of independent government. The most notable case of this is Lee Kuan Yew who became Prime Minister in 1959, retaining that position until his retirement from the premiership in 1990 from when he became Senior Minister within cabinet.

The long period of governmental stability has allowed the political philosophy of the PAP to subordinate alternative perspectives. Integrated and comprehensive economic and social planning has thus been possible and, perhaps more importantly, so has the continuous adaptation of policies to changing circumstances. Singapore has not maintained a system of national economic planning, but the inner leadership have fulfilled many of the functions of a central economic planning agency. The compact geographical scale and the concentration of administration in a few large delivery agencies has further helped policy coordination, both horizontally and vertically. The net result has been to give the state considerable freedom of action. Major infrastructure projects, for example, necessitating the removal and relocation of large numbers of urban residents, have not been constrained by the demands of sectoral lobbyists, community advocates or other interest groups as they have in other major cities of Southeast Asia (Aldrich, 1985; Neville, 1993). Similarly, it has been comparatively easy to reverse policy decisions, even where this requires abandoning once firmly held positions, as in the case of population policies (see Chapter 4).

Political stability and centralization have heightened the perceived risks associated with a change in control. The passing of political control to a 'new guard' in the 1990s, themselves exposed to a new generation of voters, has been managed carefully. This commenced in the mid-1980s with the introduction of new avenues for public involvement in policy debate, including the reintroduction of local government, although under the control of MPs and government approved representatives rather than separate municipal elections. To strengthen the cohesion of society, a set of shared national values were promulgated in 1991. Also in that year, legislation was passed to introduce an elected President with veto powers over government budgets, key public appointments and checks against government use of its powers under the Internal Security Act, religious harmony legislation and corruption investigations. The first presidential election was held in 1993 prior to which the President was an appointee of parliament with a purely ceremonial function.

This chapter provides an outline of Singapore's political system and the recent innovations made to its system of government. It examines the various ways that democracy has been managed and shaped and the extent to which its acceptance is related to the predominance of a Confucian ethic. The innovations associated with the transfer of power to a new generation of leaders are explored as well as the impact on political management of an increasingly affluent middle class.

### Major features of Singapore's political system

During the PAP government's reign, there were no opposition MPs from October 1966 until 1981 (when the Workers' Party candidate, J. B. Jeyaretnam, won the Anson by-election) and ten years later the number of opposition MPs was only four (Table 3.1). Such political dominance can be ascribed only partly to the popularity of the PAP and its success in delivering goods and services to the population. The political system has been described by one of Singapore's leading political scientists as a 'controlled democracy' (Quah, 1988). Constraints on political opposition have created a political system that facilitates an unusual degree of control and penetration of society.

**Table 3.1** General elections since 1955

| Election date | Number of seats | Uncontested seats | Party returned | Seats won | Share of total vote |
|---|---|---|---|---|---|
| *Legislative Assembly* | | | | | |
| 2 April 1955 | 25 | – | Labour Front | 10 | 26.7% |
| 30 May 1959 | 51 | – | PAP | 43 | 53.4% |
| 21 September 1963 | 51 | – | PAP | 37 | 46.4% |
| *Parliament* | | | | | |
| 13 April 1968 | 58 | 51 | PAP | 58 | 84.4% |
| 2 September 1972 | 65 | 8 | PAP | 65 | 69.0% |
| 23 December 1976 | 69 | 16 | PAP | 69 | 72.4% |
| 23 December 1980 | 75 | 37 | PAP | 75 | 75.5% |
| 22 December 1984 | 79 | 30 | PAP | 77 | 62.9% |
| 3 September 1988 | 81 | 11 | PAP | 80 | 61.7% |
| 31 August 1991 | 81 | 41 | PAP | 77 | 59.3% |
| 2 January 1997 | 83 | 47 | PAP | 81 | 63.5% |

*Source:* Singapore 1995, *The Straits Times*, 3 January 1997

Independent Singapore inherited a parliamentary system of government based on the Westminster model from Britain and then adapted this model to include extra-parliamentary constraint on challenges to the ruling party. Quah (1988) considers that only the minimum criterion for a democracy remains, namely the existence of free, fair and periodic general elections (although it might be considered unusual that the campaign period for elections can be limited to ten days). Rather than these elections being the end product of broader contests over social and political power, as would be expected in a western democracy, they tend to be the only contest (Rodan, 1993a). In a similar vein, it has been argued that Singapore's political system is best described as a 'hegemonic party system' in which other political parties are permitted but there is not provision for political competition on an equal basis (Chan, 1987, p. 147).

The impediments to political opposition comprise negative sanctions and various mechanisms for channelling political debate through government-controlled organizations. Amongst the former, the 1963 Internal Security Act allows the detention without trial or charge of persons who are suspected of involvement in subversive or communist-related activities. After the detention of two opposition *Barisan Sosialis* MPs in late 1966 for security reasons, all nine opposition members resigned their seats from whence a period of unopposed PAP control ensued. The Internal Security Act has subsequently been used to control dissent. The last widespread use of this power was the arrest of 22 people in May and June 1987.

Those arrested, who were mainly Catholic church leaders and dramatists, were alleged to be Marxist conspirators. Most were released within a few months but the manner of their detention was the occasion of international outrage, including allegations by Amnesty International of torture to elicit confessions (Rodan, 1989, p. 202; Seow, 1994).

Control of press freedom has been a further limitation on open political debate. The PAP government inherited from the 1948 Emergency Regulations the Printing Presses Ordinance which made it unlawful to operate a printing press without an annual licence that can be revoked at any time. In May 1971, the government forced the closure of two English language dailies. *The Eastern Sun* was claimed to be a fifth column communist newspaper, backed by sources in Hong Kong, while *The Singapore Herald* was said to be advocating permissiveness in sex, drugs and dress styles and dissenting attitudes to labour laws, national service and the Internal Security Act (Gayle, 1986). Concern that newspapers funded from overseas might incite conflict led to the 1974 Newspapers and Printing Presses Act giving the state greater control over newspaper management. The new Act separated financial ownership from editorial control by issuing management shares to Singapore citizens approved by the government. Through this mechanism, an official programme of media restructuring led to the eventual merger of three publishers to produce a controlled English language newspaper monopoly.

In 1986, an amendment to the 1974 Act was made to allow restrictions on the circulation of foreign periodicals and newspapers which are considered to be 'engaging in the domestic politics of Singapore'. Part of the motivation may have been the concern that the local population was increasingly turning to the foreign press for comment on Singapore affairs given the absence of this discussion in its own press (Chua, 1995, p. 211). The *Far Eastern Economic Review* (FEER) has been subject to such restrictions since the government judged the nature of its reporting on the 1987 arrests to be political. Circulation was cut from 10 000 to 500 copies. This circulation has since been raised gradually to 4000 from May 1995 (*The Straits Times*, 25 April 1995), despite ongoing government displeasure with some aspects of FEER's reporting on Singapore politics (Figure 3.1).

The extra-parliamentary channels which provide an avenue for some form of political debate have their origins in the PAP's need to strengthen its community organization (Rodan, 1993a). The PAP that was elected to power in 1959 was based on an alliance of a left-wing Chinese educated working class movement and a more conservative group of English educated middle class nationalists led by Lee Kuan Yew. The latter faction was in control of the party's executive, while the former had mass support and a grassroots organization. When the PAP split, through the formation

**Figure 3.1**  Examples of foreign press reporting that may produce circulation restrictions

---

*Foreign press reporting seen as against Singapore's interests*

---

Examples of FEER's attacks on Singapore, PM Goh

---

The High Court yesterday heard of several instances in which the *Far Eastern Economic Review* . . . mentioned Singapore in a negative light:
- In the Nov 15, 1990 issue, an article . . . was illustrated with a cartoon. It shows Mr Goh bearing Singapore on his back, atop of which sits Senior Minister Lee Kuan Yew. A tiny cartoon figure in the corner is shown saying 'Yes! Minister!'. Mr Goh said such a cartoon was unexpected in a serious journal like the *Review*.
- Another article, headlined Backseat Driver, by the same author suggested that Mr Goh would be less than completely in charge after he assumed the premiership because of Mr Lee's 'impatient presence'.
  Mr Goh said the story undermined his authority even before he could take on the post of Prime Minister. This was a very serious attack on him personally, and on the institution of the Prime Minister in Singapore.
- . . . Mr Bowring's article . . . noted that the communist powers in Hanoi had welcomed the *Review* setting up a bureau there, while capitalist Singapore had denied the publication clearance to base a correspondent here.
  Asked by lawyer Harry Elias what he thought of the piece, Mr Goh said it was 'written by a pen dipped in arsenic'.

---

*Source: The Straits Times*, 14 June 1995

of the *Barisan Sosialis* in 1961, there was a need to build an alternative community support base. A policy of 'controlled mobilization and participation' was a key part of this nation building programme involving 'the creation of various intermediary institutions which sought to absorb the participatory talents of the people, directing them to different aspects of the government's socio-political and development programmes' (Seah, 1987, p. 174). To a large degree, these institutions enabled the PAP to reduce emphasis on its own party organization by meshing the identity of the PAP with these new state agencies.

The three most important parapolitical institutions, or grassroots organizations as they are known locally, are the Community Centres (CCs), which are coordinated by the People's Association (PA), the Citizens' Consultative Committees (CCCs) and the Residents' Committees (RCs). The selection and appointment of members to these organizations are under the control of the Prime Minister's office. An important consequence of this control is that representatives of opposition political parties are at a clear disadvantage in advancing their policies, since they do not have access to the same set of intermediary agencies (Hill and Lian, 1995, p. 176). They are also part of the process whereby the public bureaucracy has become almost indistinguishable from the PAP (Rodan, 1993a, p. 81).

This process was taken a stage further with conversion of the once independent trade union organizations into a state-sponsored National Trades Union Congress in the 1960s (see Chapter 5).

Opposition from elected MPs is held in check by the absence of parliamentary privilege giving protection against prosecution for statements made in parliament. This implies a need to meet legal standards of proof to avoid the risk of prosecution, considerably raising the standards of evidence in political debate over that expected in western democracies. Government and opposition MPs are not differently placed except that it is parliament which determines whether 'dishonourable conduct, abuse of privilege or contempt' has been committed and parliament is dominated by the PAP. Within the ruling party there is no tradition of a critical backbench voice, notwithstanding the PAP's own attempts to foster internal debate (Chan, 1987, p. 74).

Collectively these developments led to the contention, advanced first for Singapore by Deyo (1981), that Singapore's political system is best interpreted as a form of corporatism. This contention sees a relationship of economic and political subordination between the state (as representative of national interests) and particular social groups (notably labour). To achieve this subordination, society is organized into a limited number of interest groups in the form of associations, societies and unions whose support of state objectives is ensured by close governmental control. Corporatism in Singapore has been viewed as a special case for two main reasons (Rodan, 1989, pp. 29–30). First, not all interests in Singapore have been brought under the control of the state; the notable exception being multinational enterprise. Secondly, the origins of corporatism in Singapore were in the actions of the ruling PAP as a strategy to consolidate its authority, rather than being a prerequisite for its political autonomy. In addition, it has been argued that the corporatist ascription underestimates the extent to which a 'return to sender' mentality has developed (Hill and Lian, 1995). The return to sender dynamic emphasizes an interactive relationship between the political elite and citizens, rather than a simple top-down process.

Singapore's own leaders favour the label 'communitarian democracy', although it has been pointed out that the communitarian model is still to be elaborated in detail (Chua, 1995, p. 200). The central idea of communitarianism is that collective interests should have primacy over individual ones. The extent to which the definition of the collective interest should be achieved through consensus or by the state is an unresolved tension in the model. Initially the definition of the collective interest was taken to be the preserve of the ruling government, justified by the imperative of ensuring 'national survival'. National interest was conflated with economic development and the improvement of material life of the population. The delivery of economic growth demonstrated 'good government' and legitimized ongoing control of the social, cultural and political environment. The government's pervasive authority is justified by its claims to embody the national interest, consequently it must take seriously representations from those who seek to be consulted. This right of consultation is different from a western liberal conceptualization of individual rights:

> Within communitarianism, constrained within the ideological/conceptual space of national interests, no individual or group can assert its own right as a basic condition of existence lest the assertion be read as unacceptable self-interest, potentially detrimental to the whole. The right to be consulted must therefore be constituted without reference to 'nature' but sociologically, on grounds that a broadly defined consensus can only emerge when all interested parties are consulted and their differences accommodated or rationalized (Chua, 1995, p. 197).

Chua detects the beginning of the institutionalization of the 'right' to be consulted since the mid-1980s. There are therefore two main phases to the PAP's political control. An initial period when it defined the political agenda with little recourse to national sentiment, and a more recent phase where it has been more sensitized to the electoral opinion. During the earlier phase, the central components of PAP belief were formed in pursuit of the core goal of economic growth.

## PAP political management

Prior to 1965 any notion of state and nation was poorly developed in Singapore given its multiracial immigrant population and the predominant expectation that independence would be a part of a larger Malayan union. The origins of PAP politics were conditioned by the urgent need to forge a Singaporean identity, and the sense of threat from its larger regional neighbours. This has both added to the urgency of nation building and limited the scope to pursue strategies that diverge radically from those of neighbouring territories. Even in the 1990s, it has been suggested that the adoption of a fully democratic system might not be acceptable to neighbouring governments (Regnier, 1991, p. 236).

The central components of PAP ideology are multiracialism, pragmatism and meritocracy, each of which is connected to the deeper origins of Singapore's controlled democracy (Hill and Lian, 1995). Multiracialism has its origins in the initial PAP goal of fostering a broad-based Malayan nationalist movement to secure independence from British colonial administration. The perspective of the most influential first-generation

PAP leaders – Lee Kuan Yew, Goh Keng Swee and Toh Chin Chye – was that Singapore's future was best secured as part of a Malayan nation that transcended racial divisions. This imperative had been sharpened during the turbulent years of Singapore's entry and subsequent ejection from the Federation two years later in 1965, which had seen Malay expectations in Singapore rise and the breakaway from the PAP of left-wing members opposed to union. Fuelled by communal politics, racial riots broke out twice in 1964 in which 31 persons were killed and over 500 injured. Although highly localized and the first such incidents of racial conflict since riots in 1950, they were alarming as 'Singapore had prided herself on her racial tolerance and communal peace' (Turnbull, 1989, p. 283). They underlined to the PAP government the dangers they had always recognized in communal politics, indicating the potential for racial conflict to destroy the stability of society, as well as jeopardizing the island's attractiveness to foreign investors. Equally important was the realization of Singapore's Malay racial minority being the majority in the region. The potential for conflict to spill into these territories made it likely that any prolonged political disorder would not be tolerated by its larger regional neighbours (Regnier, 1991, p. 236).

The building of a genuinely multiracial society from a population of diverse affiliations has required careful political management. The first President of the Republic, Yusof bin Iskak, was a Malay, and his two successors, Benjamin Sheares and Devan Nair were respectively Eurasian and Indian, and only subsequently was there a Chinese President (first Wee Kim Wee and then Ong Teng Cheong). After three official languages were recognized – Chinese, Malay and Tamil – Malay, the first national language, retained some greater standing by its use in the Singapore national anthem. Bilingualism was introduced in schools in 1966, with the core of instruction in English providing a means of communication across cultures as well as assisting international business. The replacement of Chinese dialects (such as Hokkien, Cantonese, Teochew, Hainanese) by Mandarin, a language foreign to most of Singapore's Chinese speakers, has been encouraged as a way of providing commonality between groups. While the British did not completely withdraw their military presence in Singapore until well into the 1970s, the PAP introduced compulsory military service of 24–30 months for all 18-year-old males. Military insecurity encouraged its introduction but the mixing of ethnic groups and cultures is stressed as an important reason for its continuance. Appointments to government agencies are usually balanced to ensure multiracial participation, but some deviations are allowed where this is seen to be beneficial. Malays, for example, are numerically strong in the police, the army and the judiciary, while Indians are over-represented in the diplomatic service so 'even if its ASEAN neighbours tend to regard Singapore as a Chinese emporium in a "Malay ocean", they often have to negotiate with non-Chinese representatives of the Singapore government' (Regnier, 1991, p. 250).

A pragmatic style to PAP politics is seen in its tendency to adopt policies that offer the best prospect of succeeding, whatever their ideological credentials. The origins of this style have been linked to the 'politics of survival' in the 1960s when the urgency of raising the social conditions of the masses was seen to justify a shift away from the socialist strategies earlier advocated (Chua, 1985). Others have argued that such pragmatism had a much earlier origin, reflected in the way that PAP leaders had associated with socialist ideals only with the goal of gradually harnessing their community appeal to their own political programme (Bloodworth, 1986).

Whatever the origin, pragmatism has developed into the belief that policy can be justified where there exists, from the PAP's perspective, an acceptable rational response (Hill and Lian, 1995, p. 190). One example of this in operation is the government's linking of electoral choice to public infrastructure provision. Opposition-held constituencies are openly advised that they can expect to be a lower priority for maintenance or new investment than government-held areas. Thus when a new MRT line, linking the north east of the island to the central area, was announced in 1996 the station closest to the opposition constituency of Potong Pasir was allocated only as a second phase development. Such discrimination is well established in the allocation of public housing improvements (see Chapter 8), justified on the simple grounds that it is fair from a party viewpoint and appropriate for the community since improvements are only possible because of the economic success engineered by the PAP (Hill and Lian, 1995, p. 191). In this context it is sensible to reward those who recognize this achievement and penalize those who place it in jeopardy.

The third component of PAP politics is meritocracy. One aspect of meritocracy involves promoting ability over ethnic, cultural or religious affiliation. In a society dominated racially and economically by the Chinese, meritocracy has required continual reconciliation with the goal of multiculturalism, especially given the PAP's commitment to avoid welfare measures or positive discrimination which are seen only to generate a dependence mentality. The Malay population overall has tended to lag behind the Chinese and Indian in social and economic advancement. Key positions in the police and army remain barred for Malays, as a legacy of communal troubles in 1969, reinforced when Malays protested against the Israeli President's visit to the Republic in late 1986 (Brown, 1993). Intensified Islamic resurgence in other countries as well has been the occasion of questioning by Singapore's leaders as to where the local Malay loyalty would lie in time of crisis. State sponsored self-help has, however, been vigorously pursued, including the Council for the Development of Muslims in Singapore (MENDAKI), the Association of Malay Professionals, the Chinese Development Assistance Council and the Singapore Indian Development Association. Addressing inequalities through a multiplicity of ethnic associations has also served to weaken any tendency to solidarity amongst low income groups (Hill and Lian, 1995, p. 110).

As well as the balance between meritocracy and multiculturalism, the potential for a meritocratic system to produce a generation of self-interested individuals has demanded ongoing political management. The fear of deculturalization has given rise to several projects designed to promote a value system supportive of the rigorous social discipline favoured by the PAP. Under the bilingual education programme introduced in 1966, English rapidly gained ascendancy to the extent that the survival of other languages seemed to be threatened (Kuo, 1976). The Goh Report on education published in 1979 led to greater efforts to ensure a second 'mother' language was retained. This report also identified the need to expand moral education, noting that 'a society unguided by moral value can hardly be expected to remain cohesive under stress' and that 'one of the dangers of secular education in a foreign tongue is the risk of losing traditional values of one's own people and the acquisition of the more spurious fashions of the West' (Goh, 1979, p. 5). The report's solution to the dangers of deculturalization was to suggest that children were taught the historic origins of their culture in their 'mother tongue'. It was left to the Moral Education Programme launched in the 1980s to construct the precise curriculum for this exercise which developed six options for secondary school students to choose from: Bible knowledge, Buddhist studies, Hindu studies, Islamic religious knowledge, World religions and Confucian ethics. The latter was a late addition to the list of alternatives as it was strictly outside the scope of religious education but was added at the request of the Prime Minister (Kuo, 1992, p. 6). It proved however not to be a popular choice. In 1989, when the compulsory options were withdrawn, its 17.8% enrolment of all eligible Chinese students compared unfavourably with 44.4% in Buddhist Studies and 21.4% in Bible Knowledge, while non-Chinese were absent entirely (Chua, 1995, p. 30).

As well as seeking to reward ability, meritocracy has also been used by the PAP to argue for the compartmentalization of expertise, justifying the confinement of politics to only those professionally engaged as politicians. The notion of strict spheres of competence provides a way of limiting debate on government action. Lee Kuan Yew has expressed this viewpoint in connection to the principles identifying the scope of permissible academic freedom:

First, that the teacher was a technical expert in his field. Second, that his search for truth and knowledge was disinterested. Third, that teachers in a university did not just transmit knowledge to successive generations: they were expected to advance the frontiers of human knowledge and widen the dominion of man's mind. . .Within his province, his freedom was supreme. But his special status did not extend to fields where he was not the competent disinterested explorer. And one of those fields was the heat and dust of the political arena (Josey, 1974, p. 72).

Enactment of the Maintenance of Religious Harmony Act in 1990, which attempts to circumscribe religious activity to purely spiritual and moral affairs by controlling the content of religious sermons, is a further example of the rationalization of spheres of competence. To substantiate the claim to a monopoly of specialized political expertise, PAP election candidates are said to be screened scientifically including, since 1980 the use of IQ and psychological tests intended to eliminate self-interested candidates (Clutterbuck, 1984, p. 352).

## Accommodating opposition

As the majority of Singaporeans are Chinese, an assumption that political behaviour in Singapore can be explained by the adoption of a Confucian ethic has often been made (Chan, 1976; Clammer, 1985). In this interpretation Singapore's political system is made possible by a compliant and submissive population and a successful economic performance. Such a view can overlook significant changes in political management and the difficulty of ascribing the continuance of PAP control solely to a Confucian respect of those in authority. Indeed some have even questioned whether Confucianism is important to the values of most Singaporeans.

As an immigrant population drawn originally from the displaced peasantry of southern China, Singaporean understanding of Confucianism is typically no more than 'a distilled folk version of familialism' (Chua, 1995, pp. 28–29). For the more educated migrants, their philosophical outlook was influenced by modernist movements in post-1900 China that rejected rather than supported Confucianism. Within pre-independent Singapore, the most radical and assertive political elements were drawn predominantly from the Chinese population, drawing on both professional and working classes and the student population. Moreover, it is important to note that prior to 1979, Confucian or any other traditional Asian values were rarely a subject of public discussion (Wong and Wong, 1989; Hill and Lian, 1995). In 1977, for example, a senior politician was quoted at a seminar on Asian values and modernization as saying:

> I have very serious doubts as to whether such a thing as 'Asian values' really exists – or for that matter 'Asian' anything – Asian unity, Asian socialism, Asian way of life and so on. It may exist as an image but it has no reality (Rajaratnam, 1977 quoted in Hill and Lian, 1995, p. 194).

Government advocacy revived Confucian ethics, motivated by the desire for a unifying set of values supportive of PAP politics.

Since the early 1980s the electoral domination of the PAP has declined. After a period of 15 years without parliamentary opposition, a shock by-election loss in 1981 broke the PAP monopoly. The election of Jeyaretnam, leader of the Workers' Party, brought a radically different political agenda into parliament including the advocacy of a citizen's right to 'challenge arbitrary government decisions', freedom for trade unions to protect workers' rights and questioning of the independence of the judiciary. In the subsequent general election, PAP support fell by 13% with a second opposition member returned (Table 3.1). In 1991, the first election fought after the transfer of control to the new prime minister Goh Chok Tong, the opposition share of the votes was 39%, with four members elected. The interpretation of this decline is made difficult by the fragmentation of opposition parties, of which even those with opposition MPs (the Singapore People's Party and The Workers' Party) struggle to have an existence beyond a few leading individuals. It should be noted as well that the strategy of the opposition in the 1991 election to stand in only half the electorates, so as to reassure voters that there was no risk of dislodging the PAP, probably accentuates the 'protest' nature of much of the opposition vote.

Although there is no sense in which the PAP's domination is under threat, the erosion of popularity has caused it much anxiety. Two factors are important in contributing to this concern. First, the need to manage a transfer of political power to a new generation of leaders and party members in the midst of the fall in electoral fortunes (Cotton, 1993). Secondly, the belief that growing affluence, and the generation of an expanding middle class, explain much of the loss of popularity suggesting an inevitable process of decline (Jones and Brown, 1994).

Two strategies assumed growing importance, during the 1980s, to address the weakening of PAP popularity. One involved a number of political reforms designed to increase policy consultation with the middle class (Rodan, 1996). The other was the revival of Asian values to act as a bulwark against the infiltration of liberal, western ideas. To some degree these developments can be seen as contradictory: promoting the impression of a genuine attempt to widen participation in the political process whilst also seeking to strengthen the traditional practices of deference and loyalty to authority.

As discussed in a later section, it has been suggested that this mixing of values has contributed to a peculiarly Singaporean value system supportive of corporatist government. First, however, this section continues with a review of the measures taken to contain political opposition through participatory channels, followed by the attempt to promote a national ideology of Asian values.

One of the first participatory initiatives taken was the introduction of non-constituent members of parliament (NCMPs) with restricted voting rights. Prior to the 1984 election, provision for up to three of the highest opposition losers in general elections to be so appointed was made where the total elected did not meet this tally. This move has been seen as an attempt to stem the tide of serious opposition, whilst also projecting an image of political tolerance (Rodan, 1993, p. 84). The then Prime Minister Lee Kuan Yew gave three reasons for the NCMP scheme: (i) to educate younger voters, who were not familiar with the political conflicts of the 1950s and 1960s, on the myths about the political opposition's role in Parliament; (ii) to sharpen the debating skills of the new generation of MPs; (iii) to provide a means of dispelling accusations of government corruption or wrongdoing (Quah, 1988, p. 142). The 1984 election, however, returned two outright opposition winners while both of the next highest polling candidates refused the remaining NCMP seat because of its perceived second class status. There was one NCMP after the 1988 general election, none after 1991 when four opposition members were elected and one after the 1997 election when the elected opposition MPs fell to two.

The reform measures introduced after the 13% erosion of the PAP's share of the vote in 1984 include: the establishment of the Feedback Unit in 1985; the phased introduction of town councils starting in 1986; the introduction of Government Parliamentary Committees (GPCs) in 1987; the establishment of the Institute of Policy Studies (IPS) and the introduction of the Group Representative Constituency (GRC) in 1988; the appointment of nominated MPs (NMPs) from 1990 as a fresh attempt to introduce a controlled opposition within parliament.

The Feedback Unit extended the practice of using extra-parliamentary bodies under government control to channel public grievances. It is headed by a government MP and has four stated objectives: to receive suggestions from the public on national problems; to gather information on existing policies; to facilitate prompt responses by government departments to public complaints and to instigate public information programmes. Typically in the order of 20–40 'dialogue sessions' have been held each year since 1985, targeting organized groups particularly those representing professional associations. The total number of 'inputs' logged annually by the Unit varied from 1106 to 1803 during 1985–1991, jumping sharply after the 1991 election to 3269 inputs in 1995, of which 20% were unsolicited (*The Straits Times*, 27 April 1996).

The appointment of an Economic Committee to enquire into the causes of the short-lived recession of the mid-1980s (see Chapter 4) provided a further opportunity to put this more consultative style into action. The committee was supported by eight sub-committees, each conducting their own consultations through which over 1000 individuals participated. A lasting impact of this exercise was the attention given to the local business sector which it has subsequently retained (Chalmers, 1992).

The transfer of responsibilities to town councils, which was first piloted in 1986, was achieved through the transfer of certain administrative activities previously centralized under the Housing and Development Board (HDB). When initially presented, town councils were discussed in terms of their role in encouraging participation in matters affecting the local environment (Ooi, 1990). As with the Feedback Unit and other parapolitical structures, control was vested in an MP, in this case the constituency MP, who has responsibility for selecting town councillors. Those selected are so-called 'grassroots leaders' which refers to those already involved in the management of community centres, citizens' consultative committees or residents' committees. This move therefore had a limited impact in broadening community involvement in local affairs.

The initiative, however, has become important to the government as a way of seeking to demonstrate how the PAP has a monopoly of administrative expertise. Prior to the 1988 election, the PAP stressed the need for expertise in running town councils and the availability of back-up and resources from the elected MP's political party. This was underlined by stressing how funds and HDB assistance to town councils would depend on demonstrating financial competence. Whereas the PAP may have wished to promote the risk of inferior management in opposition constituencies, no evidence of this has been produced (Rodan, 1993, p. 88). A more recent move to differentiate government from opposition appointed town councils was announced in 1996. PAP controlled town councils collectively decided to contract independently for services formerly provided to councils by the HDB. Subsequently the HDB, at three months notice, announced that it would no longer provide these services, including lift rescue, lift monitoring and the restoration of services to the four opposition councils. The danger for opposition councils is that they will not be able to match the savings expected among the larger number of government councils (*The Straits Times*, 2 March 1996).

Parapolitical channels of communication were brought closer to parliament through the revival of GPCs, of which ten were established by 1988. These comprise five or six MPs with authority to appoint a panel of up to

12 persons from outside parliament to review public policy issues. The Institute of Policy Studies was established as a small research unit with a mission to educate younger Singaporeans in public administration and private sector management about Singapore's political history and to foster open political debate. The first projects completed were at the instigation of the government. This has included a review of the role of an elected president in safeguarding national financial reserves (Low and Toh, 1989) and a study to identify national values that unite all Singaporeans (Quah, 1990).

In 1988 the GRC system was introduced under which selected constituencies are combined and the individual MPs elected as one team including at least one from a minority community. Where an opposition constituency is included in such a group, it would mean that the opposition must now obtain an overall majority across the combined electorates and where this is achieved they take all the seats. For the 1988 elections, 13 GRCs were created from 39 constituencies, including eight of the ten most marginal PAP seats from the previous election. This selection gives rise to the suggestion that GRCs were devised simply to 'dilute opposition votes by combining constituencies with dominant opposition sympathies with neighbouring constituencies which strongly support the PAP' (Lim, 1989, p. 184). The government's defence of GRCs was that they would ensure minority race representation in parliament and that by participating in electorate teams, any tendency for racial extremism would be curbed (Chan, 1989, p. 86). This justification emerged after the initial reason for the scheme (that group representation would help MPs take on additional responsibilities for running town councils) failed to stem criticism of the proposed change. The new justification was consistent with a growing assertiveness and openness in the government's handling of ethnic relations during the 1980s (Hill and Lian, 1995, p. 111). Viewed in this light, GRCs can be seen as a pragmatic response to the dispersal of minorities across housing estates (see Chapter 8) which had made it difficult for minorities to get elected from predominantly Chinese communities. However changes to the GRC system made shortly before the 1997 election, allowing combinations of up to six constituencies, raised again the suggestion that the initiative was about frustrating political opposition.

The final reform during the 1980s, the introduction of NMPs, also proved controversial, this time including doubts within the PAP itself (Rodan, 1993a, p. 88). Provision now exists for up to six NMPs to be appointed, by the President on advice from a parliamentary Special Select Committee, for two year terms with the same restricted voting rights as NCMPs. Their role is seen as providing an informed but non-partisan view in parliament, as well as offering a short-term stint in politics for those not wanting to make it their career (*The Straits Times Weekly Overseas Edition*, 20 May 1989). They were also presented as a way of underlining the limitations of an elected opposition, who were presented as tending to concentrate on the rhetoric rather than the substance of debate, and even as an alternative to the support for opposition candidates (*The Straits Times Weekly Overseas Edition*, 9 December 1989).

The common theme in these reforms was the attempt to direct dissent and dissatisfaction with the PAP or particular government policies through institutions controlled by the party or agencies that sought to depoliticize debate (Rodan, 1993, p. 89). The new Prime Minister's 'manifesto', released in January 1991 under the title *The Next Lap* (1991), endorsed the belief that a more open and accountable style of government was being looked for by the middle class. This document concluded the initiatives taken over the previous decade by offering the vision of a high tech Utopia softened by a caring and consultative style of government. The images in *The Next Lap* were much discussed prior to Goh Chok Tong's first election, including the suggestion that development priorities to date had not been sufficiently balanced. In a speech on civic society, a senior cabinet minister George Yeo from the second generation of leaders, argued that in the process of achieving sustained economic growth, it had created not an organic community but a 'five star hotel', where residents might like to spend a vacation but not a lifetime (*The Straits Times*, 21 June 1991). To build a more rounded society, the desire of 'educated and rational' people for greater participation and less authoritarianism had to be responded to. In the same speech, Yeo also compared Singapore to a banyan tree, which required cutting back so that all beneath its shade did not wither. The analogy alluded to the danger of individual commitment being sapped in an overly regulated society. As well as political management, these kinds of sentiments were reflected in a reappraisal of the contribution of arts and heritage in building a well-rounded society (see Chapter 9).

### Shared values

A concern to arrest a perceived drift from Asian to western values had been a central theme of the Moral Education Programme which, as noted above, had been launched in the 1980s. This programme had a dual purpose (Hill and Lian, 1995, p. 201). On the one hand it was designed to arrest a perceived decline in behavioural standards – problems cited by politicians included lapses in business ethics, drug and theft problems among the military, snobbery among secondary students from élite schools, aged parents being sent to welfare homes and a decline of the work ethic. On the other hand it was searching for a religious or moral value system that would encourage a dedication to economic growth. The other economically successful Asian countries of Hong Kong, Taiwan and South Korea were seen to provide a role model in this regard through their Confucian tradition. In these countries, the Confucian ethic was seen to combine an emphasis on hard work alongside a stress on social obligations and respect for authority. Confucian ethics were thought to be the Asian equivalent of the contribution of the protestant spirit in the development of western capitalism.

The Moral Education Programme, which promoted teaching of five religions as well as Confucian ethics proved unsuccessful in developing the community cohesion that the PAP was looking for. Religious revivalism grew strongly in the form of missionary Islam, fundamentalist and syncretic Hinduism, the spread of Japanese 'new religion' and a massive growth in the Christian community (Clammer, 1991; 1993). The last provoked particular alarm because of their community activism and concern about the links that some Christian groups had formed to liberation circles in the Philippines and elsewhere. The shift among young, English-educated Chinese toward the rapidly growing Christian charismatic churches also raised fears of community destabilization through the pursuit of inter-racial conversions. The government's response took several forms.

One response was to crack down on groups perceived to be acting against the interests of the community. In 1987, as noted earlier, the Internal Security Act was evoked against a group of religious activists thought to have connections to a clandestine communist network (Rodan, 1992; Seow, 1994). In 1989, the cessation of the compulsory teaching of religious knowledge in schools was also announced to avoid the heightened consciousness of religious differences (Clammer, 1993, p. 45). Subsequently, the Maintenance of Religious Harmony Act 1990 was passed to prevent religious groups and individuals from commenting on social and political matters and to outlaw inter-racial proselytism. The other initiative was to announce the construction of a set of shared national values to transcend religious and ethnic differences and help build a Singaporean identity.

The shared values project involved extensive surveys of the Singapore population (Quah, 1990) but the final version was primarily shaped by the government's own suggestions. The government's White Paper on Shared Values was issued in January 1991 containing five components: placing society above the self, upholding the family as the basic building block of society, resolving major issues through consensus instead of contention, and stressing racial and religious tolerance and harmony (*The Next Lap*, 1991). The first was later rewritten as 'nation before community and society above self' to acknowledge the existence of different ethnic communities. 'Regard and community support for the individual' was subsequently added as an amended version of an addition suggested by the survey responses gathered by Quah which had originally been proposed as 'compassion for the less fortunate'. Another value suggested by Quah, 'honest government' was not incorporated out of a view that the ideology was intended as a guide to personal rather than institutional behaviour. The amended white paper was discussed and accepted by parliament in January 1992, although it lacks any legal status to bind anyone.

The shared values project is open to various interpretations. One perspective, as argued by one longstanding observer of Singapore society (Clammer, 1993), is that its significance is primarily to preempt social change or direct it in controllable directions. He makes six observations to support this view:

1. The linkage of Singapore's exposure to alien values and lifestyles overlooks the importance of this same exposure in forming Singapore's culture and economic competitiveness.
2. The counterpoising of alien and traditional Asian ideas of morality idealizes the extent to which Asian moral values were ever part of Singapore society. It overlooks the fact that most Singaporeans are 'descendants of people who were fleeing morality, duty and society in order to find greater freedom and prosperity'.
3. The loss of indigenous culture seems to be viewed as a matter of choice rather than as a consequence of the massive social and economic changes experienced. Moreover the government's own policies (comprehensive urban renewal, public housing, language change) are significant here as well as the impacts of employment and workforce change and the internationalization of the economy.
4. The values are an uneasy mix of description and prescription. If they are a description of already existing values, it may be questioned whether they require promotion. If they are still to be accepted then operational details are missing such as whether family values are compatible with the widespread middle class reliance on poorly paid foreign domestic servants for care giving.
5. The balance between individual rights and state authority is uneasily defined leaving a wide margin of discretion to the state at the expense of the individual.
6. While purporting not to privilege any one community over another, the shared values draw disproportionately on Confucian ideas.

Clammer in particular draws attention to the following paragraph in the white paper which incorporates the Confucian conception of good government by 'honourable men': 'the concept of government by honourable men who have a duty to do right for the people, and who have the trust and respect of the population fits us better than the Western idea that a government should be given as limited powers as possible, and should always be treated with suspicion unless proven otherwise'.

A sympathetic reflection on the endeavour is offered by the Singaporean sociologist Chua Beng Huat (1995, p. 33), who describes the shared values as tending to 'float' as a moralizing statement rather than as having descriptive or prescriptive value. The practical significance of the shared values project is to identify the PAP as the defenders of a national consensus, so that challenges to the PAP can be portrayed as an attack on Singapore's collectively held values. But, according to Chua (1995, p. 37), apart from a segment of the tertiary educated minority, the government's communitarian ideology is generally supported so that the project cannot be dismissed simply as a veil for the perpetuation of authoritarianism.

## Illiberal democracy

The 1991 general election, Goh Chok Tong's first as prime minister, has been seen as a test of the PAP's measures to accommodate middle class expectations of greater political freedom. The election did not bring the result looked for with a further erosion of the PAP's share of the vote. Subsequent evaluation of the result has suggested that the direct political significance of the middle class had been overstated (Jones and Brown, 1994; Rodan, 1996). The election revealed widespread working class discontent derived from their perception that rising living costs were falling disproportionately on their income, exacerbated by the PAP's seemingly greater sensitivity to perceived middle class concerns. This resulted in a number of post-election measures designed to respond to the concerns of low and middle income voters, a group the government likes to describe as the 'HDB heartlanders'.

A Cost Review Committee was established to address concerns about rising costs of living. The Committee conducted investigations to counter the perceptions about the impact of increasing living costs. Drawing on census data, for example, the Committee argued that the bottom 20% and middle 60% of households experienced higher rates of income growth than the top 20% of households (Ministry of Trade and Industry, 1993). It acknowledged that there had been steep price rises in housing, health and private transport costs but this was seen as an inevitable consequence of being a small island state with limited land resources and a need to control congestion. (This reassurance and ongoing surveillance of cost of living changes has not, however, silenced public perception about the unfair impact of inflation. As we discuss in Chapter 10, as Singapore prepared for an election in 1996, the Cost Review Committee was once again active in investigating the impacts of rising living costs.) The government did, however, respond to some of the anxiety expressed about aspects of its pre-election 'cosmopolitan creativity'. Prior to the election a film classification system had been introduced to reduce the extent of censorship, allowing 'adult' films to be screened in cinemas. After the election the classification system was revised to ban films with purely pornographic intent and to raise the age threshold for viewing 'artistic' films containing nudity.

Outside observers of the 1991 election have used the result to question whether a liberalizing middle class actually exists, drawing as well on the experience of other Asian countries (Bell *et al.*, 1995). Rather than increasing wealth encouraging a middle class desire for liberal democracy, a form of illiberal democracy is developing which, Jones *et al.* (1995) see as comprising three distinctive features:

1. *A non-neutral state:* in contrast to the western stress on freedom of choice, East Asian society accepts widespread government intervention and control of social affairs in order to promote its interpretation of the national interest. The national interest typically being presented as a blend of development aspirations and the selective restoration of traditional values. Elections are a source of feedback on the extent to which the state's vision is retaining consensus and a test of any opposition's willingness to break away from the national consensus (in Singapore's case, for example, it is seen as acceptable to deny opposition electorates certain public services). 'In a liberal understanding, democracy succeeds when elections change governments, in the illiberal version democracy succeeds when elections legitimate the rule of an incumbent élite' (Jones *et al.*, 1995, p. 164). In the Singapore context, for example, it has been noted that electoral support is not about how well the opposition performs but rather how united the nation is behind the PAP leadership and the party's claim to be a people's movement (Chua, 1995, p. 194).
2. *Resort to legal obligations:* in a western democracy, the legal system provides a medium through which individuals or the judiciary can interrogate the activities of the state. The ideal in an illiberal democracy is that the legal system leaves 'little space for critical or creative interrogation' by the legal profession or individuals. Rather it seeks to provide

a precisely defined code of conduct, specifying the duties of citizens. Greater certainty over the implementation of legal controls tends to reduce the legal system to an administrative tool of government, although equally applied to all subjects and enforced strictly according to what is permitted in statute. The understanding of law as a legitimate part of the 'ruler's technical equipment' has drawn on Confucian conceptions and the state's assessment of its rule as apolitical, driven by the pursuit of societal interest. Hence it is not unusual to see statutes changed to better suit enforcement immediately after they were successfully contested by litigants. A case in Singapore being the removal of appeals to the Privy Council in London after a successful appeal to that body by one the PAP's political opponents (Seow, 1994, p. 253). While such turnarounds are to be found in western democracies as well, an unusual degree of 'fine-tuning' is said to be attempted in illiberal democracies.

3. *A managed civil society:* 'a notable feature of illiberal democracy consists in the existence of formal democratic procedures without politics'. Instead of rising education and affluence encouraging the formation of political parties, interest groups and critical debate, the activities of any emerging group are channelled into state-managed arenas. This results in a managerial solution to latent opposition, avoiding recourse to authoritarian coercion. The acceptance by interest groups of such capture reflects the tendency for groups to form around specialized interests, without connection to a larger political agenda, which is a product of the inherited constraints on political activity and an uncritical education system.

The model of illiberal democracy is a challenge to political analysts who would see a necessity for modernization to bring a replication of western political values. It responds to the distinctive ethnic and historic context of rapidly developing Asian economies, namely: a mix of western and diverse Asian value systems; the emergence of a middle class in a world of corporate capital and multinational enterprise, stressing team work and loyalty rather than economic individualism; the electoral popularity enjoyed by post-colonial governments and the willingness to trade off political participation in return for economic security. However, various challenges to the communitarian ideal remain which question whether illiberal democracy constitutes a sustainable form of government. In the context of Singapore the following dilemmas and pressures have been noted:

1. The PAP government is democratically elected and rules without corruption through an open parliamentary process but Singapore's politi-

cal system meets only the minimum criteria of a democratic society (Quah, 1994, p. 409). Three aspects of an authoritarian regime remain:

(i) the continuance in power of a political party whose past history includes the undemocratic suppression of opponents (Bloodworth, 1986; Seow, 1994);

(ii) a style of rule which seeks to render government decisions as expert actions outside the understanding of the public at large (a 'father knows best' mentality);

(iii) the retention of legislation that curtails democratic freedoms, including the Internal Security Act which allows the detention without trial of individuals for a renewable period of up to two years. The shadow of repression constrains the development of a genuine sense of attachment to the community which ultimately will only be built on a relationship of trust (Chua, 1995, p. 181).

2. In the absence of the growth of a politically interested middle class, other values have taken hold which can be seen to equally challenge the communitarian ideal. The expanding administrative, executive, managerial and professional groups in Singapore do not exhibit the kind of articulate, self-confident autonomy which constitutes the liberal version of the middle classes (Jones and Brown, 1994). The political environment is amongst the factors contributing to the perceived lack of critical creativity (other influences being an education system depicted as encouraging rote learning and the high dependence on careers in government or government-linked agencies). Allowed neither to pursue freely their own self-interest and cautioned against welfare liberalism, a Singaporean middle class has grown up typified by anxiety and uncertainty of their rights and responsibilities. In particular, the peculiarly Singaporean culture of *kiasuism* can be seen as a reaction to the form of political conformity demanded. *Kiasu* is a Hokkien dialect word for 'scared to lose' while *kiasuism* is generally taken to reflect an attitude that 'if you are not one up you are one down'. Behaviour of this type is frequently identified in Singapore, as when the NTUC attempted to distribute school books free-of-charge to low income parents only to be besieged by other parents concerned for their children not to miss resources allocated to others. According to Jones and Brown (1994, p. 86), such behaviour originates from an absence of self-confidence 'that makes fear of failure the dominant concern in a competitive and regulated society'. This lack of confidence provides a supportive context for PAP politics but may be less effective in building an innovative and gracious society.

3. Increasing social differentiation in the population along income, education and ethnic lines will make it harder to maintain claims about

shared values and a national consensus (Chua, 1995, p. 206). Already, notwithstanding the attempts to limit political participation several interest groups have formed which to varying degrees have sought to broaden the policy agenda and scope for political engagement. These include the Nature Society of Singapore (see Chapter 7), the Association of Women for Action and Research (AWARE) and the Association of Muslim Professionals (AMP). AWARE was formed in 1985 and while it has sought to avoid open challenges to government policy, it has taken strong positions on the government's procreation policy in the late 1980s and in a controversy over unequal benefits to female civil servants (Rodan, 1996, p. 38). The formation of AMP in 1990 was in itself a challenge to the PAP. It reflected dissatisfaction amongst some Malay professionals with Mendaki, the existing council for the development of the Muslim community. Mendaki was controlled by PAP MPs and according to the AMP was too compliant to government policies that it saw as disadvantaging the Malay community in Singapore (Rodan, 1993, p. 66). While the government has so far been successful in containing the profile of these organizations, each has had some accommodation of its interests and in changing the focus of public debate.

4. Alienation from the political system leads to a tendency for individuals to cultivate their own private interests and little desire to enter public office. This rejection has caused the PAP to express concern, particularly about the reluctance of highly qualified individuals to join its ranks (Ong, 1992). Declining membership of the PAP's youth wing has also been noted, despite commitments to offer greater consultation and to tolerate alternative viewpoints to those of the main party (Chua, 1995, p. 208). Similarly the migration outflow of professionals seemed to accelerate during the 1980s partly motivated by the search for a life in freer society (Rodan, 1993a, p. 95).

5. In a similar way, some controls on political debate create difficulties for the ruling government. Control of the press, for example, has reduced the domestic content of national newspapers to little more than an announcement service for the government. This has both reduced the capacity of the press to shape public opinions, since beyond the substantive news content interpretative arguments are apt to be ignored, at the same time denying the government a window on public opinion. As Chua (1995, p. 199) observes, by excluding contrary opinions from the national press it becomes harder for the government to respond to smouldering areas of discontent. The limits of the PAP's own feedback mechanisms for gauging public opinion were underlined in its injudicious calling of an early general election in 1991 when its optimism of growing popularity proved to be unfounded.

## Conclusion

The last decade has seen a significant evolution in political management. From their assumption of power to the early 1980s, the PAP ruled Singapore with an authoritarian blend of Confucian paternalism and meritocracy. The difficult circumstances of political independence and the successful charting of an economic future provided a large fund of electoral popularity, reinforced by assiduous emphasis on the fragility of national survival. The 1984 election evaporated much of the remaining fear of voting against the PAP. The growth in the opposition vote focused PAP attention on the need to manage a stable leadership succession and to curb a perceived drift to westernized values. A more westernized society raised anxiety about demands for political liberalization and the fragmentation of society between an affluent and outward-looking middle class and lower income groups still wedded to traditional values.

From the early 1980s, these challenges prompted the PAP leadership to adopt a new strategy of communitarian inclusionism. New channels for political discussion and competition were introduced with the dual aims of containing dissatisfaction and building political institutions to guard against the succession of an 'irresponsible' government. Through these innovations politics has been kept within a narrow range: the appointment of quasi-opposition MPs to enable controlled debate between PAP and non-PAP viewpoints; the GRC scheme and support to officially sanctioned ethnic associations ensures racial minority representation and checks racial arrogance from the dominant Chinese; the Feedback Unit and parliamentary committee procedures provide channels for constructive comment; the elected Presidency guards against fiscal profligacy by a future government. The *Next Lap* manifesto culminated these reforms and further developed the image of a more 'caring and consultative' style of rule to be followed by the new Prime Minister Goh Chok Tong.

Faced with what seemed to be a growing middle class expectation of liberal values and political participation, the PAP sought to avoid suppression through strategies of accommodation and cooption. The subsequent electoral test of the new leadership suggested that the middle class may be less of a political challenge than the perception amongst lower income groups that economic rewards and burdens are unfairly distributed. Singapore's initial elevation to a newly industrialized economy was associated with remarkable economic growth and social mobility. Greater rigidity in social structures is fuelling a sense of unfairness and challenging the PAP's adherence to meritocratic and anti-welfare values.

# 4

# Population

Fertility, mortality and migration are the three variables that shape population change. In Singapore, variations in fertility have been the main influence on demographic trends in the last four decades. Migration, either inward or outward has not involved substantial numbers, although a large workforce of temporary foreign residents has been attracted in recent decades. Similarly, with advanced medical facilities and improved hygiene and sanitation standards, mortality rates have been kept consistently low. Fertility patterns, on the other hand, have varied significantly over the post-independence years, reflecting the interaction of changing family structures and household formation patterns, typical of high income societies, and the swings in government policies from anti- to pro-natalist priorities. Indeed such is the scale of state intervention that Singapore's population social policies may well be the most stringent in the world, apart from China's (Yap, 1989, p. 467).

In examining population growth trends since independence, this chapter focuses primarily on fertility trends and the government's population policy in relation to fertility. It distinguishes two main phases in fertility patterns and population policy: (i) 1965 to 1983, a period when fertility rates declined to below replacement level, due largely to a family planning policy including financial and other incentives and disincentives to suppress fertility rates; (ii) post-1983 to the present when fertility rates continued to decline below replacement level, alerting the government to a need to address the potential problem of a declining population base. This second phase is further distinguished between an earlier period characterized by a form of *social eugenics* and a later phase of selective pro-natalist policy. The distinction is marked, for example, by a shift from childbirth incentives to graduates to incentives offered on the basis of income. These policies continue to be among some of the most controversial aspects of modern Singapore.

The second part of the chapter addresses the attempts to respond to the impact of an ageing population. In 1989 the submission to the government of a report by an Advisory Council on the Aged has been of particular significance in this context, reinforcing the emphasis on family responsibility which is another well-known aspect of Singapore.

## Family planning

The newly independent republic inherited a declining rate of population growth. This decline became more marked after 1965, dropping again from 1975 to 1983 due primarily to declining fertility rates (an initial drop in mortality rates soon stabilized) (Figure 4.1). The effects of such fertility and mortality trends were reinforced by declining migrant numbers as independence in 1965 made migration from Malaysia more difficult.

Several factors contributed to the declining fertility rates. This was a period of rapid modernization during which attitudes towards the value of children and family size were changing as the former 'agricultural mentality' waned, industrialization enabled women to join the work force in greater numbers and women's higher levels of education encouraged the postponement of marriage and childbirth (Table 4.1). Women's literacy rate, for example, increased from 33.6% in 1957 to 60.1% in 1970 and

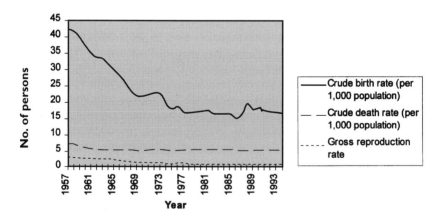

**Figure 4.1** Crude birth rates, gross reproduction rates and crude death rates, 1957–1994
*Source: Report on the Registration of Births, Deaths, Marriages and Persons, various years. Yearbook of Statistics, various years*

**Table 4.1** Female labour force participation rates, 1957–1990

| Year | Economically active (%) | Employed (%) |
|------|------------------------|--------------|
| 1957 | 19.3 | 18.1 |
| 1970 | 24.6 | 20.2 |
| 1975 | 29.6 | 27.1 |
| 1980 | 39.3 | 37.8 |
| 1985 | 44.9 | 43.0 |
| 1990 | 50.3 | 49.5 |

*Source:* Labour Force Survey, 1975, 1985; *Census of Population*, 1957, 1970, 1980 and 1990

76.2% in 1980 (Cheng, 1989, p. 167). Underlining these changes, a *Women's Charter* of 1960 made polygamy illegal followed in 1966 by the start of an active period of population policy.

The population programme reflected the broadening economic vision of the PAP administration which saw a need to concentrate education, training and housing resources if standards were to be improved. Prime Minister Lee Kuan Yew later expressed his view that negative population growth was less a threat to Singapore in its early industrialization stage than rapid population growth. If necessary, selective immigration could supplement the local labour supply if shortages emerged (Yap, 1989, p. 469).

As part of the population control programme, the Singapore Family Planning and Population Board (SFPPB) was set up in 1966 to provide family planning advisory services. Apart from mass media publicity, the Board also took population education to schools and conducted individual and group counselling in clinics and hospitals. The SFPPB claimed to have increased the uptake of family planning from around 1500 in 1965 to over 30 000 in its first year of operation (Cheng, 1989, p. 166), peaking in 1969 with 35 643 official converts to family planning, contributing to a 25% drop in the gross reproduction rate (GRR) from 1966 to 1969 (Figure 4.1). In 1969, legalized voluntary sterilization was introduced, with various incentives such as paid maternity leave, full-pay leave after sterilization, reimbursement of delivery fees, and priority in primary school registration for children of a sterilized parent.

The impetus of these first measures seemed to wane in the late 1960s as the 'baby-boomer' generation began to enter reproductive age. As a result, the government introduced other measures to ensure further reduction in fertility rates, of which the main steps were:

1. A major campaign to 'stop at two' was launched in 1971 involving a 'saturation campaign' of posters, pamphlets and television advertise-

ments encouraging small families. Slogans such as 'Girl or boy – two is enough' and 'Put some years between us' became well known throughout the island.

2. In 1970 abortion became legal under the Abortion Act. In 1974, a new act further liberalized rules and procedures. The impact was seen in the number of reported abortions: 1913 in 1970, 7175 in 1974 and 15 496 in 1975 (Cheng, 1989, p. 166).

3. In 1974, the Voluntary Sterilization Act extended existing legislation to make sterilization obtainable on request to a doctor accredited to the scheme.

4. Differential delivery fees introduced a stepped charging regime with higher fees for each additional child.

5. Maternity leave was not granted for the third and subsequent child unless the mother was sterilized after delivery, while income tax relief was allowed for up to the third child only.

6. Public housing allocation was adjusted to favour small families.

Pecuniary measures affected the majority lower and lower-middle classes more than the minority upper-middle and upper classes (Cheng, 1989, p. 166), although as later policy changes indicated, this was not necessarily a concern to the government. However it might be argued that because the population slowdown enabled standards in education and housing to be increased, lower income groups did gain from the measures.

**Social eugenics**

The anti-natalist policy remained in place for seven years after the fertility rate fell below replacement level. In 1983 Prime Minister Lee Kuan Yew, indicated in a National Day rally speech that some adjustment to the government's anti-natal stance would be introduced. This was not so much because of the overall population drop but because of its differential impact. In addition, economic considerations were influential in the partial shift to a pro-natalist policy (Drakakis-Smith *et al.*, 1993). In the Prime Minister's projected scenario, should better-educated Singaporeans fail to reproduce themselves: 'levels of competence will decline. Our economy will falter, the administration will suffer, and the society will decline' (*The Straits Times*, 15 August 1983).

This view coincided with the planning of a second industrial revolution (Chapter 5) in which skilled work was expected to displace unqualified labour.

The Prime Minister argued that it was the better educated and the higher income working women who were marrying later, or not marrying at all, and who were having less children than the less educated and those in the lower income group. For example, while only 10.3% of women aged 30 to 34 with no qualifications were not married, 28.0% of women in the same age category with tertiary education were not married (Table 4.2). The 1980 census revealed that working married women earning less than $500 a month had an average of 2.53 live births, while women earning $2000 and above per month had 1.74 (Table 4.3). Similarly, the average number of live births for women with no educational qualifications was 3.34 while that for women with tertiary education was 1.56 (Table 4.4). These trends were indicative of the effects of improved female education and participation in the work force. The Prime Minister held the view that it was nature more than nurture which guaranteed a 'high quality' population and hence his concern with what he saw as an erosion of the genetic pool of talented women.

**Table 4.2** Percentage of unmarried females by age group and educational qualification, 1980

|  | Age | | | | |
|---|---|---|---|---|---|
|  | 20–24 | 25–29 | 30–34 | 35–39 | 40–44 |
| No qualification | 55.1 | 21.3 | 10.3 | 5.2 | 4.1 |
| Primary | 68.2 | 30.7 | 16.4 | 9.3 | 7.1 |
| Secondary | 83.4 | 44.8 | 25.6 | 17.0 | 14.3 |
| Post-secondary | 90.9 | 49.2 | 25.9 | 17.6 | 11.1 |
| Tertiary | 92.8 | 57.8 | 28.0 | 16.9 | 14.0 |

*Source:* Cheng, 1989, p. 168

**Table 4.3** Working married women by monthly income and number of children born alive, 1980

| Monthly income (S$) | Total married women (%) | Number of children |
|---|---|---|
| Below 500 | 67.2 | 2.53 |
| 500–900 | 21.3 | 1.51 |
| 1000–1499 | 7.0 | 1.90 |
| 1500–1999 | 2.7 | 1.84 |
| 2000 & over | 1.8 | 1.74 |
| Total | 100.00 | 2.23 |

*Source: Census of Population,* 1980, pp. 94–95

**Table 4.4** Married women by highest qualification and number of children born alive, 1980

| Highest qualification | Total females (%) | Number of children |
|---|---|---|
| No qualification | 49.6 | 3.34 |
| Primary | 35.9 | 2.29 |
| Secondary/upper secondary | 12.7 | 1.56 |
| Tertiary | 1.9 | 1.56 |
| Total | 100.00 | 3.20 |

*Source: Census of Population,* 1980, pp. 88–89

Equally alarming to the Prime Minister were projections of likely marriage trends. It was estimated that for every ten women who go to university, four would remain single, while four out of every ten males with no qualification would have difficulty in finding wives (Table 4.5). (This assessment assumed that males prefer to marry females with lower education than themselves.) As more and more women pursue higher education (Figure 4.2), from this perspective it appeared downward fertility rates would accelerate.

In response to these concerns, several measures were introduced to encourage higher educated women to reproduce. One of the most controversial was the priority given in pre-primary and primary school registration to graduate women with three or more children, introduced in 1984. This was an about-turn from past policy in which priority was given to those with small families and those who had undergone sterilization after the first or second child (*The Straits Times*, 24 January 1984). This measure was criticized for its élitism, and was withdrawn in 1985 (after the 1984 general election had seen a drop in the PAP's share of the national vote, as discussed in Chapter 3).

**Table 4.5** Projected unmarried population by highest qualification

| Qualification | No. of male and female school-leavers each year | Single males (%) | Single females (%) |
|---|---|---|---|
| Tertiary | 2500 | 5 | 41 |
| Upper secondary | 4750 | 5 | 29 |
| Secondary | 11 250 | 5 | 3 |
| Primary | 3250 | 23 | 3 |
| No qualification | 3250 | 38 | 3 |
| Total | 25 000 | 12 | 12 |

*Source:* Adapted from Cheng, 1989, p. 169

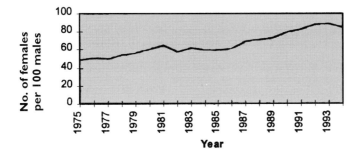

**Figure 4.2** Sex ratio of student enrolment in institutions of higher learning, 1975–1994
*Source:* Cheng (1989, p. 170); *Yearbook of Statistics,* various years

A more enduring initiative at this time was the setting up of the Social Development Unit (SDU) to promote marriage among graduates. The SDU organizes a variety of activities such as courses, trips and teas which provide singles with the opportunity to meet one another. It also provides a computer dating service. While it did not quite get off to a roaring start, the SDU has, since its early beginnings, gained a significant degree of social acceptance, with a substantial number of voluntary participants today (14 000 in 1996).

Sterilization incentives were restructured to give S$10 000 to women from low socio-economic and educational backgrounds (women under 30 with no 'O' levels, in households where the total monthly income was less than $1500) if they opted for sterilization after the birth of their first or second child. If another child was born, then the $10 000 would have to be repaid, plus 10% per annum compound interest. Delivery fees were also restructured so that different socio-economic groups would pay similar fees, although there was still some provision of subsidized wards for low-income patients.

Given somewhat adverse reactions to the selective pro-natalist policy, the government began to consider a different approach. This began in 1986 when the SFPPB was replaced by the Population Planning Unit under the Ministry of Health. In March 1987, the government announced a change in population policy from its earlier 'stop-at-two' to a pro-natalist policy in which families were encouraged to have three children or more *if they could afford it*. Affordability (or class, measured in income terms) thus overtook educational qualifications as the key criterion. This removed somewhat the educational élitism since, as First Deputy Prime Minister Goh Chok Tong said at the time:

> There are many people who might not even have secondary education, but they make up for it with diligence, hard work, special talents, skills . . . And

they may be earning very much more than those with O levels or even those who have been to university. These people can support their children (*The Straits Times*, 2 March 1987).

The measures that were introduced to encourage marriage and childbirth comprised:

1. New organizations to encourage social interaction. The People's Association (a government institution which promotes social, cultural, educational and recreational activities), for example, set up a Social Development Section which catered to secondary school leavers. The Sports and Recreation Club of the Civil Service also established its Social Interaction Unit for the same purpose.
2. To promote fertility, the 1987 Budget allowed parents of a new born third child to be granted income tax rebate of a maximum of $20 000 per couple spread over five years, with effect from the Year of Assessment 1988. Working mothers became entitled to a tax rebate equivalent to 15% of their earned income if they have a third child and, for a fourth child, the existing 'enhanced child relief' was granted. Incentives were also introduced to target working mothers, and varied according to age (*The Straits Times*, 5 March 1987). While some tax rebates were initially applicable to those with five 'O' level passes, this was later extended to those with three or four.
3. A family of three children of less than six years of age qualified for a $100 subsidy per month per child for the use of approved child-care centres. This was designed to encourage mothers to stay in the labour force at the same time as increasing family size (these subsidies have since been extended). No-pay leave for child care for married women in the civil service was extended from one to a maximum of four years. Leave provisions were also extended to enable mothers to take time off to look after their children when sick.
4. Housing allocation gave priority to families wishing to move to bigger flats on the birth of the third child. All previous disincentives against the third child in school registration exercises were removed.

Apart from such incentives and disincentives, extensive media campaigns on the benefits of marriage and family life and the undesirability of growing old alone have also been waged. Pre-sterilization counselling has also been introduced for women with less than three children. There is also compulsory pre- and post-abortion counselling in order to discourage abortions on non-medical grounds (Cheng, 1989, p. 171). This was thought to be particularly necessary because too many married women were aborting their pregnancies for non-medical reasons or contraceptive failure. For example, significant proportions of those opting for abortion were doing so because they had 'enough children', because it was 'too soon after the previous one' or because they were 'not ready' (Figure 4.3).

Over 1986–1987, the number of live births increased from 38379 to 43 616, an increase of 13.6%, while in the following two years there was an increase of 21.4% (*Yearbook of Statistics*, 1988). It was difficult to interpret this immediate change in fertility, however, as these were auspicious years in the Chinese zodiac when childbirth tends to increase, and it was the Chinese who contributed most to the growth in births (Table 4.6). Moreover, fertility rates have not since topped the 1988 (Dragon year) figure (Figure 4.1).

The longer term evaluation of the pro-natalist population policy is still inconclusive. Information collected in a survey on Singaporeans' views of the new population policy, conducted in 1992 amongst a sample population in one of Singapore's public housing estates, suggests that the response is cautious but perhaps marginally positive (Drakakis-Smith *et al.*, 1993). While almost half evaluated the policy positively, it is not clear from their response in the survey whether they would also put the policy to practice. Moreover those most negative were young adults (18–24 years), who have the greatest long-term impact on fertility rates (Table 4.7). Only about a quarter of the respondents thought that the policy would result in more earlier marriages; 34% thought that there would be earlier childbirth; and 54.4% thought there was likely to be a positive impact on family size (Table 4.8). In all cases, the younger respondents were once again least persuaded of the likely positive impacts of the pro-natalist policy. However, those who suggest that they have increased their

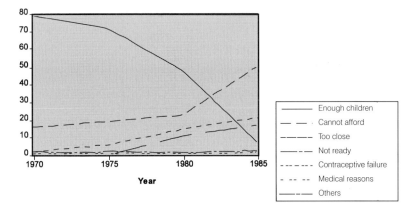

**Figure 4.3** Married women – why they abort, 1970–1985
*Source: The Straits Times, 22 April 1987*

**Table 4.6** Live-births by ethnic group, 1986–1988

| Year | Chinese | | Malay | | Indian | | Others | | Total | |
|---|---|---|---|---|---|---|---|---|---|---|
| | No. of live births | % increase | No. of live births | % increase | No. of live births | % increase | No. of live births | % increase | No. of live births | % increase |
| 1986 | 25 361 | – | 8124 | – | 3211 | – | 1683 | – | 38 379 | – |
| 1987 | 29 839 | 17.7 | 8636 | 6.3 | 3441 | 7.2 | 1700 | 1.0 | 43 616 | 13.6 |
| 1988 | 38 245 | 28.2 | 9224 | 6.8 | 3716 | 8.0 | 1772 | 4.2 | 52 957 | 21.4 |

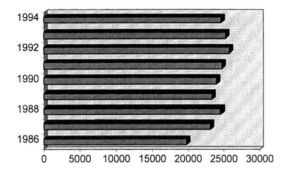

**Figure 4.4** Marriages registered, 1986–1994
*Source: Yearbook of Statistics*, various years

family size are disproportionately from the younger age group and the more highly educated higher income group (Table 4.9).

Measures to expedite marriage registration, including accreditation of more than 100 licensed 'grassroots' solemnizers, have been introduced to make marriage easier. Some suggest that a muted response to the selective pro-natalist policy is likely to continue because of the perception that the policy is unequal (Brown, 1994). While some have seen the inequality in racial terms (Siddique, 1989), others argue that the pro-natalist policy has less to do with race than with education and income (class). AWARE (Association of Women for Action and Research), one of the few active non-government organizations in Singapore, argues that social attitudes lag behind the government's population goals, and that their economic incentives need to recognize these constraints. Many women, AWARE believes, would like to have more children, 'but for constraints like lack of good childcare facilities, strain of combining both a good career and being a good mother, lack of cooperation from spouse in housekeeping and management' (Ang, 1987, p. 1). In these terms, what are needed are improvements in leave schemes, working conditions and childcare facilities, and adjustments in attitudes and responsibilities if the government is to realize its pro-natalist ambition.

### Planning for an ageing society

Average life expectancy in 1947 was 50 but increased to 74 in 1990 (Teo, 1994, p. 406). In 1957, the proportion of the population aged 60 and above was less than 4%. By 1980, this figure was 7.5% and by 1990, 9.1%. It is estimated that by the year 2030, the figure will be 26%. This trend towards an ageing population is also evident in the growing median age of the

**Table 4.7** Opinion of the pro-natalist population policy

| Age | Good/ very good | Neither good nor bad | Bad/ very bad |
|---|---|---|---|
| 18–24 | 41.3 | 37.0 | 21.7 |
| 25–29 | 45.7 | 42.9 | 11.4 |
| 30–34 | 47.0 | 42.6 | 10.4 |
| 35–39 | 44.6 | 47.3 | 8.1 |
| 40 & above | 54.5 | 32.5 | 13.0 |
| Total | 46.7 | 41.9 | 11.4 |

*Source:* Adapted from Drakakis-Smith *et al.*, 1993, p. 159

**Table 4.8** Perceived likely positive influences of pro-natalist population policy

| Age | Earlier marriage | Earlier childbirth | Family size |
|---|---|---|---|
| 18–24 | 9.3 | 19.0 | 48.8 |
| 25–29 | 24.2 | 33.3 | 48.5 |
| 30–34 | 25.0 | 32.7 | 57.8 |
| 35–39 | 25.6 | 37.7 | 54.5 |
| 40 & above | 31.4 | 38.6 | 58.3 |
| Total | 24.5 | 34.0 | 54.4 |

*Source:* Adapted from Drakakis-Smith *et al.*, 1993, p. 160

**Table 4.9** Characteristics of women reporting an increase in family size

| Age | % | Education | % | Income ($ per month) | % |
|---|---|---|---|---|---|
| 18–24 | 30.0 | None/primary | 10.7 | <2000 | 13.6 |
| 25–29 | 17.0 | 'O' levels/vocational | 16.4 | 2000–3999 | 14.4 |
| 30–34 | 22.0 | 'A' levels/diploma | 16.3 | 4000–5999 | 21.4 |
| 35–39 | 13.0 | University degree | 34.3 | >6000 | 19.0 |
| 40 & above | 6.8 | All respondents | 16.2 | | |

*Source:* Drakakis-Smith *et al.*, 1993, p. 161

population. While the population's median age in 1957 was 18.8 (Chen and Cheung, 1988), the figure had risen to 29.8 by 1990 and is expected to increase to 40.6 by 2030 (Ministry of Home Affairs, 1989). It is further projected that within the elderly population, the proportion of those aged 75 and above will grow faster than the 'young-old' aged 60 to 74. While the former is expected to grow by six times from 1985–2030, the latter is expected to grow by four times (Chen and Cheung, 1988).

As providing for an aged dependant is more expensive than providing for a young one (Clark *et al.*, 1978), these trends are a concern to government. They also raise other implications: a reduction in the relative proportion of working people in the overall population, as well as an ageing of those in work. One projection, for example, expects the median age of the work force to rise from 27 years in 1985 to 35 in 2000 and then to 43 in 2030 (Cheng, 1989, p. 170). With respect to the dependency ratio (the ratio of persons aged 15 to 59 to those aged 60 and above), it is expected to fall, from 9.1:1 in 1980 to 2.2:1 in 2030 (Teo, 1994, p. 407).

The possibility of fewer recruits to military service is a national security concern, while changes in consumption and resource needs suggest a need to redistribute investment. All of these require public policy initiatives to address the needs of the aged population, for example, in the provision of health and medical care, housing and transportation.

Singapore's first investigation of these issues was contained in the Report of the Committee on the Problems of the Aged, released in 1984. Its findings covered employment, financial security, health and recreational needs, social services and institutional care, and family relations. One of its recommendations, however, tended to get most attention, to the cost of the remainder of the report. This was the recommendation to raise the Central Provident Fund (CPF) withdrawal age in line with a proposed lifting of the retirement age from 55 to 60 and then to 65. Many Singaporeans felt that their own hard-earned money would be unfairly withheld from them if the CPF withdrawal age was raised. Coming alongside the unpopularity of its population measures, and the poor election result of 1984, this first report was not acted upon.

In 1989, a newly constituted Advisory Council on the Aged drew attention to the need for a change in attitudes. It reported that older persons were too often viewed as 'sickly, dependent and decrepit' (Ministry of Home Affairs, 1989, p. 3; see also Anwar, 1996). It recommended a strengthening of family cohesion so as to promote greater understanding and respect for elderly persons, echoing part of the emphasis in the shared values project (Chapter 3). Additional resources for existing public education programmes, including the Parent Education Programme (PEP) and the Public Awareness Programme on Ageing (PAPA), were requested and several new initiatives identified.

The Advisory Council report emphasized the need to keep the elderly population physically healthy and socially active. The Ministry of Health's 'healthy lifestyle' campaign and its efforts to interest all Singaporeans in the 'Great Singapore Workout', an annual mass exercise day, have been products of this. A variety of services are now also available, for example, free health-screening services, medical counselling, health education, and senior citizens' sports and recreation clubs at community centres (Ng, 1992). The potential for employment to give a person 'a sense of worth and dignity and financial independence' has also been taken up. The report recommended that the retirement age be raised to 60. In order to make it more attractive for employers to retain older workers, CPF contributions were reduced for older workers (Table 4.10). The government has also indicated that it is acceptable to vary employment conditions according to age, for example by replacing annual wage increments by one-off bonuses according to performance. For the aged in need of care, it was recognized that more community-based and residential care facilities would be needed. While part of this provision could be made by assisting voluntary welfare homes (for example, by reserving space for homes adjacent to public housing estates and by contributing to their setting up and running costs), it was also recognized that the sheer growth in numbers would require an increase in government-run homes (Teo, 1994). While this provision needs to be balanced against its greater wish not to do anything that might cause families to 'abandon' their elderly members, a shortage of staff to work within homes is an immediate problem for government (Shantakumar, 1991).

These measures to cope with an ageing population indicate that the government does not intend to take on the full responsibility of looking after the aged population. From its view, the financial burden on the state would be too great. Rather its aim has been to 'create structural and social conditions conducive to the sharing of the costs of caring for elderly persons' (Teo, 1994, p. 412). As discussed in Chapter 8, public housing allocation has long been designed to keep families together. A further step in this direction was the imposition of a legal obligation on children to maintain their parents. This idea had first been put forward by the 1984 Committee on the Problems of the Aged. In 1995, after much discussion in parliament and in other public arenas, the Parents Maintenance Act was passed in 1996.

**Table 4.10** Central Provident Fund contribution rates

| Age | Employer's contribution (%) | Employee's contribution (%) | Total (%) |
|---|---|---|---|
| For younger workers | 20 | 20 | 40 |
| For older workers | | | |
| 55–59 | 12.5 | 12.5 | 25 |
| 60–64 | 7.5 | 7.5 | 15 |
| 65 and above | 5.0 | 5.0 | 10 |

*Source:* Ministry of Home Affairs, 1989, p. 30

To help families meet the greater cost of looking after the old in their own homes, the Advisory Council recommended that the dependant's tax relief should be doubled for persons aged 75 and above. One of the criticisms of the measures so far introduced is that they have yet to give support to care givers in the same way as support has been extended to women caring for their children (Teo, 1994). As the international experience is that the main caregivers within the family are women, regardless of who is being cared for (Brody, 1990; Arber and Ginn, 1991), the shift to family-based care can be seen to impose an uneven burden. AWARE, as noted above, is one group campaigning for this to change.

### Conclusion

There are varied interpretations of Singapore's population policy experience. One view is that policy-making has displayed an excessive concern with short-term considerations, reflected in the way that the government appears:

> . . . to have paid scant attention to the theoretical and empirical relationships between development, motivation to control fertility, and decline in the population growth rate . . . The failure of the 1984 attempt to raise fertility among the better-educated segments of society is perhaps one indication of the strong influence of development on the motivation to control fertility (Yap, 1989, p. 470).

This parallels a view that the government operates on the basis of a crisis consciousness, that is, if the population does not produce more or less babies (depending on the specific economic situation and labour requirements), the economy will not be able to survive and the country will be thrown into crisis conditions (Cheng, 1989, p. 172). Drakakis-Smith *et al.* (1993) take this point further and argue that the motivating force behind the attempts at population engineering and control is the desire to sustain economic growth. Their evaluation of the success of these measures may be worrying to government: 'exhortations and controls to ensure that there are enough players, who are healthy and trained enough to do the right thing at the right time, seems to be beginning to chafe with some younger Singaporeans' (Drakakis-Smith *et al.*, 1993, p. 162). Future population policy may need to be introduced more gradually than in the past to avoid 'the disruptive effects of accordion-like waves of growth and contraction' (Yap, 1989, p. 473). Another area where the state may need to compromise is its emphasis on self-help and family care for the aged. There is a substantial proportion of the elderly population at the moment and in the near future that will require other assistance. This is because they may never have been employed (especially true of women) or their wages may have been so low in the past that their CPF savings are extremely small (Yap, 1989, p. 471). Policies will thus have to be thought through to suit the different cohorts of elderly persons who will have different needs.

# 5

## Economic growth

Singapore is an economic success story. Since 1965, it has achieved an annual average growth rate of 9% and now has a GNP per capita that exceeds many developed countries. Along with the economic performance of Japan and the East Asian newly industrializing economies (South Korea, Taiwan and Hong Kong), Singapore's emergence as an economic force accords with the view that a new world economy, centred around the Asian Pacific rim, is taking shape. Few commercial decisions relating to Southeast Asia are now taken without reference to Singapore; almost any multinational enterprise, whether in manufacturing or services, planning to expand outside North America, Western Europe or Japan would naturally consider it as a location. To many, Singapore offers a role model of economic development, combining efficient and far sighted government economic management with a reliance on private enterprise and personal initiative. It can be overlooked, however, that Singapore commenced independence as an already comparatively modern metropolis. Its economic progress is remarkable but not a miracle (Huff, 1994, p. 31).

In the 1950s, Singapore was the most important communications centre in the region, for shipping and the rapidly developing airline and telecommunications links. As well as a thriving entrepôt, it was also the home of international trading markets for rubber and tin and a major distribution centre for oil (Rowe, 1965; Coates, 1987). There was an established ship repair industry, a reservoir of skilled labourers and a record of strong and stable government. It was a comparatively affluent society which, as it recovered from the impact of the Second World War, had been steadily growing in wealth. This inheritance has not surprisingly been downplayed by Singapore's post-independence rulers. As with other new governments, additional political hegemony was sought by encouraging an image of order and progress replacing disarray and stagnation (Huff, 1994, p. 33). The immediate circumstances of independence were challenging, but the contemporary economy has much continuity with the island's long established role as a trading emporium (Regnier, 1991).

Separation from the Federation of Malaysia in 1965 made the strategy of import substitution, being pursued by the Federation, untenable for Singapore alone. This change unsettled development intentions but the new strategy adopted – export-orientated growth through the attraction of foreign investment – was consistent with the island's established role as the gateway between Southeast Asia and the international economy. The challenge was in extending this role to the manufacturing sector. At the time, few locally-owned manufacturing enterprises of any significance existed. Local capital was in abundant supply but immobilized either through a preference for savings or for short-term investment in the profitable and more familiar sector of trade and commerce (Taylor and Neville, 1980, p. 57). An abundant labour supply existed but unemployment was high as were wages.

Local circumstances were a challenge to the economic prospects of independent Singapore, but the world economic environment was highly favourable. In 1966, as Singapore started its search for export-orientated foreign investors, a new international division of labour was taking shape (Rodan, 1985, pp. 180–83). Foreign multinationals were actively starting to use offshore locations for the assembly of low value-added goods for use in the multinational's home market or other export destinations. Countries such as the United States helped this development by making special tariff provisions for offshore assembly. From the outset, a high proportion of the investors attracted to Singapore were making electronics goods for the United States. The electric and electronic industry remains the largest concentration of manufacturing activity, accounting for around 40% of value added in the mid-1990s. While North America remains the principal market, Japanese investment has grown to rival American capital. Another change has been a gradual increase in the capital intensity of production and the sophistication of products assembled. Across the manufacturing sector, low value-added and labour intensive operations moved out to other parts of Southeast Asia and increasingly to China, leaving Singapore as the control and coordination centre for multinational subsidiaries located across the region.

The inherited foundations for growth and compatibility with the changing structure of the global economy make it hard to determine precisely the role of the PAP government in the achievement of growth. This is further complicated by the pervasiveness of government intervention.

Presently, the focus is on the provision of a services infrastructure and human resource base capable of making Singapore the so-called 'brain centre' of Southeast Asia, managing foreign subsidiaries and supporting the regionalization of domestic enterprise. The comprehensive battery of instruments used by the government to influence change are not all equally influential or necessary. For example, tax incentives designed to encourage organizations to open regional offices are given to already established offices (Dicken and Kirkpatrick, 1991). Attempts to accelerate technology transfer through investments in high technology companies overseas had reportedly resulted in huge losses by the early 1990s (Kanai, 1993). On the other hand, the efficient and non-corrupt decision-making of its economic development agencies has been a key factor in the island's favour.

This chapter continues by outlining the main phases in Singapore's post-independence economic development, followed by a profile of the economy in the mid-1990s. The key agencies and tools used to promote economic development are then outlined, followed by a discussion of the government's impact on economic growth. This is followed by an outline of the most recent departure in economic strategy, promoting the regionalization of the economy through offshore investment by Singaporean organizations. The regionalization programme is being led by government-linked investment in infrastructure projects, underscoring the continuing importance of the state in influencing economic progress.

## Stages of growth

Singapore's recent economic development can be summarized into four main phases according to differences in performance and management (Figure 5.1). The immediate period post-separation from the Malaysian Federation was the time of most rapid growth. During 1966–1973, average annual GDP growth accelerated to 12.7%. The foundations for this growth had been laid prior to the separation. Investment incentives had first been introduced in 1959 under the Pioneer Industries (Relief from Income Tax) Ordinance and Industrial Expansion (Relief from Income Tax) Ordinance. New investors which met certain criteria were accorded pioneer status and were entitled to tax exemption for five years, and approved existing firms were given tax incentives to invest in the expansion of productive capacity. To administer the tax incentives, as well as to invest in industry and infrastructure development, an economic development agency was set up in 1961, known as the Economic Development Board (EDB). This agency set about implementing proposals recommended in a develop-

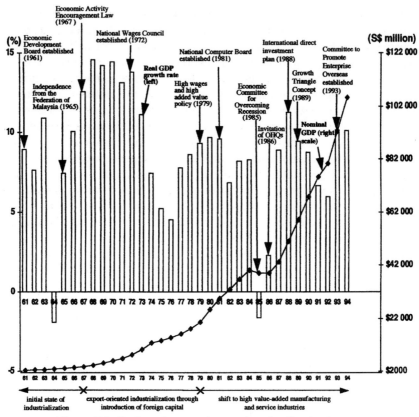

**Figure 5.1**  Outline of economic growth and policy development

ment plan produced by the United Nations, subsequently integrated into the First Development Plan 1961–64. As part of this plan, industrial sites and advance factories were constructed in Jurong, although it was only from 1967 that foreign companies started to arrive in significant numbers (Huff, 1994, p. 309).

Independence brought changes in business incentives and labour market conditions. In 1967, the Economic Expansion (Relief from Income Tax) Act superseded the earlier incentives, taxing the profits of export industries at 4%, instead of the usual 40%, for between 10 and 15 years. In addition, the government reinforced the liberal investment regime, renewing the island's free port status and limited controls on foreign investment, ownership and profit repatriation.

Up to the mid-1960s, Singapore was a high-cost producer by Asian standards with wages '20–30% too high for world markets' according to the United Nations (UNISM, 1961). The government changed this perceived misalignment through two acts of legislation in 1968, the Employment Act and the Industrial Relations (Amendment) Act. The Employment Act increased standard working hours from 39 to 44; reduced public holidays from 15 to 11; reduced entitlements to holiday leave and other benefits and made them contingent upon disciplined behaviour in the workplace; and reduced eligibility for retrenchment benefits by increasing the qualifying period of employment to a minimum of three years (Anantaraman, 1990, p. 124). The Industrial (Amendment) Act reduced the influence of trade unions by, amongst other changes, removing rights to negotiation over redundancies and job reorganization. The scope for industrial action was further circumscribed by doubling the minimum duration of collective agreements to three years. From a peak of over 400 000 person days lost through industrial stoppages in 1961, the days lost fell to under 10 000 in 1969. Also by 1969, wages in the electronics industry had fallen below those in South Korea, Taiwan and Hong Kong and were less than one-eleventh of the United States' level for equivalent productivity (Huff, 1994, p. 324). To maintain control over wage levels, a tripartite National Wages Council (NWC) was established to make recommendations on wage increases and the structure of payments. The status of these recommendations was raised by amending the Industrial Relations Act in 1972 to allow the Industrial Arbitration Court to enforce the NWC's recommendations (Anantaraman, 1990, pp. 174–80).

The EDB's initial investment promotion did not prioritize preferred industries, although value added, skill requirements and capital intensity were increasingly scrutinized. After some early concentration in the apparel and textile sectors, the electronics sector rapidly assumed dominance. From the late 1960s, United States and later European electronics companies increasingly favoured Singapore as an offshore assembly base. Compared with other locations in the region, Singapore's administrators attained a reputation for fast and fair decision-making, while the island's geographical advantages and well-developed communications and shipping services offered further advantages. From 1967 to 1973, textiles and garments and the production of electronics and electrical goods generated about half the manufacturing employment growth (Table 5.1). The Vietnam war and the development of energy resources in Southeast Asia provided further sources of growth (Regnier, 1991, p. 5).

In 1973, for the first time, direct manufactured goods – goods with some part of their value added through manufacture in Singapore – exceeded primary commodity exports excluding petroleum (Huff, 1994, p. 312). Foreign firms were almost wholly responsible for this reorientation, establishing control of almost three-quarters of manufacturing output. The tripling of manufacturing employment from 1966 to 1973 helped

**Table 5.1** Manufacturing employment and output, 1967-1993 (%)

|  | 1967 | 1973 | 1984 | 1990 | 1993 |
|---|---|---|---|---|---|
| *Employment* | | | | | |
| Textiles & garments | 13.1 | 17.6 | 10.8 | 8.8 | 6.7 |
| Printing & publishing | 8.5 | 3.9 | 5.2 | 4.5 | 5.0 |
| Petroleum refineries & products | 1.1 | 1.6 | 1.3 | 0.9 | 1.1 |
| Transport equipment | 10.3 | 12.8 | 9.6 | 7.4 | 9.2 |
| Machinery except electrical & electronic | 3.5 | 3.9 | 7.1 | 6.9 | 7.1 |
| Electrical machinery & apparatus | ) | ) | 6.0 | 6.3 | 5.4 |
| Electrical products & components | ) ) 3.2 | ) ) 22.4 | 26.4 | 34.9 | 33.1 |
| Instrumentation equipment & photographic & optic goods | – | 3.3 | 1.9 | 2.2 | 2.3 |
| Others | 60.3 | 34.5 | 31.5 | 28.1 | 30.1 |
| Total employment | 58 347 | 198 574 | 274 391 | 351 674 | 355 367 |
| *Output* | | | | | |
| Textiles & garments | 3.6 | 7.6 | 3.3 | 3.0 | 1.9 |
| Printing & publishing | 4.1 | 2.1 | 2.3 | 2.5 | 2.6 |
| Petroleum refineries & products | 21.6 | 24.8 | 30.3 | 15.9 | 12.8 |
| Transport equipment | 5.5 | 9.7 | 4.8 | 5.3 | 5.2 |
| Machinery except electrical & electronic | 1.8 | 2.6 | 4.7 | 4.7 | 4.2 |
| Electrical machinery & apparatus | ) | ) | 3.6 | 3.4 | 3.2 |
| Electrical products & components | ) ) 2.5 | ) ) 15.8 | 23.4 | 39.1 | 45.4 |
| Instrumentation equipment & photographic & optic goods | – | 1.6 | 0.7 | 1.1 | 1.2 |
| Others | 60.9 | 35.8 | 26.9 | 25.0 | 23.5 |
| Total output ($m) | 1 687.2 | 7 938.1 | 41 077.9 | 71 333.2 | 87 727.7 |

*Source: Report on the Census of Industrial Production* (various years)

to cut unemployment by half to 4.5%, a level close to full employment. The share of manufacturing in GDP rose from 16.3% in 1966 to 22.5% in 1973. Exports provided the market for manufacturing growth, rising from 31% of total manufacturing sales in 1967 to 54% in 1973 (Huff, 1994, p. 320).

The second phase of development (1974–1984) is distinguished by slower overall growth and changes in investment promotion. Less favourable circumstances existed in the world economy than in the earlier period, partly associated with the two international oil shocks. Even so, economic growth remained high and the EDB was able to exercise increased discretion in the allocation of investment incentives. As early as 1969, the EDB had recognized that when assessing development proposals:

> more demanding criteria and critical examination will have to be applied to ensure that growth is directed towards making maximum use of resources and advantages. The main emphasis and priority will be given to those types of industries and operations that can make the most significant contribution in skill development with good potential for technological advance. The products must be marketable on a worldwide basis with prospects for future growth (*EDB Yearbook*, 1969, p. 15).

This strategy was reflected in the raising of investment thresholds for taxation incentives, the expansion of technical training and efforts to upgrade local industry. A priority industry list was published in 1975 and while this had few exclusions from the range of activity already attracted (Low, 1993, p. 74), a transformation in the manufacturing sector did take place. Domestic-market and low value, labour intensive industries such as food and beverages, textiles and wood products declined in relative importance. Industries which expanded rapidly included chemical products, fabricated metal products, electrical and electronic products and components as well as machinery and precision equipment (Tan, K. Y., 1995, p. 57).

Petroleum refining was another industry to grow rapidly in this period. From 1892 to 1960, Singapore served as the storage, transshipment and distribution centre for the Far East. Its role as a refining centre started in 1961 when Shell opened a small refinery of 20 000 barrels capacity per day. By the early 1980s, capacity was over 80 0000 barrels per day with refineries operated by Shell, Esso, Mobil, British Petroleum and the Singapore Refining Company (a consortium including Caltex, BP and Singapore Petroleum Company, a partly government-owned joint venture with Japanese and other partners) (Doshi, 1988). Through this investment, Singapore became the petroleum refining centre of the Asia-Pacific region (from the Persian Gulf across to Northeast Asia, and from Australia across to the United States West coast). It filled a niche by complementing national refining capacity and its ability to fill product deficits within its extensive market area. Singapore thus emerged as the 'swing' refiner, balancing out the disparities between supply and demand for specific petroleum products (Doshi, 1989). In the early 1980s, Singapore provided almost half of the gasoline and fuel oil, over two-thirds of the jet kerosene and diesel and about a quarter of the naphtha imported by countries in the Asia-Pacific region (Doshi, 1988, p. 88).

Singapore's role as an international financial centre also consolidated during the 1970s. Here Singapore had distinct advantages for growth, giving economic planners greater scope to select activities for promotion than in manufacturing (Huff, 1994, p. 341). Among the beneficial attributes were location on the world's main east–west communication network, an established core of international financial institutions and the world-wide growth of financial intermediation to service expanding multinational business networks. These advantages were capitalized on through taxation changes to create an Asian Dollar Market in 1968, providing the regional equivalent of the London Eurodollar market. The assets held in Asian Currency Units, banks dealing in the Asian Dollar Market, rose from US$30.5 million on inception to over US$128 billion in 1984 (equivalent to about 12% of the value of the Eurodollar market at the time). The initiation of 24-hour international foreign exchange trading helped Singapore emerge as a foreign exchange dealing centre, crossing the time zone gap between New York/London and Hong Kong/Tokyo. Singapore also developed a role as a funding centre, acting as an entrepôt between deposit centres like Bahrain in a region of surplus funds and arranging centres like Hong Kong close to the ultimate borrowers (Huff, 1994, p. 341).

In the late 1970s, sustained economic expansion, which by now was resulting in an increasing dependence on foreign workers (Table 5.2), led the government to embark on a 'second industrial revolution'. Compared with industry in other Asian NICs – Hong Kong, Taiwan and Korea – the Singapore economy seemed to be slow in intensifying the use of capital and skills (Tan, K. Y., 1995, p. 63). Fear of the economy sinking between these apparently more productive economies and lower cost locations opening up in the region (such as Malaysia and Indonesia) led the government into a bold strategy. In a dash for restructuring, a 'wage correction policy' was engineered by the NWC resulting in a 40% increase in unit labour costs from 1979–1984. This was intended to force the pace of technological upgrading by increasing the incentive to raise productivity. As well as increases in direct labour costs, the compulsory contributions made by employees and employers to the state administered savings and pensions fund (the CPF) were raised simultaneously, partly to prevent higher wages fuelling inflation.

To reinforce the upgrading, incentives to attract technology-intensive industries were introduced along with product development assistance. Pioneer status was restricted to priority industries and a local industry upgrading scheme was introduced to strengthen the subcontracting sector. R&D capacity and technical skills were given special attention. Government development expenditure on education was increased ten-

**Table 5.2** Foreign workers in Singapore 1985–1994

| Year | Total workforce | No. of foreign workers |
|------|-----------------|------------------------|
| 1985 | 1 135 000 | 100 000 |
| 1988 | 1 332 000 | 150 000 |
| 1992 | 1 576 000 | 200 000 |
| 1994 | 1 680 000 | 300 000 |

Data not available pre-1985
*Source:* Ministry of Labour, Annual Report; 1994 estimate cited in Chew and Chew (1996, p. 197)

**Plate 5.1** Labour shortages result in plentiful factory jobs

fold, principally to accommodate more engineering students (Rodan, 1989, p. 149). New centres for technical skills training were opened with German, Japanese and French collaboration. In 1979, a Skills Development Fund was established through a compulsory levy on wages to provide central-ized training for lower-income workers. Government R&D funding expand-ed, including support to a new Software Technology Centre and the opening of a Science Park.

The economic transformation looked for did not eventuate as planned: in the third phase of development (1985–1986) real GDP declined in the only recession so far encountered by independent Singapore. Net invest-ment commitments in the manufacturing sector fell by over a third in

1985, although the total received stayed above $1 billion, and real exports fell by 5%. The reasons for the recession are not entirely to do with the wage correction policy, but it was an important contributor. Expectations of high wage increases stayed beyond the correction period, encouraged by the tight labour market and higher costs reduced competitiveness against other Asian NICs. However these problems were mitigated by international economic conditions in which foreign investment in competitor economies was slowing down as well.

Other judgements on the second industrial revolution see some positive achievements and suggest it was 'a case of a little too much a little too soon' (Wilkinson, 1994, p. 47). The high wages policy did arrest labour demand and helped accelerate annual productivity growth, from 2 to 3% in the 1970s to 4% in the early 1980s (Lim and Pang, 1984, p. 27). Automation made some inroads: in 1984, one assessment found 564 CNC machine tools in use, 86 industrial robots and 220 CAD/CAM stations with most of these technologies installed after 1981 (Chng et al., 1986). Over this period, the semiconductor industry became a testing and regional logistics centre, with routine assembly operations relocated into neighbouring countries (Scott, 1987; Henderson, 1989).

Government reaction to the recession came through the appointment of a ministerial committee, instructed to identify the causes of the downturn and to identify 'new directions' for growth. The Committee's immediate impact was to order a wage freeze and a cost cutting programme, reducing the employer CPF contribution (from 25% to 10% of wages), corporate taxes (from 40% to 33%) and various public utility charges. The Committee, nonetheless, did not view production costs as the fundamental cause of the economic slowdown:

> . . . a more meaningful perspective is to recognize that this slowdown marks a transition from one stage of development to another, characterized by the following turning points: (a) a more competitive international market due to slow world economic growth; (b) our having reached or approached the limits of some key resources, such as labour and land; (c) satisfaction of domestic infrastructure demand such as housing, commercial building etc; and (d) a standard of living where we are no longer cheap (Economic Committee, 1986, p. 163).

As well as the cost-cutting measures introduced from 1986–1988, the Committee proposed various diversification strategies. Continued expansion of the R&D base was recommended as part of the strategy for upgrading manufacturing activity. The service sector was identified as a new area for promotion, which was partly a recognition of it having contributed a greater share of GDP than manufacturing since the launch of the second industrial revolution (Table 5.3). Particular opportunities were identified to attract the regional operational headquarters (OHQs) of multinational companies, which it was hoped would in turn stimulate demand for business services. An OHQ incentive scheme was introduced, designed to make Singapore's taxation environment for regional head offices competitive with Hong Kong, while other service activities became eligible for the investment incentives previously reserved for manufacturers. The Committee also talked about the importance of invigorating local enterprise and reducing government business ownership. The main change in strategy was, however, contained in the idea of building a 'total business centre' in which:

> Singapore aims to become an important strategic node of global companies for the Asia-Pacific region . . . we would like companies to do more than production. On the one hand, they should integrate backwards into activities such as production engineering, product design, research and development; on the other hand, they should integrate forwards into marketing, technical support, after sales services and ultimately regional management (EDB, 1988, p. l2).

By January 1989, two and half years following the start of the OHQ incentive, 20 OHQs had been designated, which was above the target of six designations a year (Dicken and Kirkpatrick, 1991, p. 177).

The immediate post-recession recovery, however, was driven primarily by strong manufacturing growth, more than the expanding role as a regional office centre. After contracting in the previous two years, manufacturing output grew by 23.6%, 22.8% and 11.2% over the period 1987–1989 while direct manufactured exports almost doubled in value. This growth came in large part from economic recovery in the United States, reviving the demand for electronic products and components, and the restructuring of other Asian economies (Rodan, 1993b, pp. 232–33). The sharp yen appreciation following the Plaza Accord (an agreement reached by France, Germany, Japan, the United Kingdom and the United States to seek a managed appreciation of currency values relative to the US dollar) of September 1985 encouraged a surge of offshore production relocation from Japan. One estimate suggests that in 1989, Japanese organizations committed US$1900 million to new investment projects in Singapore, or over half the total value of all Japanese foreign direct investment made in 1986 (Fukushima and Kwan, 1995, p. 6). From 1985 to 1990, Japan's share of cumulative foreign investment in the manufacturing sector jumped from 22.3% to 31.2% (Table 5.4). The growth of Japanese investment in neighbouring economies was a further stimulus to Singapore through its emerging role as the regional coordination centre for Japanese MNCs (Aoki and Tachiki, 1992). The regional headquarters of Sony, for

**Table 5.3** Sector output and employment distribution (%) 1960–1994

| Industry | Output | | | | | Employment | | | | |
|---|---|---|---|---|---|---|---|---|---|---|
| | 1960 | 1970 | 1980 | 1990 | 1994 | 1957 | 1970 | 1980 | 1990 | 1994 |
| Agriculture & mining | 3.9 | 2.7 | 1.5 | 0.4 | 0.2 | 8.8 | 3.8 | 1.7 | 0.4 | 0.3 |
| Manufacturing | 11.7 | 20.2 | 28.1 | 27.8 | 25.6 | 14.1 | 22.0 | 30.1 | 29.1 | 25.6 |
| Utilities | 2.4 | 2.6 | 2.1 | 1.8 | 1.5 | 1.2 | 1.1 | 0.8 | 0.4 | 0.5 |
| Construction | 3.5 | 6.8 | 6.2 | 5.3 | 7.1 | 5.2 | 6.6 | 6.7 | 4.3 | 5.1 |
| Commerce | 33.0 | 27.4 | 20.9 | 16.3 | 16.1 | 24.2 | 23.4 | 21.3 | 8.0 | 6.6 |
| Transport & communication | 13.6 | 10.7 | 13.5 | 12.6 | 11.4 | 10.6 | 12.1 | 11.1 | 9.5 | 10.6 |
| Finance & business services | 14.4 | 16.7 | 18.9 | 26.5 | 28.1 | 4.6 | 4.0 | 7.4 | 10.9 | 12.0 |
| Other services | 17.6 | 12.9 | 8.7 | 9.5 | 9.9 | 30.6 | 26.8 | 20.8 | 19.7 | 21.4 |

*Source:* Department of Statistics, *Economic & Social Statistics Singapore 1960–1982*, *Yearbook of Statistics* (various years)

example, employed a staff of over 300, involved in product design, marketing distribution, finance, legal services and logistics coordination.

Overall, however, despite some diversification in investment sources, the period of recovery did little to alleviate the vulnerability of the manufacturing sector. This issue has absorbed greater attention in the most recent phase of economic development, partly because of the perceived political risks of poor economic performance at a time of leadership succession. At the end of 1990, Lee Kuan Yew stepped down as prime minister, to be succeeded by Goh Chok Tong. A batch of new economic strategies characterized the early 1990s of which the central document was the Strategic Economic Plan (MTI, 1991).

The Strategic Plan was partly a restatement of established goals. It spoke of positioning Singapore as a global city, by making it a 'total business hub' for the Asia-Pacific and offering a business location on a par with other leading global cities. The attraction of high tech, knowledge-intensive industries was to be intensified, along with investment to

**Table 5.4** Cumulative foreign and local investments in manufacturing by country (gross fixed assets, $m) 1970–1994

|  | 1970 | 1975 | 1980 | 1985 | 1990 | 1992 |
|---|---|---|---|---|---|---|
| United States | 343 | 1118 | 2091 | 4656 | 8037 | 9678 |
| Japan | 68 | 454 | 1187 | 2943 | 7546 | 9093 |
| Europe | 423 | 1170 | 2992 | 4480 | 7161 | 8331 |
| – United Kingdom | 199 | 481 | 1172 | 1796 | 2583 | 2860 |
| – Netherlands | 183 | 473 | 1292 | 1663 | 2818 | 3367 |
| – Germany | 3 | 105 | 243 | 245 | 488 | 666 |
| – France | 8 | 22 | 57 | 190 | 484 | 563 |
| – Other European | 40 | 89 | 226 | 586 | 788 | 876 |
| Others | 161 | 638 | 822 | 1081 | 1388 | 1463 |
| Local | na | na | 3469 | 7100 | 8682 | 10 604 |
| Total cumulative foreign | 995 | 3380 | 7092 | 13 160 | 24 133 | 28 565 |
| Total cumulative | na | na | 10 561 | 20 259 | 32 815 | 39 168 |

Source: EDB, Annual Yearbook (various years)

**Plate 5.2** Caltex House in the CBD. Photo courtesy of the URA

enhance labour skills and innovation capacity, partly through more emphasis on teamwork and tripartite cooperation. The division of the economy into clusters of related activity, identifying perceived strengths and opportunities for growth, was the more novel aspect of the Plan, reflecting the influence of the fashionable American business guru of the time, Michael Porter (Table 5.5).

The 14 clusters identified were commodity trading, shipping, precision engineering, electronics, information technology, petroleum and petrochemical, construction, heavy engineering, finance, insurance, general supporting industries, tourism, international hub (meaning regional headquarters and corporate support services) and domestic industries. It was recommended that participants in these clusters should be integrated through workshops and some form of institutionalized planning process. In December 1993, a $1 billion Cluster Development Fund was set up to

**Table 5.5** Implementation action from the Strategic Economic Plan 1991

| Policy target | Agency responsible | Programmes |
| --- | --- | --- |
| Human resource improvement | MTI | International manpower programme |
| Promote national teamwork | MTI | Economic panel established |
| Become internationally orientated | EDB | Prepare Singaporeans for international assignments. Promote Growth Triangle and business alliances within ASEAN. Develop information infrastructure |
| Conducive environment for innovation | NPB (now PSB) | Review government rules hindering innovation |
| Develop business clusters | Each cluster assigned agency relevant to activity, includes TDB, PSA, EDB, NCB, MAS, CIDB or STPB | Implement cluster-based development plans; strengthen cluster cohesion through data reporting and improving employer/employee relation |
| Economic redevelopment | EDB with other agencies | Identify new growth opportunities |
| Maintain international competitiveness | MTI | Establish competitiveness monitoring group |
| Reduce vulnerability | MTI | Establish scenario analysis group. Strengthen home base character of MNCs. Encourage positive attitude to local enterprise within government agencies and review institutional support |

*Source:* von Alten (1994, p. 128)

promote development within clusters. By January 1996, $225 million had been committed to eight projects of which the largest was outside Singapore, a joint venture project with Daimler Benz to open a car assembly plant in Vietnam (*The Straits Times*, 31 January 1996).

## The economy in the 1990s

Three decades of modernization have brought limited diversification to the Singapore economy. Within the service sector, a major shift has occurred from commercial to financial and business services (Table 5.3) reflecting the island's evolution as a regional headquarters centre. After an initial expansion up to the early 1970s, manufacturing has retained its contribution to GDP at around 26–28%. While a number of local business groups, mostly government-linked have grown, overall the reliance on foreign investment remains (Table 5.4). Foreign companies account for around three-quarters of production, of which one-third are American and one-fifth are Japanese (Table 5.6). Of the 50 largest locally-owned private enterprises (judged by a range of financial indicators), 23 had no overseas earnings in 1995 while 13 of those with overseas earnings were primarily distributors and traders of electronics, computer and clothing goods (*The Business Times*, 10 February 1996).

The electric and electronic industry remains the largest concentration of manufacturing activity, accounting for around 40% of value added (Table 5.7). Within the sector, there is a significant specialization on four product areas: disc drives (24% of production value), computer peripherals (11.3%), semiconductors (10.6%) and audiovisual equipment (9.7%). Each segment is primarily an export activity, with North America being the principal market. Of these sectors, Singapore is of most international significance in disk drive manufacture for which it is the base for over half of the world's production of 2.5", 3.5" and 5.25" disk drives (EDB, 1994a).

After electronics, the chemical products and petroleum refining sectors produce the next highest share of manufacturing value added at 16.2%. The petroleum refining industry is largely controlled by multinational petroleum companies, with only 4 out of 15 refining sites owned by local interests (Doshi, 1989). Nearly 60% of the output is exported with other major markets being fuel supply to ships and the locally-based, but primarily foreign-owned petrochemical industry. The next most important sectors, transport equipment and metal products, are closely linked to the petroleum sector as they are dominated by marine engineering. Three government-linked companies – Sembawang Engineering, Keppel Corporation and Jurong Shipyard – along with Hitachi Zosen account for two-thirds of dock capacity. Ship repairs is the dominate activity with Singapore undertaking around 60% of the world market in repairs to very large cargo carriers (EDB, 1994b). The metal product industry is primarily a locally-owned supporting industry to the marine sector and other manufacturing and construction.

**Table 5.6** Foreign and Singaporean contributions to the manufacturing sector 1993

| Nationality* | No. of Companies | Share (%) | No. of Employees | Share (%) | Added value ($m) | Share (%) | Exports ($m) | Share (%) |
|---|---|---|---|---|---|---|---|---|
| Singapore | 3135 | 78.5 | 159 299 | 44.8 | 8286 | 29.3 | 7863 | 14.8 |
| Foreign | 858 | 21.5 | 195 876 | 55.2 | 20 001 | 70.7 | 45 158 | 85.2 |
| – United States | 175 | 4.4 | 78 688 | 22.1 | 9664 | 34.2 | 25 337 | 47.8 |
| – Japan | 312 | 7.8 | 65 637 | 18.5 | 4516 | 15.9 | 9682 | 18.2 |
| – European Community | 149 | 3.7 | 32 141 | 9.0 | 4479 | 15.8 | 6576 | 12.4 |
| – Europe other | 41 | 1.0 | 5098 | 1.4 | 435 | 1.5 | 693 | 1.3 |
| Other foreign | 181 | 4.5 | 14 312 | 4.0 | 906 | 3.2 | 2868 | 5.4 |
| Total | 3993 | 100 | 355 175 | 100 | 28 287 | 100 | 53 022 | 100 |

*Note:* *50% equity used as cut off

*Source:* Report on the Census of Industrial Production 1993

**Table 5.7** Singapore major manufacturing sectors 1993

| | % total manufacturing | | |
| --- | --- | --- | --- |
| | Output | Employment | Value added |
| Electronic products & components | 45.4 | 33.1 | 39.0 |
| Petroleum | 12.8 | 1.1 | 7.1 |
| Chemical products | 5.7 | 3.0 | 9.1 |
| Fabricated metal products | 5.6 | 9.2 | 6.7 |
| Transport equipment | 5.2 | 9.3 | 7.7 |
| Non-electrical machinery | 4.3 | 7.2 | 5.0 |
| Electrical machinery & appliances | 3.2 | 5.5 | 3.7 |
| Printing & publishing | 2.6 | 5.1 | 4.8 |
| Others | 15.2 | 26.5 | 16.9 |

*Source:* Report on the Census of Industrial Production 1993

Financial and business services rank slightly ahead of manufacturing in terms of GDP contribution but employ considerably fewer (Table 5.3) and provide higher income. Singapore is now among the top ten international banking centres, accounting for around 5% of international banking activity (Regnier 1990, p. 120). Out of 137 banks in Singapore, 35 possess a full licence (24 of these being foreign-owned banks) with the remainder only engaging in restricted domestic banking activity as well as non-resident and inter-bank trading activity. Banking activity is still dominated by the Asian dollar market, which remains largely an inter-bank market with the funds recycled to end users in other locations. Other important financial markets are foreign exchange, financial futures as well as other merchant banking services to business and a newly developing role as a fund management centre. The latter activity is being promoted partly by allowing individuals to transfer some of their CPF savings into approved funds. As well as the financial sector, Singapore's importance as a regional headquarters centre (see Chapter 1) helps support a wide range of business services. Of the new investment in service activity that is tracked by the EDB, over 50% was linked to operational headquarters from 1990 to 1993 (*EDB Yearbook 1994*).

A third key component of the economy comprises transport, travel and tourism. Port, distribution and warehousing activity continue to benefit from the island's strategic location in relation to international commerce. In terms of tonnage of ships handled, Singapore became the world's busiest port in the 1980s, surpassing Rotterdam and Kobe and is the largest container terminal operation, recently exceeding that of Hong Kong. A much greater volume of ships than those docking make use of Singapore as a shipment point for fuel, supplies and labour. Re-exports account for just under a third of the value of total imports. This statistic, however, does not reflect the extent to which Singapore is used by multi-national organizations as a storage and distribution point for goods and equipment.

All Southeast Asian international airports benefit from their strategic location in relation to European–Australasian air traffic, but Singapore has been the most successful in encouraging travellers to break route at its airport. Assisted by this, Singapore International Airlines has grown into one of the world's leading carriers. In 1994, the airline was the world's sixteenth largest by operating revenue, but the most profitable despite not ranking among the top 24 in terms of the size of its air fleet or passenger volume (*Air Transport World*, June 1995). Singapore's airline alone contributes around 5% of GDP while the tourist sector as a whole is estimated to contribute 10.3% of GDP (Singapore Tourist Promotion Board, 1995). Singapore has had a surplus in its travel balance (travel export minus travel import) since 1960. This surplus increased from 0.7% of GDP in 1960 to a high of 10.2% in 1981 (Hall, 1994, p. 104). The balance had dropped to 5% in 1994 (Singapore Tourist Promotion Board, 1995), reflecting the increasing number of Singapore residents travelling over-seas for business and leisure, but with a resident population base of less than three million, the travel balance is likely to remain in surplus for many years to come.

In 1994, there were almost 6.9 million visitor arrivals, representing over a fivefold increase since 1975. Of major significance to Singapore has been the perceived safety of the destination which has made the country extremely attractive to first time travellers, especially Japanese and other Asian women travelling alone or in groups (Economist Intelligence Unit, 1990). One of the main issues in the development of Singapore as a tourist destination is the appropriate balance between the retention of the old city landscape and the creation of the modern metropolis orientated to inter-national commerce (see Chapter 9). For future expansion, one of the mar-kets targeted is the meetings, incentives, conventions and exhibition trade, as reflected in the opening of a second major convention facility (the Singapore International Convention and Exhibition Centre) in 1995 which, unlike the existing centre, is located downtown in the heart of the central hotel and shopping district. To make up for the oriental charm and mystique lost in the redevelopment of Singapore, tourist resorts are being developed in the nearby Riau islands as part of the growth triangle project (see Chapter 6).

### Government role in the economy

The Singapore economy has variously been seen as predominantly *laissez faire* (see Rodan 1989, pp. 25–30) and as an economy under extensive state regulation and control (Henderson, 1993). Such opposing interpretations are partly a product of the unusual characteristics of the economy and the uneven scope of government intervention. The island is essentially a free port in respect of trade and manufacturing investment, with few restrictions on the use of professional expatriate labour and no performance requirements on recruitment of local personnel. It is also the case that, unlike neighbouring countries, after the first development plan, covering 1960–1964, there is no formal development plan process. On the other hand, key components of the domestic economy are in full or partial public ownership and subject to government direction, as are the conditions of employment for the domestic workforce and a high share of personal incomes. The close coordination of economic development exercised by senior ministers and civil servants is one reason that formal development planning has been dispensed with (Toh and Low, 1993, p. 232). The nature of the intervention exercised can be summarized with respect to five modes of intervention: agencies, incentives, infrastructure, workforce control and economic management.

*Agencies*

Without a strong indigenous business sector, the state has relied heavily on a number of agencies and government-linked companies to modernize the economy. The range of agencies involved in economic promotion is extensive and has tended to keep multiplying with the development ambition of the state. The following discussion identifies those agencies with the most prominent roles directly affecting the economy.

*Economic Development Board.* The EDB has operated since 1961 and is the longest established and most powerful economic promotion agency. It functions as the development arm of the Ministry of Trade and Industry and oversees the work of most of the other development agencies. The EDB operates as an investment promotion agency, seeking to encourage inward investment and the expansion of established enterprise. It is assisted by a wide range of taxation and investment incentives, a network of overseas offices and a wide ranging capacity to monitor technologies and companies that might be attracted to Singapore. As well as investment promotion, the EDB also operates as an employment agency, sourcing Singaporeans overseas and foreign nationals in areas of skill shortage. Compared with similar industrial development agencies found around the world, four aspects of the EDB's operation are of note.

First, the EDB has great discretion over the way it determines eligibility for the taxation and other assistance it administers. While assistance is packaged under specific programmes, these typically leave a large area for discretion in determining the eligibility of individual applicants (Chia, 1989). This gives the EDB considerable leverage over companies to participate in development schemes as it can be perceived that failure to cooperate will risk access to other incentives and government cooperation. Secondly, the agency has authority to initiate new business ventures, either directly as an investor or, where particular expertise is sought, by directing subsidiary agencies and government-linked companies to be involved. Thirdly, the extensive web of incentive schemes and information sources provides opportunity to coordinate activity and ensure opportunities are not lost to Singapore. For example, major MNCs are surveyed annually to determine their development intentions and operating needs. This survey information is then used to identify new markets that local enterprise can be assisted to enter using incentives and support provided in its 'local industry upgrading programme'. Fourthly, the agency is a branch of government and reports directly to senior ministers. This means that there is little challenge to the prestige or authority of the organization through independent scrutiny or public review of its effectiveness.

Collectively, these attributes indicate the high status obtained by the agency which, in turn, become reasons for investors to seek its recognition. Endorsement by the EDB, through participation in one of its incentive schemes has been seen as a route to preferential treatment from other government agencies and private financial institutions, as well as assisting in the recruitment of local staff (Bando, 1990). How far these additional benefits are obtained in practice is unclear, but their perceived importance is indicative of the authoritative reputation acquired by the EDB. Joint industry-agency committees, to incorporate private business managers in policy development, are a further way of extending influence over private business. It should be noted, however, that the sense of the

EDB's all pervasive influence may be a source of difficulty, as a recent example illustrates. In 1996, Singapore Technologies – a government linked company set up to develop and acquire defence technologies – acquired the Singapore operations of the United States disk drive manufacturer Micropolis. Seagate Technology, a disk drive manufacturer with major subsidiary operations in Singapore (collectively it is one of the island's largest employers), voiced concern that the managing director of Singapore Technologies was also the deputy chairman of the EDB, an agency with which they were expected to share information to acquire access to their assistance. Perceiving that there was now a risk in sharing company information with the EDB, the Seagate chairman alleged that they were now faced with competition 'from a country'. He threatened that future investment might be redirected to other locations (*The Straits Times*, 2 May 1996).

The scope of the agency's activity had grown as a consequence of the mid-1980s recession. Until this setback, while there had been recognition of the scope for promoting services, investment incentives and the wider promotion of the EDB stayed focused on manufacturing. Subsequent diversification has taken three directions. In 1986, a Services Promotion Division was set up within the EDB to oversee the efforts to promote Singapore as a regional headquarters centre and to attract other service industries. In the same year, increased attention to supporting indigenous enterprise was given through the establishment of a Small Enterprise Bureau, changed in 1990 to the Enterprise Development Division. The third diversification aims to build an 'external wing' to the Singapore economy by assisting the outward investment of local capital. This initiative is now overseen by the International Business Development Division. Other new priorities are reflected in a biotechnology promotion unit and a consultancy unit to sell the EDB's expertise to agencies and governments outside Singapore.

More recently the EDB has commenced a set of programmes to concentrate effort in five main areas up to the year 2000: (i) maintaining the manufacturing sector's share of national output and ensuring annual growth of at least 7%; (ii) to increase the number of 'significant regional headquarters' from 80 to 200; (iii) to promote the growth of larger locally-owned enterprises, with a target of helping 50 to 70 'promising local enterprises' each with turnover in excess of $100 million and a core of locally-owned multinationals; (iv) to expand the network of overseas industrial parks with economic linkages to Singapore (see below); (v) to participate in industrial projects in the region. To support these initiatives, the EDB was allocated a budget of $4.3 billion for 1996–2000, more than double that allocated in the previous five year budget (*The Straits Times*,

31 January 1996). In addition, the EDB manages an investment fund of $1.3 billion (expected to be enlarged several times by the end of the century), now prioritized to cluster development and joint venture investment with local and foreign companies.

*Trade Development Board.* The TDB was established in 1983 to promote international trade by providing assistance to local and foreign companies through Singapore and overseas offices. It has acquired a business development role by assisting the representation of local companies in international trade fairs and the access of foreign buyers to local sources of supply. More recently, it has taken charge of a number of schemes offering taxation incentives to companies involved in ship fleet management, aircraft leasing and international commodity trading. Among recent initiatives is a programme to help 15–20 local trading companies grow into 'mega-traders', envisaged as operations akin to the Japanese *sogoshoshas* or Korean *chaebols* (*The Straits Times*, 1 May 1995).

*Singapore Productivity and Standards Board.* The PSB is the newest agency to be established having started operations in 1996. It was formed through the amalgamation of two longer-established organizations: the National Productivity Board (NPB, established in 1972) and the Singapore Institute of Standards and Industrial Research (SISIR, established in 1969). The amalgamation of the agencies was designed to integrate previously divided responsibilities for training and certification. The new agency is to release a ten year national productivity plan in 1997 which will include a certification system to recognize skills obtained at work and to identify skill development paths for a wide range of occupations. The new agency will continue previous activities of the original bodies. In addition, it has acquired the EDB's responsibilities for promoting SMEs (firms of less than 200 employees and $5 million net fixed assets). The latter underscored the EDB's renewed concentration on strategic investments and big business.

The NPB had been concerned with promoting productivity growth in the workplace through what is called a 'total approach to productivity'. The tools utilized include training programmes, social campaigns, management guidance and financial incentives to encourage companies to train employees and upgrade their production facilities. The Skills Development Fund (SDF), established in 1979 as part of the attempt to foster the second industrial revolution, continues to resource much of the training. The fund collects compulsory levies from employers. These contributions are then recycled to employers through two channels. First, approved training courses are designated to which employers obtain a rebate on course fees, with many of these courses provided directly by the

NPB. Much of this training provision is targeted at basic skills, aiming to reach the lowest paid workers who might otherwise be excluded from company training provision. Secondly, in-house training programmes are subsidized including special programmes to encourage the retraining of middle-aged workers (aged 40 and above) and to assist small and medium-sized companies.

Starting in 1980, at the instigation of the Office of the Prime Minister, the NPB orchestrated a productivity consciousness campaign in an attempt to replicate Japanese and Korean workplace commitment and methods in Singapore (Wilkinson, 1994, p. 62). The timing of the campaign was connected to political unease at a perceived loss of respect for traditional 'Asian values' and the launch of a moral education programme in schools (see Chapter 3). The productivity campaign has had a lasting impact in the ongoing support of a national quality circle movement. Individual quality circles are registered with the NPB to participate in annual awards, training courses and social programmes. In 1995, 8.7% of the workforce were claimed to be members of registered quality circles, compared with 2–4% for other advanced Asian economies (*The Straits Times*, 7 May 1996). This promotion is now augmented by more modern productivity ideas such as total quality management and ISO certification promotion. A new departure is the establishment of the Franchise Development Centre to encourage the conversion of local enterprise into franchise groups, with the perspective that franchising can raise productivity among small firms.

SISIR was established in 1969 as an offshoot of the EDB. Its original purpose was to foster the competitiveness of Singapore-made products by establishing quality standards. The new agency inherits SISIR's role as a standards authority, developing local systems of accreditation and acting as an examining agency for overseas standards authorities. It will also link the new responsibilities for SME assistance with SISIR's experience in technology transfer, which had included an incubator centre for new technology-based enterprise and research centres specializing in materials technology, microprocessor applications and a product and process technology centre. The remit of these centres is to upgrade methods of quality verification, originate standards for new products and develop new technologies that can be taken up by local industry. For example, SISIR had adapted a range of ethnic foods for canning and designed automated semiconductor inspection systems.

*National Computer Board.* The NCB, established in 1980, is responsible for promoting the use of information technology and promoting the development of the information technology industry. It invests in R&D and training in information technology skills. A National Information Technology Plan, completed in 1986, has guided much of its subsequent activity. Projects completed arising from the Plan are the computerization of state bureaucracies and the development of several electronic data exchange networks for use by specific sectors. The largest such network, known as TradeNet, links businesses in the international trading industry including shipping companies, freight forwarders, regulatory agencies and port administrators. Other networks have been designed for the legal, medical and construction sectors where standardized document exchange exists (see Chapter 6). Training in computer skills is provided in collaboration with the NPB and a range of incentives administered to encourage private industry investment in information technology.

*National Science and Technology Board*. The NSTB took over the functions of the Science Council in 1991 to expand the latter's role in promoting R&D activity. A National Technology Plan was released by the enlarged agency in 1991 which established new targets and resources for R&D promotion. Under this plan, the NSTB was allocated a $2 billion Research and Development Fund to be spent over five years through grants to research institutions and private industry. This fund is in addition to the administration of a Research and Development Assistance Scheme offering tax concessions against industry R&D expenditure. A range of research institutions are now overseen by the NSTB, usually affiliated to the NCB or a university. These institutes cover information technology, systems science, computer integrated manufacturing, microelectronics, molecular and cell biology, wireless communications, magnetics and environmental technology. As part of the government's concern to raise the private sector contribution to R&D, the NSTB has encouraged these institutes to form joint industry-government research centres. Outcomes of this have been the Glaxo-Institute of Molecular and Cell Biology Centre and the Apple-Institute of Systems Science Centre.

*Jurong Town Corporation*. JTC has taken direct responsibility for the development of Singapore's industrial infrastructure. The facilities provided include an industrial port, facilities for the petroleum and petrochemical industry, most of which are located on nearshore islands, shipyards, industrial land and factory accommodation. In 1995, the corporation managed 30 industrial estates, accommodating 6500 companies and a workforce of 350000 or around 80% of the total manufacturing workforce. Around half of this provision is in Jurong, the original industrial estate in the south western tip of the island. A subsidiary agency, Jurong Environmental Engineering, now works extensively overseas as part of the EDB's regionalization strategy.

**Plate 5.3** Singapore Science Park. Photograph courtesy of the URA

*Government-linked companies.* Most of Singapore's larger locally-owned enterprises are government controlled. The national airline, shipping line, the three major shipyards and parts of the petrochemical industry are majority government-owned. In total, the government has an ownership interest in over 500 companies, comprising over half the 500 largest businesses in Singapore (von Alten, 1995, p. 208). Total assets of the 15 largest statutory boards and the 47 largest GLCs amounted to $167.4 billion in 1993, equivalent to two-thirds of Singapore-owned business assets (Vennewald in von Alten, 1995, p. 212). The origins of this investment are in the early period of industrialization when government investment in joint ventures was used to attract strategic industries. Most of the early projects in the Jurong industrial estate arose in this way, such as National Iron and Steel Mills, Jurong Shipyard, National Grain Elevator and Sugar Industries of Singapore. This motive for government enterprise continues to be used to bring new technologies to Singapore.

In the semiconductor industry, the government, concerned by Singapore's failure to attract integrated production facilities, took the lead role in the formation of two joint venture plants. In 1989, to secure a Singapore presence in wafer fabrication, the EDB through Singapore Technologies, entered a joint venture, known as Chartered Semiconductor, with Sierra Semiconductor and National Semiconductor of the USA. The joint venture was 74% owned by Singapore Technologies and absorbed over $120 million of investment by 1991 when, unexpectedly, the American partners withdrew. In the same year, the EDB orchestrated a second joint consortium, Tech Semiconductor, comprising itself (26% share), Texas Instruments (26%), Hewlett-Packard (24%) and Canon (24%). This consortium is developing a 16MDRAM chip manufacturing plant at a cost of $300 million. In November 1995, Chartered Semiconductor announced investment in two new wafer fabrication plants in Singapore involving total investment of up to $4 billion (*The Business Times*, 7 November 1995). EDB investment in wafer fabrication further expanded in 1996, as part of the renewed impetus to manufacturing, through a new joint venture with Hitachi and Nippon Steel in a $1.33 billion project and with the announcement of further plants to be built by its existing consortium (*The Straits Times*, 14 June 1996). Government participation in new petrochemical investment, through the Petroleum Corporation of Singapore, also continues as in a joint venture with Sumitomo and Hoechst to expand ethylene production (*The Business Times*, 8 April 1996).

The GLCs are mainly administered through three holding companies – Temasek Holdings, Singapore Technology Holdings and Health Corporation Holdings – or a statutory board. Ownership is tiered such that these ultimate controllers have a direct ownership interest in the first tier companies; the second tier comprises companies in which one of the first-tier companies is dominant, and so on to a sixth tier. The holding companies are exempt from requirements to submit reports and accounts to the Registrar of Companies, providing a buffer to public and parliamentary surveillance, although the government is often only part owner of individual GLCs which may also be public companies. Government influence is maintained though a small group of politically loyal senior civil servants appointed to the boards of GLCs. One study, for example, identified a group of 13 persons each of whom were members of at least 18 boards of directors, mainly drawn from top civil service posts and with government careers starting in the 1950s and 1960s (Vennewald quoted in von Alten, 1995, p. 208). GLCs are expected to operate profitably and it is suggested that subsidizing ailing enterprises would not be entertained (Castells *et al.*, 1990, p. 182). They are, in practice, a significant source of government revenue. Perhaps of greater significance to government, however, they provide a way of marshalling the private sector behind economic planning imperatives.

A privatization programme was announced as part of the Economic Committee's response to the 1985 recession. This committee believed that government investment was frustrating the emergence of stronger private sector groups, partly through the special privileges obtained by some

GLCs. The Public Sector Divestment Committee announced a ten-year privatization programme in 1987 guided by three principles:

1. To withdraw from commercial activities which no longer need to be undertaken by the public sector.
2. To add breadth and depth to the Singapore stock market by the flotation of GLCs and statutory boards and through secondary distribution of government-owned shares.
3. To avoid or reduce competition with the private sector (Ministry of Finance, 1987, p. 12).

The divestment programme included 17 complete privatizations and 15 public listings, usually involving a partial sale of the government's holding. This compares with the total of 495 GLCs identified in 1988 (Thynne, 1989, p. 29). Rather than indicating a 'rolling back of the state', the privatization programme is tending to reorganize government holdings given the EDB's expanded resources for investment and participation in new projects. As the Minister for Finance, Dr Richard Hu, is quoted as saying, there is no hurry to accelerate privatization as 'compared to some other countries, we don't need the money' (Low, 1991, p. 189).

*Incentives*

Extensive use of tax incentives and subsidies continues to be practised. This commenced with pioneer status and expansion incentives and has since grown into a multiplicity of schemes (Table 5.8). The original pioneer incentive survives, as well as the post-pioneer tax status. The 421 manufacturing establishments with pioneer status in 1993 generated 74.4% of all direct manufacturing exports with the share rising to 90% in the key electronic products industry (*Yearbook of Statistics 1994*). In addition, tax incentives designed to target specific activities have multiplied, such as different types of international trading, or the promotion of particular forms of development such as offshore investment. The EDB argues that tax incentives are needed to negotiate with potential investors, including organizations already established in Singapore that they wish to see expand (Hughes, 1993, p. 19). This rationale reflects the proactive soliciting of investment practised by the EDB. When its officers seek to persuade companies to develop according to their plans, some form of incentive is needed. In practice, the extent to which incentives change investment behaviour is unclear.

A survey of 119 large firms in the manufacturing sector conducted in 1967 concluded:

**Table 5.8** Major tax incentives managed by the EDB 1995

| Tax incentive | Scope | Eligibility requirements | Tax concession |
|---|---|---|---|
| Pioneer status | Manufacturing and services | 1. The project is above current average levels of industry technology, skills or know how; and 2. No companies in Singapore perform a similar activity without being awarded pioneer status. | Exemption of 31% tax on profits arising from pioneer activity. Tax relief period is 5–10 years with possible 'post-pioneer' extension at 15% for 5 years |
| Expansion incentive | Manufacturing and services | For manufacturers, a minimum $10 million investment in new machinery and production equipment. Specified investment to be made within 5 years | Exemption of 31% tax on profits arising in excess of pre-expansion level. Tax relief period is 5 years |
| Investment allowance | Manufacturing and services, certain R&D and construction projects, approved projects designed to reduce drinking water consumption. | | Exemption of taxable income of an amount equal to a specified level, up to 50% of new fixed investment |
| Operation headquarters incentive and Business headquarters incentive | Regional headquarters and service centres of foreign companies, head offices of local MNCs | OHQ – minimum qualifications set in terms of office expenditure, employment and regional subsidiaries supported. BHQ – regional management of activities outside of Singapore with commitment to expand this activity | OHQ – income arising from the provision in Singapore of approved services taxed at 10%; other income from overseas subsidiaries or associated companies may be eligible for similar tax relief. Award for 5–10 years, with extension possible. BHQ – regional office activity given eligibility to other tax incentives |

*continues overleaf*

**Table 5.8** (*continued*)

| Tax incentive | Scope | Eligibility requirements | Tax concession |
|---|---|---|---|
| Export of services incentive and warehousing and servicing incentive | Services | Services must be delivered overseas from a Singapore base; company must derive at least 20% of earnings overseas. | Tax exemption of 90% of chargeable income for the qualifying export activity, for up to 10 years. Exemption of 50% in case of warehousing and servicing. |
| Venture capital | Investors (individuals or companies) in innovative new ventures. | Companies must be at least 50% owned by Singapore citizens or PRs, and incorporated and resident in Singapore for tax. | Losses from sale of equity can be offset against the investor's other taxable income. |
| International direct investment | Investment by eligible companies in approved overseas projects. | Companies must be at least 50% owned by Singapore citizens or PRs, and incorporated and resident in Singapore for tax. | Losses from sale of equity can be offset against the investor's other taxable income. |
| Approved foreign loan | Manufacturing and services | Minimum loan of $200 000 from a foreign lender for the purchase of productive equipment, providing that the tax relief does not increase liability in a foreign country. | Exemption of withholding tax on interest. |
| Approved royalties, fees and development contributions | Manufacturing and services | Tax relief should not increase tax liability in a foreign country. | Full or partial exemption of withholding tax on interest. |

... foreign investors, almost without exception, stated that taxation concessions and pioneer status did not play a significant role, and for the most part
played no role at all, in bringing them to Singapore. The majority of the
firms which could qualify took advantage of the tax concessions available,
although a few preferred not to do so because they wished to be free from
government 'red tape' (Hughes, 1969, p. 183).

Economic literature about tax incentives for economic promotion suggests that incentives are more likely to be effective in respect of export-orientated investment rather than local-market directed investment
(Guisinger, 1985; 1986). From this perspective, the changing structure of
the Singapore economy, which is moving from an export platform to a
regional control and coordination function, would suggest that Hughes'
finding continues to apply. Some evidence for this exists from surveys
completed in the early 1990s that examined the influence of tax incentives
to regional offices and commodity traders. While differences existed,
overall the three schemes examined were found to have had little impact
on investor decisions (Perry, 1992; 1994).

As well as taxation privileges, low interest loans and a wide range
of investment subsidies are available to local enterprises at all stages
of development (Table 5.9). To qualify as a local enterprise, as little as
30% local ownership is required. Although evidence of benefit to the
Singapore economy is a criterion for the allocation of assistance, the low
ownership threshold effectively makes assistance available to foreign-
controlled companies. Further, the local industry upgrading programme
is designed to build the competence of supporting industries in their role
as suppliers and subcontractors to foreign MNCs. Under the programme,
the EDB funds a manager from an MNC to assist its suppliers in upgrading their operations. Since its inception in 1986, 32 MNCs and 180 local
companies had taken part in the programme by 1995.

### Infrastructure

The government, through various statutory boards, is the sole supplier of
infrastructure (see Chapter 6). An ability to invest in advance of immediate demand has contributed to the high standards of provision and
ensured economic growth has not been frustrated by infrastructure constraints. The government's control of personal savings and ability to
mobilize these resources for domestic capital formation provides the
resources to keep ahead of current demand. Over the next 25 years, the
Port of Singapore Authority plans to complete a new container terminal
on reclaimed land, increasing the island's overall container handling

**Table 5.9** Assistance to local companies at different stages of development

*Start up stage*
Local enterprise computerization programme
Local enterprise finance scheme
Product development assistance scheme
R&D incubator programme
Skills development fund
Venture capital

*Growth stage*
ISO 900 certification
Local enterprise computerization programme
Local enterprise finance scheme
Local enterprise technical assistance scheme
Local industry upgrading programme
Market and investment development assistance scheme
Product development assistance scheme
Pioneer status/investment allowance
Skills development fund
Software development assistance scheme
Venture capital

*Expansion stage*
Automation leasing scheme
Brand development assistance scheme
Business development scheme
Franchise development assistance scheme
ISO 900 certification
Local enterprise computerization programme
Local enterprise finance scheme
Local enterprise technical assistance scheme
Local industry upgrading programme
Market and investment development assistance scheme
Product development assistance scheme
Pioneer status/investment allowance
Skills development fund
Software development assistance scheme
Total business plan
Venture capital

*Going overseas stage*
Business development scheme
Double deduction for overseas investment development expenditure
Franchise development assistance scheme
Local enterprise finance (overseas) scheme
Local industry upgrading programme
Market and investment development assistance scheme
Overseas enterprise incentive/overseas investment incentive

*Source:* 'Growing with enterprise: a national effort', EDB (1993, p. 23)

capacity almost threefold to 36 million TEUs (twenty-foot equivalent units). A third runway and terminal are to be added to Changi Airport for use by the early years of the next century. Expansion of the submarine optic fibre cable network and satellite communications is planned. While space is being found for transportation expansion, other infrastructure capacities are coming up against space constraints, particularly water and waste disposal.

*Workforce control*

Government influence on the labour market is extensive, encompassing industrial relations, wages, skill formation, productivity performance and the recruitment of foreign workers. Industrial relations are controlled through legislation and the close relationship between the government and the National Trades Union Council (NTUC). The initial changes introduced by the Employment Act and the Industrial Relations (Amendment) Act in 1968 have been reinforced by the Trade Union (Amendment) Act 1982 and the Employment Act 1984 which, according to one assessment, collectively 'make for exceptional employer prerogatives and leave employees with little in the way of legal safeguards or bargaining rights' (Wilkinson, 1994, p. 64). Since 1977, there has been one industrial stoppage although individual disputes have increased (Table 5.10).

Trade union membership is low in Singapore at around 14% of the total employed workforce. This share has fallen from 25% in 1975. The NTUC, to which all recognized unions must affiliate, is nonetheless an influential body through its role in the National Wages Council (NWC) and as an agent for other aspects of labour market policy. The NWC makes recommendations to government on three issues: (i) annual wage increases; (ii) development of the wage system to promote economic and social development; (iii) the design of incentive schemes to promote productivity. The annual wage recommendation has been based on a basket of considerations – productivity, exchange rate, inflation, economic performance (Tan, K. Y., 1995, p. 63) – designed to keep a close control on wage movements. While not mandatory, the recommendations have been widely followed, partly because they are fully adhered to in the public sector which sets a benchmark for other pay rises. As well as this control, the NWC has designed a 'flexible' wages system to further maintain control over wage costs in the wake of the 1986 recession. Flexibility in this context means that around 20% of wages are paid in the form of discretionary annual bonuses (see Sharma and Lan, 1994).

**Table 5.10** Industrial disputes 1970-1991

|  | Industrial stoppages | Man days lost due to industrial stoppages | IAC awards[a] | Trade disputes[b] | 'Individual' disputes[c] |
|---|---|---|---|---|---|
| 1974 | 10 | 5380 | 89 | 1091 | 855 |
| 1975 | 7 | 4853 | 73 | 709 | 1991 |
| 1976 | 4 | 3193 | 57 | 694 | 2465 |
| 1977 | 1 | 1011 | 33 | 640 | 2228 |
| 1978 | 0 | 0 | 35 | 548 | 2000 |
| 1979 | 0 | 0 | 73 | 577 | 1635 |
| 1980 | 0 | 0 | 94 | 484 | 1332 |
| 1981 | 0 | 0 | 100 | 392 | 1335 |
| 1982 | 0 | 0 | 82 | 311 | 1588 |
| 1983 | 0 | 0 | 59 | 353 | 1466 |
| 1984 | 0 | 0 | 48 | 338 | 1400 |
| 1985 | 0 | 0 | 35 | 340 | 2185 |
| 1986 | 1 | 122 | 74 | 317 | 2730 |
| 1987 | 0 | 0 | 39 | 275 | 2960 |
| 1988 | 0 | 0 | 22 | 366 | 2818 |
| 1989 | 0 | 0 | 38 | 353 | 2516 |
| 1990 | 0 | 0 | 46 | 303 | 3835 |
| 1991 | 0 | 0 | 31 | 323 | 4197 |
| 1992 | 0 | 0 | 18 | 353 | 4967 |
| 1993 | 0 | 0 | 9 | 370 | 6786 |
| 1994 | 0 | 0 | 10 | 333 | 4659 |

*Notes:*
[a]The Industrial Arbitration Court hears and determines the outcome of referred trade disputes.
[b]'Trade disputes' refers to industrial disputes which have been referred to the unionized disputes section of the Ministry of Labour for reconciliation.
[c]'Individual disputes' are registered when a dispute between an individual and an employer is referred to the individual disputes section of the Ministry of Labour for reconciliation.

*Source:* Ministry of Labour, *Singapore Yearbook of Labour Statistics*, various issues.

The EDB maintains a coordinating role in respect of skill formation through the Council for Professional and Technical Education (CPTE). The CPTE monitors labour market trends and recommends enrolment targets and the corresponding staffing and financial requirements of the universities, polytechnics, vocational and technical institutes and training centres (Soon, 1993, p. 254). This network of training resources makes use of foreign technology and investment. There are four training institutes, established from 1979 to 1982, co-funded and co-managed by the EDB and foreign governments: the German-Singapore Institute for Advanced Manufacturing and Automation Technology; the French-Singapore Institute for Electro-technical Engineering; the Japan-Singapore Institute of Software

Technology; the Japan-Singapore Technical Institute for Electronics Engin-eering. In addition, there are several training centres established with individual MNCs of which the longest running is with Philips. Under its transnational approach, the EDB encourages several MNCs to cooperate in establishing small training units in areas of advanced technology. The number of trainees in these various collaborative centres is small in comparison with the polytechnics, around 1500 and 10000 respectively. Their special significance is in bringing foreign technology to the training environment, both in terms of hardware and the workplace culture of the partner nation.

The control of foreign worker inflows is a further area of government influence over the labour market. The shortage of labour in many parts of the economy and the high share of temporary foreign workers in the labour force, around 20% (350000) in 1996 (*The Straits Times*, 22 August 1996), make this control of great significance. Government regulation dis-tinguishes between two types of foreign worker. Employers are generally free to recruit foreign professional workers on three-year employment passes and, providing the employment pass is granted to a male, that per-son's family will be able to reside in Singapore for the duration of the employment. These workers, particularly if they are from another Asian country, may be granted permanent residence. To qualify, a foreign work-er must have, as a minimum, a secondary education, monthly income of at least $1500 (roughly half the average professional wage in 1994) and five years working experience.

Unskilled workers, which account for the greater share of foreign workers, are primarily from Malaysia, Thailand, South Asia and the Philippines. They are given a two-year work permit without entitlement for dependants to reside in Singapore during the employment period. In addition, employers pay a levy for each unskilled foreign worker and are restricted to a set quota of foreign workers. The levy varies according to the quota of foreign workers employed, their skill level and sector. The highest levy, currently $450 a month, is paid in the manufacturing sector by employers with over 35% foreign workers. The permissible quota varies from 20% and 45% in services and manufacturing to a ratio of one local to five foreign workers in construction.

The controls of foreign worker employment are partly to prevent for-eign workers becoming permanent separate communities, competing with the local population for housing and health care. Even with its con-trols, the Ministry of Labour was recording around 2000 arrests of illegal workers a year in the early 1990s (*Ministry of Labour Annual Report 1994*). In 1989 an amnesty granted to illegal Thai workers brought forward almost 10000 workers (Sullivan *et al.*, 1992). Under 1996 amendments to the Immigration and Employment of Foreign Workers Acts, employers of illegal foreign workers can be held responsible for illegal workers on their premises. In one subsequent case, a construction company was fined over $1.5 million for 188 Indonesian and Malaysian illegal workers found at one of its sites (*The Straits Times*, 30 August 1996).

Controls on foreign workers are also designed to restrict them from being used as an alternative to raising productivity and paying higher wages. In practice, the bulk of unskilled foreign workers are contained within sectors of the economy not favoured by locals (unlike the professional sector), notably construction and domestic service. In these sectors, foreign workers accept wages well below the national norm, with daily wages of $20–$40 typical amongst construction workers. Although theoretically extended the same protection as local workers, their temporary status, limited resources and unfamiliarity with legislation creates a pool of low cost, compliant labour. Foreign construction workers, for example, are generally housed in temporary plywood shacks or converted shipping containers, located on the construction site where they are working. As well as reducing the cost of infrastructure, foreign workers provide a buffer against unemployment for Singaporeans. In 1985, when there was a net loss of 96 000 jobs, three-fifths of those affected were foreign workers (Huff, 1994, p. 348). In 1987, as the economy recovered, there was a 1% increase in foreign workers compared with a 2% increase in Singaporean workers (Sieh Lee, 1988).

A third category of expatriate worker comprises immigrant labour, as compared with the two types of guest labour just discussed. Immigrant labour are granted permanent residency and encouraged to take root in Singapore. The Tiananmen incident on 4 June 1989 spurred the Singapore government to offer permanent residency status to 25 000 skilled workers from Hong Kong. As they are perceived as being hardworking and enterprising, it is thought that such an inflow will help improve the work ethic in Singapore (Chew and Chew, 1995). The government has also shown interest in encouraging talented Indians to take up permanent residency, particularly to fill positions in engineering and software occupations. This selective marketing of permanent residency however is a sensitive issue because of the need not to upset the existing racial balance. It is difficult to promote similar opportunities to Malays as they would need to be sourced in Malaysia.

Singapore government attitudes to foreign labour have been informed by the experiences of Europe and Japan. To avoid the social problems perceived to have arisen in Europe, there are stringent controls on settlement and tight policing of overstayers. It differs from a similar stringency employed in Japan through the willingness to accept immigrants, although selectively. Even with its tight control, foreign workers have been a source of political difficulty, particularly associated with allegations of their poor living conditions and excessive criminal punishments enforced against their nationals. After the hanging of a Filipino maid in 1995, for example, the outpouring of resentment against Singapore led the Philippines to impose a temporary ban on women leaving to work as maids in Singapore.

*Economic management*

Macro-economic management has aimed to keep inflation low and coordinate investment to maintain economic growth. This has been achieved through the use of tools that are typically not available in other states, helped by certain peculiarities of the economy and the acceptance of state intervention (Huff, 1994, p. 345). The key to economic management has been the state's capture, directly and indirectly, of a substantial share of national income which is then allocated to savings and investment according to prevailing economic, social and political objectives (Castells *et al.*, 1990, p. 176).

The public sector is the largest source of savings derived from the government's budget surplus, together with the surplus realized by statutory boards (Table 5.11). The private sector contribution to savings has largely been through the CPF, the social security scheme inherited from the former colonial administration (Chapter 2). As a provident fund, the CPF pays benefits to individuals according to past contributions from themselves and their employers, plus interest. (This contrasts with 'pay as you go' schemes that make payments to retirees by collecting money from those still working.) Participation in the scheme is compulsory for residents. Consequently the value of the fund has grown with increasing workforce participation and through changes in the share of income extracted in CPF contributions. At its peak in the mid-1980s, the CPF took 50% of wages (shared equally between employer and employee) which was subsequently reduced and then raised to its present level of 40% in 1991. In addition, the state has voluntarily obtained a large share of private savings through deposits with the Post Office Savings Bank by exempting interest from tax and paying higher interest than commercial banks.

The government has invested public savings in social and physical infrastructure, public corporations and in investments abroad. The offshore investment of public monies is mainly to allay fears about the vulnerability of the Singapore economy (Castells *et al.*, 1990, p. 181). The diversification of assets and broadening of financial and industrial depen-

**Table 5.11** Sources of gross national savings 1974–1985

| | Gross national savings | Public sector savings | | Private sector savings | | | |
| | | | | CPF | | Other | |
| | $m | $m | %GNS | $m | %GNS | $m | %GNS |
|---|---|---|---|---|---|---|---|
| 1974 | 3220 | 736 | 22.8 | 643 | 20.0 | 1841 | 57.2 |
| 1975 | 3985 | 1362 | 34.2 | 821 | 20.6 | 1802 | 45.2 |
| 1976 | 4580 | 1470 | 32.1 | 831 | 18.1 | 2279 | 49.8 |
| 1977 | 5079 | 2021 | 39.8 | 888 | 17.5 | 2170 | 42.7 |
| 1978 | 5928 | 2230 | 37.6 | 1027 | 17.3 | 2671 | 45.1 |
| 1979 | 7300 | 2801 | 38.4 | 1534 | 21.0 | 2965 | 40.6 |
| 1980 | 8282 | 3407 | 41.1 | 2036 | 24.6 | 2839 | 34.3 |
| 1981 | 10 483 | 4261 | 40.6 | 2599 | 24.8 | 3623 | 34.6 |
| 1982 | 12 885 | 5936 | 46.1 | 3506 | 27.2 | 3443 | 26.7 |
| 1983 | 16 306 | 8649 | 53.0 | 3849 | 23.6 | 3808 | 23.4 |
| 1984 | 18 596 | 11 291 | 60.7 | 3166 | 17.0 | 4139 | 22.3 |
| 1985 | 16 543 | 11 052 | 66.8 | 4159 | 25.1 | 1332 | 8.1 |

Comparable data not available post-1985 due to changes in official statistics.

*Source:* Huff (1994, p. 333)

dencies provides protection against a sudden shrinkage of world trade and foreign direct investment. Outside of these investment funds, about one-quarter of total government revenue is retained within a government development fund to stabilize the economy and allow for strategic government expenditures.

The high savings ratio contribution has had two benefits for macro-economic management. First, government-forced savings dampen inflationary pressure by restricting an individual's purchasing power. This control is reinforced by the ability of the NWC to control wage increases which seek to limit wage rises to productivity gains. Secondly, domestic savings gathered by the government provide a non-inflationary method of funding infrastructure development. It has avoided the need to incur government deficits and borrowing, thus restricting the growth of money supply. Inflationary pressure has been further minimized by exchange rate control exercised by the Monetary Authority of Singapore to restrict international trading in the currency. This is achieved through the imposition of a withholding tax on interest earned by non-residents on Singapore dollar accounts and through directives to the banking system (Huff, 1994, p. 346).

A necessary condition for the effectiveness of the government's economic management has been the public's willingness to accept enforced saving through the CPF. The spread of subsidized home ownership facilitated by CPF, and gradual relaxation of the eligible uses for which CPF funds may be applied (Table 5.12), has helped obtain compliance. Similarly, the withdrawal of private savings into public assets and government reserves has been possible through the high inflow of foreign direct investment to fund private productive capital. Both processes have been criticized by some Singaporeans, the former for encouraging over-investment and the unwarranted sacrifice of consumption and the latter for crowding out local entrepreneurship (Lim and Associates, 1988).

## Evaluation of state intervention

The pervasiveness of state intervention in the economy points to the importance of the government in promoting Singapore's economic development, but this is debated. Analysts including Harris (1986) and Rodan (1985, 1989) claim that Singapore's growth is a product of fortuitous external events. At two critical times in the republic's recent history, supportive external economic trends have provided opportunities for growth.

**Table 5.12** Schemes introduced for use of CPF savings

| Application | Year | Scheme |
|---|---|---|
| Home ownership | 1968 | Approved housing scheme |
| | 1981 | Approved residential property scheme |
| Investment | 1978 | Singapore Bus Services Ltd Share Scheme |
| | 1986 | Approved investment scheme |
| | 1993 | Basic investment scheme |
| | 1993 | Enhanced investment scheme |
| Insurance | 1982 | Home protection insurance scheme |
| | 1989 | Dependants' protection insurance scheme |
| | 1990 | Medishield scheme |
| | 1990 | Medishield II scheme |
| Education | 1989 | Financing of tertiary education in Singapore |
| | 1992 | Edusave |
| Others | 1984 | Company welfarism |
| | 1984 | Medisave scheme |
| | 1987 | Minimum sum scheme |
| | 1987 | Topping up minimum sum scheme |

The first coincidence was the separation from Malaysia with the rise of the export-orientated foreign investment at the time when the republic's need for inward investment was first expressed. Prior to the 1960s, few MNCs had established overseas branches simply for the purpose of carrying out one stage of a production process, assembling components for use at home or in a third market. This strategy was used extensively in the electronics industry to Singapore's great benefit. The republic itself did not influence the impetus to export processing investment. It originated in changes in home-country conditions and technology and affected other places apart from Singapore.

A second coincidence came during the mid-1980s recession when two developments in the Southeast Asia region opened opportunities for growth unforeseen by the second industrial revolution (Rodan, 1993b, p. 234). The first was the emergence of a 'regional focus' in the corporate strategy of many multinational corporations (Ng and Sudo, 1991). This resulted in the decentralization of an extended range of business functions to the region, allocating Singapore a coordination and servicing role for regional MNC investment. Secondly, the decentralization of foreign investment to nearby countries offering lower production costs than Singapore extended the viability of export platform investment. It both transferred production to places with more abundant labour forces than Singapore and offered opportunities to integrate investment in the region. For example, Toyota now uses Singapore to coordinate procurement from among four supplying bases in Thailand, Malaysia, the Philippines and Indonesia (Fujita and Hill, 1995).

The existence of external opportunities and historic specificity provides one reason to suggest that Singapore's development experience may not provide a model that other states could replicate. According to Rodan (1989, p. 208), the export orientated strategy 'was feasible because of opportune historic conditions, not because this strategy made universal sense'. Two objections to this point of view may be cited, however, which suggest that the role of good government is not so easily dismissed. First, other states pursuing a similar development strategy have different opportunities to take advantage of according to their historic conditions (Rigg, 1991, p. 200). For example, in the late 1980s, Thailand was able to attract considerable volumes of inward investment from Japan at a time when Japanese companies were shifting resources offshore. Secondly, the existence of external opportunities should not belittle the conversion of those opportunities into sustained growth. This is particularly the case as after the initial flow of inward investment, and the achievement of full employment, Singapore ceased to be simply a passive recipient of inward investment. Active measures were taken to support the gradual upgrading and restructuring of foreign investment as well as to obtain some transfer of technology to local enterprise.

The elevation of Singapore's development experience into a model for use by other countries nonetheless remains questionable as its growth is based on more than a combination of economic policies. Huff (1994, p. 355) identifies four ingredients that have provided the conditions for successful implementation of economic policy: (i) government autonomy from interest groups; (ii) stability, both initial and perpetuated by a favourable sequencing of events; (iii) material gains for the bulk of the population which, combined with expectations of stability, promote acceptance of government control; (iv) good economic judgement and policy selection.

A government that is autonomous of any particular interest group has the chance to pursue its economic strategy without compromise or negotiation. This autonomy was obtained by setting a development strategy which required neither the support of the local business élite nor an active trade union movement. The pursuit of growth through the acceptance of foreign direct investment relieved economic policy from the need to accommodate local business interests. At the same time, the reliance on MNCs to deliver growth allowed most directly productive activity to remain in private ownership and avoided dependence on state-owned capital. The established trade union movement was transformed through legislation into a government-controlled body that ceased to articulate an independent position.

The second and third factors – the combination of stability and the rapid delivery of material gains – provided the conditions under which strong government was accepted. In 1959, a successful economy and efficient administration was inherited. The new government added to these inherited strengths by creating the various development promotion agencies to support inward investment and by rigorously curtailing the scope for public dissent. The potential for special interest groups to form along racial or dialect lines was constrained by an educational approach which made English the first language in all schools (as well as the sole university that remained in the 1980s) and the rehousing programme. Threats to the stability of policy are also contained through controls on the mass media and through the government's other measures to manage dissent. This authoritarian regime obtained acceptance through ensuring the distribution of economic gains, through the maintenance of full employment and the housing and other welfare programmes, as well as by maintaining a perception of the ongoing vulnerability of these economic achievements to external and internal instability.

The final factor has been the calibre of top economic decision makers. Perhaps of more importance than individual abilities has been the retention of key decision making within a small group – not above 50 in number according to sources quoted in Huff (1994) – from the period from independence to 1990, when Lee Kuan Yew retired as Prime Minister. Typically, the same men served as directors for a host of public enterprises and government development initiatives, ensuring loyalty to the government and further tightening its control.

## Limits of state intervention

While Singapore's economic planners are generally credited with setting the conditions in which growth has been maintained, not all its strategies have proved effective. The wage correction policy effected from 1979 to 1982, introduced as part of the second industrial revolution, is one example of a policy that had to be reversed and which has been judged 'an unmitigated disaster' (Tan, K. Y., 1995, p. 72).

The lateness, compared with Taiwan and South Korea, in promoting indigenous R&D has been seen as a cause of Singapore's relative failure to develop indigenous industrial capacity (Wong, 1995). Singapore has maintained a liberal environment for foreign direct investment (FDI) largely avoiding the imposition of performance requirements whilst retaining generous taxation incentives. While a desire to encourage R&D intensive activity has existed, as reflected in the setting up of the science and technology agencies discussed above, the investment involved was until recently well below that made by governments in Taiwan or South Korea. Taiwan, for example, has combined greater selectivity in FDI acceptance with the promotion of indigenous technological capabilities, including extensive support for public–private collaboration to develop targeted technologies. One consequence of the contrasting approaches is that local SMEs in Taiwan were able to enter the electronics sector and other labour-intensive assembly industries on a larger scale than in Singapore. The continued dominance of large MNCs in Singapore, according to Wong (1995), has acted to crowd out local industry development, partly in the way the cost of labour was bid up and the workforce became less willing to work in local SMEs.

Workforce issues connect to another area where government intervention has brought limited success, namely the attempt to promote productivity through greater employee involvement in the workplace. This lack of impact is worth elaboration as it indicates how various elements of government strategy can be mutually conflicting as well as identifying a gap in the economic progress so far achieved.

In the light of complaints from employers about the lack of loyalty and commitment displayed by Singaporean workers, the government embarked on a productivity campaign in the early 1980s (see Wilkinson, 1986; 1994). These complaints appeared in reports from the EDB and Ministry of Labour in 1979 and 1980. Allegations included a tendency for Singaporean workers to be too individualistic; too reluctant to work over-time, accept menial or unpleasant tasks; unwilling to work beyond nar-row job responsibilities, although efforts to gradually erode managerial authority were seen as a further problem; and that they lacked loyalty. At the time, labour turnover had reached 6% to 8% a month, substantiating a central weakness identified by employers.

The government response was a campaign to promote Japanese and Korean productivity methods and employee devotion to their place of work. The NPB was given the responsibility of coordinating the campaign which as well as consciousness raising, through such methods as a cam-paign mascot ('Teamy the Bee'), songs, films and ministerial speeches, sought to spread participation in quality control circles (referred to as work improvement teams in the public sector) and encourage company provision of welfare services and consultation committees. Other mea-sures brought into play were the introduction of a compulsory course in human resource management to be taken by all university undergradu-ates; SDF-supported training with a human relations emphasis; employer access to the CPF records of job applicants, so that checks could be made on any history of 'job hopping'; changes to CPF regulations enabled employers to channel a share of their CPF contribution into a company trust fund for employee welfare programmes. Finally, the NTUC and the Singapore National Employers' Federation endorsed the promotion of enterprise unionism.

According to Wilkinson (1994, p. 71), these initiatives to replicate a Japanese-style worker loyalty have been a 'dismal failure' and the achievement of an industrial community is still far away. This judgement was based on several observations of the limited diffusion of actual work-place-based productivity initiatives. The campaign to establish 'work excellence committees' as a vehicle for labour-management communica-tion on non-employment contract conditions, resulted in fewer than 20 committees being set up. As noted above, there has been a high rate of quality circle participation, but it seems they have been of little practical significance in promoting productivity and workplace commitment (an impact not unexpected by quality circle experience in other countries (Hill, 1991)). Limitations reported range from the unwillingness of man-agers to take employee participation seriously to their use by employees as simply a vehicle for voicing grievances. Before the reductions in CPF made in 1986, only six companies had introduced company welfare schemes. The subsequent CPF contribution reductions rendered the company welfare option less realistic as a tool for promoting company allegiance. In the 1991 Strategic Economic Plan it was noted only four companies were still implementing it. Enterprise unionism has made little progress. The enterprise unions which exist are mainly in the public sector or GLCs. More generally, the workforce as a whole has continued to drift away from union participation and labour turnover continues to be high.

Even Japanese companies have made little attempt to transfer the three 'sacred treasures' of their home industrial relations – lifetime employment, seniority-based pay, and enterprise unions (Milton-Smith, 1986; Lim, 1991). Japanese employers recognise that in a tight labour market, secure employment policies and the prospect of gradually increasing remuneration are insufficient to win the loyalty of employees. Other influences as well have frustrated the emergence of the kind of industrial community that has been seen as necessary to promote workplace productivity. First, engendering employee loyalty to a foreign-owned company – the predominant ownership context amongst large private sector workplaces – is more challenging than obtaining loyalty to a national company. External ownership raises doubts about the extent of local management control and makes it harder to equate company loyalty with national duty than when working for a home country firm. Secondly, Chinese values are said to emphasize loyalty to family above employer, which foreign ownership is again likely to accentuate. Thus while Japanese cultural values may support company devotion, Chinese 'economic familism' does not (Lee, 1978). Thirdly, the containment of trade union activity within a narrow, non-threatening role allows employers to maintain distanced relationships with their workforce. This is facilitated as well by the setting of employment conditions through national wage recommendations and industrial relations legislation.

Certain incompatibilities in the Singapore development model are suggested by the way reliance on foreign companies, tight control of labour unions and strong support for family loyalty frustrates the achievement of a more participative work culture. It should be noted, however, that while some aspects of the Japanese management system are not to be found, this has not been a barrier to the introduction of other Japanese work methods in some Japanese companies (Rodgers and Wong, 1996). Just-in-time production systems can be found along with workplace participation in continuous improvement initiatives, but this seems to depend on a high use of expatriate management. A stronger productivity culture is important, therefore, to encourage greater skill transfer and workplace innovation in local enterprise and to increase local workers' promotion to positions of responsibility within foreign companies.

## Regionalization – the future of Singapore

During the early 1990s the government launched a concerted effort to promote the regionalization of the economy. Developing a so-called 'external wing' is not a novel departure, but it has now become a central objective of economic policy. This is reflected in both the investment of public money in regionalization projects and in a host of inducements for local business to internationalize their operations. Senior Minister Lee Kuan Yew has explained government thinking behind regionalization in terms of two main considerations (see Kanai, 1993). First, while companies from other Asian NICs had built up significant foreign direct investment portfolios in China and Southeast Asia since the mid-1980s, Singapore companies had been much less active in this area (Table 5.13). Secondly, it was argued that unless specific steps were taken to encourage outward investment, Singapore was likely to fall further behind its Asian competitors. There was, the Senior Minister argued, a shortage of people willing to take risks in running enterprises, as well as a reluctance among Singaporeans to leave their country's safe, clean environment to live and work somewhere else. The Senior Minister's suggested strategies to overcome the reluctance included: (i) a relaxation of government regulations that might be a disincentive to overseas investment, and help with information to assist investment; (ii) tax incentives to provide an additional inducement to go offshore; (iii) the establishment of schools and other facilities for expatriate Singapore children and employment search assistance to the wives of expatriate men on their return to Singapore.

A Committee to Promote Overseas Enterprise was established in early 1993, shortly after the Senior Minister's suggestions. Prior to the report of this committee, the budget announced seven reforms in the taxation system that provided favourable treatment of overseas investment. These measures included wider exemptions from taxation on income and dividends earned overseas; double deduction against expenditure associated with the initiation or development of approved investments outside Singapore and easier criteria for overseas investment incentives. The budget also made provision for companies (provided they are registered in Singapore and at least 50% locally owned) to be eligible for tax exemption on overseas income, rather than the company requiring case-by-case approval. The Committee's report further endorsed the strategies proposed by Senior Minister Lee and recommended that the government

**Table 5.13** Direct investment (US$ million) in selected Asian countries by Asian NIEs and Japan 1987–1992

|  | 1987 | 1988 | 1989 | 1990 | 1991 | 1992 | 1987–1992 |
|---|---|---|---|---|---|---|---|
| Malaysia |  |  |  |  |  |  |  |
| – Singapore | 103 | 160 | 338 | 331 | 405 | 174 | 1511 |
| – Hong Kong | 35 | 114 | 130 | 139 | 218 | 31 | 667 |
| – South Korea | 1 | 16 | 70 | 240 | 661 | 39 | 1027 |
| – Taiwan | 96 | 317 | 797 | 2344 | 1312 | 589 | 5455 |
| – Japan | 284 | 467 | 993 | 1557 | 1348 | 1054 | 5703 |
| – Total | 818 | 1863 | 3194 | 6529 | 7361 | 4618 | 24 383 |
| Thailand |  |  |  |  |  |  |  |
| – Singapore | 64 | 274 | 411 | 591 | 623 | 482 | 2445 |
| – Hong Kong | 125 | 451 | 562 | 1072 | 340 | 140 | 2690 |
| – South Korea | 13 | 109 | 171 | 270 | 49 | 28 | 640 |
| – Taiwan | 299 | 850 | 868 | 765 | 572 | 291 | 4794 |
| – Japan | 965 | 3045 | 3524 | 2706 | 1760 | 1968 | 13 968 |
| – Total | 2634 | 6249 | 7966 | 8032 | 4988 | 10 027 | 39 896 |
| Philippines |  |  |  |  |  |  |  |
| – Singapore | 1 | 3 | 24 | 14 | 3 | 5 | 50 |
| – Hong Kong | 28 | 27 | 133 | 208 | 8 | 13 | 417 |
| – South Korea | 1 | 2 | 17 | 21 | 45 | 42 | 128 |
| – Taiwan | 9 | 110 | 149 | 141 | 12 | 9 | 430 |
| – Japan | 29 | 96 | 158 | 306 | 210 | 72 | 871 |
| – Total | 167 | 473 | 804 | 961 | 783 | 284 | 3472 |
| Indonesia |  |  |  |  |  |  |  |
| – Singapore | 6 | 240 | 166 | 264 | 346 | 454 | 1476 |
| – Hong Kong | 135 | 239 | 407 | 993 | 278 | 1021 | 3073 |
| – South Korea | 23 | 199 | 466 | 723 | 301 | 618 | 2330 |
| – Taiwan | 8 | 910 | 158 | 306 | 210 | 72 | 871 |
| – Japan | 532 | 247 | 789 | 2241 | 929 | 1509 | 6246 |
| – Total | 1457 | 4409 | 4719 | 8750 | 8778 | 10 313 | 29 648 |

| | 1987 | 1988 | 1989 | 1990 | 1991 | 1992 | 1987–1992 |
|---|---|---|---|---|---|---|---|
| China | | | | | | | |
| – Singapore | 70 | 137 | 111 | 103 | 155 | 997 | 1573 |
| – Hong Kong | 1947 | 3467 | 3160 | 3833 | 7215 | 40 044 | 59 666 |
| – South Korea | - | - | - | - | 171 | 417 | 588 |
| – Taiwan | - | - | - | 890 | 1389 | 5543 | - |
| – Japan | 301 | 276 | 439 | 457 | 812 | 2173 | 4458 |
| – Total | 3709 | 5297 | 5600 | 6596 | 11 977 | 58 124 | 91 303 |

*Source*: Kanai (1993, p. 22)

should cooperate with private investors by seconding experts, forming joint ventures and providing leadership in infrastructure projects.

As noted above, these initiatives are not entirely new. Increased promotion of overseas investment was among the new economic directions proposed in the report of the Economic Committee (1986). In 1988, the EDB initiated an overseas direct investment plan, giving financial support for overseas investments that were designed to provide access to new technology or foreign markets. This was supported by the setting up of an International Business Linkages Unit within the EDB. In 1989, the government announced that local businesses would be helped to form alliances for international expansion with government-linked companies.

The initial internationalization strategy differed from that currently underway in being focused on globalization, emphasizing expansion into Europe and North America. Until recently, overseas investment was still being seen as a way of promoting a shift to higher value-added activities. Three factors have changed the emphasis to regionalization, implying a narrower focus on expansion within the Asian region. First, economic growth and changes to foreign investment controls among the countries of Indochina and China have generated many business opportunities. Secondly, with respect to investment in these markets, Singapore's leaders see themselves as having a privileged access to Chinese business networks and government officials. For example, the President of Singapore Technologies Industrial Corporation (STIC) is quoted as saying:

> If you are a multinational in Europe or elsewhere, involved in technology and want to come to Asia then we suggest you look at us as a possible partner. STIC has an established network in the regional market. We also have all important guanxi (connections) in China (Cooke quoted in Yeung, 1994, p. 1940).

A third reason for the shift in overseas focus is that the investment encouraged in Europe and North America, as a strategy for technology transfer, was not successful. During 1989–1991, over $1.2 billion was invested in North America and Europe under the EDB's international direct investment programme (*The Straits Times*, 13 December 1991). A high proportion of this was linked to STIC, and involved investments in semiconductor and computer companies. Most of these investments have failed to take off successfully, generating enormous accumulated losses (Kanai, 1993). A similar fate affected less high tech investments too, as in the Temasek-Yeo Hiap Seng (a Singapore food and beverage manufacturer) acquisition of an American food company Chun King.

The current phase of the regionalization strategy is again being led by GLCs but is placing greater emphasis on overseas infrastructure provision to provide a supportive environment for the expansion of local companies. Industrial estates are now under construction in India, China and Vietnam. As well as infrastructure provision, the government endeavours to export the 'software' to manage the property according to Singapore administrative practices by training Chinese officials in various urban administration tasks. This is both to exploit its reputation for efficient, non-corrupt administration and to further ease some aspects of regional expansion for local ventures.

In 1994, to underscore the government's commitment to the new investment strategy, it was announced that initially 2–3% of the republic's financial reserves would be directed to infrastructure projects in Asia but after 10 to 15 years this share could grow to 30–35%. This indicates the high confidence in the viability of the intended projects and a shift from traditional practice of investing the financial reserves in blue chip stocks and bonds in industrialized economies.

The single largest overseas infrastructure investment is the development of the Suzhou industrial township, six kilometres inland from Shanghai. The development plan, to be completed over 20–30 years, envisages a town of 600 000 people, covering 70 square kilometres and a workforce of 350 000. In return for Singapore investment capital, the investors have obtained delegated approval authority for new investments and preferential incentives that are said to better those given to some provincial governments (Tan, C. H., 1995). The project commenced as a 65:35 partnership with the majority capital provided by 19 Singapore organizations, with the balance provided by Suzhou municipal government, but subsequently additional Singapore partners have joined including EDB Investments. As well as the direct economic commitment the project is of symbolic and strategic significance as a sign of the mutual goodwill and trust between the partners (Kwok, 1996). The Suzhou pact was signed in January 1994 between Singapore's Senior Minister and China's Vice-Premier, with the respective Prime Minister and Premier in attendance. About 50 kilometres from Suzhou, the Wuxi-Singapore industrial park is under development which is one of several smaller projects linked to Singapore's economic development agencies. As well as the profit from real estate development, these projects are being used to push the overseas expansion of a range of Singapore enterprises including taxi firms, medical clinics, warehousing services and retailing.

Through infrastructure provision, Singapore is also extending its linkages into the Indian economy. Singapore is seeking to promote its role as India's gateway to the Asia-Pacific. In 1994, the first phase of the Bangalore Information Technology Park was opened as a forerunner of satellite townships and industrial estates to be developed in joint ventures with Singaporean investment. Among other projects in India, Temasek Holdings with an Indian joint venture partner, are building a small township near New Delhi to be known as Sentosa City. In September 1994, joint venture projects between Singapore and India in third party countries (mainly in ASEAN and China) were reported to be worth $1.5 billion (Kwok, 1996, p. 293). In 1996, construction commenced on a Singapore–Vietnam Industrial Park located 20 kilometres outside Ho Chi Minh City with the completed park expected to provide 50 000 jobs (*The Straits Times*, 15 May 1996). Other government-linked infrastructure projects have been completed or are at various stages of implementation in Thailand, Cambodia and Burma.

To further its regional strategy, the Singapore government has recently promoted the formation of bilateral business councils with overseas governments. The purpose of these councils is to identify and evaluate third-country marketing and investment opportunities. For Singapore, these forums provide opportunity to market the use of its overseas industrial parks. Such councils now exist with Britain, France, Germany and most recently Australia. As further support to the Singapore–Australia Business Alliance Forum, government agencies from both sides of the alliance have contributed to a A$2 million 'joint feasibility study fund'. Opportunities for joint tourism promotion have been identified as one area to be supported.

## Conclusion

Singapore's economy over the last 30 years has succeeded in combining high growth with a significant restructuring of its economic role. From its initial expansion as an export manufacturing base it has developed into a regional control and logistics centre. This shift partly builds on the long-established status of Singapore as the most advanced metropolis of Southeast Asia and the geographical centre of regional business flows. It has, however, demanded the development of new infrastructure, business services and technical skills. While manufacturing activity has moved away from low value assembly work, the pace of technological upgrading has been slower than that desired by the state's economic planners. Making Singapore the R&D base for multinational organizations and acquiring an independent technological capacity, under its own control, remain key objectives of public policy.

The regionalization strategy, which aims to exploit Singapore's financial wealth and high esteem with multinational business leaders, as well as its privileged position within the Chinese business world, may be a more realistic development target than high technology. It also offers a way of strengthening local enterprise and escaping the reluctance of foreign capital to fall in with all aspects of the state's economic ambition. If the Suzhou model succeeds and is successfully replicated in other locations, Singapore's external economy has many new growth opportunities. Of course, given the vagaries of the international economy and geopolitical relations, and the turbulence in Asian domestic politics, this success cannot be guaranteed. To minimize the risks, the Singapore state is required to invest considerable political capital in maintaining partner government cooperation and protection of its investments. This holds the danger of political alliances that may jeopardize links with western countries. It may also require over-optimistic presentation of overseas investment opportunities to individual investors. While the government is currently promoting the excellent prospects offered by Suzhou, for example, a recent survey of Singapore-based investors in China found that on average they were less than satisfied with their investments (*The Straits Times*, 25 May 1996). Acceptance of these risks can be seen as part of the growing confidence of the Singapore state.

# 6

# Land use and communications

The use of land and competition for space are major issues in Singapore. A shortage of land makes self sufficiency in basic resources such as food and water unattainable, making reliance on good relations with regional neighbours necessary to sustain the economy. Economic growth has resulted in wholesale changes in the use of land and demanded the comprehensive assessment of land functions to ensure that development opportunities are maximized. Since the early 1960s, extensive coastal reclamations have expanded the land area by almost 10% to accommodate growth. The coastal geography has been further altered through impounding to create estuarine reservoirs for freshwater storage. The transformation of land use and destruction of the natural coastline have attracted little community reaction or resistance to the state's development intentions. The disciplined, rigorous, centrally planned economic and social regime has been fundamental to allowing a radically altered pattern of land use to take shape. Only as the last vestiges of natural territory have lost their ecological integrity, and global awareness of environmental responsibilities has grown, has opposition to some land use plans turned into active campaigning against state development priorities.

Infrastructure provision demands a disproportionate allocation of land by metropolitan city standards because of Singapore's multiple status as a global city, city state and nation state (Neville, 1993). The combined land area of telecommunications, utilities, domestic transportation, ports and airports exceeds the space occupied by housing. Singapore's regional and global service roles demand large amounts of space for roads, port and airport facilities and, as these services continue to be viewed as central to the island's economic future, they continue to assume priority in land use allocation. On the other hand, stringent efforts have been made to manage

internal travel and minimize congestion problems. Despite growing affluence, private car ownership has been kept low by international standards.
As well as the normal duties and road taxes paid by car owners, would-be
car owners must first purchase an entitlement to own and operate a vehicle. These charges, alongside extensive public transport provision, have
helped Singapore avoid the urban traffic congestion characteristic of other
Asian cities, although they have added to the prestige of vehicle ownership and not prevented a widespread desire for car ownership.

Increased integration of places of work, education, shopping and residence has become an established strategy to contain the demand for
mobility. As well as traditional land use planning solutions based around
self-contained neighbourhoods, greater use of information technology is
being promoted partly to offset lifestyle constraints, as well as to reinforce
economic goals. Under a strategy to make Singapore an 'intelligent island',
investment in broadband fibre optic cable is underway to make it possible
to work, shop and bank from every home using information technology.
A network of computerized neighbourhood information kiosks, delivering services such as theatre booking, travel tickets and news reviews, is
planned by the end of the century.

This chapter examines these related issues of land use change, infrastructure and telecommunications. It commences by a review of the major
changes in land use since the 1960s and the extensive reclamation projects
completed and planned. The central role of the Land Acquisition Act in
enabling the government to manage the process of land use change is
explained as well as the emergence of an environmental campaign which
has achieved some impact in modifying state plans for land use. The
chapter then examines key infrastructure provision for air and maritime
traffic, internal transport and telecommunications. The 'growth triangle'
project, linking the economy of Singapore with Johor, the southern state of
Malaysia, and the neighbouring Indonesian islands that form part of the
Riau province, is then discussed in relation to its contribution in helping
Singapore overcome some of its land and infrastructure constraints.

## Land use change

Land use patterns have changed significantly since 1967 with industry,
housing, transport and utilities the main functions to expand their use of
space (Table 6.1; Figures 6.1, 6.2). The overall pattern has seen a substantial drop in agricultural land, major expansions in other economic land
uses along with institutional and infrastructure uses and little change in
the proportion devoted to living space.

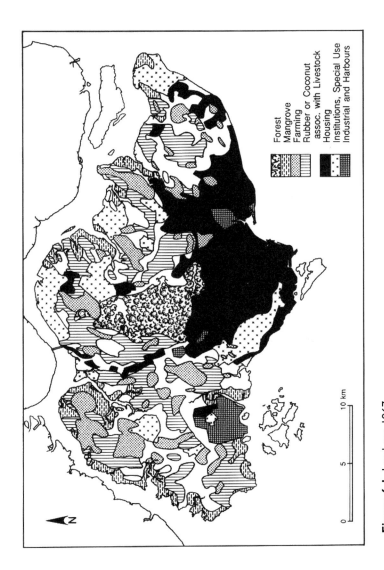

**Figure 6.1** Land use 1967

*Source:* Reprinted from *Geoforum*, 42, 2, Warwick Neville, 'The Impact of Economic Development on Land Functions in Singapore', 143–163, 1993, with kind permission from Elsevier Science Ltd, the Boulevard, Langford Lane, Kidlington OX5 1GB.

Forest
Mangrove
Farming
Rubber or Coconut
assoc. with Livestock
Housing
Institutions, Special Use
Industrial and Harbours

10 km

5

0

**Figure 6.2** Land use 1990

*Source:* Compiled in the Department of Geography, National University of Singapore from various government sources.

**Table 6.1** Land use change

| Land use | 1967[a] | | 1988 | | 2030[b] | |
|---|---|---|---|---|---|---|
| | sq km | % | sq km | % | sq km | % |
| **Living space** | | | | | | |
| Residential | 76.0 | 13.0 | 80.0 | 12.8 | 151.0 | 20.6 |
| **Working space** | | | | | | |
| Industrial | | | | | | |
| & warehousing | 11.0 | | 54.0 | | 110.0 | |
| Commercial | 7.2 | | 8.0 | | 12.5 | |
| Agricultural | 146.7 | | 53.0 | | 24.0 | |
| Subtotal | 164.9 | 28.3 | 115.0 | 18.5 | 146.5 | 20.0 |
| **Community uses** | | | | | | |
| Open space | 13.0 | | 18.0 | | 31.0 | |
| Institutional | 15.0 | | 41.0 | | 61.0 | |
| Subtotal | 28.0 | 4.8 | 59.0 | 9.5 | 92.0 | 12.6 |
| **Infrastructure** | | | | | | |
| Transportation | 20.6 | | 62.0 | | 81.0 | |
| Utilities & | | | | | | |
| telecommunications | 4.4 | | 12.0 | | 23.0 | |
| Ports and airports | 14.1 | | 19.0 | | 41.0 | |
| Subtotal | 39.1 | 6.7 | 93.0 | 14.9 | 145.0 | 19.8 |
| **Other uses** | | | | | | |
| Central catchment | | | | | | |
| & drainage | 91.7 | | 53.0 | | 53.0 | |
| Cemeteries[c] | 183.3 | | 223.0 | | 145.5 | |
| Subtotal | 275.0 | 47.2 | 276.0 | 44.3 | 198.5 | 27.0 |
| Total | 583.0 | | 623.0 | | 733.0 | |

*Notes:*   [a]The internal subcategories are estimated; subtotals are compatible to subsequent years.
[b]Assumes population of 4 million.
[c]Includes land under clearance or development, military and other special uses.

*Source:* Neville (1993)

In the competition for space, housing more than any other sector has been forced to recognize the scarcity of land (Neville, 1993, p. 148). Whereas residential uses typically account for around 40–50% of land space in European and North American cities (see Kivell, 1993, pp. 65–70), in Singapore the share has remained at around 13% since the 1960s (Table 6.1). In the early 1970s, it was estimated that if every family was allotted a 30 foot by 50 foot housing plot (9.1 by 15.2 metres), a population of 4 million could be accommodated on around a quarter of the island's then land

area (Gamer, 1972). From the inception of the HDB construction programme (see Chapter 8), however, high density, high-rise housing has
been the overwhelming provision, surpassing and influencing considerations of design, location or consumer preference. Consequently, despite
the scale of the HDB construction programme, with 680 000 new apartments added from 1960–1990, land was saved by rehousing the mass of
the population at higher densities than they left behind. The intensive use
of residential land accommodated a net increase of over 260 000 housing
units in the period 1967–1988 with only a 5% increase in the land allocated to residential functions. As reclamation expanded Singapore's total
land area over this period, residential uses actually came to occupy a
smaller proportion of the island.

The future provision of housing space anticipates a near doubling of
the area occupied by housing as the population reaches the target level
of four million, expected around 2030 (see Chapter 7). Some relief from
the monotonous multi-storeyed apartment block housing environments is
being planned. The main impact will be felt from the increased reliance on
private sector housing construction which favours smaller-scale development, although still often in the form of apartment blocks. The share of
private housing in the total stock is expected to be 30% in 2030, compared
with 17.5% in 1990, although the increase is partly expected through the
privatization of some existing higher quality public housing developments (Lim *et al.*, 1994, p. 22).

In comparison with the containment of the living environment, industrial uses have expanded their share of the island territory. Reflecting the
emphasis on industrialization in the post-independence development
strategy, industrial development has recorded by far the largest relative
expansion in land allocation up to 1988. The five-fold increase in industrial land area now makes it the third largest user of space in the built up
environment. Most of industrial activity takes place on land leased from
Jurong Town Corporation (see Chapter 5). Since its establishment in 1968,
JTC has planned, developed and managed more than 6000 hectares of
industrial land, of which over two-thirds has remained under its ownership (*JTC Annual Report 1994*).

Multi-storeyed factory accommodation accounts for almost half of the
1.9 million square metres of factory space retained by JTC, indicating how
the limitations of space have moulded the industrial landscape. But while
most types of light industry have adapted to multi-storey accommodation,
petrochemicals and shipbuilding, important factors in the island's industrial growth, are extensive land users. Much of the petrochemical industry
was sited on small islands, close to the Jurong industrial area. These are
now fully developed and to enable further expansion of the petrochemi-

**Plate 6.1** Jurong industrial estate. Photograph courtesy of the JTC

cal sector, seven of the occupied islands are being joined through recla-mation to create 300 hectares of additional production space (Figure 6.3).

The land area devoted to all types of commercial activity is modest and, even with the island's expansion as an international business service centre, grew by only a little over 10% in the period 1967–1988 (Table 6.1). The reconfiguration of the central business district has been one major contributor to the economy in commercial space. In the 1960s, the central area contained a highly diverse mix of land uses accommodated within streets of shophouses typical of Asian cities (Bellett, 1969). Redevelopment of the central area has left few buildings more than 20 years old and trans-formed the skyline through the spread of high-rise tower blocks. These new buildings predominantly accommodate financial and business ser-vices. Future expansion of the financial district has been provided for through the reclamation of waterfront land which is expected to satisfy

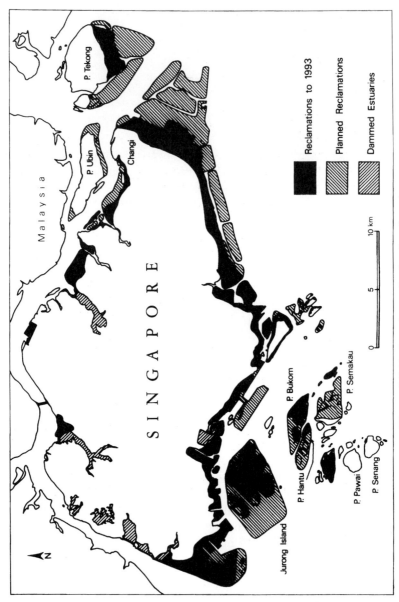

**Figure 6.3**  Reclamation realized and projected
*Source:* Hilton and Manning (1995)

the demand for central city office space up to 2050. Retailing activity in the central area has reduced largely to tourist and fashion markets supplied by international retail chains. Small scale retail outlets have been rehoused in large shopping complexes and malls located along major routes out of the central area and in suburban locations. Supermarket retailing was provided in the new housing areas mainly through centrally located stores, minimizing travel needs and encouraging day-to-day shopping trips. Competition for retail space was minimized by HDB rental concessions to the NTUC supermarket chain.

Although it has never been an agriculture economy, commercial agriculture long comprised the island's single major land use. At its peak in the mid-1930s, nearly two-thirds of the country was under cultivation (Neville, 1992, p. 245). At this time agriculture comprised two largely separate activities: commercial cash crop production primarily for export and more intensive food crop production for the local market. Rubber dominated the former and covered about 70% of the cultivated area (Humphrey, 1982). Despite being relegated to residual space, food crop production supplied the bulk of the country's fresh food requirements prior to the early 1930s. Increased demand for food and the declining viability of rubber plantations encouraged the expansion of intensive pig and vegetable farming. In 1964, self sufficiency existed in poultry, eggs, pork and some leafy vegetables mainly from intensively cultivated small holdings (Blaut, 1953), but from this point local food production has reduced although the recent designation of agrotechnology parks aims to strengthen selected activities.

The loss of agricultural land took place in three main phases (Figures 6.4–6.6). In the 1960s, housing construction acquired large areas of land outside the central area eliminating many intensive farm holdings on the fringes of existing suburban areas. In the mid-1970s, environmental conflicts led to the resettlement of pig farming to a designated estate in the east of the island at Punggol. As well as resolving land use conflicts, investment in pollution control and rearing equipment was envisaged to raise overall efficiency. The pollution problems proved to be greater than expected and starting in 1983, pig farming was phased out across the whole island.

In 1986, the Ministry of National Development instituted a comprehensive reorganization of the whole agricultural sector. Whereas in 1986 less than 2% of farm holdings were in units of over 0.6 hectares, the plan set a minimal holding size of two hectares to be adhered to by 1995 (Ministry of National Development, 1989). The consolidation of individual holdings was achieved through the relocation of activity to newly designated agrotechnology parks covering 2000 hectares. Of the space

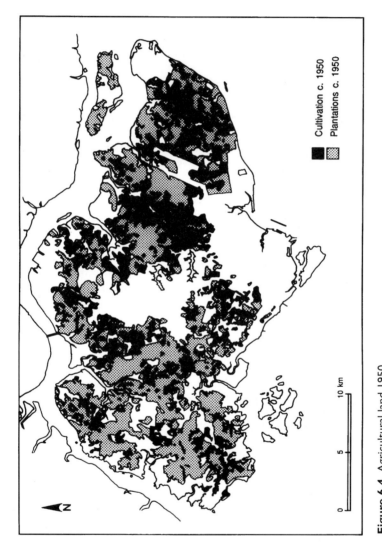

**Figure 6.4** Agricultural land 1950
*Source:* Reprinted from *Journal of Rural Studies*, 8, 3, Warwick Neville, 'Agribusiness in Singapore: a Capital-intensive Service', 241–255, 1992, with kind permission from Elsevier Science Ltd, the Boulevard, Langford Lane, Kidlington OX5 1GB.

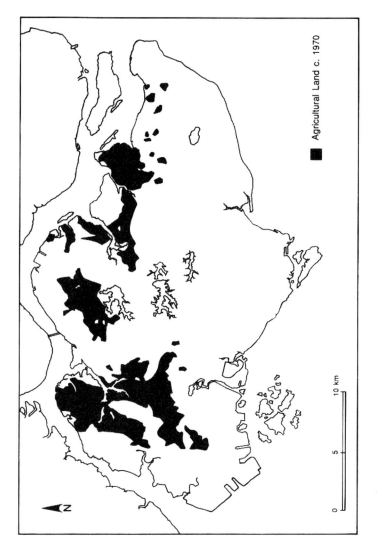

**Figure 6.5** Agricultural land 1970
*Source:* Reprinted from *Journal of Rural Studies*, 8, 3, Warwick Neville, 'Agribusiness in Singapore: a Capital-intensive Service', 241–255, 1992, with kind permission from Elsevier Science Ltd, the Boulevard, Langford Lane, Kidlington OX5 1GB.

**Figure 6.6**  Long-term agricultural land

*Source*: Reprinted from *Journal of Rural Studies*, 8, 3, Warwick Neville, 'Agribusiness in Singapore: a Capital-intensive Service', 241–255, 1992, with kind permission from Elsevier Science Ltd, the Boulevard, Langford Lane, Kidlington OX5 1GB.

allocated, 839 hectares had been developed by 1994 with a further 573 hectares under development. Space in the parks is allocated to high investment, high technology operations that are judged capable of building a regional research, development and servicing centre and intensive production units. Once fully operational, output is expected to exceed previous volumes in the selected production areas (Table 6.2) although only eggs and ducks will be close to self sufficiency. For local fresh food needs, the government is encouraging Singapore companies to invest overseas. Such operations have already been established on Pulau Bulan (a small nearby Indonesian island) which is expected to provide 20% of Singapore's pork demand, near Medan (Sumatra) and Pontianak (Kalimantan).

Infrastructure, especially transport and water storage, has taken much of the former agricultural land. The protected catchment together with several of the major central reservoirs covers 2059 hectares (Corlett, 1991, p. 142) but local sources supply only slightly above half the consumption with the balance imported via pipeline from Malaysia. Impounding of coastal estuaries has contributed to the loss of marine farming sites along

**Table 6.2** Projected quantity and value of production in agrotechnology parks

| Activity | Net area (ha) | Planned production | Planned contribution to domestic demand | Actual production 1994 |
|---|---|---|---|---|
| *Livestock* | | | | |
| chickens | | | | |
| (broilers etc) | 80 | 12.0m birds | 15% | |
| hens (eggs) | 110 | 574.2m birds | 87% | 32% of domestic |
| ducks | 92 | 6.0m birds | 87% | consumption |
| dairy cattle | 23 | 6.3m litres | | |
| others | 50 | | | |
| | | | | |
| *Horticulture* | | | | |
| vegetables | 262 | 39 300 tonnes | 20% | 5644 tonnes |
| orchids | 295 | 88.5m stalks | | 32.8m stalks |
| ornamentals | 145 | | | 188m plants |
| | | | | |
| *Fisheries* | | | | |
| ornamental | 312 | | | |
| consumption | 367 | 17 600 tonnes | 20% | 11 280 tonnes |
| Total | 1736 | $650m | | |

*Source:* Neville (1992); Department of Statistics, *Yearbook of Statistics 1994*

*environ*

with the extensive coastal reclamations for other infrastructure projects (Hilton and Manning, 1995). Of around 80 kilometres of coastal mangrove forest existing in the 1960s, less than three survive (World Resources Institute, 1986). The threefold increase in land allocated to transport is partly responsible for the fragmentation of remnant rainforest in the centre of the island, whose ecological viability is now in doubt. Some of the most ecologically significant land is now found within the extensive military training areas in the west of the island and Pulau Tekong, the largest offshore island and now closed to public access.

### Land acquisition

When the PAP assumed power it inherited land holdings from the colonial government amounting to around 44% of the island's territory. State ownership had increased to 76% in 1985 and to 80% in 1992 (von Alten, 1995) through acquisition and to a lesser extent through land reclamation. State purchase of land has been regulated by the Land Acquisition Act, 1966, which has been one of the principal extensions of state power since independence. The Act provides that land may be acquired for:

(a) any public purpose;
(b) any work or an undertaking by any person, corporation or statutory board, which, in the opinion of the Minister of National Development is of public benefit or of public utility or in the public interest; or
(c) any residential, commercial or industrial purpose.

As the third clause permits state acquisition of private land without the need to demonstrate public benefit, grounds for appeal against expropriation are severely contained (Khublall, 1991). The state also acted to minimize the cost of acquisition by setting compensation to a historic value and disregarding any increase in land value arising from public investment in the vicinity of the site to be acquired. During 1974–1988, the compensation was pegged to the site's 1973 value (unless the current value was lower); from 1993 compensation has been pegged to its 1 January 1992 valuation before being updated again in 1995.

At the same time, restrictions on the sale of rented property were retained up to 1988 and then only gradually phased out (Phang, 1992, p. 28). Under the Control of Rent Act 1947, property rents on private premises built before 7 September 1947 were pegged to 1939 or when the property was first let. This legislation was originally intended as a way of protecting tenants at a time of housing shortage. As it was also a disincentive to improve controlled property, it became a further way of acquiring land at low compensation rates and of restricting private sector real estate trading.

These controls on private property speculation illustrate the basic philosophy of the PAP government that the good of society collectively is more important than individual rights. As Lee Kuan Yew when Prime Minister is reported as saying in 1985:

> . . . the PAP in its early days broke the law to break the back of the housing problem we . . . therefore, took overriding powers to acquire land at low cost which was in breach of one of the fundamentals of British constitutional law – the sanctity of property. But that had to be overcome because the sanctity of society seeking to preserve itself was greater. So we acquired at sub-economic rates (Neville, 1993, p. 155).

Compulsory land acquisition limited speculation, kept development costs low and enabled the government to plan, develop and construct modern industrial zones, housing and satellite towns in which affordable home ownership was possible. The controls did however add some sources of instability into the property market which reached a peak in the 1985–1986 recession.

The right of state peremption at low compensation made owners of private land fearful of acquisition. This concern was heightened by land banking and speculative acquisition by state agencies. In the late 1970s and early 1980s land was purchased for housing and construction projects that were brought forward to counter the slow-down in global economic growth in the aftermath of the second oil crisis. The subsequent over-supply was a contributor to the sharp drop in property values from 1981–1985, by a third for newly-built flats and by almost two-thirds for offices (Ministry of Finance, 1986, p. 28). Land banking also became controversial as it questioned the justification for the original acquisition, particularly where surplus land was sold off. Sales of land (or more usually, the sale of a 99-year lease) to a MNC or statutory board were made at current market prices, producing a surplus at the expense of the original owner whose land had been acquired at below market value. A government inquiry completed by the Committee to Review Government Tender and Land Acquisition Procedures reported in 1987 that of the land acquired by four statutory boards (HDB, URA, JTC and PSA) from 1976–1986 only 29% had been developed (Ministry of Finance, 1987, p. 29). It recommended that land holding be limited to five years and that compensation levels be periodically updated, as has become the practice.

*Land reclamation*

The expansion of the land area by around 7.6% from 1960–1990 would be remarkable in a large country, but in Singapore this effort has added just 44 square kilometres at a cost of $4.25 billion. Although there are substantial inward areas of land still to be developed, the reclamation schemes have typically accommodated functions that required a coastal location or favoured in situ expansion. The resiting of the international airport on reclaimed land at Changi allowed building height restrictions in the central area to be removed (incidentally making economic, reclamation of land to accommodate expansion of the central financial and business service district). Ports and wharves have been constructed along the southern coast and waterfront land extended to concentrate industry in Jurong. In the case of Jurong, reclamation made use of earth removed through the flattening of land. The original siting of the petrochemical industry on offshore islands has required ongoing reclamation efforts to provide space for expansion. One offshore island has been reclaimed for use as a pig holding station, completing the phase out of mainland pig rearing. Other small islands have been reclaimed to improve harbour navigation facilities and for recreation purposes.

**Plate 6.2** Factories on reclaimed land at Tuas in the island's south west corner. Photograph courtesy of the JTC

Some momentum exists within the reclamation programme from the economies of keeping expensive equipment and construction plant in use (Wong, 1992, p. 245). This was, for example, a factor in the continuance of reclamation along the East Coast. The growth in solid waste collected, from 2100 tonnes in 1975 to around 4000 tonnes in 1990, and change from tipping to incineration of the waste has provided a source of fill material for use in reclamation projects (Vickridge, 1992, p. 409). Increased inciner-ation ash generation is driving some new offshore island reclamation pro-jects, although other material obtained from land and seabed sources will continue to be the main material utilized.

Under prevailing technology, the 15 metre water depth contour marks the limit of viable reclamation. Together with the need to retain space for sea traffic, the reclamation projects identified in the 1991 Concept Plan (Chapter 7, Figure 7.3) will exhaust reclamation opportunities. By this stage the land area is expected to have grown to 736 square kilometres, adding over a quarter to the land area of 1967.

## *Land use conflict*

The transformation in the Singapore landscape has been the subject of little outward public concern. Although certain land use decisions have at times been challenged, rarely has this caused the state's development objectives to be modified. The redevelopment of old burial sites and new provision for traditional burial practices was a source of complaint among religious and ethnic groups affected. Chinese burial grounds are more extensive users of space compared with other ethnic groups and were consequently identified by urban planning authorities as a particularly wasteful use of land (Yeoh and Tan, 1995). Despite the continuing desire to preserve their customary practices and sacred space, since indepen-dence the groups affected gradually acceded to the states nation-building priorities and accepted alternative provisions and the exhumation of nearly 120 000 graves by the HDB prior to 1985, rendering 21 cemeteries 'free of encumbrances for development' (Neville, 1993, p. 158).

A more recent challenge to the state's internalization of land use decisions has come from a growing public concern with the loss of Singapore's few remaining areas of wildlife habitat. In this case, opposi-tion has been organized by the Singapore Nature Society, which has open-ly campaigned to protect several areas proposed for development, incidentally becoming one of the few examples of attempts to organize public opposition to government decisions. In the early 1960s, the Nature Society (when it was the Singapore branch of the Malayan Nature Society) was unsuccessful in persuading the government to conserve one of the southern islands (Chia and Chionh, 1987). The Nature Society began a more high profile conservation campaign in the late 1980s, encouraged by the vulnerability of surviving areas, which in 1990 amounted to only around 100 hectares of primary forest and 600 hectares of mangrove forest (Briffett, 1990). While the island's indigenous fauna has been reduced largely to several varieties of bat, shrew, rat, snake and tree frog, overall the tropical environment supports a rich biodiversity (Turner, 1994). The number of flowering plant species, for example, equals that of New Zealand, a country 400 times larger in area. Many rare and endemic species exist precariously in the remaining fragments of undeveloped land. Of 180 resident species of birds (species that breed or have bred in Singapore) 35 became locally extinct prior to 1940, another 39 from 1940 to 1991, while a further 52 are considered at risk of extirpation (Lim, 1992). The loss of the Serangoon estuary to development, then the island's most bountiful bird sanctuary resulted in the Society submitting proposals for nature reserves in areas thought to be at risk from development (*The Straits Times*, 29 June 1991).

The Nature Society's conservation priorities were collectively submitted to the government in 1991 in a Master Plan for Conservation, including 11 high priority areas for conservation. As we discuss in the following chapter, it subsequently organized a number of high profile campaigns to support its conservation priorities. In response to this activity, as part of the strategy of channelling opposition into government-controlled organizations, senior members of the Nature Society have been invited to join the boards of public agencies. This includes the National Parks Board and the National Council on the Environment, an organization sponsored and appointed by the Ministry of the Environment to promote environmental awareness. These appointments encourage the Society to work within official channels rather than campaign independently.

### Infrastructure

Efficient infrastructure is widely cited in surveys of managers' location decisions as a key factor encouraging business expansion in Singapore (Taylor and Neville, 1980; Perry, 1992; 1994). The threefold increase in land area occupied by infrastructure during 1967–1988 is a reflection of the priority given to upgrading provision. As well as meeting domestic demands, infrastructure provision reflects the regional and global service functions that Singapore performs as a consequence of its strategic position at the meeting place of sea and air routes. This has necessarily amplified the capacities of the road network, ports, air terminals and telecom-munications industries. Provision of these facilities has been realized by statutory boards (Table 6.3). Although partial privatization of CAAS, PSA, PUB and TAS was proposed by the Public Sector Divestment Committee (Ministry of Finance, 1987), by 1996 this had only occurred in the case of telecommunications through the creation of Singapore Telecom. A vari-ant to privatization, as recognized by the Public Sector Divestment Committee, in which revenue rather than ownership is privatized (where-by the government relies on consumer charges rather than tax revenue to finance operations) has been used in the case of SMRT. In addition, private operators have been given access to some activities controlled by the Boards, as in the formation of joint venture companies to provide airport-related services (Thynne, 1989, p. 51) and the leasing of some port facili-ties to private companies (Low, 1991, p. 173).

*Seaport*

Throughout its history, sea trade and other maritime activity has been the primary basis of the economy. This role has been further consolidated in

**Table 6.3** Main statutory boards for infrastructure provision

| Board | Year established | Responsibility |
|---|---|---|
| Public Works Department | 1951 | Road development and management; regulation of private building works |
| Public Utilities Board | 1963 | Production and distribution of water, electricity, and piped gas |
| Port of Singapore Authority | 1964 | Provision and maintenance of port facilities |
| Civil Aviation Authority | 1971 | Operation and management of Singapore Changi Airport |
| Telecommunication Authority of Singapore[a] | 1974 | Regulator and promoter of telecommunication and postal services |
| Mass Rapid Transit Authority | 1985 | Construction of MRT; regulation of licensed operator |

*Note:* [a]In 1993 Singapore Telecommunications Ltd took responsibility for the provision of telecommunications

its modern era through the expansion of port and oil industry installations. As well as its advantageous location along one of the world's busiest waterways, it benefits from strong tidal currents through the Straits of Singapore. These currents provide natural dredging of the shipping channels although maintenance around the deep modern berths is still required (Chia, 1989). During the Second World War and the Japanese Occupation, port facilities fell into disrepair. When the Singapore Harbour Board resumed control in 1946, extensive repairs and improvements were made to re-establish the port. A more extensive investment programme was commenced when the Port of Singapore Authority (PSA) took control of all port operations in 1964, particularly as the success of the industrialization strategy began to indicate the need to upgrade shipping services.

The PSA now manages infrastructure comprising six terminals handling all types of vessels (container ships, bulk carriers, cargo freighters, coasters, lighters and passenger liners), 15 kilometres of quays and specialized facilities, 600 000 square metres of covered warehouses and a labour force of over 7000 workers. In addition, there are extensive oil terminal facilities operated by major refining companies (Shell, Esso, Mobil, British Petroleum and Caltex) as well as two separate oil storage terminals. The large number of oil tankers calling at these various installations account for Singapore's ranking as the world's busiest port, when measured in terms of the tonnage of shipping passing through the port and the volume of bunkering supplied. Container traffic has, however, been the largest source of growth over the last decade (Table 6.4) and measured in terms of volume of containers handled, Singapore is the second largest terminal after Hong Kong with more than double the container volumes of the largest ports (Kaohsiung and Rotterdam).

The volume of traffic has not compromised turnaround times which, at an average of around 13.5 hours are low in comparison with other ports (Table 6.5). Speed, combined with the low port charges, have helped Singapore achieve top ranking amongst 15 industrializing nations, ahead of Hong Kong and South Africa, in a survey of port user satisfaction (IIMD/WEF, 1993). In 1993, 92 477 ship arrivals were handled at the port. As well as the number of arrivals, almost 30% of vessels undertake multiple tasks while in port such as receiving supplies, bunkering, crew changes or undergoing repairs. Many other vessels obtain such services without calling at the port.

A major expansion of port capacity commenced in 1993 with the start of reclamation work to construct a new container terminal of 50 berths. When fully completed in 2018, the PSA's container handling capacity is expected to increase four-fold to 36 million TEUs. The viability of this

**Plate 6.3** Container terminal. Photograph courtesy of the URA

investment is partly reliant on the corresponding expansion of facilities in neighbouring countries, as the enlarged capacity will exceed the ability of regional ports to handle the increased volumes of freight expected to be generated within the region. Congestion in the Straits of Malacca, and the increased risks of pollution and tanker collisions, are further constraints to expansion (see Valencia, 1991 for discussion of the management of mar-

**Table 6.4** Sea freight cargo handled 1980–1994 (,000 freight tonnes)

| Year | Total containers | Unloaded Mineral oil | Other[a] | Total | Loaded Mineral oil | Other | Total |
|------|------|------|------|------|------|------|------|
| 1980 | 12 550 | 31 633 | 18 490 | 50 122 | 20 859 | 15 318 | 36 178 |
| 1985 | 23 862 | 38 430 | 23 658 | 62 086 | 25 181 | 18 569 | 43 750 |
| 1990 | 76 631 | 53 335 | 52 888 | 106 223 | 33 571 | 45 996 | 81 567 |
| 1994 | 142 000 | 76 200 | 88 200 | 164 400 | 47 800 | 77 800 | 125 600 |

*Note:* [a]Includes general and bulk cargo, containerized and conventional.

*Source:* Department of Statistics, *Yearbook of Statistics*

**Table 6.5** Indicators of comparative port efficiency, 1991 or latest

| Port | Shipcalls per employee | Crane rate | Ship rate | TEUs per crane | Shipcalls per tug | TEUs per berth metre | occupancy (%) | TEUs per area (ha) |
|---|---|---|---|---|---|---|---|---|
| Rotterdam | 33.4 | 30.2 | 30.2 | 73 517 | 2225 | 314 | 51 | 21 860 |
| Kaohsiung | 4.5 | 21.0 | 27.0 | 112 844 | 1147 | 656 | 70 | 17 444 |
| Hong Kong | 2.0 | 21.0 | 36.0 | 104 835 | 814 | 874 | 71 | 25 926 |
| Singapore | 10.8 | 40.0 | 50.0 | 135 870 | 2647 | 1639 | 72 | 28 579 |
| Bangkok | 1.0 | 20.0 | 20.0 | 146 337 | 242 | 944 | 62 | 12 269 |
| Zeebrugge | 61.7 | 25.0 | 40.0 | 31 127 | 2246 | 186 | 52 | 12 229 |
| Melbourne | 2.6 | 15.0 | 28.0 | 47 509 | 310 | 190 | 38 | 10 616 |
| Jakarta | 8.0 | 25.0 | 25.0 | 76 347 | 615 | 445 | 47 | 17 240 |
| Klang | 2.0 | 25.0 | 26.4 | 99 305 | 175 | 502 | 75 | 10 344 |
| Manila | 1.0 | 16.0 | 23.4 | 28 073 | 804 | 51 | 50 | 3365 |
| Auckland | 3.4 | 18.0 | 20.0 | 49 450 | 530 | 221 | 40 | 7492 |

*Source:* Tongzon and Genesalingam (1994)

itime traffic in the Straits of Malacca). A long-term solution to this congestion, discussion of which is revived periodically, is the construction of the Kra canal across southern Thailand, which would remove the need to circumnavigate the Malay peninsula (Regnier, 1991, p. 106).

Attempts have been made by neighbouring countries to divert traffic to their own ports. The most direct competition has come from Malaysia. The port of Pasir Gudang was developed in the 1970s in southern Johor in an attempt to capture traffic from Singapore, reinforced by Malaysian restrictions on freight movements across the Singapore–Johor causeway. More recently, Malaysia has proposed the development of a new container terminal, to the west of Singapore at Tanjung Pelepas, to be completed by 2020 (Figure 6.7). To date, however, Singapore's dominance of maritime traffic has been unaffected by regional competition (Regnier, 1991, p. 103). Landing costs in Malaysia are inflated by customs and port dues (Table 6.5) and neither Port Klang nor Pasir Gudang are able to accommodate tankers of more than 80 000 tonnes whereas Singapore's offshore buoy moorings can service tankers of over 300 000 tonnes. The dominance of Singapore is reinforced by the emergence of round-the-world container shipping, first introduced in 1984. These services use large, high-speed container vessels and depend for their efficiency on a rapid turnaround time at a limited number of ports (Rodrigue, 1994). The size of Singapore's merchant fleet also helps protect the importance of the port. At the end of 1994, the fleet comprised 2647 vessels making it the twelfth largest among major maritime nations, one-fifth controlled by the state-owned Neptune Orient Lines.

*Airport*

Changi Airport was opened in 1981 with one runway and one terminal. In his 1989 National Day address, the Prime Minister Lee Kuan Yew indicated that the success of this US$800 million investment was a particular source of pride among his development decisions. It required writing off considerable investment in the existing international airport and having confidence in the revival of air traffic growth beyond a slump in the mid-1970s when the decision to proceed was made. The optimism proved to be justified. A second runway began operating in 1984 and a second terminal in 1990. This gave a capacity of 24 million passengers a year of which 90% was utilized in 1994, but already development of a third terminal and runway is planned to bring capacity up to 36 million passengers a year by 2010. In 1994, 66 airlines used the airport linking Singapore directly to 124 cities in 56 countries through 2800 scheduled flights per

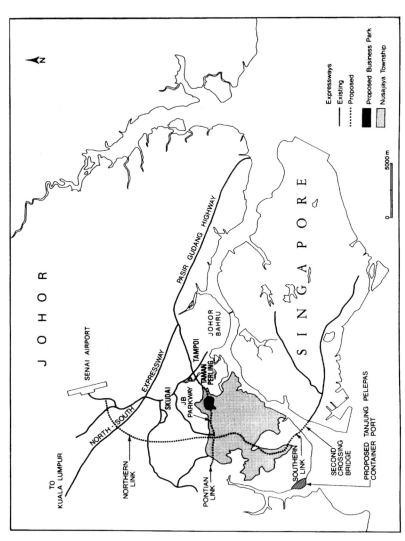

**Figure 6.7** Second crossing and linked development projects proposed in Johor

week. In addition, the airport has five air freight terminals, two opened since 1993. Connectivity, efficient throughput of travellers and ease of travel to and from the airport has helped it win numerous awards from business traveller and other international magazine-reader polls (*Singapore 1995*).

Singapore's role as the regional hub for air transport has been less controversial with its regional neighbours than its seaport dominance (Regnier, 1991, p. 109). This is helped by a so-called open skies policy that allows regional airlines to compete for passengers in Singapore. A large number of international airlines wish to use Changi as a transit stop between Europe and the Asia–Pacific. This demand has placed the national airline in a strong negotiating position to obtain reciprocal landing rights to overseas destinations. Consequently the expansion of the national airline carrier Singapore International Airlines has not required the monopoly of regional traffic. Similarly, as Singapore only serves as a transit stop for tourists, its success as a break-journey point is generally welcomed by neighbouring tourist industries. The number of persons arriving and departing through Singapore has grown at a faster rate than transit passengers (Table 6.6) which provides a growing market for regional travel.

*Land transport*

Despite the island's small size, the average commuter was still travelling over ten kilometres a day in 1990 (Chin, 1992). Prior to the 1970s, transport planning had received relatively little attention compared with the priorities of jobs and housing (Varaprasad, 1989). The centralization of trans-

**Table 6.6** Air traffic 1980–1994

| Year | Aircraft landing | Passengers | | | Air cargo (tonnes) | |
|------|---------|---------|-----------|------------|-----------|---------|
| | | Arrival | Departure | In transit | Discharged | Loaded |
| 1980 | 37 956 | 3 140 723 | 3 151 032 | 1 002 794 | 90 713 | 91 062 |
| 1985 | 36 600 | 4 323 587 | 4 397 908 | 1 135 335 | 167 388 | 132 631 |
| 1990 | 48 803 | 7 237 233 | 7 166 347 | 1 217 178 | 324 157 | 299 684 |
| 1994 | 37 956 | 10 134 000 | 10 069 000 | 1 442 040 | 529 334 | 480 430 |

*Source:* Department of Statistics, *Yearbook of Statistics*

port planning and control in the Ministry of Communications and Registry of Vehicles provided the administrative apparatus for bringing order to a previously neglected component of the city infrastructure. The integration of private bus company operations and the licensing of taxi operations in the early 1970s (to eradicate pirate taxi operators) were among the first actions carried out by the new administrators. These initiatives were intended to help relieve traffic congestion by improving other transport modes compared with the private car. However the rapid expansion of work in the central business district exposed the inadequacies of a road network that had not received any significant investment since the mid-1950s. Piecemeal road improvements and management solutions were introduced, including staggered work hours and car pooling, but the level of congestion, which made travel by bus unattractive, demanded a more radical solution.

In 1975, Singapore became one of the first cities in the world to introduce a form of road pricing. As well as a willingness to act, certain practical considerations made such a scheme relatively easy to introduce, including the relative isolation of the city from outside traffic and the preponderance of commuting by public transport even before the scheme was implemented (Holland and Watson, 1982). The scheme introduced a supplementary private car licence for access to the core downtown area

**Plate 6.4** MRT train pulls into a station. Photograph courtesy of the URA

during the peak morning flow (7.30 am to 9.30 am, later extended to 10.15 am) by private car, unless upwards of four passengers were being conveyed. Monthly or daily licences could be purchased by any driver but, as a further disincentive to the commuter, parking charges were raised in the central area, especially on long-stay parking, and the availability of on-street parking reduced. The aim of the area licensing scheme was to reduce peak-hour traffic by 25–30%. The target was exceeded during the peak morning flow, but to the surprise of the scheme's planners the evening peak did not subside. Consequently, the scheme was later extended to the evening peak as well, and in 1994 a lesser charge was introduced for off-peak entry throughout work days.

The area licensing scheme addressed central city congestion. Import duties, registration fees and road taxes were raised simultaneously to constrain the growth in private car ownership. These charges meant that owning a car became as expensive as owning a four bedroom HDB flat (*HDB Annual Report 1992*). The scope of the charges levied on vehicle ownership has progressively been extended to provide tighter control over the net growth in vehicles on the road. Initially import duties on new vehicles were raised, followed by the introduction of an additional registration fee (ARF) for new cars, paid as a proportion of vehicle value. In 1975, when the ARF was 100%, a preferential registration fee (PARF) was introduced to encourage the scrapping of vehicles over ten years old. Under this scheme, a purchaser of a new vehicle simultaneously scrapping or exporting a vehicle of less than ten years old, pays the ARF at a preferential rate. At its peak, the ARF was set at 175% of the new vehicle value. A Parliamentary Select Committee on Land Transport concluded, however, that high financial penalties alone were not giving sufficient control over the growth in car ownership.

In 1990, a quota system was introduced to regulate the number of new vehicles entering the road system. Under this scheme, an intending purchaser of a new vehicle must bid for a 'certificate of entitlement', this gives the right to purchase a new vehicle and to retain its ownership for ten years. In the first year, a total of 50 000 COEs were auctioned, allocated over eight vehicle categories. This quota provided a net growth close to the average annual rate of 4.3% over the previous 15 years. The intention is to manipulate the quota volume according to changing traffic conditions. After the whole-day extension of the area licensing scheme in January 1994, for example, a 15% increase in COEs was released making up for previous cutbacks in the quota. Over the first four years of the scheme, bid prices for COEs have risen to levels that have added 50% to the price of car ownership (von Alten, 1995, pp. 158–59). To reduce some of the inequality in access to car ownership, a 'weekend car' scheme (later changed to the off-peak car scheme) was introduced in 1991, offering reduced fees for vehicles used only during off-peak times. This allowance was an interim measure prior to the introduction of electronic road pricing, for which trials commenced in 1996 covering the central area (replacing the area licensing scheme), congested ring roads and expressways.

Despite the comprehensive measures so far employed, private car ownership has not been constrained to the target average of one per twelve people, as announced in 1981 (Spencer and Chia, 1985, p. 306). A ratio of one to ten existed in the mid-1990s. While this ratio is still low in comparison with other cities of comparable income, the high demand for vehicle ownership is to some degree perpetuated by the subsidized housing environment (Varaprasad, 1989, p. 429). The discretionary funds available for car purchase are further increased by the type of housing provision, which provides limited scope for expenditure on improvements. At the same time, the concentration of living and work environments within a small part of the island now makes it hard to accommodate a growth in vehicle density. In much of the built-up area, the road network is reaching the limit of above-ground development and vehicle numbers per kilometre exceed international levels: in 1990, average figures were 81 vehicles per kilometre in Singapore, compared with 62 in the United Kingdom, 43 in Japan and 27 in the United States (Lee quoted in Neville, 1993, p. 159). A computerized traffic signal control system has been in place in the central area since 1988 and is being progressively extended to other localities as a way of maximizing road capacity. To accommodate further increases in traffic, increasingly costly engineering solutions are required as reflected in over $1 billion committed to the road building programme of 1990–1995 and the construction of underground road tunnels to divert traffic otherwise crossing the central city.

The density of residential and commercial development has, on the other hand, been a benefit to public transport provision. The Mass Rapid Transit (MRT) came into operation in 1990, covering a 67 kilometre network of three lines and 42 stations. A 16 kilometre extension to Woodlands in the north of the island, close to the causeway, opened in 1996. The system carried around a fifth of all public transport trips in 1994 (von Alten, 1995, p. 79), but has obtained most patronage from former bus travellers rather than capturing former car travellers (Chin, 1992). Further extensions of the MRT are planned but under its commercial funding arrangements construction depends on confidence that operating costs will be covered by commercial revenue. (Capital costs are partly offset by the government capturing increased land values arising from MRT construction.) Consequently when a new line was agreed in 1995, to run from the World Trade Centre west of the city centre to Punggol in the northeast, uncertainty over potential patronage led the government to indicate higher fares might be charged on this line compared with the existing ones.

The causeway crossing between Singapore and Johor Baru is a final important aspect of Singapore's land transport infrastructure. It is important to the viability of the freight distribution industry, facilitating the daily commuting of around 25 000 workers into Singapore, providing an outlet for car drivers frustrated by Singapore's limited road space and making Johor an important recreation and shopping location for Singaporeans. Over 7.5 million day trippers cross the causeway from Singapore annually. Improvement of the causeway has however lagged behind the growth in traffic flows, largely because Malaysian authorities have tended to view increased integration of the two economies as more advantageous to Singapore (Kamil *et al.*, 1991). For example, while Singaporeans' use of Johor as a weekend leisure location generates substantial income for the state, the intrusion of a wealthier group who allegedly 'do not behave as they do at home' is also a source of tension (Parsonage, 1992). A less critical perception of Singaporean influence has developed under the growth triangle initiative (see below) of which one result has been Malaysian agreement to the construction of a second crossing. The new bridge, construction of which started in 1995, will link Singapore to southwest Johor through the industrial zone of Tuas on the Singapore side (Figure 6.7).

*Telecommunications and information technology*

As with air and sea traffic, Singapore is one of the leading intersections of international telecommunications and again this has a long history. In 1871, a submarine cable linking Singapore to Madras was completed allowing direct telegraphic communication to Europe via India. A year later, telegraphic communication was extended to Australia and Hong Kong. This early privileged position in the international communications infrastructure was an important factor in the growth of the port (Chia, 1989, p. 315). The information and communication infrastructure that retains Singapore's international connectivity today includes three satellite earth stations, submarine fibreoptic links to Malaysia, Hong Kong, Taiwan and Japan, from where there are onward connections to other regions, as well as three international digital gateways. Some indication of the importance of these connections to the contemporary economy is given by the growth in outgoing international telephone calls from 3.5 million in 1980 to 146 million in 1994.

Information technology infrastructure has been the focus of improvement since early 1981 when the National Computer Board (NCB) was established to lead a national computerization effort. It commenced with the computerization of the civil service and other projects to expand the use of information technology (Corey, 1991). As part of the 1986 National Information Technology Plan, efforts turned to encouraging electronic data interchange (EDI) for the distribution of business documents. TradeNet was the first EDI network to become operational and since the pilot version commenced in 1989, the number of subscribers has grown to 12 000. TradeNet was designed in collaboration with the NCB, PSA, TDB and CAAS with the aim of reducing the cost and turnaround time involved in the preparation, transfer and processing of trade related documentation. Participation in the network has become necessary for shipping companies submitting trade declarations, permit applications and related documents to government agencies that are part of the network. Subsidized training and software was given to participants and for small companies, grants and subsidized loans are available to purchase computer hardware (Tan, C. H., 1995). Total annual savings for both government agencies and the trading community have been estimated at $1 billion, based on the assumption of productivity savings of between 20–30% within individual trading offices.

As well as communication between participants in the international trade sector, TradeNet provides access to local and international databases and other computer networks. One such connection links TradeNet to PortNet, another NCB-supported network. PortNet gives access to the PSA's database for vessel, cargo, container and shipping information as well as access to similar databases of major overseas ports. Other computer networks established are: Spectrum, for air cargo services; MediNet, for the health care industry; LawNet, for communication between legal offices and on-screen access to government statutes. CoreNet, to link participants in the property and construction industry, is being developed. Studies have been conducted of the feasibility of networks in the manufacturing and retail sectors, but the absence of standardized business documents and procedures remains a barrier to EDI in these sectors.

A second plan completed by the NCB, called IT2000, has guided further investment in information infrastructure since 1992. IT2000 set out a vision of an 'intelligent island' where information technology and computer networking are pervasive in business and at home (NCB, 1992). By the end of the century, the NCB's target is to have facilitated a computer infrastructure that makes it possible to work, shop, bank and learn from home. The most tangible sign of this commitment is the upgrading of the telephone cable network which, already entirely digital by 1994, is being converted to a Broadband Integrated Services Digital Network to enable multiple simultaneous transmissions to each household, business and other organization. Other projects being completed as part of IT2000 are the upgrading of, and computer access to, library resources; 'SingaTouch' information kiosks located in all neighbourhoods; and a video-on-demand service delivered through the telephone network.

High population density in a confined geographical space makes it economic to consider such information technology infrastructure. It is seen as important to the economic viability of the island and as a way of raising information technology skills, although this also depends on the expansion of training and the use of computers in education. Investment in information technology infrastructure is also justified to offset the constraints on car ownership and the limitations of apartment dwelling. Fear that such constraints may encourage skilled and affluent professionals to depart Singapore is motivating a search for alternative ways of satisfying lifestyle ambition. However, others have pointed out that providing freer access to information services is at odds with government wishes to maintain control over sources of ideas (Johnstone, 1995).

### The Singapore–Riau–Johor Growth Triangle

In the early 1990s, the Singapore–Indonesian border zone became seen as a possible solution to some of Singapore's land and resource constraints. To the south of Singapore, across a narrow stretch of water, the Riau archipelago has remained sparsely populated, although the two larger Riau islands, Batam and Bintan, are both close to Singapore (Figure 1.2). The potential for these islands to become closely linked with Singapore-based activity had been recognized since the 1970s but hardly exploited beyond a small amount of weekend tourism. Although an investment accord had been signed between Singapore and Indonesia (Table 6.7) this brought no immediate change to the islands. Until the 1990s, the islands remained free of industrial development apart from some support activity to Indonesia's offshore petroleum industry (Rice 1989; Esmara, 1975). In 1989, total employment on Batam was 11 000, mainly concentrated in local services, tourism and oil-related firms using Batam as a service base (Batam Industrial Development Authority, 1991).

Interest in the possibility of the Riau islands supplying additional production space for activity linked to Singapore was revived by the Indonesian government in 1989 (Scherschel, 1991). This time, as a precondition for its development cooperation, the Singapore government obtained changes to the investment regime in Batam designed to make

**Table 6.7** Development initiatives in the Riau islands post-1970

---

*Period of development by Indonesia*

| | |
|---|---|
| 1971 | Batam Island Development Agency (BIDA) established |
| 1978 | Batam designated as a tax free bonded zone for export industry |
| 1979 | Industrial development master plan released for development up to 2006 |
| 1980 | Indonesia–Singapore Batam development agreement |

---

*Period of development by Indonesia and Singapore*

| | |
|---|---|
| Oct 1989 | President Suharto and then Prime Minister Lee Kuan Yew discuss Batam's development; foreign investment restrictions modified |
| Oct 1989 | Growth Triangle idea announced by then Deputy Prime Minister Goh Chok Tong |
| Jan 1990 | Singapore–Indonesia joint venture established to construct Batamindo Industrial Park |
| Aug 1990 | Economic cooperation and investment protection agreement signed by Singapore and Indonesia to promote development of the Riau province |
| 1991 | Establishment of Bintan Resort Management for joint venture resort, industrial park and water projects |
| Apr 1992 | BIP officially opened |
| Dec 1994 | Partial opening of Bintan resort development |
| Dec 1994 | Memorandum of Understanding signed by trade ministers of Singapore, Malaysia and Indonesia to govern cooperation in the growth triangle |
| Apr 1995 | Indonesia proposes construction of 50km of highways and bridges to link islands south of Batam, creating Barelang Bin |
| Mar 1996 | Expansion of growth triangle to other states in Malaysia and Indonesia proposed by these countries |

---

the island attractive to multinational capital (Vatikiotis, 1991). In the Batam Economic Zone (Batam plus five neighbouring islands) 100% foreign ownership is now possible, subject to the divestment of 5% to local ownership after 5 years; this compares with the need to divest 51% of ownership after 15 years elsewhere in Indonesia. Restrictions on the private development and control of industrial estates were relaxed to allow Singapore government companies to manage industrial estates, so reducing uncertainties associated with the security of land tenure (Perry, 1991). A Board of Investment Office was opened in Batam with decision-making autonomy from the head office in Jakarta. Finally, duty payments were restricted to the value of imported raw materials, rather than the finished product, making the island more viable as an export base to other parts of Indonesia. The Singapore government failed to achieve the introduction of tax incentives, such as pioneer status, but the measures taken were sufficient to secure their cooperation and make Batam a privileged investment location in Indonesia.

This cooperative initiative was broadened by inclusion of the southern Malaysian state of Johor, forming the so-called growth triangle or Sijori (Lee, T. Y., 1991). Economic cooperation between Malaysia and Singapore has a long history. Singapore is provided with around half its daily water requirements from reservoirs and water purification plants in Johor. Under an agreement signed in 1962, and renewed in 1987, Singapore manages these facilities and re-sells part of the supply to the local administration in Johor (Regnier, 1991, p. 72). Johor has also received significant industrial investment from Singapore as businesses have sought to evade rising production costs. During the 1980s, Singapore was the source of over a fifth of the investment in new industrial projects in Johor. Nonetheless, as noted above, Malaysia's federal government has remained ambivalent towards Johor's greater dependence on Singapore, partly from a perception that investment flows are disproportionately beneficial to the Malaysian Chinese, at the expense of ethnic Malays (*bumiputras*).

Inviting Johor into a tripartite regional scheme with themselves and the Riau island accorded with Singapore's interest in sharing its economic growth among its Indonesian and Malaysian neighbours (Regnier, 1991, p. 80). But while Johor state was enthusiastic (the concept of twinning development with Singapore was incorporated in the Johor State Economic Plan 1990–2005 (MIER, 1989)) the Federal Government delayed commitment. Three factors contributed to Malaysian hesitation: (i) a reluctance to accept a subsidiary economic status to Singapore, as implied by the respective roles of the three partners in the triangle; (ii) a regional development programme including dispersion away from existing growth regions as one of its goals; (iii) uncertainty over the potential for economic cooperation with Indonesia, since both were competing for foreign investment. It was not until December 1994 that a formal framework was agreed for trilateral cooperation including Malaysia, by which time there had already been substantial development in the Riau islands.

Following a memorandum of understanding between Singapore and Indonesia in 1989, covering Batam and the neighbouring island of Bintan, the Indonesian government allocated US$450 million to the Batam development plan for projects including the upgrading of sea and airport facilities and public utilities. The memorandum also released Singapore government investment in Batam's infrastructure, most directed at the development of Batamindo Industrial Park in a joint venture between Singapore Technologies Industrial Corporation and Jurong Environmental Engineering (40%) and Indonesian investors led by the Salim Group. The

Singapore contributors took control of the design, physical development and management of the estate which as well as 125 factory units, includes service infrastructure, workers' accommodation, recreational facilities and a town centre. A Salim Group subsidiary took responsibility for labour recruitment, bringing in mainly young female workers from mainland Indonesia, hired on to factory tenants on two-year contracts.

Although Batamindo Industrial Park is the eighth industrial estate to be authorized by the Batam Industrial Development Authority, it was the first to see actual development. By October 1994, 57 companies were employing 27 000 workers on the estate within four years of the first tenant moving in (Fukuda, 1995). Much of the investment has come from Singapore-based organizations that have opened low-value assembly operations in the island to access lower labour costs and to expand production to supply the Indonesian market. To consolidate the Park's development, Batamindo is developing executive housing and a golf course to improve facilities for executives. Other developments on the island include expansion of the airport's capacity, a deep-water cargo terminal and the development of a commercial centre. A water pact signed in June 1991 established a joint venture between the PUB and Indonesian investors to develop water resources in the Riau province, including mainland Sumatra, in addition to the Riau islands. This pact is designed to ensure that development planned for Batam and Bintan will have sufficient water capacity as well as providing Singapore with an additional supply of imported water to that obtained from Johor (Parsonage, 1992).

The Batamindo partnership has been replicated to develop a similar park on the neighbouring island of Bintan. The first ten tenants, mainly textile and clothing companies, commenced operation there in 1994. Fully developed, the Park is planned to cover eight times the area of the Batam Park (Table 6.8). An area of 23 000 hectares in the northern part of Bintan has been set aside for tourist projects. Ferry services to Singapore have been upgraded and in 1995, plans for a car ferry link were announced. A number of resorts and hotels opened in 1994 and 1995 with the ultimate target of creating a comprehensive leisure centre attracting regional and international visitors.

The four Karimun islands have been designated for shipyard and oil base facilities. The Sembawang Group, a Singapore GLC, is building a shipyard and oil base in a joint venture with Jurong Environmental Engineering and the Salim Group. Work has also commenced on the construction of an oil storage depot.

In a short space of time, the growth triangle has radically transformed the development outlook for the Riau islands. Further ambitious plans have been devised by the Batam Industrial Development Authority, includ-

**Table 6.8** Comparison of the Riau islands

|  | Batam | Bintam | Karimun |
|---|---|---|---|
| Distance from Singapore | 20 km | 45 km | 40 km |
| Travel time from Singapore | 45 min | 45–60 min | 60 min |
| Area (km$^2$) | 415 | 1030 | 133 |
| Timing of major new projects | 1989–95 | 1991–96 | 1994–98 |
| Investment priorities | Electronic industries, Singapore linked | Light industries, including clothing, leisure | Petrochemicals and oil, ship repair and heavy engineering |
| Key projects | Batamindo Industrial Park (500ha) Southlinks Country Club (golf course and executive housing) | Bintam Beach International Resort (23 000ha divided over 20–30 projects, supplying 3000 hotel rooms by 2000 and sports facilities) Bintam Industrial Estate (4000ha) | Karimun Industrial Complex (3600ha) |

ing the construction of seven ocean-spanning bridges to connect the islands extending southwards from Batam (Figure 6.8). As a contribution to relieving resource constraints in Singapore, however, there are evident limitations to what can be achieved through the growth triangle. One problem is that the Riau islands are water scarce, limiting their capacity to supply Singapore and restricting the scale of development possible on the islands. Partly for this reason, the islands are unlikely to serve a major role as an industrial adjunct to the Singapore economy, particularly Bintan where the priority industries are not key sectors for Singapore. As an outlet for leisure and recreation activity, however, the islands offer opportunities to satisfy some of the lifestyle aspirations lost in Singapore's congested environment.

Beyond satisfying Singapore's resource needs, the growth triangle has been viewed as indicative of a form of subregional cooperation particularly suited to Asian conditions (Tang and Thant, 1994; Chia and Lee, 1992). Low levels of intra-regional trade, the diversity of economic sys-

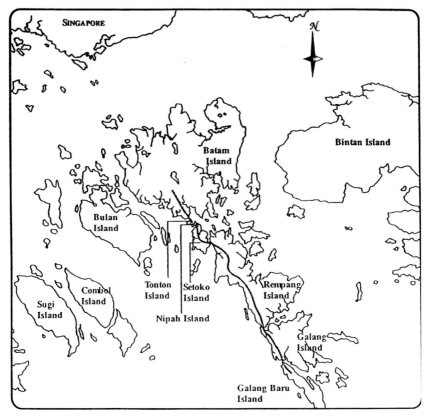

**Figure 6.8** Bridges to connect Barelang (Batam–Rempang–Galang)

tems, disparities in income levels (for example, the *per capita* income of Japan is about 40 times that of the Philippines and 100 times that of Vietnam), geographical dispersion and sometimes poor communication infrastructure prevent regional integration of the depth obtained in Europe and North America. Growth triangles, on the other hand, involve little change in national and institutional arrangements and may even operate, as in the case of Sijori, without formal treaties or changes in domestic regulations. Moreover, rather than economic disparities being a constraint on cooperation, advocates of growth triangles see the existence of economic disparities as a tool for development (Tang and Thant, 1994; Lee, T. Y., 1991). This does, however, rely on the existence of a congested core economy that wishes to divest low-value added and labour intensive activities, and has the capacity to bring additional investment to neighbouring economies. While Singapore may have this strength, it is less certain that some of the other subregional groupings that have been proposed can replicate these conditions. Further, Singapore's willingness to invest in the Riau islands is partly conditioned by their island status. Physical isolation provides a means of controlling population inflows and squatter settlement development enabling close management of the environment, although even on Batam these problems exist. The security offered to international investors by the guarantee of Singapore's political weight and commitment has been no less important. Nonetheless, despite what might be the rather special circumstances of Sijori, interest in the possibility of engineering development in this way is growing as indicated by proposals for a northern ASEAN growth triangle (comprising the northern states of Malaysia and Sumatra and southern Thailand) and an east ASEAN growth triangle linking regions in the Philippines, Sulawesi and Malaysia (Thant *et al.*, 1994; Kumar and Siddique, 1994).

For Singapore's economic planners, the growth triangle has been an important development experience which contributed to the confidence to launch a more ambitious programme of regional investments (see Chapter 5). The development of Batam illustrated the capacity of the Singapore government to influence the investment trajectories of multinational capital. It also indicated how the infrastructure development expertise and wide experience of accommodating multinational capital by agencies such as JTC and the EDB have become a potential export industry for the state. Other Asian countries now look set to see a multiplication of 'mini Singapores' as the state seeks to capitalize on its expertise in infrastructure provision and investment promotion.

## Conclusion

The operation of the land market has tended to be an overlooked contributor to Singapore's economic success. The British bequeathed vast areas of state-owned land, including prime sites, to the new administration. This greatly reduced the financial cost to the state in building new towns and industrial estates. This advantage was reinforced by the harsh provisions of the Land Acquisition Act, designed under the general dictum in Singapore that the needs of society, as defined by the government, supersede those of the individual. This legislation simplified the development process, reduced development costs and provided significant revenue that helped maintain low taxation. At the same time, the CPF provided a further source of resources for infrastructure development. These forced savings collected at their peak 50% of gross wages. These deductions were accepted without the resentment that a similar volume of taxation would cause, partly for the simple reason that the contributions remain in the contributor's name and can be used for housing purchase.

But while the land market has so far been an important buttress to the state's economic and political programme, signs of tension are becoming evident. As levels of affluence have grown, and development has consumed more of the limited space available, the government has been increasingly challenged to accommodate expanding lifestyle aspirations. Concern with the protection of the few remaining areas of wildlife habitat has encouraged one of the few examples of organized campaigning against government intentions. Among other sections of the population, the desire for private car ownership and more diverse housing environments outside the monolithic HDB estates present other challenges to the highly regulated landscape. In this context, the expansion of leisure space in the Riau islands and the creation of a so-called intelligent island are projects of great importance to the continuing willingness of those with the possibility of emigration to live within the highly structured landscape of contemporary Singapore.

# 7

# Planning and environment

One of the major hallmarks of modern Singapore lies in its intensively planned environment. The city's rapid transformation from a landscape of slums and squatters in the immediate postwar years to a self-styled 'tropical garden city' of apartment blocks and skyscrapers has often been attributed to the success of land use planning or what McGee (1972) calls 'deliberate urbanization'. Indeed, it has been argued that in the context of Singapore, planning is 'essential to the nation's survival' given, first, the country's scarce land resources (physical limitations in terms of both size and natural resources) and the need to optimize land utilization to meet different demands (such as housing, industries, commercial uses, communications, defence and security, and water supply) and, secondly, the need to constantly maintain a balance between facilitating economic and urban growth and providing a good living and working environment (Tan, 1972, p. 2; Cheong-Chua, 1995, p. 110). Planning seeks 'to influence spatial development' and is 'integrated into a wider national policy' where 'the overall planning goals are expressed in national rather than in communal or individual terms' (Teo, 1992, p. 171). According to the *Revised Master Plan, Report of Survey* (1985, p. 4) published by the Ministry of National Development, planning is necessary to facilitate the optimal use of Singapore's scarce resources and the resolution of development conflicts 'in the overall interest of the state for the common good'. Land use planning has thus been a *sine qua non* in all government development programmes and a major influence on private developments. The planning machinery is assisted by over 80% of the land being government-owned (Chapter 6).

Similar arguments are used to justify Singapore's 'pragmatic but effective' environmental planning and management policies: economic and industrial growth must be accorded the highest priority in order to ensure a high standard of living for the people but the physical environment must be protected given the country's land and natural resource constraints which leave no margins for error. As argued in a recent plan to create a 'Model Green City': 'The physical environment should not suffer because of strong economic growth and rapid urbanization. We have actively pursued policies to safeguard the environment by adopting an integrated approach on the environment and development' (quoted in Koh, 1995, p. 164).

In Singapore it is accepted that the key to sustainable urbanization and development is 'proper planning and control' (Hui, 1995, p. 26). Indeed, the current political leadership's manifesto is inextricably linked to a carefully planned and consciously visionary future which envisages the creation of 'a tropical city of excellence'.

This chapter examines land use planning and environmental planning in turn. For each type of planning, the general goals as well as strategies and measures used by respective planning agencies to carry out their plans are discussed. Planning cannot be conceived simply as a technical exercise which generates physical solutions; instead, it is inevitably locked into a wider political framework. As Bristow (1992, p. 26) observes, land use planning is 'an intensely political activity. . . . Allocations of land, or decisions about its use, give benefits to some and impose costs on others: the purpose of a land-use planning administrative system is to cause such decisions to be taken in the public domain, and usually to make them subject to democratic and in varied ways, participatory control'. To examine some of these issues and illustrate the politics of planning, we focus on several areas of debate on planning issues in a final section.

## Planning a 'Tropical City of Excellence' – land use plans

*The Master Plan*

The land use planning system in Singapore is an amalgam of colonial, mainly British ideas and formulations as well as local influence. As discussed in Chapter 2, while British ideas on the future development of Singapore conceived in the waning years of colonial rule and contained in the Master Plan of 1958 did not survive independence, the statutory basis and general framework of proposed land uses stayed in place. The concept of regulatory control through zoning envisaged in the Master Plan remains the basis of land use control. The planning system introduced through the Planning Ordinance of 1959, because it depended on the discretionary powers of administrators to approve or reject each development proposal on a site by site basis, actually proved ideally suited to Singapore's transition to an independent state (Bristow, 1992, p. 28). It proved flexible enough to 'accommodate the new policy preferences of the incoming PAP government' and at the same time 'enabled development to go ahead despite the rapid outdatedness of the Master Plan's zoning proposals'.

In the post-independence period, provisions were made for a mandatory quinquennial review of the Master Plan to take into account the changing socio-economic needs of the country. It has in fact undergone five revisions, in 1965, 1970, 1975, 1980 and 1985. By providing the statutory basis for controlling physical development, regulating land values and the levy of development charges, the Master Plan facilitates the coordination of physical development within the country, both private and public, and the reservation of adequate and appropriate sites through zoning for different commercial, industrial, residential and social needs of the country (Figure 7.1). Since the early 1960s, physical development projects of the government and statutory boards have been exempt from the limiting constraints of the Plan. In the case of private development, the Master Plan is a reference point for control rather than an absolute constraint. Development at densities in excess of the limits identified in the Plan or which deviates from the zoning prescriptions is permitted on the payment of a development charge calculated according to a standard formula.

*The Concept Plan*

Although the Master Plan is reviewed every five years, it is inadequate as a guide to large-scale or long-term public developments. In view of this, a new planning idea – the Concept Plan – was sought in the 1960s to guide long-range public developments which could generate an increased supply of housing and job opportunities. The Concept Plan grew out of a 1967 State and City Planning Project, launched with the assistance of the United Nations Development Programme to study land use and transportation needs, with the aim of drawing up long-range plans for land allocation and development according to estimated needs. The Concept Plan encourages planning efficiency by providing statutory boards and other public agencies with a coordinating framework, elevating planning to essentially 'a technocratic exercise and as a matter of process' (Teo, 1992, p. 177).

**Figure 7.1** Master Plan of 1958

The Concept Plan is flexible to accommodate changes, for example, in projected population growth trends, as it is an advisory plan rather than a statutory document for urban development as in the case of the Master Plan. It does however form the basis for the quinquennial reviews of the Master Plan (Gamer, 1972, pp. 138–46; *Revised Master Plan, Report of Survey*, 1980, pp. 6–7; *Ministry of National Development Annual Report*, 1987, p. 15).

The first Concept Plan or Ring Plan (Figure 7.2), envisaged the development of a ring-cum-linear urban form, with the water catchment area at the centre of the ring. Selected from several alternative strategies, it aimed at facilitating economic growth and satisfying housing requirements and basic social needs of the population. Key infrastructural provisions included a new international airport at Changi, and improvements in land transportation through a network of expressways and a Mass Rapid Transit (MRT) System. The plan envisaged high-density public housing concentrated along corridors close to high capacity transportation routes and at the same time within easy reach of industrial centres and other work areas. The central area, located in the southern part of the island, was to be cleared of residential population and industries through a policy of deliberate decentralization while a programme of urban renewal was conceived to revitalize the city core and develop it into an international financial, commercial and tourist centre. The Ring Plan helped to economize on transport infrastructure, cater to the people's housing needs, divert competition for space away from the city centre and generally maximized space for economic activity (Teo, 1992, p. 173). Major housing areas developed in line with the ring concept included the New Towns of Bishan, Ang Mo Kio, Yishun, Woodlands and Bukit Batok.

## The Revised Concept Plan and New Master Plan

Following a re-evaluation of Singapore's future economic, social and demographic development, a Revised Concept Plan (Figure 7.3) was formulated and released in September 1991 (published by the Urban Redevelopment Authority). It maps out the vision for Singapore's land use and long-term development in three stages, Year 2000, Year 2010 and Year X, the point when Singapore's population is expected to reach four million. In substance, it provides the physical framework, the 'blueprint' for 'living the next lap', a catchphrase encapsulating the hopes of a better quality of life as Singapore achieves developed country status (see Chapter 10). Major changes envisaged include four regional centres at Woodlands, Tampines, Jurong East and Seletar, each serving up to 800 000

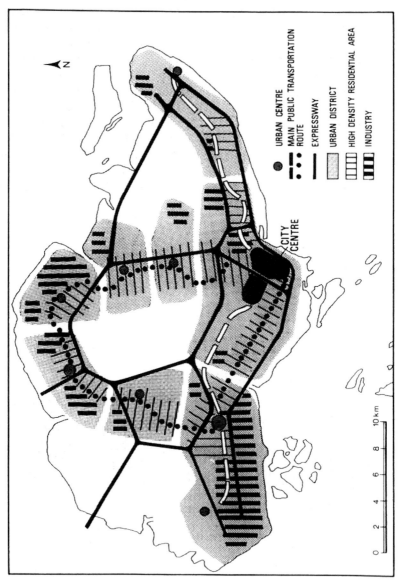

**Figure 7.2** Ring Concept Plan of 1971

people in new 'satellite regions'; a new world-class downtown area around Marina Bay which is not only to be an international business hub but also a 'showcase' of hotels, offices, shops and nightlife; more business parks located within 'technology corridors' close to major transportation nodes and regional centres; an extended and improved transport system with new expressways and semi-expressways, an extended MRT network, a new light rail system, a new ferry system, and more cycleways and walkways; better quality housing including a greater proportion of low-rise and medium-rise homes to complement high-rise housing; and a widening of leisure and recreational facilities afforded by incorporating more green spaces and water into the urban fabric as well as more cultural and entertainment centres (*Living the Next Lap*, 1991, p. 6). In spirit, the plan encapsulates three strands of thought which have become increasingly evident in post-independence planning principles: the vision of Singapore as a global city; the issue of Singapore's national survival in the light of its physical limitations and economic and political viability; and the articulation of national goals as a strategy for energizing individual and national effort (Teo, 1992).

The broad vision of the Revised Concept Plan is translated into specific proposals in localized plans called Development Guide Plans (DGPs). DGPs take into account the development potential of the area in making

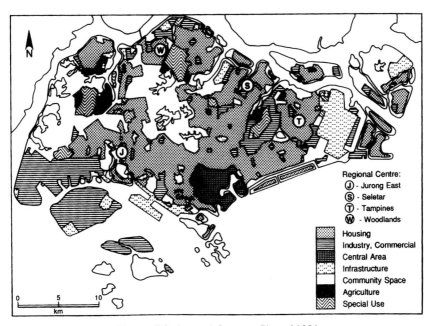

**Figure 7.3** Revised Concept Plan of 1991

provision for housing, commerce, industries, transportation, institutional uses such as schools, hospitals and places of worship, parks and open spaces as well as spelling out the intensities of development allowed for the various land uses (Figures 7.4 and 7.5). At this planning level, Singapore is currently divided into several DGP Regions further subdivided into a total of 55 planning areas, each to be the subject of an individual DGP. As each DGP is completed, it is gazetted as the revised statutory Master Plan and replaces the corresponding part of the 1985 Master Plan. All 55 DGPs are expected to be completed by the end of 1997, when they will collectively form the new Master Plan covering the whole of Singapore. In 1990, the five major residential DGP Regions (North, North-East, East, West and Central) accommodated 99.3% of the total population; it is anticipated that these five Regions will continue to absorb nearly all the population up to the year 2020 (Cheng, 1995, p. 99).

## Land use planning agencies

The planning system in Singapore is concerned with the making of plans and with the control of development (that is, the control of change in land use and buildings). Given the predominance of public agencies in the land development process, development control has played a less important role in the statutory planning system than in Britain, from where the design of the planning system was inherited and where private land ownership and development is the norm. While the Master Plan and Concept Plan set out land utilization policy, development control is concerned with the day-to-day implementation of that policy and is carried out through the legal machinery operating under the Planning Act. The primary objective of statutory planning is to prevent undesirable development of land and to ensure that the public interest is considered prior to change occurring in the development of land, an aim which is open to interpretation and inevitably carries political overtones. Where statutory planning control is deemed inadequate to facilitate the desired level of control, the government has recourse to the land acquisition machinery (discussed in Chapter 6) where land may be compulsorily acquired from private owners and subsequently disposed of under leasehold grants subject to restrictive covenants and other terms and conditions. The administration of planning, including development control, is generally the responsibility of the Planning Department of the Urban Redevelopment Authority (URA). Other authorities with a role to play in physical land use planning include Jurong Town Corporation, mainly through its interest in industrial land, and agencies which provide community facilities.

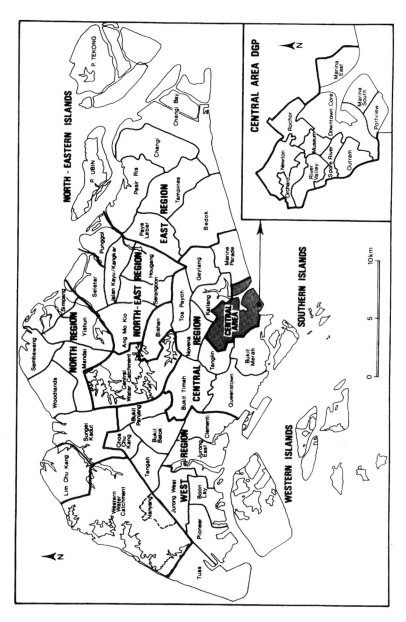

**Figure 7.4** Development Guide Plan areas

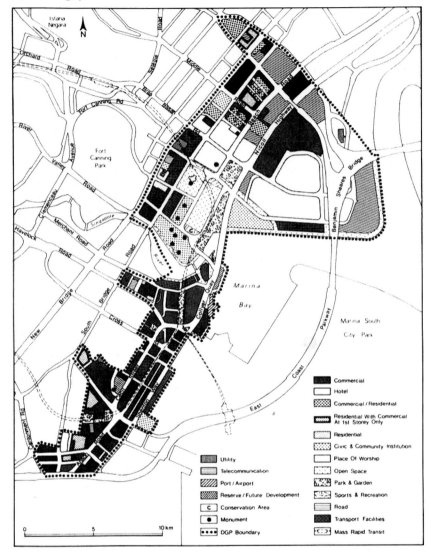

**Figure 7.5** The Downtown Core planning area

*The Urban Redevelopment Authority*

As Singapore's national planning and conservation authority, the URA is responsible for implementing the long-term land use and development strategies of the Revised Concept Plan. Its predecessor, the Urban Renewal Department (URD), a branch of the Housing and Development Board (HDB), was formed to combat urban problems such as severe overcrowding, housing shortages and unhealthy living conditions which had plagued the central area since pre-independence days (see Chapter 2). In 1974, the URA was constituted as a separate statutory body by the Urban Renewal Act to take over the functions of renewal and redevelopment of the URD and also to take on increased planning responsibilities and wider functions. In 1989, it was amalgamated with the Planning Department and the Research and Statistics Unit of the Ministry of National Development to become the national planning and conservation body, widening its purview from the city centre to the whole country.

In the early years, the imperatives of nation building and the need for rapid development dictated the planning agenda. The priorities of urban renewal were to provide a 'healthier environment for the population of Singapore as well as to make better usage of the land for commercial, industrial, residential and recreational purposes' (*HDB Annual Report*, 1963, p. 27). This involved the clearing of slums, rebuilding of obsolete properties and comprehensive planning for traffic and circulation systems in central areas; the planning and designing of public housing and other amenities such as shops, markets, hawker stalls, offices, car parks, open spaces, sewers, drains, water mains and so forth. Slum clearance and redevelopment were given priority not simply on environmental grounds but because slums were thought to be breeding grounds of communism and hence deserving clearance, according to the HDB commemorative volume *The First Decade of Housing in Singapore 1960–1969*. For the purposes of urban renewal and comprehensive planning, the central area was subdivided into 20 'precincts' to be dealt with sequentially. The priority accorded to each precinct depended on the availability of land, conditions of its present living environment, the need to undertake public and other infrastructural improvement and its prospect of acting as a catalyst in stimulating redevelopment in the surrounding areas (Chua, 1973, p. 42). Precinct South I and Precinct North I, located amidst highly congested, slum-ridden areas south and north of the Singapore River were selected as pilot areas for conversion into 'modern residential-cum-business complexes with their full complement of social amenities such as markets, hawker centres, car parks, schools, landscaped parks and pedestrian malls' (Choe, 1975, p. 108).

In the 1960s, the main impediments to comprehensive redevelopment of the city centre were the fragmentation of land ownership, congested slums and squatters. The Land Acquisition Act introduced in 1966 (see Chapter 6) gave the government the power to acquire land on a compulsory basis for public development, 'with little room for owners to challenge an acquisition gazette order once this was in force' (Cheong-Chua, 1995, p. 121). There was little, if any, scope for challenging an intended acquisition, only a process of appeal on the quantum of compensation,

**Plate 7.1** Eu Tong Sen Street (Chinatown) in the 1960s. Photograph courtesy of the URA

which was circumscribed by the framework of the Act. Apart from a tough policy on land acquisition, slum clearance also entailed massive resettlement of affected families and businesses. By comparison, resettlement benefits for occupiers of land (as opposed to owners) were generous.

As well as the scale of public housing construction, families resettled obtained cash compensation, priority in the allocation of space in one of the new planned estates and incentives that made owner occupation an attractive option (see Chapter 8). Shopkeepers affected by resettlement schemes were accorded priority in renting alternative HDB premises at subsidized rates (Choe, 1975, p. 105). The Controlled Premises (Special Provisions) Act of 1969 was a further stimulus to slum clearance. It assisted the revitalization of rent-controlled areas where landowners had difficulty selling or developing their land because sitting tenants demanded high awards for moving out. The Act enabled landlords to recover possession of rent-controlled premises in a designated development area, established a Tenants' Compensation Board to hear applications for recovery of possession of such premises, and determined the amount of compensation to be paid to tenants and subtenants on account of such recovery of possession. In 1970, the provisions of the Act were applied to 32 hectares of commercial land in the heart of the Central Business District involving 770 properties, a tract of land subsequently known as the 'Golden Shoe', in view of its high value and shape. Along with the sale of the adjoining vacant reclaimed state land, rent decontrol in the Golden Shoe area has been 'jointly responsible for the growth and transformation of the Central Business District during the last two decades' (Phang, 1992, p. 29).

An important tool in URA's planning machinery is the URA Sale of Sites programme initiated in 1967. This approach promotes a form of public–private sector collaboration for the development of new offices, retail complexes and hotels in the city centre and is best carried out by the private sector. Under this programme, the government provides the infra-structure and releases the land through a public competitive tender system. The private developer bids for the land and provides capital and expertise to realize the development project. As the clearing of slums and

**Plate 7.2** Eu Tong Sen Street (Chinatown) after redevelopment into the People's Park Centre. Photograph courtesy of the URA

squatters from the central area proceeds, land is freed and small plots reassembled into parcels for release and comprehensive redevelopment.

In the earlier sales programme of the 1960s and 1970s, the focus was on redeveloping the central business area to create a modern financial district. Many of the projects along the Shenton Way financial corridor like Shenton House, Robina House and UIC Building were sold (Chua, 1989). Other sites in New Bridge Road and Outram Road, for example, were sold to encourage the development of medium-priced shopping and office space and apartments. Hotel sites were also sold to provide the necessary infrastructure for tourism projects, creating hotel belts near the Singapore River and along Orchard Road. Condominium projects were also sold through the programme. More recently, recreational projects have been sold on the reclaimed land known as Marina South on shorter leases so that the land can be put to interim use until such time as the land is required for the expansion of the financial and business service centre. After the URA assumed the role of national conservation authority in the 1990s, projects have also been sold for conservation, the largest single project thus far being the Clarke Quay riverside conservation project covering 2.1 hectares. Initially, financial incentives, such as tax concessions and an instalment scheme, were used to attract the appropriate types of development in designated areas. As economic prospects were transformed, such incentives were withdrawn. By the end of 1993, a total of 520 land parcels totalling 246 hectares had been sold under the Sales programme since it began in 1967 (Cheong-Chua, 1995, pp. 122–23).

Through the sales programme, the government controls the location, pace and type of urban development. By controlling the release of land, the government attempts to ensure that sufficient land is made available to ensure that development proceeds at a steady pace to sustain economic growth, so minimizing the possibilities of property market gluts and shortages. Urban design objectives are accommodated through conditions attached to the tender documents that control the form and scale of buildings. For example, buildings along Shenton Way were required to have a low podium of four storeys to provide visual uniformity and human scale. Continuous covered walkways and overhead pedestrian bridges were also required to safeguard pedestrian access as well as extensive landscaping and plaza spaces to improve the general environment of sale sites (Cheong-Chua, 1995, p. 123). In order to introduce greater flexibility in the planning system, a recent innovation is the designation of selected sites as 'white sites' where developers can subsequently change the use of the land in response to changing market conditions without having to pay a differential premium (*Business Times*, 26 October 1995). In essence, this allows developers to opt for any type of development as long as the permissible gross floor area is not exceeded.

**Plate 7.3** Robina House in the Golden Shoe financial district. Photograph courtesy of the URA

Where development does not involve recently sold land, development control gives the URA influence over the use of space. Private developers wishing to initiate projects can consult the Master Plan to determine the areas they are permitted to build. They submit both ground layouts and building blueprints to the Development Control Division which checks that the plans conform to building specifications and zoning regulations and that the site has not been potentially designated for public purposes (Gamer, 1972, p. 52). In 1987, in order to streamline planning procedure so as to shorten processing time for applications, a Simplified Planning Approval System was introduced. By simplifying submission requirements and allowing plans to be simultaneously submitted for planning and building control approval, processing time is shortened to six weeks (Khublall and Yuen, 1991, p. 86).

Both the Sale of Sites programme and development control involve either harnessing or controlling private sector development. In the case of proposed public developments, whether on private or state land, evaluation is first undertaken by the URA in the light of the long-range objectives of the Concept Plan, the provisions of the Master Plan or DGP and national development objectives. On completion of the evaluation, a report is submitted to the Master Plan Committee (comprising the Chief Planner and representatives from various public bodies) and ultimately to the Minister for National Development for consideration and approval. Once approval is granted, the URA acts to help ensure that the site becomes available for public development and that the use of adjoining sites is compatible with the intended development. The relevant agency will then implement the approved development, a procedure which involves either the acquisition of land by the government if it is in private ownership, or the vesting of the land in the relevant development agency in the case of state land (Khublall and Yuen, 1991, p. 190).

With the launch of the Revised Concept Plan, the URA's sights shifted from slum clearance and urban renewal to a more visionary role to create an urban design that would complement Singapore's aspirations of becoming a global city on a par with the first league of developed nations. This is evident in the URA's revised Mission Statement which is 'to plan and facilitate the physical development of Singapore as a city of excellence with a distinctive identity reflecting on geographical location, cultural heritage and meeting the economic, social and political aspirations of Singaporeans'. In pursuit of an aesthetically more pleasing living environment, urban planning is inextricably linked with environmental planning.

### Planning the 'Environment City'

Environmental concerns featured early in the post-independence years in Singapore and the 'green vision' has formed part of the evolving planning agenda. In 1963, a tree-planting campaign was initiated by the then Prime Minister, Lee Kuan Yew while the notion of a 'Green and Clean City' has been the declared goal of the government since 1968. In terms of institutional machinery, an Anti-Pollution Unit (APU) was formed under the auspices of the Prime Minister's Office in 1970 to ensure that rapid industrialization did not destroy the quality of ambient air. A fully-fledged Ministry of Environment (ENV) was set up in 1972 to improve sanitation services including sewerage and drainage, promote public health and to address problems of solid waste, air and water pollution, industrial water production, and environmentally hazardous chemicals. It is one of the first Ministries specifically for the protection of the environment in the world (Hui, 1995, p. 14). Apart from the Ministry of Environment, other government bodies also play a role in managing and protecting the environment including the Ministry of National Development which is responsible for urban renewal, development and planning, public housing, public works, parks and recreation, construction industry development, building control and land development.

Up to the early 1970s, Singapore's environmental achievements were mixed. In the immediate post-independence years, the government's environmental concerns were primarily with public health issues, for example, the provision of low-cost public housing (see Chapter 8) with the emphasis on a more hygienic alternative to overcrowded slums and squatters, rather than ecological ones. Savage (1991, 1992) argues that during these early years, the government's stance was 'quasi environmentally deterministic' in that the environment was only of interest to the extent it affected public health, and ultimately, the productivity of the labour force. Similarly, the greening campaign can be seen as part of a beautification policy to prevent rapidly industrializing Singapore from degenerating into an urban nightmare and to assist the creation of national pride and identity for Singaporeans.

A 1972 United Nations sponsored report on the Human Environment gave credit to the government's attempt to promote a green Singapore through its tree-planting programme. Less positively, it noted gross pollution of rivers, canals and the marine environment as a result of indiscriminate dumping of agricultural, industrial and domestic waste as well as the deteriorating air quality as a result of sulphur dioxide emissions from major oil refining centres (Bankoff and Elston, 1994, p. 49). Environmental legislation was inadequate, enforcement ineffective and overall, environmental concerns not only played second fiddle to economic ones but were perceived to detract from economic development. In the last 20 years, however, the environment has emerged as a major consideration in government planning. Indeed, most writers who have commented on Singapore's overall environmental standards in recent years not only applaud the country's modern environmental infrastructure and effective environment management systems but attribute successful environmental protection programmes to government management and Singapore's 'political culture of ecological consciousness' (Savage and Kong, 1993, p. 39; Hui, 1995, p. 13; Koe and Aziz, 1995, p. 219). The government's increasing concern with environmental issues can be closely linked to the 'reassessment of the role of the environment as an economic factor of importance in the development of the national economy' in three ways

(Bankoff and Elston, 1994). First, as Singapore's economic development is highly dependent on international capital and overseas markets, it behoves the government to be aware of changes in, and attempt to conform to, internationally accepted environmental standards. Thus, Singapore is a signatory of international treaties such as the 1985 Vienna Convention for the Protection of the Ozone Layer and the 1987 Montreal Protocol on Substances that Deplete the Ozone Layer, an important treaty for Singapore in view of the widespread use of chlorofluorocarbons in the electronics industry. Second, environmental improvement is part of the 'increasingly strong economic imperative' to meet the environmental aspirations and recreational demands of skilled and mobile professional and managerial workers in order to stem the small but significant emigration of these key participants in the island's economic success. Third, with increasing worldwide interest in eco- and heritage tourism, the environment is now perceived as a profitable 'commodity in its own right'.

In general, two main directions can be discerned in the formulation of environmental policy in Singapore: the eradication of pollutive and insanitary landscapes, and relatedly, the creation of a clean and green city. These two strands in the making of Singapore's interpretation of an 'environment city' will be discussed in turn.

## Eradicating pollutive landscapes

As already indicated earlier, the imperative to remove unhygienic activities from the city provided part of the rationale for the clearance of slums and squatter settlements from the central area and the relocation of people and businesses into the new, controlled environments of public housing satellite towns. Along with slum clearance and the provision of public housing, other major environmental improvement schemes include stringent control of sources of pollution; the construction of hygienic hawker and food centres; the clearing out of pollutive activities in association with the cleaning of rivers.

The environmental control of land-based sources of pollution is a key criterion in land use planning decisions so as to minimize and regulate the effects of pollution. About 5% of the main island of Singapore around the reservoirs of MacRitchie, Seletar, Upper and Lower Peirce have been set aside as protected water catchment areas where development is not permitted. In addition, about 36% of land comprising the catchments of Kranji, Pandan, Sarimbun, Murai, Tengeh, Poyan, Sungei Seletar and Jurong Lake are also developed as unprotected water catchment areas where only clean industries are allowed. Apart from protecting catchment areas,

all proposed new developments are also screened by the Pollution
Controls Department (PCD) of the ENV for the environmental impact of
the development and its compatibility with the surrounding land use.
New industrial developments, for example, are assessed by the PCD to
ensure that measures are incorporated into the manufacturing processes
to minimize the generation of industrial effluent and treatment of such
effluent according to prescribed procedures and standards (Koe and Aziz,
1995, p. 205). In addition, for major developments like potentially pollutive industries, industries storing and handling large quantities of hazardous chemicals, port development and landfill development which are
likely to have a significant impact on the environment, an environmental
impact assessment (EIA) covering possible adverse impacts of the development and the measures recommended to eliminate or minimize the
impacts may be required by the ENV. Hesp (1995, p. 136), however, suggests that there is a degree of cynicism about EIAs amongst the public,
NGOs and other environmental groups as these are not made available to
the public and only carried out if the government deems them necessary.
There is also 'a strong tendency to approve a Government sponsored project first, and perhaps, then conduct an EIA'.

Beyond the planning stage, a battery of legislative controls have been
enacted to control pollution. These include the Prevention of the Pollution
of the Sea Act which controls oil pollution and other contaminants; the
Clean Air Act which stipulates that emission levels from all industrial and
trade premises must be kept within the standards set for various air pollutants; the Water Pollution Control and Drainage Act which controls the
discharge of waste water from domestic, industrial, agricultural and other
premises; and the Environmental Public Health Act which regulates, *inter
alia*, the collection, conveyance and disposal of solid waste. The philosophy behind this legislation is the 'polluter pays' principle (Hui, 1995,
p. 16). To ensure that sources that generate pollution are responsible for
the cost of pollution control, legislation requires factories to install and
operate pollution control equipment in order to comply with the emission
limits (for air pollutants) and effluent limits (for water pollutants) stipulated by the regulations. Environmental policy is essentially gradualist in
its approach: as control technology improves, standards are progressively
raised over the years. Legislative controls are backed by systematic monitoring of air and water quality and stringent enforcement in the form of
both regular inspections and spot checks on factories and other premises.
The ENV also works with other government agencies to control pollution
at its sources as in the case of the regulation of car ownership where
efforts are made jointly between ENV, the Registrar of Vehicles and the
Traffic Police to control smoke emission from vehicles.

Success in regulating air pollutants has been uneven: while the levels of total acidity and urban smoke have declined in the last two decades, nitrogen oxide and dust fallout levels have been more variable (Ooi, 1995, p. 141). It has also been noted that while Singapore has built up 'a reputation' for high air- and water-emission standards and effective waste treatment facilities, a major area of neglect is the problem of the release of large sediment loads into the coastal waters as a result of 'unconfined dumping of earth spoils, harbour-dredging operations, and on-going reclamation works', leading to the degradation of mangrove forest and coral reefs in Singapore's coastal environment (Hilton and Manning, 1995, p. 316).

Street hawkers and vendors, considered sources of pollution in many Third World cities, were the main targets of a campaign to sanitize the city from colonial days (see Chapter 2). They were frowned upon by official sources for a litany of reasons: traffic obstruction; water and environmental pollution caused by trade effluent and waste products such as poultry droppings, fish, vegetable, fruit and food wastes and dregs; the danger of food-borne diseases such as typhoid and cholera resulting from unhygienic handling of food, prompted by conditions of high temperatures and humidity; and the encumbrance of land which could be given over to other national development projects (Thoo, 1982, pp. 102–3). According to one official source, in 1980, there were 27 000 hawkers with a large number operating in the central area, particularly in side streets, city streets and along five-foot-ways (*Revised Master Plan, Report of Survey*, 1980, p. 33). This large number still prevailed despite the fact that some 19 300 hawkers had already been resettled in purpose-designed centres by 1979. Control measures including a licensing policy have been introduced, allowing the relevant state departments to keep track of the number and type of hawkers and to cap the numbers where necessary. The most concrete and visible impact on the landscape has been the relocation of street hawkers, both itinerant and stationary, to purpose-built markets and food centres well supplied with electricity, piped water, refuse receptacles, sewerage systems and storage facilities. For example, in 1983, one of the oldest and biggest agglomerations of street hawkers in Singapore located in the heart of Chinatown was cleared and rehoused in the Kreta Ayer Market and Food Centre (Yeoh and Kong, 1994).

Another notable success in terms of pollution control is the cleaning up of the Singapore River and the Kallang Basin catchments which cover about one-fifth of the total land area of Singapore. Over the years, the Singapore River and its tributaries had slowly degenerated into open sewers and rubbish dumps as all forms of waste were discharged into them by industries, farms, unsewered premises and hawkers located within the catchment area. Pollution was further aggravated by the rapid growth in population, industrialization and urbanization in the 1960s and 1970s. Mooted by the then Prime Minister, Lee Kuan Yew, the government embarked on a ten-year comprehensive programme in 1977 to clean up these watercourses. The main objective was 'to remove the sources of pollution and eradicate filth and stench permanently in the rivers and canals so that aquatic life could thrive once again in them . . . in keeping with Singapore's resolve to be clean and green' (Hui, 1995, p. 19). An action plan coordinated by ENV but also involving various other agencies like the URA, HDB, PSA, the Parks and Recreation Department and the Primary Production Department entailed phasing out pollutive activities such as pig and duck farming, the resettlement of squatters, backyard trades and industries and farmers contributing to the pollution of the river, extending the sewerage system and redeveloping run down areas, apart from the actual cleaning up of the river itself. About 90% of the pollution load identified was eliminated from the catchments within ten years, resulting in improved water quality and the return of aquatic life in the rivers.

## Creating a garden city

In the mid-1960s, the concept of a 'Garden City' was introduced to guide the planning and development of an island with abundant greenery. In

**Plate 7.4** Singapore River in the 1970s. Photograph courtesy of the URA

the words of the then Minister of Health, Chua Sian Chin, during a 1968 Parliamentary session: 'The improvement in the quality of our urban environment and the transformation of Singapore into a garden city – a clean and green city – is the declared objective of the Government' (quoted in Koh, 1995, p. 148).

The western 'Garden City', as proposed by the visionary Ebenezer Howard in the late nineteenth century, suggested a systematically laid out town of limited size surrounded by a permanent belt of agricultural land serving as a buffer zone and developed on land held in common by the community (Cherry, 1988, pp. 64–69). The 'Garden City' in Singapore was more literally interpreted to mean introducing plants into the city to procure a green mantle. This was achieved through the large-scale planting of trees and shrubs all over the island, which complemented the annual Tree Planting Day, initiated in 1963 by the then Prime Minister, Lee Kuan Yew. The primary rationale behind what was to develop into a comprehensive programme for 'the greening of Singapore' was clearly as a means of improving the quality of the environment, in view of the heightened activity in the building industry, rapid urbanization and massive alteration of the landscape in the post-independence period.

At the institutional level, various committees and departments were created to take the responsibility for creating an aesthetically pleasing

**Plate 7.5** Singapore River in the 1980s, Clarke Quay on the right prior to conservation. Photograph courtesy of the URA

Garden City. In 1965, a Garden City Action Committee was formed to implement the Garden City Concept, taking on an overall policy making role. This committee comprised representatives from all the main agencies with a role in land development as well as the Parks and Recreation Department and the URA. In 1968, the Parks and Trees Division of the Public Works Department (PWD) was formed to undertake the task of greening Singapore. In 1973, it merged with the Singapore Botanic Gardens to form the Parks and Recreation Division under the PWD. Reflecting the increasingly important role of this division, it became in 1975 an independent department under the Ministry of National Development. In 1990, with further acknowledgement of the importance of nature areas in Singapore, the National Parks Board (NPB) was set up to administer the Botanic Gardens and Fort Canning Park as national parks and the nature reserves. In the mid-1990s, the Parks and Recreation division also became a department under the NPB. The number of official departments and committees set up over the years to bring to fruition the green vision reveals the level of government commitment to this vision and the determination to see it realized (Kong and Yeoh, 1996).

At the legislative level, the Parks and Trees Act was introduced in 1975. This piece of legislation provided for the 'development, protection and regulation of public parks and gardens and for the preservation and growing of trees and plants' (Parks and Trees Act, 1985, p. 2) in the Republic. It spelt out specifically that any proposed development had to meet with certain standards in landscaping and tree planting, subject to control by the Parks and Recreation Department and the PWD. The Act also required that landowners spruce up their property and made it an offence to wilfully destroy trees, plants and turf areas (Kong and Yeoh, 1996).

In the 1960s and 1970s, the Garden City idea was pursued by establishing a green mantle across the island to provide shade and to keep the environment cool (Lee, 1995, p. 133). The planting of trees, particularly those of the fast-growing 'instant' variety such as the Angsana, Pong Pong, Rain Tree and Yellow Flame, along roadside verges and road dividers, in open spaces, public gardens, parks, recreational grounds, approaches to public buildings including amidst heavily built up areas such as the Central Business District, soon cloaked parts of the city in abundant greenery. As the programme progressed and Singapore attained a reputation as a 'green' city, the aesthetic qualities of introducing nature into a highly urbanized area were given new directions in the 1980s. In 1980, for example, Lee Kuan Yew foresaw that:

> By the 1990s, Singapore can become a green, shady city filled with fruits and flowers; a city worthy of an industrious people whose quest for progress is matched by their appreciation for the beauty of nature. The harshness of tar-

mac and concrete can be softened by nature's trees, flowers and birds (quoted in Lee, 1995, p. 130).

A few strands can be discerned in the shift in vision for the Garden City in the 1980s and 1990s. First, the aim of 'colouring' the island to create an aesthetically pleasant environment received further attention. Specifically, the Parks and Recreation Department increasingly introduced a variety of ornamental trees and flowering shrubs brought from other countries and more kaleidoscopic colours in the choice of vegetation. Plants are introduced to camouflage concrete structures in order to soften the harshness, and in particular creepers and climbers are trained on to retaining walls, lamp-posts, flyovers and overhead bridges. Ironically, until recently, the authorities have been concerned with clearing away what was seen as extraneous growths on wayside trees such as ferns, algae and other epiphytes on the excuse that these caused branches to rot or served as a breeding ground for mosquitoes (Wee, 1990, p. 531). In the Singapore idea of the Garden City, fruit trees are also given some emphasis, not simply for adding variety but also in order to provide educational opportunities for the younger generation growing up in an urban setting to observe nature at work, and to inculcate 'social discipline' among residents responsible for managing fruit trees planted in their neighbourhoods (Lee, 1995, p. 137). Neighbourhood parks created in different parts of the city emphasize and capitalize on the aesthetic quality of nature. For example, Mount Faber Park and Kent Ridge Park take advantage of the panoramic views from hill and ridge tops while West Coast Park and East Coast Park make use of sea front views. As part of a plan formulated by the URA in 1976 and revised in 1980 to guide the design and use of open spaces in the central area, planting strips have been incorporated within road reserves to form green buffers along major roads so as to ensure a visually pleasant streetscape with a variety of colours and shades. The aim is to use nature as a landscaping tool to 'give the illusion of being in a city that has sprung out of a garden' (*Living the Next Lap*, 1991, p. 28). In sum, urban vegetation is carefully managed to meet aesthetic and architectural criteria; far less attention is given to spontaneous vegetation which provides food and protected nesting sites for birds and insects. The most popular street trees, for example are legumes with fruits inedible to birds and pesticides are liberally used to control insects (Corlett, 1992, p. 210).

Apart from a stronger focus on harnessing the aesthetic quality and variety of nature in urban areas in the 1980s and 1990s, there is also increasing emphasis on nature as a setting for recreational activities as part of the notion of living in a tropical Garden City. The vision is not only for 'a city and homes wrapped in tropical foliage to give a heightened

**Plate 7.6** Greenery to landscape urban expressways

impression of a Garden City' (*Living the Next Lap*, 1991, p. 7), but to cultivate nature as a 'playground' within easy access of residents. A hierarchy
of parks is a feature of HDB new towns: town parks of 5 to 10 hectares
each, neighbourhood parks of 1 to 1.5 hectares each, and precinct gardens
of approximately 0.2 hectares each. These form the recreational green
spaces in HDB new towns and are equipped with a range of facilities:
jogging tracks, children's playgrounds, playing fields, multi-purpose
courts, fitness corners, and landscaped areas with seats and shelters.
More recently, 'recreation in nature' is evident in the Park and Recreation
Department's proposal to link all parks in Singapore into a network
through the development of park connectors (Lee and Chua, 1992). These
parks and connectors act as buffer zones between two developments, creating a sense of spaciousness and offering new recreational opportunities.
When the network is completed, the island will in the planner's vision
approximate 'a single large playground and garden' as it will not only
create many green trails for jogging and strolling but allow a cyclist to
cycle from one park to another across the island. A variety of parks with
different themes – coastal parks, nature parks, riverine parks, reservoir
parks and adventure parks – also provide a wide range of leisure opportunities to suit different demands. For example, the Singapore River
Redevelopment Plan aims to turn the three major bodies of water and

their waterfronts into a grand stage for outdoor recreational activities, settings for water-based recreation, such as powerboat and dragon-boat races, swimming and boating (*URA Annual Report*, 1988/89, p. 4).

In sum, the planned vision is to make Singapore an 'Environment City', a city which is, in the words of Professor Tommy Koh (later chairman of the 1992 Earth Summit in Rio), 'like New York built inside Central Park' (Briffett, 1990, p. i). Toward this end, a major policy review on environmental concerns was carried out in the early 1990s and the result of the exercise published by the ENV in May 1992 as *The Singapore Green Plan – Towards a Model Green City* (1992). This was presented as Singapore's national-al plan in support of Agenda 21, a global action programme to achieve the goals of sustainable development and other environmental agreements reached at the Earth Summit in Rio de Janeiro in June 1992. The green plan was formulated at a time when 'the basic needs of Singaporeans have been met and rising affluence demands a corresponding increase in the quality of life . . . [including] a quality environment' (Lo and Quah, 1995, p. 226). It 'carried a vision of a city in the year 2000 with high standards of public health, with clean air, land, water and a quiet living environment – a city conducive to gracious living, with people who are concerned about and take a personal interest in the care of both the local and global environment, a city that will be a regional centre for environmental technolo-

**Plate 7.7** Greenery is encouraged to grow on overhead bridges

gy' (Hui, 1995, p. 25). Beyond continuing to emphasize the eradication of pollutive landscapes and the greening of the city as already discussed, the Green Plan also advocates new elements of environmental consciousness such as product recycling, green consumerism and eco-education. Recent surveys of environmental behaviour among Singaporean students and women have shown that Singaporeans are generally ignorant of and resistant to incorporating environmentally friendly practices in everyday life such as minimizing domestic waste, using recycling bins and buying environmentally friendly products (Lau, 1992–93; Ng, 1993–94; Savage, 1995). In general, 'the government's vision of a Garden City is couched in the still larger and more holistic perspective of turning Singapore into a fully-developed country inhabited by a cultivated people' (Yeh, 1989, p. 831). In pursuance of the plan, six inter-ministerial work groups have been established with a view to drawing up action programmes in the areas of environmental education; environmental technology; resource conservation; clean technologies; nature conservation; and environmental noise.

## Debates in urban and environmental planning

The government, statutory authorities and public agencies are the dominant influence over the pace and direction of urban growth. Indeed, Kian (1988) argues that Singapore's 'unique planning culture' is based on a 'dynamic, centralized, and top-down "action planning" approach to urban design and planning'. In the planning process, a high premium is set on allocative efficiency and order. As already discussed, planning goes beyond a question of physical coordination and carries ideological weight: it is firmly interwoven into the pursuit of national goals; it is a panacea to a country disadvantaged by scarce resources and central to Singapore's economic success; and it is rationalized by the rhetoric of the 'common good'.

Similarly, in the case of environmental planning, ecological imperatives are weighed in the balance against 'strategic' or 'national' interest, the latter usually interpreted in economic terms. The primacy of economic objectives in environmental planning is evident in four ways (Hilton and Manning, 1995, pp. 319–20). First, the government has been reluctant to implement EIA legislation despite the fact that this is widely accepted as a tool which facilitates better resource allocation and mitigates the adverse effects of development projects. Briffett and Malone-Lee (1992) argue that this is attributable to the government's concern that EIAs might hinder economic development. Secondly, nature is valorized mainly for its economic value, for example, as a tourist or recreational resource, and relatedly, confined to 'carefully selected sanctuaries' such as nature reserves (Kong and Yeoh, 1996). The government justifies this by emphasizing Singapore's land scarcity and finite resource base, a stance which legitimizes the rapid eradication of biodiversity outside nature reserves as 'inevitable', ignores 'more imaginative conservation, possibly involving habitat restoration or development/conservation integration', and privileges 'productive land uses that yield short-term economic returns'. Thirdly, areas designated as 'Nature Areas' in the Concept Plan have no legal status and are susceptible to disturbance or development if other competing uses of 'national or strategic interest' arise. According to the ministerial work group on nature conservation, 'a more pragmatic approach to nature conservation' is required as 'land is limited in Singapore'. Fourthly, the government tends to equate, erroneously, the gains from pollution control with 'conservation' and 'sustainable development'; instead, they argue that while the 'cleaning and greening' of Singapore have created an aesthetically pleasing environment, this has been 'at the expense of the indigenous terrestrial and marine habitats, ecological health, and indigenous biota'. This reflects an 'ecological pragmatism' (Savage, 1992, p. 207) where 'pragmatic' interest outweighs 'ecological' considerations.

Urban and environmental planning is thus orchestrated primarily around the *leitmotif* of economic development. The extent to which this legitimacy of the government's approach to planning has been accepted by the population at large has been the subject of much debate, particularly in respect of three issues which we discuss below: the approach to urban renewal of the city centre; the degree of public consultation in the planning process; and the role of NGOs in environmental planning.

*Urban renewal by demolition or rehabilitation*

The dramatic impact of urban renewal in the 1960s and 1970s on the city centre landscape is clearly evident. The complex patchwork of shophouses, backyard industries and street activities which characterized the old city has been razed to make way for high-rise commercial structures, middle class apartment blocks and hotels in less than two decades. While this transformation has been hailed as a success in presenting Singapore with a 'fully functional' city centre 'with adequate infrastructure and facilities' (*URA Annual Report*, 1986–87, p. 2) in official (and other) sources, others have been more critical.

Writing in the early 1970s, Gamer (1972, p. 131) argued that while Singapore's approach to land use planning is 'politically astute', 'fiscally sound', 'administratively convenient' and produces 'speedy results', it does not have the 'long-term merits of solving basic human problems'. More specifically, he contends that urban renewal based on the demolish-and-rebuild concept as practised by planners in the 1960s and early 1970s disrupted livelihoods, destroyed small retail establishments and marginal industries and accentuated class, language and racial rifts among the people. In his view, urban renewal should not mean wholesale demolition of structures but should include conservation, rehabilitation and rebuilding; in particular, the old city should be rehabilitated rather than demolished. This alternative approach was in fact proposed by two separate United Nations consultancy teams in the early 1960s. In 1962, United Nations consultant Erik Lorange conducted a six-month study on the feasibility of urban renewal in Singapore and was of the view that the old city should not be condemned as a slum but looked upon 'more positively as the location of many improvable businesses and buildings' (Gamer 1972, p. 139). A second United Nations team comprising architect and planner Otto Koenigsberger, legal adviser Charles Abrams and traffic economist Susumu Kobe who issued their report the following year also 'rejected the idea of wholesale demolition of large quarters', a decision 'motivated primarily by the desire to minimize the social upheaval and the suffering that would result from the dislocation of large numbers of people and business undertakings' and based on 'the recognition of the value and attraction of many of the existing shop houses and the way of living, working and trading that produced this particular Singapore type of architecture' (quoted in Gamer, 1972, p. 142). The team was of the view that 'every big city needs escape hatches from sameness and order, and areas like Chinatown can emerge into important examples if they are treated with something more subtle than the steam shovel' (quoted in Gamer, 1972, p. 142).

More than a decade later, Kian (1988) echoes the view of Gamer (1972) as well as others such as architect William Lim (1975) that urban renewal has 'helped create a clean, crystalized [sic] well ordered but drab and colorless environment in the CBD'. While the 'technocratic planning culture' has worked well as 'a socio-political and economic tool to counter adverse national development trends and to preserve and strengthen the middleman, entrepreneurial role of a "global city", it has 'all but destroyed the "spirit of the place" of [the] central area'. These critics recommend dismantling the 'tight plan, brick and mortar' approach to urban renewal and advocate a number of 'humanist' measures such as incorporating community inputs in the planning process, 'particularly [from] among the least articulate residents and marginal businesses of central area neighbourhoods'; using infill redevelopments of a variety of scales and types as opposed to large-scale demolition and rebuilding; and proceeding at a moderate pace to allow for 'continuous learning and avoidance' of planning mistakes and the 'natural reintegration of the city in time' instead of harking mainly to economic imperatives.

The views of these critics who draw inspiration from humanistic values and bottom-up approaches to development went unheeded by administrators and planners in the first two decades of urban redevelopment. Where the general public is concerned, a recent survey of people's views as to whether the demolish-and-rebuild approach to urban renewal (and the sidelining of conservation) in the 1960s and 1970s was justifiable found respondents fairly divided in their opinions (Kong and Yeoh, 1994). About half took the view that in the early years of Singapore's independence, economic development and the concomitant urban redevelopment, including wholesale demolition, had to take precedence. Only in recent years since the flourishing of Singapore's economy could attention be paid to the luxuries of conservation. Another group (slightly less than half) expressed regret that many buildings and areas that had already been demolished in the name of urban renewal could never be replaced.

In the late 1980s, there were signs of some rethinking regarding new directions for the growth and redevelopment of the city. With growing confidence that Singapore's 'bread and butter' issues have been resolved alongside greater concern with questions of national identity and heritage, new issues such as conserving the old and harnessing the city's legacy became more prominent on the urban planning agenda. Urban planning in the 1990s is not only emphasizing modern functionality and economic growth, but the creation of a 'distinctively Asian city' befitting 'a culturally vibrant society with people living a more gracious life' (*URA Annual Report*, 1987–88, p. 2; 1988–89, p. 4). This new thrust is discussed further in Chapters 9 and 10.

*Planning as an expert or participatory process*

While government rhetoric in the 1990s continues to stress rationality, pragmatism and efficiency as opposed to Gamer's (1972) and Kian's (1988) 'community inputs' and 'citizen participation' in the planning process, some commentators contend that there is now a higher degree of public consultation in the urban planning process. Teo (1992, p. 183), for example, noted a trend towards greater public consultation and participation in the planning process in the case of the Simpang and Kampong Bugis DGPs on the basis that these 'were exhibited for public viewing and dialogue was sought with the private sector'. Similarly, in URA's publicity flyers such as one entitled *The Making of the New Master Plan*, it is asserted that 'public consultation and feedback are important features of the DGP planning process'. Public feedback is usually sought at the outline DGP stage through an exhibition and a public dialogue, following which 'feedback is analysed and carefully considered, so that the final Master Plan best reflects both the national aspirations and the concerns and desires of all Singaporeans'.

While there is arguably a certain level of transparency in an attempt to incorporate the people into the planning process – a strategy essential to the ideological work of building 'hegemony/consensus' (Chua, 1991, p. 33) around a vision of Singapore as a 'tropical city of excellence' – the real extent to which citizen voices are counted *vis-à-vis* planning expertise is unclear. Others have argued that the provisions of planning do not cover 'detailed ramifications relating to the exercise of administrative discretion' (Khublall and Yuen, 1991, p. 1). In a city which owes its administrative efficiency in policy implementation to the increased powers vested in the administrative and bureaucratic sector (what Chan (1975) terms an 'administrative state'), 'administrators do not merely serve, they also wield decision-making power without the mandate'. In view of the power of the administrative layer in the planning process, there can thus be considerable slippage between planning intents and effects, a state of affairs which further marginalizes the voices of the citizenry.

*The role of environmental NGOs*

Writers such as Kong (1994) and Mekani and Stengal (1995) have argued that in many public arenas in Singapore, the government 'plays an inordinately large role in defining the agenda and identifying and facilitating the implementation of the solutions, often, though not invariably, to good effect'. However, while the process of agenda-setting is largely an 'undemocratic' one dominated by the government, the environmental arena is one where a few environmental NGOs and near NGOs have featured in recent years, if not in challenging the government's agenda then at least by participating in it.

Arguably the most controversial issue in recent years which has galvanized environmental groups to take up proactive stances sometimes at odds with that of the government is the question of how nature should be conserved or incorporated into the urban fabric. While the vision of 'bringing [a carefully managed] nature into urban development' (Liu, quoted in Kong and Yeoh, 1996, p. 42) in order to facilitate Singaporeans living in a tropical island paradise with close-to-nature housing, resorts and marinas is one of the mainstays of Singapore's urban planning, the government has been less receptive to other conceptions of nature (such as untamed nature containing bio-diversity) championed by environmental groups such as the Nature Society of Singapore (NSS), a long-standing group dedicated to 'the study, conservation and enjoyment of our natural heritage' (Briffett, 1990, p. 7). As Allen (quoted in Mekani and Stengal, 1995, p. 287) observed, 'when it comes to nature conservation, . . . the weakness of Singapore's Government lies in its unshakeable belief that everything can be managed and that one can create nature just as one can create townships, ports and airports'. Indeed, in view of the acclaim of Singapore's open zoo, night safari, bird park, botanic gardens as well as the ubiquitous mantle of green which decorates the cityscape, it has been claimed that 'no other country matches Singapore as far as "managed" nature is concerned' (Mekani and Stengal, 1995, p. 285). After setting aside 5% of land 'of ecological merit' to 'conserve the diversity of our flora and fauna and protect their natural habitats' (a total of 19 'Nature Areas') (*The Singapore Green Plan*, 1992, p. 30), the government is of the view that developmental concerns should prevail elsewhere in land-scarce Singapore. In contrast, NSS has expressed concern that designated Nature Areas are 'certainly not sufficient to ensure the long-term survival of existing diversity of species in Singapore' (*The Straits Times*, 22 November 1991). The Society has since proposed an alternative Green Plan that argues for the protection of several other areas (Figure 7.6) to widen the range of habitats to ensure that the principle of bio-diversity is seriously respected.

In sum, the debate on nature in Singapore is not so much whether there should be nature in urban areas but which *form* of nature – whether as 'manicured lawns' or 'untamed wilderness' to quote a journalist (*The Sunday Times*, 3 November 1991) – best suits modern urban Singapore. A recent furore arising out of the Public Utilities Board's proposal to build an 18-hole golf course in the Lower Peirce Reservoir illustrates the ideological difference. An EIA report produced by the NSS calculated that to build the golf course on the site, a total of 163 species of plants (including 40 000 mature trees belonging to 82 different species) and 485 species of animals (of which 44 are considered endangered) would be lost (Wee, 1992, p. 3). Furthermore, forest clearance on the site could also threaten the adjoining Nee Soon freshwater swamp forest, home to several species of animals unknown elsewhere in Singapore. The NSS led a petition against the building of the golf course (*The Sunday Times*, 10 May 1992) arguing that Singapore 'is now affluent enough to make a sacrifice in favour of nature' and should uphold its image as 'a civilized nation and responsible world citizen' responsive to the worldwide call to preserve bio-diversity (Wee, 1992, pp. 8–9). The project has since been put on hold.

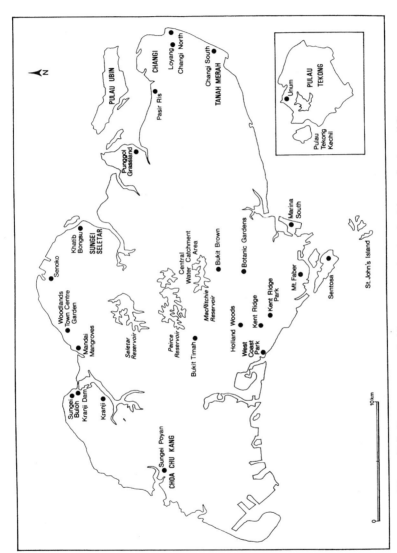

**Figure 7.6** Sites recommended for conservation by the Nature Society of Singapore
*Source:* Briffett (1990)

There have been other recent instances where NSS appealed against government plans to develop areas noted for bio-diversity. In May 1992, the Nature Society appealed to the government to reconsider its decision to fill in certain duck ponds in the reclaimed Marina South area as these were the breeding and feeding grounds of several water-fowl species. This was turned down as the area, earmarked for future urban development, was 'too commercially valuable to be set aside as a bird sanctuary' (*The Straits Times*, 12 May 1992). In another case, the ENV announced in 1992 that landfills in Singapore were rapidly filling up and that it would start dumping non-incinerable waste within a 350 ha area between the southern islands of Pulay Semakau and Pulau Sekeng, the site of some of the most intact coral fringing reefs in Singapore waters (Hesp, 1995, p. 139). The NSS, along with recreational diving groups and others, have opposed the construction of the dumping ground, expressing concern over the pollution, increased sedimentation and smothering of coral reefs, but these have largely gone unheeded. Terms of reference for tenders to undertake an EIA on the effects of disposing dredged sediments in various parts of Singapore including Pulau Semakau were issued in August 1994. To observers such as Hesp (1995, p. 139) this was 'a cynical exercise, coming as it does, years after the decision was taken to develop the dumping ground'. More generally, Hilton and Manning (1995) estimate that given the current rate of coastal ecological destruction, little of Singapore's original mangrove and coral reef habitats will remain in the year 2030 beyond degraded and fragmented remnants. In yet another recent instance, NSS initiated a public collection of 25 000 signatures to save Senoko, an important bird habitat in terms of both species and numbers located in an area scheduled for housing and transport development. The Society proposed conserving 168 ha of the Senoko site, though later suggesting that a compromise 75 ha core area be conserved, arguing that designated Nature Areas of little ecological value such as heavily modified urban parks should be excluded to allow biologically richer sites such as Senoko to be included in the '5% strategy' adopted by the Green Plan (Hilton and Manning, 1995, p. 318). The appeal, however, was laid aside as 'people's needs [are] more pressing' (*The Straits Times*, 19 March 1994; 21 October 1994). In the government's words, 'if the Nature Society's request to conserve . . . Senoko was acceded to, the opportunity cost would be in the order of 17 000 HDB flats and around 40 ha of industrial land' (*The Straits Times*, 13 April 1994). In Hilton and Manning's (1995, p. 320) assessment, 'government agencies zealously pursue elements of environmental management that relate to the provision of services and secure the physical well-being of Singaporeans, but have been reticent to take tangible steps to maintain the Republic's ecological diversity'.

Beyond the substantive question of how much and what form of nature should be conserved, the ultimate impact of NGOs on environmental planning has also been debated. Kong (1994) classifies environmental groups including the NSS in Singapore as 'insiders', those who have some access to and dialogue with the bureaucracy but which must also play by the rules the bureaucracy sets down. From insider positions, the actual influence of environmental groups on the agenda is rather weak. Kong (1994, pp. 281–83) describes the typical scenario:

> . . . the group is cast in the role of providing information [before a govern-ment-led committee]. It is not defining and negotiating the nature of the problem. The group becomes one voice among many. When the committee hearings are over, the committee becomes the new experts and authorities on the subject. The environmental group has lost itself in this process, and it is the committee report that defines the issues.

In contrast, Mekani and Stengal (1995, pp. 288–300) are more optimistic that environmental NGOs have 'a big role to play', not so much in setting the agenda but in acting as a 'bridge' between the government and the private sector 'to educate, exert pressure on monopolies, give the right signals to producers and build awareness'. Not only are they of the view that an 'Asian-style of non-governmental activity' based on cooperation with the government is the only viable alternative in Singapore as NGOs will not have the people's support without official blessing, they argue that a 'proactive and conflicting approach' has no place in Singapore as the government has upheld a strong record for championing environ-mental issues and 'not only listened . . . but included' the concerns of NGOs in the national agenda (Mekani and Stengal, 1995, p. 297). In areas of disagreement such as the extent of nature to be conserved, they advo-cate gentle pressure as opposed to confrontation.

Environmental NGOs such as the NSS have certainly carved out a niche for themselves in raising environmental issues and participating in environmental planning. Their roles in supporting government pro-nouncements and programmes are firmly in place. What is less clear is the extent of their influence on issues where there is no accord.

## Conclusion

Urban and environmental planning has formed one of the major cor-nerstones of Singapore's development over the last four decades. Planning is also one of the key strategies in the making of a vision for Singapore in the twenty-first century. Singapore has evolved a highly intricate bureaucratic machinery to generate plans and put them into effect. Its achievements in terms of creating a physically superior environment to meet growing aspirations among the people have attracted many accolades. However, hitherto, the planning process from the formulation of visions and goals to the fine tuning and enforcement of regulatory policies have been largely state-dominated. As has been noted, 'Singapore's clean environment is upheld not only by numerous officers of the Ministry of Environment but also a fleet of cleaners and gardeners' (Mekani and Stengal, 1995, p. 286). Other voices – experts with alternative views, NGOs and the general public – have played much more subdued roles. Yet as visions soar and agendas widen in the 1990s, it is debatable whether government-led planning and its reliance on legislative and fiscal measures can continue to satisfy the standards of urban living set by rising aspirations. Changes might have to be made to the political culture of planning to include more voices.

# 8

## Housing environment

Singapore's housing environment is distinctive because of the dominance of public sector provision. In the early 1990s, 86% of the population was housed in public housing provided by the Housing and Development Board (HDB). State control of the housing market has provided important means through which overall land use has been influenced. It has also given the state a direct means of determining changes in living standards in a highly controlled fashion. As the rest of the chapter explains, the progressive uplifting of housing conditions has been achieved through changes in physical aspects of the housing stock, rules and regulations regarding access to state-subsidized housing, and increasingly through how much space is given to private sector housing. This chapter concentrates on the period from 1959, when the PAP took over internal self-government and the HDB became the main provider of housing. This will be followed by a section discussing the role of public housing in state ideology and a discussion of everyday life within an HDB housing estate. While the HDB and its changing policies provide the main focus of the chapter, private housing provision is also reviewed as this sector accommodates a growing proportion of Singaporeans, and is the aspiration of many more.

### Public housing in context

As many observers have pointed out, the visual impact of modern (public) housing in Singapore is impressive by comparison with most other large cities in the world (see, for example, Pugh, 1989, p. 833). Singapore's public housing programme has also been recognized for the excellence of its management. In 1995, the HDB received the *Asia Management Award in Development Management* from the Asian Institute of Management in recognition of 'excellent achievements of Asian management' which were said to have created 'substantial positive impact on target beneficiaries through innovative, sustainable and effective management' and to have improved the quality of life of people (*The Straits Times*, 17 October 1995). This award was also a recognition of how rapidly the HDB had turned around housing conditions. When the PAP came to power in 1959, housing in the central city was old, badly degenerated and lacking in adequate sanitation (see description in Chapter 2).

Squatter settlements and congested slums are the scenario typical of many urban areas in developing countries that are experiencing rapid urbanization (Todaro, 1979). Plagued by economic problems, Third World governments have tended to treat housing needs as a social problem that can be handled after economic progress has been achieved. Industrial programmes to stimulate the economy have had the first call on resources, in the belief that wealth will gradually trickle down to urban dwellers and produce a gradual improvement in housing conditions. From the outset, Singapore's planners saw the need to improve the living environment as a prior condition for economic success. In reversing the order of development, Singapore had the advantage of being devoid of a rural hinterland and the population pressure resulting from internal migration. After its exit from the Federation in 1965, the conversion of the causeway into a customs border also gave the new state tight control over international migrants. Even so, the commitment of Singapore's newly elected government to tackle the housing problem has deservedly given the state credit, as well as explain why overseas governments frequently send delegations to study the efficiency of its public housing programme.

From the time the PAP took over internal self-government, Singapore's public housing has been handled mainly by the HDB. It was set up in 1960 to replace the Singapore Improvement Trust (SIT) as the main housing authority. All administrative units in various parts of the bureaucracy that handled public housing and related programmes were integrated under the HDB, centralizing decision-making to give greater organizational efficiency and coordination. At the same time, functions that had burdened the SIT were transferred to separate planning departments under the Ministry of National Development. As well as the clear sense of purpose, the HDB was allocated an enlarged budget compared with the SIT. With its mission and resources in place, the HDB set about its task through a series of quinquennial development plans. Reflecting the five year policy cycle over which targets and policy evolved, this chapter reviews the HDB's contribution by contrasting its priorities and policies across four decades.

## First decade of public housing: 1960s

Given the severe shortage of decent housing in 1960, the HDB's first task was to build as many housing units as possible within a short time. In the First Five-Year Plan (1960–65), the Board's target of 50 000 units was exceeded by 5000, thus allowing 23% of the total population to be housed in HDB flats by 1965. This represented the first step towards tackling the housing problem and was an indication of the HDB's capacity to deliver.

These first HDB housing estates were located around areas of heavy population concentration within easy reach (six to eight kilometres) of the city centre. Large scale urban renewal in the congested central city area meant moving existing residents. To obtain their cooperation, it was important to provide them with alternative housing close to their existing places of work and social association, which were predominantly in the city centre. Examples of these early housing developments include Queenstown, Whampoa and Kallang (Figure 8.1).

Resettlement mainly affected low income persons. To make housing available to them, construction costs were kept low by building basic flats. HDB housing standards are primarily measured in terms of the number of rooms per dwelling. Generally the number of rooms refers to the combined total of bedroom, sitting room and dining room. The early units were all standardized: they were either one-room (emergency), two-room, or three-room flats. A one-room flat had about 140 sq ft of bed-cum-sitting room and a 80 sq ft service area consisting of a bathroom and toilet combined, cooking area and a balcony for eating, washing and drying purposes (*HDB Annual Report*, 1961, p. 3). Some of the one-room flats had communal or semi-communal toilet and kitchen facilities. Rentals and selling prices were further minimized by a government subsidy that aimed to keep rentals at about 15% of the average household's income (*HDB Annual Report*, 1969, p. 16). Eligibility for HDB flats was restricted to Singapore citizens above 21 years of age, whose income did not exceed $500 and who did not own land or property. A minimum household size of five family members and a combined household income not exceeding $800 per month were also fixed (*HDB Annual Report*, 1962, p. 4). These stipulations have changed through the years, and are a means by which the government can encourage or discourage certain norms and behaviour that it deems desirable.

Although the main concern in the early 1960s was to meet construction targets measured in terms of housing units, other amenities were not neglected. From the start, the neighbourhood principle as developed in British new town planning was adopted. The idea was to minimize travel outside the neighbourhood by providing each neighbourhood with essential amenities such as shops, clinics and playgrounds.

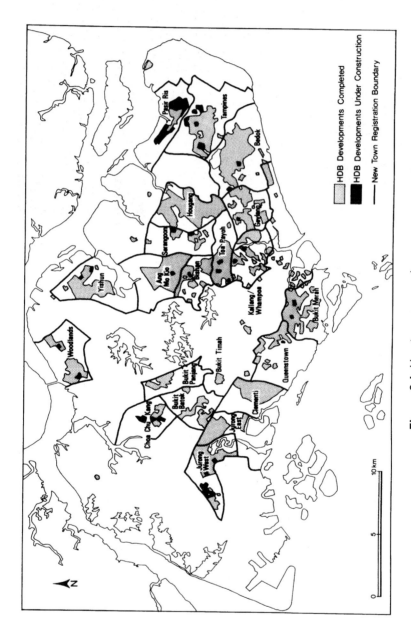

**Figure 8.1** Housing estates and new towns
*Source: Compiled from HDB Annual Reports*

**Plate 8.1**   First generation HDB housing in Queenstown

In 1964, the Home Ownership Scheme was introduced to encourage Singaporeans to buy their flats as part of the drive to create a property-owning democracy extending to the lower middle income groups (*HDB Annual Report*, 1964, p. 9). It was believed, among other things, that people would look after their own properties better than rental units, thus reducing estate management problems in the long run (*The Straits Times*, 26 February 1984).

Housing conditions improved dramatically over the First Five-Year Plan, although there were still large amounts of substandard housing remaining. In the Second Five-Year Plan (1966–70), the housing target was lifted to 60 000 units or 1000 units per month (*HDB Annual Report*, 1965). As well as increasing the rate of construction, the quality of provision gained more consideration than in the preceding five years. This was reflected in several ways. In terms of the types of units constructed, the Board stopped constructing one-room emergency flats with communal facilities while three-room 'improved' flats were built with new features such as larger floor space, and separate bathrooms and toilets. Four-room flats were also constructed for the first time, as were 'point block' flats (in which staircases serve only two units on each floor to allow for greater privacy as compared with staircases which serve about ten units, all of which share a common corridor) (Teh, 1975).

Rising standards were secondly reflected in greater investment in the external living environment offered in the new housing estates as well as the internal space. This is seen in the greater emphasis on the provision of open spaces, landscaping, car park facilities and recreational facilities such as playgrounds and sports facilities. The HDB also paid more attention to the provision of employment opportunities within housing estates by putting aside 10 to 15% of land in housing estates for small-scale labour-intensive industries such as garment, textile and electronics factories (*HDB Annual Report*, 1970, p. 56). These plans for more comprehensive and self-sufficient estates took shape, for example, in the planning and construction of the first two satellite towns, Queenstown and Toa Payoh, completed in 1965 and 1971 respectively. Each housed a bigger population (160 000 and 180 000 respectively) but also provided a larger number of amenities and light industries than the estates completed previously (*HDB Annual Report*, 1965, p. 23; *HDB Annual Report*, 1971, p. 44).

The Home Ownership Scheme, which had initially met a poor response, was given a boost in the Second Five-Year Plan by permitting purchasers to use their Central Provident Fund (CPF) savings to pay for both the downpayment and monthly instalments if they desired from 1968. By taking housing loan payments out of CPF contributions housing purchase might mean no extra outlay beyond their existing CPF contribution and not surprisingly therefore became an attractive option. In addition, existing tenants enjoyed a concessionary downpayment of 5% of the purchase price of the flat rather than the regular 20% (*HDB Annual Report*, 1968, p. 16). Other incentives to encourage home ownership were introduced in later years, including periodic revision of the household income ceiling for eligibility, first to $1200 in 1969, and up to $8000 in 1996. Regulations have also been adjusted to ensure that individual social groups have fair access to HDB housing, as in the decision to allow senior civil servants not to pay the initial 20% downpayment if they were not on the CPF scheme (when the revised CPF scheme commenced in 1965, civil servants had the option of staying in their own scheme).

At the end of the first decade of public housing, the HDB had constructed more than 110 000 units and provided residents with modern amenities such as direct water and electricity supplies, sanitation and rubbish disposal systems which made for much better public hygiene. Gross overcrowding became a thing of the past. In 1951, the average number of rooms per household was 0.8, by 1970 it was 2.2 (Gee and Chee, 1981, p. 102). As a consequence, health conditions were significantly improved. In a survey conducted by the HDB in 1968, 26% of residents felt that life had become very much better; 44% said that it was somewhat better; 18% reported that conditions had remained the same as before; 11% indicated that things had changed somewhat for the worse; while 1% felt that change had made life very much worse (Yeh, 1972, p. 107). Where dissatisfaction existed, it typically arose from the perception that the HDB had failed to protect a sense of community, neighbourliness and identity, and contributed to the breaking up of the extended family. Other complaints had to do with the inadequacy of communal facilities, inefficient lifts and public transportation, and noise (Yeh, 1972). These issues were all to be taken up in subsequent decades.

## Second decade of public housing: 1970s

The 1970s produced a peak in applications for public housing of both rental and purchase flats as a result of the various incentives to encourage home ownership, the widening differentials between private and public housing costs (Teo and Savage, 1991) and increased household formation as more young married couples chose to live separately from their families. In response to accelerating demand, the HDB constructed about 110 000 housing units in the Third Five-Year Programme and 131 000 units in the Fourth Five-Year Programme (Pugh, 1989, p. 848).

In the second decade of public housing provision, the HDB had to respond to a new group of home owners with different expectations beyond mere shelter. Bigger and better designed flats in choicer locations, as well as good infrastructural support in the form of efficient transportation, adequate retail and recreational facilities and other amenities became the preference (Teo, 1986). To accommodate these expectations, the design of flats and new towns began to change. For example, flats were now designed with a dining room and an attached bathroom for the master bedroom while new designs of three- and four-room flats (for example, with storerooms) were also introduced. In 1971, five-room flats were introduced for the first time, comprising three bedrooms, a dining room and a living room, in addition to a kitchen, bathrooms and toilets. Whereas flats came in standard regimented slab blocks in the first decade, architectural variations were now introduced, such as uneven rooflines and circular blocks to help give distinctiveness and identity to the housing environment.

As housing standards increased, suburbanization was necessary to enable a more spacious living environment to be provided, resulting in a second generation of new towns, such as Clementi, Bedok, Woodlands and Ang Mo Kio. All of these are located at a distance from the city centre and are much larger than the housing estates of the 1960s, housing about 150 000 to 250 000 persons. Each new town is made up of several neigh-

**Plate 8.2** Three-room flats above shops: typical provision of the 1970s

bourhoods, and each neighbourhood houses between 1000 and 5000 families. Neighbourhoods are interlaced with open spaces, recreational facilities, such as jogging tracks, artistic landscaping and facilities including post offices and libraries. Each new town is served by a central bus terminal, connected to different parts of the new town by feeder services as well as being linked to the city centre by new roads and expressways.

Greater financial support from the government underpinned the HDB's improved construction in the 1970s so that rents and prices of flats could be kept low (*HDB Annual Report*, 1970). The financing of public housing siphoned off massive financial resources. It has been alleged that the expansion of the construction sector was at the expense of investment in productive capital which was already attracting less interest because of the recession in the oil crisis years of 1973 and 1974 (Castells *et al.*, 1990,

p. 323). However, this view may overlook the benefits of channelling consumer spending into the highly controlled housing sector where inflationary pressures could be kept in check.

The 1970s saw the question of community spirit and neighbourliness enter the agenda of issues to be tackled in the new housing estates. This was prompted by the recognition that social ties between HDB neighbours were rather ritualized, superficial and transitory, in some cases, not extending beyond 'casual ritual greeting' (Hassan, 1977). In 1977, Residents' Committees (RCs) were piloted in two new towns, Tanjong Pagar and Marine Parade as an experiment to encourage the growth of community cohesion and neighbourliness. Since then, RCs have been introduced in every estate to provide residents with opportunities for social interaction. Various activities are organized for residents, including social and recreational programmes (such as excursions and get-together parties) and educational ones (such as forums and exhibitions). Other forms of service to the community include the organization of senior citizens' programmes and tuition classes.

Community centres (CCs), although existent since the early 1950s, were also more actively harnessed during this time to bring residents together in shared activities. They cater to various social and recreational needs of residents (Wong, 1988). Like RCs, they organize a range of recreational (such as Chinese chess), vocational (dressmaking), cultural (musical instruction) and educational (talks) activities. At the same time, community centre groups served not only as organizers, community centres were themselves places for interaction.

Alongside the attention paid to developing community spirit, the differentiation between the older estates and the more recent new towns also attracted attention as younger people, aspiring to better living conditions, were tending to shun the older areas. In an attempt to contain such movements and retain the social balance of communities, the HDB began to demolish some of the one-room emergency flats to make way for new developments and convert others into larger self-contained flats. This can be seen as the first property 'upgrading' exercise but as we discuss below, it was in the 1980s that upgrading efforts gathered real momentum.

The impact of housing relocation on family relations was addressed in 1978 through two new schemes (a joint balloting scheme and the mutual exchange of flats scheme) to help married children and their elderly parents to live in adjoining flats or blocks within the same estate. Those who applied for a flat as a three-tier family were given incentives, such as a three-year retrospective priority over other applicants, a longer loan repayment period and a smaller deposit payment for those with insufficient CPF savings (*HDB Annual Report* 1978–79, p. 7). Another policy

**Plate 8.3** The uneven skyline of Bishan is intended to give it a distinctive identity

introduced in the same year was the concession for single senior citizens (defined as males over 55 and females above 40) to purchase a flat, or rent one if they were willing to share it with someone else, not necessarily a relative. These policies can be seen as among the first responses in Singapore to an ageing population and, in this respect, they show the state's preferred solution of using care from friends and relatives as an alternative to state assistance (*HDB Annual Report*, 1978–79, p. 7).

Finally in this decade, the creation of the Housing and Urban Development Corporation (HUDC) as a subsidiary of the HDB in 1974 catered to the interests of a growing middle income group. This group had a total household income exceeding the ceiling that would qualify them for HDB flats but were priced out of the private housing market. To meet their needs, HUDC-constructed flats followed the condominium concept, with maisonettes and flats in an estate within which communal amenities such as children's playgrounds and outdoor ball courts are provided. The developments proved popular, largely because they were 'exclusive developments away from those sprawling HDB look-alikes, and priced at a considerable discount compared with private property' (*The Straits Times*, 2 September 1995). Construction of HUDC estates continued into the 1980s, resulting in a total of 16 estates.

## Third decade of public housing: 1980s

After the rapid building in the 1960s and 1970s, the emphasis in the 1980s was on promoting new town character to create a stronger sense of community, identity and belonging. As the basic principle of high rise, high density construction was not varied, change was to be achieved through block designs of varying building height to break the monotony of the skyline. Greater use was also made of traditional forms such as pitched roofs, overhanging eaves and tall windows typical of a tropical building and the division of estates into pedestrian-linked precincts of 600 to 1000 dwelling units. By being smaller than a neighbourhood, the precinct was seen as a way to encourage meaningful social interaction among residents. In furtherance of this, each precinct was equipped with an area to function as a focal point for community activity, usually a landscaped square with recreational facilities surrounded by a kindergarten, eating places and local shops. These design principles can be seen in the layout of Bishan New Town which was substantially completed in 1990–1991.

Questioning of the HDB's organizational efficiency began to surface in the 1980s as problems of high staff turnover and poor morale became evident (Castells *et al.*, 1990, p. 325). Part of the problem was diagnosed as the sheer size of the organization and its consequent 'distance' from individual residents. It was partly in response to this that devolution of some aspects of estate management to newly created town councils took place. Following a pilot project in Ang Mo Kio New Town, the Town Councils Act was passed in 1988 (Ooi, 1990). Each town council is headed by an elected Member of Parliament (MP); in the case of Group Representation Constituencies (GRCs) where there is a group of up to six MPs standing for election as a team (Chapter 3), one of the MPs will chair the council while the others will serve as town councillors. Residents can take part in the day-to-day running of their estates by serving as town councillors, although it is typically existing grassroots leaders who are chosen for this task (as they are approved by their MPs) or by participating in dialogue sessions organized by their MPs and town councillors. The precise significance of town councils is open to discussion (see Chapter 3). They were presented as a way 'to help Singaporeans to forge stronger community spirit and identity' (Ministry of National Development, 1988, p. 1). As the dialogue is channelled through PAP-controlled organizations, town councils may alternatively be viewed as a way of containing debate and preventing the appearance in communities of interest in opposing the state.

Managing dangers of social differentiation between the older estates and the new with their greatly improved amenities also became a priority in the 1980s. Upgrading of older estates involved a range of actions:

**Plate 8.4** The precinct concept was applied in a number of estates, including this one in Bishan. A few blocks share one focal point, in this case, a meeting area where residents might meet and chat

1. Old flats were demolished so that land could be made available for redevelopment. From 1978, for example, out of the 19 408 units or 88 blocks of one-room emergency flats built in the early 1960s, 10 976 flats in 53 blocks were to be demolished. These include areas such as Redhill, Bukit Ho Swee, Kampong Tiong Bahru, Macpherson, Alexandra Hill, Mountbatten and Aljunied. After clearance, bigger flats were constructed (*HDB Annual Report*, 1978–79, p. 24).
2. Older one-room flats were converted during this period into larger three- and four-room self-contained flats by knocking down the walls between the old flats. This took place, for example, in Fort Road, Kallang Basin and Tanjung Rhu.

3. Additional facilities were provided for the older estates so as to ensure that they had their share of improved facilities. At the estate level, for example, Toa Payoh was provided with a commercial complex with fast food restaurants and offices, a new bus interchange, the Mass Rapid Transit line stopping in the town centre, and the first government mini-hospital of 40 beds. At the level of individual buildings and units, new lifts were added; casement windows were installed to existing flats with open balconies; central television antennae were added; and rewiring and reroofing took place (*HDB Annual Report*, 1979–80, pp. 6–7).

4. Rules on flat alterations were liberalized. Owners were allowed to make minor alterations themselves. For example, owners of five-room flats were allowed to install windows in their open balconies; residents on ground floors were allowed to extend their courtyard shelters to keep out the rain; the space in recessed entrances and along common corridors could also be sold so that residents could turn them into mini-gardens or playgrounds and have improved security and privacy.

Finally in the 1980s, another important initiative was the introduction of explicit rules controlling the racial composition of estates. After the massive relocation of population affected by the housing programme, it was observed that different racial groups were congregating in particular housing estates. For example, Ang Mo Kio and Hougang had a larger share of Chinese than the national profile. In turn, there was a larger than average concentration of Malays in Tampines, Marine Parade and Bedok. In 1989, rules regarding the racial mix in new towns and individual blocks of flats were introduced to ensure that their racial mix should reflect roughly the racial proportion in the total population. Where a particular group was over-represented, any flat that was to be sold must be sold to someone in the racial group that was under-represented (Ooi, 1993). This is enforced by rules which require all sales of HDB property to be processed through the agency.

## Public housing in the 1990s

In the 1990s, quality and service became the HDB's emphasis, involving the provision of bigger flats, and more comfortable and up-to-date physical environments. In this regard, a variety of measures have been taken, such as the introduction of a formal upgrading programme involving individual units and blocks of flats as well as entire estates; the introduction of executive condominiums and housing cooperatives; and the privatization of HUDC estates.

Apart from the ongoing upgrading efforts that took place from the late 1970s to the 1980s, in July 1989, the government announced a formal, large scale plan to upgrade existing HDB estates. This was presented as the second phase of upgrading which would allow 'a complete change in the perception of public housing' (S. Dhanabalan, then National Development Minister, quoted in *The Straits Times*, 12 July 1989). The project is intended to last 15 years from 1991 and benefit 95% of HDB dwellers (*The Straits Times*, 12 July 1989). By and large, upgrading would take place without residents relocating.

This formal upgrading plan was introduced for a variety of reasons. First, it was to fulfil people's rising expectations of an improved quality of life, in short, the government's way of delivering living standards for a population with growing aspirations. Secondly, it would raise the value of HDB flats. Thirdly, it was a means by which to retain the population balance in the older estates by stemming the tendency for young people to shun the older estates in preference for a new flat. This would ultimately save on resources if the upgrading stopped the 'death' of an estate. Fourthly, it was a way of ensuring that the population shared some of Singapore's economic growth, in a way that they would easily recognize (Teo and Kong, 1997).

The decision to accept upgrading is given to residents as they are required to pay from 8%–21% of the cost (depending on the size of the flat and the total upgrading cost), the balance coming from the government and town councils. A 75% vote in favour is required with, at least thus far, no opportunity for a second ballot. Whilst the programme initially obtained a mixed response, the demonstration effect of completed upgrading has created strong support for upgrading, notwithstanding the considerable disruption experienced by residents during the construction period. Upgrading involves a number of changes. At a broad level, precincts are created where they did not previously exist. Each precinct will have its own multi-storey car park, landscaped gardens and children's playgrounds. Each block will have additional architectural improvements to make them individually distinct. Lift lobbies and entrances will be enclosed to improve security. Staircases and corridors will also be upgraded, with tiled rather than cemented floors. For the flat itself, a space will be added, for example, an extra toilet or bathroom for flats with only one bathroom/toilet. The kitchen area may also be expanded.

As well as whole estates, individual older blocks around the central area are now subject to selective upgrading under the *Selective En Bloc Redevelopment Scheme* (Sers) introduced in 1995. The decision to selectively redevelop lies with the Ministry of National Development and is not subject to voting in the same way that upgrading is because in these cases the government has an overriding desire to see redevelopment. From the state's perspective, these older properties have not kept pace with surrounding land values so that there is now an imperative to intensify the use of their site. Residents are compensated at a preferential rate for their old flats and offered a new one at a 20% discount. In one Sers scheme, 16 blocks of low-rise flats in Boon Tiong Road in Tiong Bahru were selected for upgrading. Although there are many other similar old SIT flats in the vicinity, these were chosen because of the availability of empty plots of land nearby on which the HDB can build first. Residents can then move to these new blocks before their old flats are demolished and new ones built in their place. In this way, the physical living environment can be improved and the community kept intact. The desire to keep people in place also responds to the selectivity in the renewal process by encouraging those benefiting to reinvest their compensation in the locality rather than profiting from their 'windfall' in ways that others might resent. It is partly for this reason as well that those affected by redevelopment play no part in the decision making. Their views are not sought, and many homeowners are often left guessing whether they would be relocated at relatively short notice. This is particularly a problem when they have spent large amounts of money on home renovations, only to find that they are to be relocated.

Town centres are the latest target of upgrading. In these cases as well, the decision to upgrade will lie solely with the Ministry of National Development, after views are heard from residents and grassroots leaders. The first plan to be unveiled in this respect was a comprehensive strategy to rejuvenate Toa Payoh town centre. The plan, to be realized within five years from 1995, includes the construction of a new $700 million commercial complex offering 118 000 sq m of office space and 10 000 sq m of retail space and a 7799 sq m office block in the town centre. In addition to giving the town centre more space, it is also intended that pedestrian malls in Toa Payoh Central will be improved. New road linkages will be introduced to improve access to Toa Payoh; and new housing will be constructed on vacant state land and land cleared when rental blocks are freed of tenants. Two blocks of rental flats with elderly residents will also be refurbished with new non-slip tiles, pedestal toilets, hand rails and alarm systems. At the same time, three community centres in the town will be upgraded (*The Straits Times*, 2 September 1995). After Toa Payoh, the Ministry will turn its attention to drawing up plans to redevelop Bedok and Ang Mo Kio, two new towns built in the 1970s.

In 1995 a second attempt to address the interests of the 'sandwich class' was introduced, this time in the form of executive condominiums. About 2000 units are to be commenced in the first year of the scheme, each measuring 100 to 120 sq m with facilities such as a swimming pool and tennis court. While designed to approximate the standards in a private development, the price range of S$500 000–$660 000 is said to be 15–20% cheaper than comparable private apartments in similar locations (*The Straits Times*, 30 August 1995). First-time buyers will be given a $40 000 grant but they cannot use HDB loan financing for the purchase and they lose entitlement to purchase a new HDB flat. Resale conditions restrict any sale within five years and ownership is restricted to Singaporeans and permanent residents. Only after ten years are ownership restrictions to be removed. The first 540 units will be in Jurong East and Pasir Ris.

Initial response to executive condominiums was lukewarm mainly as the price was more than double that for a HDB executive flat, even though the latter are one-sixth to nearly one-half bigger. Those expressing interest are drawn by the prestige of private property and the private recreational amenities (*The Straits Times*, 31 August 1995). Provision is to be expanded by allowing housing cooperatives to undertake construction. One agency immediately taking up this opportunity was the National Trades Union Congress (NTUC) (*The Straits Times*, 21 October 1995). Alongside the executive condominium programme, the privatization of HUDC estates commenced in 1995 which represents another response to the need for middle income housing (see Teo and Kong, 1997).

New solutions were introduced in 1995 in response to the continuing preference among young couples for new property. The waiting list for new property can be 3–5 years and so many couples respond by getting married early to register a place in the queue and then have their formal wedding ceremony when the property is ready. The revised Transitional Rental Housing Scheme makes it easier for first-time HDB flat applicants to rent a unit while waiting for their own flats to be ready by reducing rentals for them. Further, to help these first-time buyers, they are given priority over those seeking to upgrade in the selection of rental flats and given units with more fittings such as a kitchen stove, water heater and refrigerator, in addition to those already available, namely, kitchen cabinets, grilles, gates and light fittings. The number of rental flats was also increased by 25% to 500 units per quarter (*The Straits Times*, 27 August 1995). Changes were also made to the CPF Housing Grant Scheme in 1995 to make it more attractive to first-time buyers to buy second hand (resale) flats. Grants were increased from $30 000 to $40 000, and if the resale units are near a parents' home, the figure goes up to $50 000, regardless of whether the parents live in HDB flats.

**Plate 8.5** Upgraded flats in Clementi provided with a new multi-storey car-park, extra design features on the frontage of the block, a new lift, and a new name – West Coast Court

## Public housing and state control

Housing in Singapore is clearly about more than a place to live. The housing programme has not only addressed the functional problem of providing shelter but also made it possible for other ideological goals to be achieved. This argument is elaborated in this section through a discussion of the way public housing has helped to: (i) promote economic development; (ii) enhance social integration and hence maintain social stability; (iii) perpetuate moral and traditional values; and (iv) maintain the PAP's political legitimacy and domination.

*Housing to promote economic development*

Chua (1995, p. 108) argues that state ideology has been couched within the terms of a discourse on 'national survival', which is fed in turn by the country's 'perceived economic non-viability; a Chinese enclave in the Malay Sea; mounting domestic difficulties of unemployment, high demographic growth rate and poor public health and housing conditions; and finally, absence of political identification with the new nation by a population of different individuals, each orientated to their own respective homelands'. Public housing helped focus this potentially divided community on the goal of economic growth and survival by:

1. Keeping operational costs low for multinational investors since cheaper public housing lowers the cost of living. By keeping rents and prices low, it relieves the pressure on wages without lowering the quality of labour. At the same time, another attraction for multinational investors is the fact that Singapore's public housing entails the planning and development of a complete network of urban infrastructure as well, such as the provision of factory sites for light and non-polluting industries in the new towns and the construction of transport networks (expressways and roads).
2. Controlling inflation by controlling the housing supply and supply of financing through the way most individuals rely on their CPF contributions for house purchase. At the same time, when wages increase, CPF contribution rates increase, so that the net increase in wages is effectively reduced and spending power curbed.
3. Public housing provision creates employment in the construction sector. As the construction industry is highly labour-intensive, and as it demands both skilled and unskilled workers, it was an extremely important employer in the 1960s when unemployment was high (Pugh, 1989, pp. 837–38). The building and construction industry employed an average of 10% of the total non-professional labour force between 1960 and 1965, and about 7% between 1966 and 1970 (Yeh, 1972, p. 189), as well as generating multiple effects in transport and other related industries. In addition, the HDB provides sites for employment to give labour intensive industry ready access to female labour. It was reported, for example, that ten major factories in Toa Payoh provided employment for about 16% of the working population living in the estate in 1972 (*HDB Annual Report*, 1972).
4. Home ownership ties the household into a regular mortgage structure that requires monthly payments. This can be met only by a steady monthly salary that can be earned through participation in the work force, helping to maintain a disciplined attitude to work (Salaff, 1988).

*Housing for social integration and national identity*

In Raffles' 1822 town plan, the city was segregated racially, with Chinatown for the Chinese and the Kampong Glam area for the Malays. HDB new towns were intended to be the means by which racial mixing could be encouraged. With public housing and different races being housed in the same block of flats, opportunities for intercommunity mixing have become higher at a daily interpersonal level. By introducing controls to ensure a racial mix in each new town, and even in each block of flats, it has furthered inter-racial mixing and added barriers to communally-based politics. The deliberate attempt at racial mixing finds its parallels in deliberate class mixing. Within estates, and indeed, within blocks, different income groups are mixed through the construction of differently-sized flats. This reduces the 'ghetto effect' (Chua, 1995, p. 141) while providing opportunities for the better educated to offer their leadership and services to the lower income and less educated groups.

These efforts at social engineering have had some success. In order to obtain updates on the profile, needs and expectations of residents, the HDB conducts a survey every five to six years. In 1993, it was reported that, on average, each HDB resident knew 11 neighbours but was close to only one or two. Only 2.6% said that they did not know anyone in their neighbourhood, a drop from 6.2% in 1981, while 50% of the residents exchanged food and gifts with their neighbours; 40% said that they helped others watch over their flats and 15% helped with child care (*The Straits Times*, 14 July 1995).

At a more general level, home ownership is provided to build a sense of commitment to Singapore. As Prime Minister Goh Chok Tong has suggested: 'The best stake we can give to Singaporeans is a house or a flat, a home. It is the single biggest asset for most people, and its value reflects the fundamentals of the economy' (*The Straits Times*, 27 August 1995). More recently, upgrading entails residents voting for and financially participating in the programme (Hill and Lian, 1995, p. 120). An individual's stake in society is therefore raised and, the state hopes, so too is their commitment to stay and work for Singapore's success.

*Perpetuating acceptable social values*

The state uses public housing policy as a major tool in encouraging those values that it deems acceptable and desirable for Singapore. The family as the basic unit of society is one of the five tenets in Singapore's shared values (Chapter 3). Although it was formally introduced in the National Ideology only in 1989, it had always remained an unwritten 'text' in Singapore's ideological discourse, and public housing policy has always reinforced the traditional family. Public housing is available only to households. Young single individuals are not entitled to public housing. This is in line with the government's pro-family policies. It is argued that to make public housing available to singles is to help in breaking up families prematurely. Only those deemed to be unlikely ever to marry may purchase their own HDB flats. In the past, this referred to men over 50 years old and women above 40. Since 1991, the policy has been that two singles, at least 35 years of age, can jointly purchase a flat in certain outlying areas. At the same time, since 1978, extended families have priority in their application to purchase flats.

Further reinforcing the family as the cornerstone of society, the HDB gives allocation priorities to keep families in close contact. As some measure of the impact of this, in 1993, 19.5% of married children lived with their parents while 45.2% lived near their parents, either next door, in the same block, within walking distance, in the same estate or in a nearby estate. This was described as 'intimacy at a distance', in which the benefits of an extended family can be enjoyed without sacrificing the independence of a nuclear family (*The Straits Times*, 14 July 1995).

As illustrated in Chapter 4, the government has a very large role in Singapore's population planning and one of the chief ways in which the desired effects are achieved is through the control of public housing policies. In the early 1960s, for example, to qualify for a flat, the minimum household size was five persons. This was because of the housing shortages then and the desire to ensure that flats were fully occupied. When it was decided in 1966 that the population policy would emphasize small families, given the rapid population growth rate at that point, the minimum household size was revised downwards to two adults. Another way in which housing policy was used to encourage small families, imposed in 1973, concerned female work permit holders who were married to Singaporeans. For these couples, one of the spouses must be sterilized after the birth of the second child or lose government housing subsidy and other concessions (Tai, 1988, p. 114).

Housing allocation has also been modified to influence marriage. In the late 1980s when it was observed that Singaporeans were marrying later, and the birth rate was dropping (Chapter 4), policies were introduced to make it easier for couples to marry earlier. As noted above, the 1995 revision of the Transitional Rental Housing Scheme made it easier for first-time HDB flat-buyers to rent flats while waiting for their own, thus encouraging young couples to start their families earlier. As Prime Minister Goh Chok Tong noted, many first-time buyers were mainly young couples who held off their marriage till they had their own flats. It was hoped that improving their rental opportunities would reduce the delay in marriage and child rearing (*The Straits Times*, 27 August 1995).

*Housing as a means of political legitimation and dominance*

Public housing has also been used as a means by which the government hopes to achieve political legitimation and dominance. In the early years of Singapore's independence, public housing provision was held as testimony to the newly elected government's commitment to bettering the material conditions of Singaporeans (Chua, 1995, p. 131). In later years, new blocks of flats became powerful symbols of government success (Pugh, 1989, p. 837; Chua, 1995, p. 139). Yet, as Chua (1995, p. 137) pointed out, the fact that the HDB is a statutory board allows the PAP government to also distance itself from public criticism of the HDB when it is politically expedient to do so. In another sense, the effort to encourage community spirit and identity through RCs and CCs also serves a political function: that of controlling the means and manner of citizen participation in civil life. These organizations act as channels through which government policy can be explained to the masses and means through which people can be mobilized for community projects (for example, for participation in National Day Parades). Public housing has also been wielded as an object of political patronage. For example, Teh Cheang Wan, then Minister for National Development (the ministry to which the HDB belongs), threatened in 1985 that those who supported opposition parties would be discriminated against in the delivery of some public estate maintenance services, arguing that: 'This is a very practical political decision. . . . It's fair from our party point of view that we should give priority to the constituencies with PAP MPs and give lower priority to opposition MPs. . . . But they will not be denied the service.' Similarly, when introducing the Town Council Act, the government cautioned residents regarding their choice of MPs, stating that 'it would be in the interest of the residents to be very careful whom they choose to be their representative in Parliament' (Ministry of National Development, 1988, p. 15), the implication being that a poor candidate (presumably from an opposition party) will not be able to run the estate as well as a highly-qualified (PAP) candidate.

The latest innovation, the introduction of executive condominiums, may also be interpreted as the government's attempt to satisfy Singaporeans' growing desire to own private property, one of the signs of the constant desire 'to get ahead, to pull away from the crowd, and to be seen to have done so' (*The Straits Times*, 2 September 1995). In recent years, the inability to do so, because of prohibitively expensive private housing (and cars), has raised fears of a disgruntled middle class. In order to contain any such dissatisfaction, schemes such as the executive condominiums help meet their expectations (Teo and Kong, 1997).

## Living in the HDB heartland

Life in a HDB estate is a microcosm of the stresses and strains of everyday life in Singapore. These have been observed by Lai (1995) who has spent considerable time observing life in the new towns. Of youths, she observes the sharing and negotiation of play spaces as a way of life, highlighting the absence of a clearcut racial identification or monopolization of spaces. Instead, there is a sense of equity and ethics, with certain basic principles that operate: first-come-first-served, ground-sharing for simultaneous play, joining forces if the game is the same, or agreement on the duration of a game or day and time of play or practice. In the mutual understanding and give-and-take attitudes evident, it may well be said that the accommodation and negotiation practised in this microcosmic way augur well for race relations in Singapore.

Shared everyday life for older residents takes mainly the form of chatting in public spaces such as coffee shops, hawker centres, void decks (the open space on ground floors of HDB flats), open corridors, benches in neighbourhoods, community centres and senior citizens' corners. Lai's observations of Marine Parade reveal how coffee shop talk can be a measure of public opinion of controversial political issues although participants are often careful not to become embroiled in highly sensitive

**Plate 8.6**  Forfar House – an early example of HDB high rise

and overly emotive discussions. More innocuous are reminiscences of life in the past, of personal histories which often also shed light on social histories.

Communication among elderly persons is not the only observed interaction in HDB estates. As Tai (1988) and others have illustrated, HDB estates are characterized by a range of interaction styles among neighbours, ranging from nods of acknowledgement to chats along common corridors to sharing of food, and leaving of keys and/or children with neighbours. Such levels of interaction, however, are observed to be less intense and lacking in a certain warmth, particularly when compared with past patterns, leading to the conclusion that the spirit of earlier *kampung* living has dissipated to a large extent with high rise, high density living (Yeoh and Kong, 1995).

Life in HDB estates can also be colourful in its cultural diversity, though requiring of residents a spirit of acceptance, accommodation and appreciation of the 'other'. This is evident, for example, in celebrations and ceremonies. Lai cites several occasions where cultural differences add colour to life in HDB estates, but run the risk of inciting heightened racial and religious tension if improperly handled. She illustrates the case of a Malay wedding and a Chinese funeral wake. Visitors to HDB estates are likely to encounter, every now and again, the celebration of a Malay wedding in an HDB void deck, elaborate, ceremonious and colourful, accompanied by music. This is part of the rhythm and life in an HDB estate. However, some degree of management of such events is needed. Use of void decks must be booked in advance with the Town Council that manages the estate. The difficulty arises when these void decks are needed for Chinese funeral wakes as well, which due to the contingency of the situation, do not allow for advance booking. Chinese custom further dictates that if a coffin is already placed in one spot, it must not be moved. Thus, it is entirely possible that a Malay couple may have applied to use a void deck on a particular day, only to find that an hour earlier, a coffin had been placed there due to a neighbour's sudden demise. In handling such a situation, the authorities run the risk of being accused of discrimination if the inviolability of Chinese custom is upheld against the Malay's needs. The solution has been to privilege bureaucratic rules over cultural beliefs, so residents are unequivocally expected to abide by pragmatic booking procedures.

Other public displays of cultural practices may also add colour to HDB estates, such as the celebration of the seventh lunar month or the Hungry Ghost Festival by the Chinese. Joss papers are burnt, very often on grass verges; marquees are pitched, sheltering offerings of diverse sorts; and stages for street performances are set up, with Chinese operas or singing at night for the 'hungry ghosts' who visit this earth in the seventh month. Complaints of noise, incense ash and burnt grass are not uncommon during this period, and can well be the occasion for religious tension and strife if not for continued counsel of religious and ethnic understanding and accommodation.

Living in the HDB 'heartlands' is not without some shared problems. For example, the cleanliness and maintenance of common properties such as lifts and staircases becomes an issue if residents do not act responsibly. Problems such as irresponsible people urinating in lifts, leaving rubbish at lift landings and 'killer litter' (the act of throwing fragile, large and/or heavy items such as flower pots from higher floors out of the window, thus endangering the lives of those passing by downstairs) are common enough trials that residents have to battle. They point to a people lacking in social graces, common courtesy and consideration for others, an issue which we will pick up again in our concluding chapter.

**Private housing**

The larger part of this chapter has discussed public housing since 86% of the population live in HDB flats. Private housing (comprising condominiums, apartments, bungalows, semi-detached and terrace houses) remains one of the unrealized goals of many young Singaporeans. Greater allocation of space for private development is being given, but with escalating cost and competition from foreign investors and expatriate workers the competition for this sector is also increasing.

In the 1960s, housing provision for the higher-income groups was concentrated mainly on developing bungalows, semi-detached and terrace houses in the suburban areas, including the prime residential districts of Bukit Timah and Katong (Sim and Yu, 1992). These landed properties were space-consuming and affordable only to the very wealthy. In the 1970s, in an attempt to maximize scarce land resources while satisfying the demand for private housing, the government encouraged the condominium concept based on apartments and townhouse blocks with shared recreational facilities such as swimming pools, tennis courts, squash courts and children's playgrounds, as well as other communal amenities, for example, a mini-mart and launderette.

Official guidelines regarding the development of condominiums were issued in 1972. To ensure success, the government took the lead in developing condominiums by releasing two parcels of land in 1974. In 1978, two other parcels of land were released, followed quickly by another in 1979. All these were in the prime residential districts of 9, 10 and 11 at the fringes of the city centre, chosen precisely because of convenience, accessibility and prestige. Although a new and untried formula, the condominium concept nevertheless attracted sufficient developers such that by 1980, there were a total of 14 projects in the prime areas and 12 in the rest of the island (Sim and Yu, 1992, p. 5).

In the early 1980s demand for condominium housing increased from both locals and foreigners. Buoyed by rapid economic growth, Singaporeans enjoying higher incomes aspired to own and live in private properties. At the same time, even those who may have been satisfied with HDB housing found that their monthly household incomes exceeded the ceiling set by the HDB and turned therefore to private housing. Externally, the demand from foreigners increased as the healthy economy attracted multinational corporations which sent their staff members to branches here. Expatriate staff therefore contributed significantly to the rental market. At the same time, a proportion of interest in condominiums also came from investors and speculators (Sim and Yu, 1992).

The tremendous interest in condominiums led to escalating prices and a rush for land for condominium development in the early 1980s. The first of these projects was marketed at the end of 1983, by which time the property market had begun to slump. It was not until 1989 that the condominium market began to show signs of recovery, so much so that by 1992, there was another boom in the market (except for a marginal slowdown during the Gulf War). The pickup in the condominium market in the 1990s was helped by the release of much more land for private housing under the provisions of the Revised Concept Plan, which included space for private housing in HDB new towns. Like the recent HDB innovations in the form of executive condominiums, these allocations reflect the attempt to meet the demands of Singaporeans with aspirations for private housing. However a significant part of the demand for private property is driven by speculation and investment motives. While the stock of private housing remains small big profits have been obtained from the rising value of private property during the 1990s, attracting purchases from Hong Kong and other Asian countries as well as wealthy Singaporeans. A particular feature of the speculation has been the use of 'soft launches' in which real estate developers give first option to preferred clients before releasing the property on the open market at its full price. To some Singaporeans this practice underlines a growing inequality in society.

### Conclusion

Singapore has come a long way from 1960 when the HDB was first established to deal with the massive problems of overcrowding and unhygienic conditions in slums and squatters. For the last three and a half decades, the HDB worked to provide Singaporeans with a living environment that is the envy of many. Home ownership has been achieved to a very large extent, and an HDB flat remains, for most Singaporeans, the biggest asset that they have, consuming most of their CPF contributions. At the same time, housing policy has served as one of the state's ideologically hegemonic tools in building consensus and achieving political legitimation. As Singapore reflects on its economic development, the state's task in providing public housing is no longer the provision of a roof over Singaporeans' heads. Singaporeans are increasingly looking for a living environment that approximates that of private housing estates. It is in this light that recent policy introductions – of upgrading, privatization, and executive condominiums – must be viewed.

# 9
# Urban conservation and heritage management

Since the mid-1980s, urban conservation has taken on a more visible profile in the government's plans for the city's development. From independence to the limited activities of the Preservation of Monuments Board (PMB) in the 1970s, urban conservation was accorded little if any attention and redevelopment took precedence as the means by which to propel Singapore towards 'growth and progress, providing not only environmental improvement, but also better employment and investment opportunities' (*URA Annual Report*, 1974/75, p. 7). In other words, the imperatives of a rapidly developing economy (to provide housing, serve the transportation and other social service needs of the population; facilitate employment and hence further economic development at minimum cost and maximum speed) dictated the planning agenda. In the words of Lim Chee Onn, Chairman of the National Heritage Board:

> There was simply no time to rearrange the furniture in the sitting room while pressing matters have to be attended to in the kitchen. Indeed on quite a number of occasions there were fires in the kitchen that had to be put out promptly. In the 60s and 70s it was not surprising that conservation did not feature highly, if at all, in our national agenda (quoted in *Roots: A Newsletter of the Singapore Heritage Society*, 1994, p. 2).

Thus, while the three indispensable elements of urban renewal were recognized to be rebuilding, rehabilitation and conservation (Choe, 1975, p. 99) and the 'preservation of Singapore's historical and architectural heritage' was explicitly written into policy guidelines (*URA Annual Report*,

1974/75, pp. 2–3), little of these intentions were translated into action prior to the 1980s.

The hint of a shift in policy occurred in 1976 when the Urban Redevelopment Authority (URA) initiated area-wide studies of conservation and rehabilitation opportunities. Chinatown was the most prominent among the large areas then under study (*URA Annual Report*, 1976/77, p. 31). It signified the first steps towards conceptualizing a conserved area to retain its distinct identity and character, but brought little practical change until the mid-1980s when a commitment was made to conserve a number of historic areas.

This chapter explains the emergence of urban conservation within the broader framework of national ideology, reflecting how urban conservation is inextricably locked into a wider political framework (see, for example, Tunbridge, 1984; Bromley and Jones, 1995). This context has been especially significant in Singapore where changing policy to the urban environment has been timed to fit the government's perception of how far reminders of the past will be a help or a hindrance to nation building. The chapter also explains practical aspects of conservation in Singapore, including specific preservation and conservation schemes initiated by various government agencies. The final part of the chapter reviews the debate about alternative strategies for heritage conservation and whose interests conservation should promote.

### The material and ideological weight of urban conservation

The increased emphasis on urban conservation as a means of preserving heritage in the 1980s coincided with changes in the ethos of the state and society. Among some sections of the population, the emergence of 'nostalgia' and a harking back to the past during the 1980s and 1990s was a reaction to the relentless drive of economic development and the consequent 'industrialization of everyday life' (Chua, 1995). However, while it may well be that the move to conserve the city's historic resources forms part of this groundswell of public opinion in favour of the past, the impetus for conservation came more directly from the hand of the government. Having created 'a sparkling new Singapore with no trace of the past' (Dhanabalan, quoted in Lau, 1992, p. 51), the reclamation of lost heritage began to assume 'an urgency that is narcotic' (Warren, 1986, p. 326). Part of this impetus arose from a concern among governing élites with the westernization of Singapore society.

Though westernization had served Singapore well in its quest for industrialization, it had also brought in its train values which were perceived to be incompatible with traditional Asian values. This unease over what Kwok (1993, p. 7) calls 'the complexity of our cultural condition' took the form of pronouncements and debates in both official and public discourse on a number of themes urging the preservation of 'Asian' and 'traditional' values and the maintenance of 'local' cultural identity and heritage. Political leaders, for example, highlighted the dangers of Singaporeans losing their Asian roots and the consequences for society. For example, Goh Chok Tong, then First Deputy Prime Minister, declared in 1988 that:

> We are part of a long Asian civilization and we should be proud of it. We should not be assimilated by the West and become a pseudo-Western society. We should be a nation that is uniquely multiracial and Asian, with each community proud of its traditional culture and heritage (Goh, 1988, p. 15).

As a defence against the infiltration of western values, interest grew in developing a set of national 'core' or 'shared' values to bind Singaporeans together and provide them with direction and identity (Ong 1990, p. 1). According to George Yeo (1989, p. 48), then Minister of State (Finance and Foreign Affairs):

> To be great, a nation must have a sense of its destiny. As we trace our ancestries, as we sift through the artefacts which give us a better understanding of how we got here, as we study and modify the traditions we have inherited, we form a clearer vision of what our future can be.

Heritage and traditions were drawn upon to provide 'the substance of social and psychological defence'. Thus, Lee Hsien Loong, then Minister for Trade and Industry and Second Minister for Defence, noted in 1989 that Singaporeans should:

> retain our heritage but examine it for values which need to be modified, and scrutinize foreign traditions for ideas which can be incorporated, but do so cautiously. Our roots are important. We should not be root-bound, but neither should we abandon our roots. They anchor us, and will help us grow (quoted in Lee, 1989, p. 33).

A Committee on Heritage was set up in April 1988 to assess the progress made in identifying, preserving and disseminating heritage awareness and to propose measures to encourage Singaporeans to be more widely informed and appreciative of their multi-cultural heritage. Singapore's 'unique heritage', reported the Committee, 'can play a vital part in nation building' for an understanding of one's roots and the lessons of history can help younger Singaporeans 'balance our Asian values and western influences', appreciate and 'draw inspiration' from the city's multicultural diversity and 'constantly renew work values and maintain the adaptiveness which underlies our economic success' (*The Committee on Heritage Report*, 1988, pp. 6–8).

According to the Committee, Singapore's 'heritage' comprises five categories: nation building heritage including the experience of living under, and the people's response to, the British colonial administration, the Japanese Occupation, the post-war struggle for independence, and the struggle against Communism; heritage of economic success which focuses on the values of our migrant predecessors who came to Singapore and their economic achievements; multi-cultural heritage expressed in the lifestyles, customs and traditions of the different ethnic communities; heritage of the created environment comprising buildings, landmarks and other visible and tangible links to our past in the physical landscape; and heritage of the natural environment which defines our territorial identity and our location within the Southeast Asian ecological region (*The Committee of Heritage Report*, 1988, pp. 27–29). For the Committee, therefore, heritage involved more than the British colonial imprint and was of more than local significance. Rather it consists of both tangible and intangible forms bequeathed by the past which are perceived to contribute to 'our shared experience of becoming a nation'. Of the different categories, it was often argued that heritage inscribed in the built environment is of particular significance as without 'visual landmarks', 'all other records of the past remain abstract notions, difficult to understand and link to the present'. 'It is clear therefore,' continued the Report, 'that the conservation of buildings, structures and other districts which provide the sign posts from the past to the present is critical to the psyche of a nation.'

The search for new economic directions after the recession of the mid-1980s (Chapter 5) became a further stimulus to the conservation of heritage. Recession led to the strategy of promoting Singapore as an international business and service centre, of which a component was tourism (Chang *et al.*, 1996). As well as manufacturing, tourism had been a casualty in the economic slowdown with a 3.5% fall in tourist arrivals in 1983. The fall in arrivals was blamed in part on 'the lack of colour in the increasingly antiseptic city-state' (Burton, 1993, p. 36) caused, according to the Tourism Task Force, by the loss of 'Oriental mystique and charm best symbolized in old buildings, traditional activities and bustling road activities' in the effort to construct a 'modern metropolis' (Wong *et al.*, 1984, p. 6). Recommendations from the Task Force were later incorporated in the Tourism Product Development Plan of 1986 (Pannell, Kerr and Forster, 1986). The plan included the expenditure of US$223 million for the redevelopment of *inter alia*, ethnic enclaves such as Chinatown, Little India and Kampong Glam, the Singapore River, a Heritage Link which encompasses all historic buildings in the city area of colonial origin as well as specific projects such as the upgrading of Raffles Hotel (the *grande dame* of colonial hotels in Singapore), the redevelopment of Fort Canning (formerly a fort turned park, museum and arts centre), the restoration of Emerald Hill (a residential street distinguished for Peranakan (local hybrid culture comprising Chinese, Malay and colonial British elements) architecture) and the rebuilding of Bugis Street (an open-air site famous for its raucous street life and local food prior to its demolition). Heritage conservation thus became intimately connected with redevelopment strategies designed to cater to tourist demands for uniqueness and to improve urban aesthetics (Teo, 1994; Chang *et al.*, 1996). As the Committee on Heritage noted, heritage 'makes us different and interesting for visitors' (*The Committee on Heritage Report*, 1988, p. 30).

### Preservation and conservation strategies and schemes

The strategy to recover heritage inscribed in the built environment moved from an early concern with preserving individual landmarks to a more concerted effort to conserve whole cultural and historic streets, areas and districts, and most recently, to a widening of interest to museums and other repositories of heritage in artefact and documentary forms. The discussion below follows these different stages in the development of a strategy to retain and inject a sense of the past in the modern cityscape.

*National monuments*

Preservation efforts relating to individual buildings and structures were initiated as early as the 1950s under the former colonial powers. *The Master Plan Written Statement* (1958, p. 35) published by the Ministry of National Development included a list of 30 structures which were proposed for preservation but befitting the mood in the 1960s of progress and development rather than preservation, little was done beyond amending the list with a few additions and deletions (*The Straits Times*, 3 August 1969). Indeed, one of the proposed buildings on the list, No. 3 Coleman Street, an early nineteenth century Anglo-Indian bungalow built by and lived in by the well-known colonial architect J. D. Coleman, succumbed to the bulldozer in the name of 'slum clearance' (*The Straits Times*, 5 December 1965).

Centennial milestones often play a major role in fostering a receptive climate of public opinion for conservation (Ashworth and Turbridge, 1990, p. 12) and this was no exception in Singapore. The celebration of the 150th anniversary of Singapore in 1969 provided the catalyst for further consideration of the preservation question. The Institute of Architects and the Historical Association of Singapore held a public meeting to discuss the concept of creating a civic organization to preserve historic buildings. Out of this initiative, a six-person committee was appointed to draft the constitution for the organization and further the proposal for 46 structures, including government and religious buildings as well as statues, to be preserved. Subsequently, it was announced by the then Minister for Law and National Development, E. W. Barker, that a National Monuments Trust would be formed (*The Straits Times*, 12 August 1969).

In January 1971, the PMB was established by an Act of Parliament to take charge of the gazetting and preservation of national monuments with four objectives: to preserve monuments of historic, traditional, archaeological, architectural or artistic interest; to protect and augment the amenities of those monuments; to stimulate public interest and support in the preservation of those monuments; and to take appropriate measures to preserve all records, documents and data relating to those monuments (Preservation of Monuments Act, 1985). A 'monument' could take the form of 'any building, structure or other erection, any memorial, place of interment or excavation or any part or remains of a monument'. Currently, over 30 structures, mainly religious and public buildings with a small number of commercial buildings, have been gazetted as national monuments (Table 9.1) while another 60-odd are safeguarded for consideration.

A designated national monument must be deemed to be of outstanding historical importance to the nation. The preservation process begins with the conservation section of the URA, the technical arm of the PMB reviewing the relative merits of buildings and structures with potential claims for preservation as national monuments. The identification process involves research and documentation, checks and verifications of historical and architectural significance, and consultations with other organizations such as the Ministry of Information and the Arts, the National Museum and the National Archives before the recommendations are put before the PMB for consideration and endorsement. To qualify as a national monument, a building or structure must be judged of 'architectural' and 'historical' significance and must satisfy criteria relating to 'rarity' and 'contribution to the environment'. Final approval before a building or structure can be gazetted as a national monument rests with the Minister of National Development. Meanwhile, PMB is consulted

**Table 9.1** List of national monuments and dates gazetted

| | National monument gazetted | Date |
|---|---|---|
| 1. | Old Thong Chai Building | 6 July 1973 |
| 2. | Telok Ayer Market | 6 July 1973 |
| 3. | St Andrew's Cathedral | 6 July 1973 |
| 4. | Thian Hock Keng (Temple) | 6 July 1973 |
| 5. | Armenian Church of St Gregory the Illuminator | 6 July 1973 |
| 6. | Cathedral of the Good Shepherd | 6 July 1973 |
| 7. | Hajjah Fatimah Mosque | 6 July 1973 |
| 8. | Sri Mariamman Temple | 6 July 1973 |
| 9. | Nagore Durgha (Shrine) | 6 July 1973 |
| 10. | Al-Abrar Mosque | 29 November 1974 |
| 11. | House of Tan Yeok Nee | 29 November 1974 |
| 12. | Tan Si Chong Su (Temple) | 29 November 1974 |
| 13. | Jamae Mosque | 29 November 1974 |
| 14. | Masjid Sultan (Sultan Mosque) | 14 March 1975 |
| 15. | Hong San See (Temple) | 10 November 1978 |
| 16. | St George's Church | 10 November 1978 |
| 17. | Sri Perumal Temple | 10 November 1978 |
| 18. | Abdul Gafoor Mosque | 13 July 1979 |
| 19. | Siong Lim Temple | 17 October 1980 |
| 20. | Raffles Hotel | 6 March 1989 |
| 21. | Goodwood Park Hotel Tower Block | 23 March 1989 |
| 22. | Telok Ayer Chinese Methodist Church | 23 March 1989 |
| 23. | CHIJ Chapel and Caldwell House | 22 October 1990 |
| 24. | Attorney-General Chambers | 14 February 1992 |
| 25. | City Hall | 14 February 1992 |
| 26. | Istana | 14 February 1992 |
| 27. | Parliament House | 14 February 1992 |
| 28. | Supreme Court | 14 February 1992 |
| 29. | St Joseph's Institution | 14 February 1992 |
| 30. | National Museum | 14 February 1992 |
| 31. | Victoria Theatre and Concert Hall | 14 February 1992 |
| 32. | Empress Place Building | 14 February 1992 |
| 33. | Sun Yat Sen Villa | 28 October 1994 |

before any state development work by other government agencies is undertaken where gazetted or safeguarded structures are involved.

Soon after the PMB's establishment, priority was given to religious buildings (Table 9.1). As well as places of worship being among the oldest and most important survivals of the Raffles era, these buildings were selected because of their importance as community centres where people 'exchange news of home' (*The Straits Times*, 19 August 1980) and as tangible emblems of the government's support for freedom of worship, commitment to multiculturalism, religious tolerance and harmony (Kong, 1993, pp. 32–33). The 1980s saw the diversification of the conservation

**Plate 9.1**  The Sultan Mosque: gazetted a national monument in the 1970s

effort to include buildings that were characterful and architecturally inter-
esting, as well as buildings that were part of the 'official' history or of religious importance. Reflecting this trend, the first structures to be gazetted
in that decade were two hotels, Raffles Hotel and part of the Goodwood
Park Hotel. In the 1990s, the PMB embarked on gazetting public buildings
(for example the National Museum, City Hall, Parliament House, Supreme
Court) and schools (for example the former Convent of the Holy Infant
Jesus and St Joseph's Institution) as national monuments. Another 60
buildings and other structures (including bridges and fountains) were
also recommended for gazetting as national monuments (*The Straits Times*,
26 April 1991).

The PMB's success in the 1970s was limited: buildings which were
gazetted came on stream intermittently and attracted little public attention while redevelopment continued relentlessly to wreak destruction on

the historic form and fabric of the city. One problem was the lack of financial and manpower resources allocated to the agency. For example, the application of the PMB Act to residential properties was often limited to the identification of the property to be preserved. As there were no funds to acquire such property or arrange viable financial alternatives, the designated property had to be released after one year (*The Committee on Heritage Report*, 1988, pp. 50–51). Some success was obtained in securing the participation of private organizations in the preservation programme. Among those which have responded to the preservation cause are Mobil, Lee Foundation, Lien Foundation and Jones Lang Wootton. This sponsorship, however, did not make up for the basic lack of resources.

Critics of the PMB have also felt that gazetted national monuments and their significance should be presented in more imaginative ways to arouse interest and understanding among the public, as 'history should be linked to everyday life – it is not just a mass of names and dates' (*The Straits Times*, 14 March 1983; 19 August 1983). A recent study (Ho, 1993–94 showed that among members of the public, while visual identification of monuments is strong, the specific names of these monuments are often overlooked and historical knowledge of them is rather shallow. The PMB encourages members of the public to actively support preservation efforts, 'to take pride in the monuments and recognize them as part of

**Plate 9.2** Supreme Court, a public building gazetted as a national monument

[Singapore's] multi-faceted heritage' (*The Straits Times*, 16 December 1988), but some of its methods have perhaps been rather formal. These include depicting national monuments on postage stamps (in 1978 and 1984); a commemorative edition of MRT tickets in 1996; inscribing them on silver ingots sold between 1 September 1978 and 1 April 1979; listing them in the official street directory, talks on the radio and television, and posters distributed to schools, community centres and other public institutions. Lectures revolving around the significance of national monuments are also held for tourist guides registered with the Singapore Tourist Promotion Board (*The Straits Times*, 19 August 1983).

*Conservation areas and historic districts*

By the mid-1980s, saving the occasional building was seen as a token concession to the importance of conserving the city's 'roots'. In its place, whole 'historic districts' or 'ethnic areas' became the target of conservation in the belief that this would better safeguard the 'richness of the cityscape' (*URA Annual Report*, 1983–84, p. 13; 1984–85, p. 3). The first project reflecting the new ethos was the refurbishment of an ensemble of low-rise Malaccan style terrace houses in Emerald Hill, a residential street leading off Orchard Road, Singapore's main shopping belt. Pedestrianization and landscaping was complemented by the development of Peranakan Corner, a commercial complex to house shops selling antiques, Nonya restaurants and a display centre featuring the Peranakan way of life at the junction of Emerald Hill and Orchard Road (*URA Annual Report*, 1983–84, pp. 22–23). Following in the wake of this project, detailed studies were completed for Chinatown, Singapore River, Little India and Kampong Glam in 1985 and subsequently included in the URA's Conservation Master Plan, publicly announced in December 1986 (*MND Annual Report*, 1987, p. 35). The plan covered more than 100 hectares, including the four areas mentioned, the Civic and Cultural District as well as the completed project at Emerald Hill (Figure 9.1). Plans for the Civic and Cultural District were given further attention in the form of a Master Plan (Figure 9.2) released to the public in March 1988, with aims to develop the area into a major historical, cultural and retail centre, as well as a venue for national ceremonies and functions (*URA Annual Report*, 1987–88, p. 2).

In the same year that the Master Plan for the Civic and Cultural District was released, conservation manuals and guidelines for the historic districts of Chinatown, Kampong Glam and Little India were also published. Each was designed to enable the public to understand the historical character and planning of, and architectural intentions in each district and

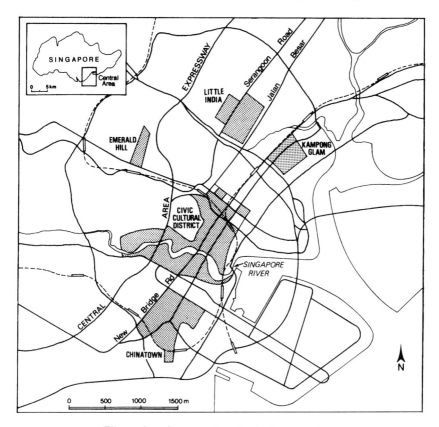

**Figure 9.1** Conservation sites in the central area

assist them in conserving their properties. Recognition and acknowledgement were accorded to all these efforts in 1989 when the Planning Act was substantially amended and the URA was made the national conservation and central planning authority. The amended Act formalized the URA's main tasks with regard to conservation – in effect, what the URA had already been doing for the last three to four years. These included identifying buildings and areas of historical interest for conservation; preparing a conservation master plan; and guiding the implementation of conservation by the public and private sectors (Sections 10(6)(c), 13, 14 and 15, Planning Act, 1990).

The URA now controls Singapore's conservation efforts, from the selection of sites and buildings to the specification of guidelines to control development in designated areas. Where the government is a major landowner, the URA directly undertakes to restore property, such as in the case of the pilot projects in Tanjong Pagar and Kreta Ayer (sub-districts in

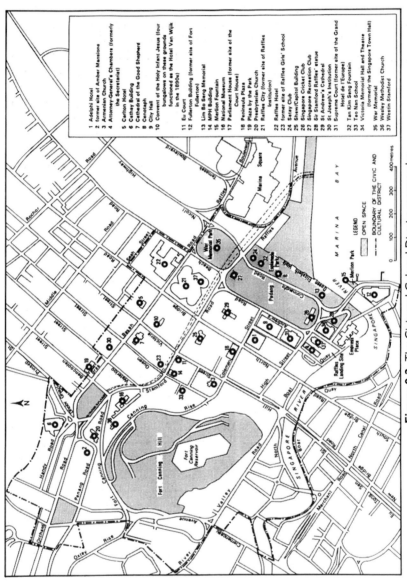

**Figure 9.2**  The Civic and Cultural District master plan

Chinatown). Where private ownership dominates, the URA works close-ly with the private sector, either by encouraging owners to restore their own buildings or tender them out to other developers.

With its responsibilities with respect to conservation established, offi-cial designation of ten areas as 'conservation areas' quickly followed. These are Kreta Ayer, Bukit Pasoh, Telok Ayer, Tanjong Pagar, Little India, Kampong Glam, Boat Quay, Emerald Hill, Cairnhill and Clarke Quay (*Republic of Singapore Government Gazette*, March 1989, No. 1154, p. 2343). In September 1991, the number of designated conservation areas was doubled by the addition of Joo Chiat, Geylang, Jalan Besar, Blair Plain, River Valley, Beach Road, Bukit Pasoh Extension, Desker Road, Petain Road/Tyrwhitt Road and Race Course Road/Owen Road (*Republic of Singapore Government Gazette*, September 1991, No. 3867, pp. 7025–6).

A further important extension of the conservation effort arose from the extension of the definition of conservation in section 3 of the Planning Act (1990) as 'the preservation, enhancement, or restoration of (a) the charac-ter or appearance of a conservation area; or (b) the trades, crafts, customs and other traditional activities carried on in a conservation area'. This expansion in the scope of heritage conservation represents a considerable challenge given the dependence on private redevelopment and enterprise for the revitalization of conservation areas and declining viability among traditional trades in Singapore.

As far as possible, the government seeks to avoid public investment in conservation projects, preferring to see them as opportunities for local enterprise so as to ensure that conservation pays its way. Government support for conservation has been achieved through the relaxation of reg-ulations, rather than direct assistance. For example, rent control (Chapter 6) has been phased out since it is the chief reason for the lack of mainte-nance of many buildings (Khlublall and Yuen, 1991, p. 134). Owners are now encouraged to restore their buildings through the relaxation of plan-ning controls, such as the waiving of development charge and parking requirements. Owners may also apply to the URA for assistance in relo-cating single elderly tenants judged to be at risk of becoming homeless to one- or two-room HDB rental flats (*Procedures for Recovering Possession of Rent-Controlled Premises*, 1990, p. 8). While encouraging and facilitating private sector involvement, the URA typically also sets strict guidelines regarding *inter alia* building material, design characteristics, acceptable trades and services, and the time limit for the completion of any project (see for example *A Manual for Chinatown Conservation Area* (1988) pub-lished by the URA). The views of the public and professional organiza-tions are sought for the purpose of refining some of these guidelines, but the URA eventually sets the rules. In general, the government's involve-

**Plate 9.3** Contrasting skylines in Chinatown

ment is confined mainly to masterplan design, policy guidelines and infrastructural and environmental improvements while the private sector is actively encouraged to provide 'the enterprise and the creativity' in undertaking conservation and determining land use mixes (*A Manual for Chinatown Conservation Area*, 1988). More recently, to increase the commercial viability of a conservation area in the case of the revitalization of Clarke Quay, a project which involved the redevelopment of 60 shophouses and godowns (warehouses), the entire site was sold *en bloc* to a single private developer to create an upmarket restaurant and entertainment area taking advantage of the riverside setting.

*Chinatown*

Of the conservation schemes already in place, historic districts in the central area have been accorded priority. The material effects of conservation are already visible in different parts of Chinatown, the earliest designated districts. Prior to urban renewal, the Chinatown landscape was characterized by tightly packed rows of shophouses, numerous clan-based institutions, traditional Chinese trades and festivities, and a bustling street life. The daily rhythm of the place combined both residential, community and commercial activities. In the 1960s and 1970s, urban renewal strategies such as the demolition of shophouses to make way for modern commercial and residential blocks and the clearance of street hawkers (Chapter 7) destroyed some of the fabric of the place. In the 1980s, Chinatown was described in government publications as an area which exemplified a range of urban problems including dilapidated structures of good architectural value, tenanted properties under rent control, fragmented land ownership and declining traditional trades (*A Manual for Chinatown Conservation Area*, 1988). Conservation was viewed as a strategy which would not only improve the general physical environment but also strengthen traditional trades and activities while introducing new features which would enhance the identity of the place.

The Chinatown conservation area covers approximately 23 hectares and 1200 structures of which about 700 are privately owned. It is subdivided into four smaller districts (Figure 9.3): Kreta Ayer (a commercial area centred around Trengganu and Pagoda Streets where the largest day and night street market used to be held until the early 1980s and the site of the Janae Mosque and Sri Mariamman Temple, both gazetted national monuments); Telok Ayer (the main landing point for nineteenth-century immigrant labourers; distinctive for the number of Chinese trading com-

**Plate 9.4** Sago Street, conserved shophouses in Chinatown. Photograph courtesy of the URA

panies set up here as well as prominent landmarks such as the Thian Hock Keng Temple, the Nagore Durgha Shrine and the Hokkien Huay Kuan), Tanjong Pagar (formerly a residential area for labourers working in the port nearby) and Bukit Pasoh (formerly a residential area and also the site of the Ee Hoe Hean Club, a recreational club for the wealthy Chinese). In general, the focus in the Chinatown Historic District is on traditional buildings such as shophouses. Once viewed as obsolete structures incompatible with the needs of a modern, dynamic city, shophouses are now seen to 'create a sense of human scale, rhythm and charm not found in much of our modern architecture' while 'the variety of building facades exhibit . . . creative use of the multi-cultural resources', providing relief from 'the monotony of a high-rise environment' (*Conservation within the Central Area with the Plan for Chinatown*, 1985, pp. 13, 15). Chinatown is now identified with the pioneering spirit and enterprise of early Chinese immigrants to Singapore and showcased as a distinctively Chinese cultural area which 'brims over with life, capturing the essence of the old Chinese lifestyle in its temples and shophouses and nurturing a handful of traditional trades [such as] herbalists, temple idol carvers, calligraphers and effigy makers . . . in the face of progress' according to the *Official Guide* (1991, pp. 28–29) to Singapore published by the STPB. Against a backcloth of shophouses and temples, large scale festival activities, fairs, *wayangs*, puppetry and trishaw rides can be 'staged' to provide both locals and tourists with 'a different kind of experience' (*Conservation within the Central Area with the Plan for Chinatown*, 1985, p. 15). Particularly during Chinese festivals, lion and dragon dances are brought in; national Chinese calligraphy competitions and exhibitions are held; ancient Chinese lantern quizzes are hosted; and Cantonese operas are performed, both for the tourist gaze as well as for locals in search of the vanished past (*The Straits Times*, 19 February 1985).

While the shophouse as an architectural form continues to provide much of the character of the place, Chinatown after conservation has lost the residential population which used to occupy these shophouses. The original local community of long-time residents, a community bonded by social interaction and affective ties, has been dispersed. As a result, there are few residents left in the conservation area to support the development of a local service centre or to contribute to the life of its streets. The local community has been replaced by an aesthetic and nostalgic notion of the Chinese 'community' less to do with local people than with local buildings and more to do with the remembered past as opposed to the lived present (Yeoh and Lau, 1995). It is this version of 'community' that is being presented to tourists and non-resident Singaporeans visiting the conservation area.

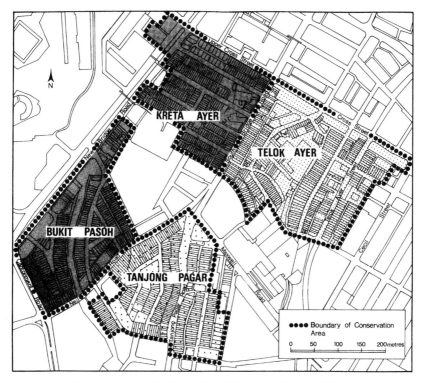

**Figure 9.3** Sub-districts of the Chinatown Historic District
*Source: A Manual for Chinatown Conservation Area* (1988)

## Little India

In similar fashion, the conservation of Little India, the traditional hub of Indian community life as its name suggests, is intended to showcase Indian cultural life and trades. This area around Serangoon Road was a flourishing centre for cattle trading activities in the second half of the nineteenth century, an economic activity dominated by Indians at all levels from ownership to labour supply. As immigration peaked in the late nineteenth and early twentieth century, Little India served as a reception and absorption centre for Indian and other immigrants. The population expanded, generating its own demand for retail and service activities which catered to the ethnically specific needs of the population. Commercial activities soon outstripped cattle trading as the main focal point in Serangoon Road. By the 1940s and 1950s, the area had developed into a commercial-cum-residential district with an ethnically mixed population but including a very high concentration of Indians. With urban renewal and relocation of the residential population to public housing from the 1960s, Little India became a predominantly commercial centre catering to Indians island-wide with some dormitory-type housing for Indian labourers working in the commercial enterprises. Today, the area is well-known for Indian food and traditional products and continues to feature as the hub of local Indian festivals. On weekends, the place serves as a meeting point and service centre for Bangladeshi, Indian and Sri Lankan foreign workers. According to the URA, the main aim of conservation is to 'preserve traits of historical development, both in form and variety and such that traditional activities can continue to take place in an authentic environment . . . [while allowing] new expressions to develop and contribute to the continuing evolution of the area' (*A Manual for Little India Conservation Area*, 1988, p. 28).

The conservation area (Figure 9.4) covers about 16 hectares of land on either side of Serangoon Road and includes 860 structures, of which about 640 are privately owned. It comprises mainly two-storey shophouses dating from as early as the mid-nineteenth century built in a variety of architectural styles, a number of religious buildings including the Abdul Gaffoor Mosque, a gazetted national monument, and several Hindu temples, as well as a few examples of nineteenth-century European bunga-

**Plate 9.5**  Conserved shophouses in Serangoon Road, Little India with a Sunday night gathering of foreign workers in the foreground

lows that once occupied part of this conservation area. Among the first areas addressed by the conservation authorities was the designated core around Buffalo Road comprising 28 shophouses and a bungalow which were restored in 1989 at a cost of $3.8 million. The intention was to create a 'festival plaza' which would 'take full advantage of the backdrop of fine street architecture [comprising shophouses] . . . for the staging of ethnic festivals and outdoor cultural performances' and to preserve the 'bazaar' effect achieved by the juxtaposition of numerous commercial activities such as the shops selling Indian *saris* (women's traditional dress), jewellery, garlands, curry powder, traditional foods, *dhobies* (laundry shops), and *mamak* shops (street-side stalls) (*A Manual for Little India Conservation Area*, 1988, p. 28). It has been reported, however, that not only is there an

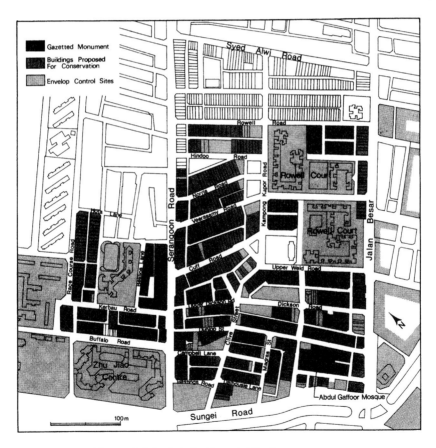

**Figure 9.4** Little India Historic District
*Source: A Manual for Little India Conservation Area* (1988)

/incursion of new uses such as pubs and bars which bring a different character to the area but the business in traditional goods has been poor in
contrast to the throb of activity in other parts of the Serangoon thorough-
fare where shophouses have not been restored (*The Sunday Times*, 2
August 1992). Despite the lack of success in the core area, conservation is
proceeding apace in other parts of the historic district. In line with the
view to encourage private sector involvement, for example, a recent project in the conservation area is the refurbishment of 26 shophouses to form
The Little India Arcade, a new shopping complex for Indian traditional
trades jointly developed by the Hindu Endowments Board and DBS land.
This project appears to be aimed primarily at tourists although it does
attract some local business, particularly at the time of Indian festivals.

### Kampong Glam

Similar design features such as the creation of a festival street and the
encouragement of traditional activities are also in the pipeline for the third
historic district, Kampong Glam, the traditional residential and business
quarter for Malay, Indonesian and Arab traders (*A Manual for Kampong
Glam Conservation Area*, 1988). This is a nine hectare site comprising 630
structures, mainly shophouses, of which about 500 are privately owned. It
is characterized by streets of two- or three-storeyed shophouses contrast-
ed with pockets of relatively large spaces housing prominent landmark
buildings of historical and architectural value such as the Masjid Sultan,
the most prominent mosque in Singapore and a gazetted national monument, and the Sultan's Palace, built in the 1840s as the residence of the
then Sultan of Johore. The conservation landscape is centred around the
area's 'historic hub' comprising the Sultan Mosque; a proposed show-
house featuring Malay heritage and culture at the site of the Sultan's
Palace; a proposed teahouse at No. 73 Sultan Gate, the former residence of
the *bendahara* (one of the Sultan's officials); a proposed community house
at the former Pondok Java; a 'festival street' (Bussorah Street) and a 'trading spine' (Arab Street); as well as the Alsagoff Arab School (Figure 9.5).
While some of the shophouses in the area have been restored, details for
the restoration of the proposed historic and cultural centres have not been
announced.

### Civic and Cultural District

Described as a 'rich historical area' containing a 'valuable collection of
architecturally and historically significant buildings' such as the Supreme

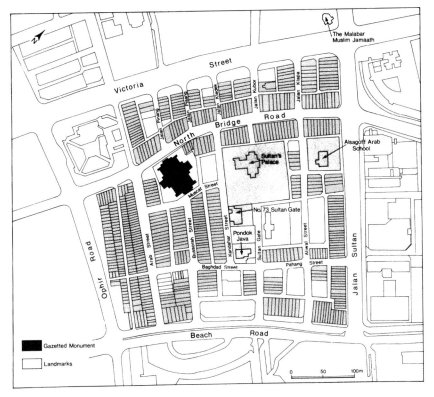

**Figure 9.5** Kampong Glam Historic District
*Source: A Manual for Kampong Glam Conservation Area* (1988)

Court, City Hall, National Museum, Victoria Theatre and Concert Hall, and a number of churches and former schools of colonial origin, the Civic and Cultural District on the north bank of the Singapore River represents the seat of the former colonial and civic government (Figure 9.2). Conservation activities in this district are aimed at revitalizing the district as a key cultural and retail magnet of the city; establishing and enhancing the distinctive qualities of the district as the historical colonial hub of the city; accentuating the special function of the district as a venue for national celebrations and ceremonies; and providing a physical framework for drawing up Singapore's Culture Master Plan for the adaptive reuse of old buildings (*Master Plan for the Civic and Cultural District*, 1988).

*Quayside projects*

Apart from the conservation of ethnic areas and the civic district, three quayside projects have also been undertaken, with the two nearest the Singapore River mouth, Boat Quay and Clarke Quay, having been completed (Robertson Quay is further inland). Until the redevelopment of the central area in the 1970s, the Singapore River was the hub of commercial and transport activities where lighters transhipped cargo from the riverside warehouses and trading establishments. Boat Quay has been revitalized as a riverside dining and entertainment street boasting a smorgasbord of pubs and restaurants serving international and ethnic cuisines. Clarke Quay opened in November 1993 as a riverside 'festival village' of shops, restaurants, pubs, push-carts offering traditional foods and crafts, pedicabs, bumboat river taxis and street architecture such as waterfront gas lamps to recreate the mood of the 1930s (Lim, 1993). Its centrepiece is a Disney-style bumboat ride housed inside air-conditioned, renovated godowns whisking visitors through moving exhibits comprising scenes from Singapore's past.

Despite some attempt to introduce heritage elements such as architectural facades, street furniture and bumboats, little of the quays' historic

**Plate 9.6** Clarke Quay riverside entertainment centre and conservation area. Photograph courtesy of the URA

character remains. Instead, they now feature as upmarket leisure areas for the well-heeled. Located close to the financial and business centre, these quayside projects cater in the day to professionals and office workers. In the evenings, the upmarket dining outlets, pubs and bars are patronized by yuppies, expatriates and tourists. Billed as a 'waterfront marketplace', Clarke Quay's 170 shops sell items ranging from designer to casual wear, electronics and souvenirs while traditional trades such as clog-making and push-carts selling titbits feature as embellishments. Boat Quay has been described by one journalist as 'an unremitting row of watering holes' with a reputation for drunkenness and teenage catfights with little to remind one of 'the toil and tears of the immigrant generation of Singaporeans' who used to work on the river (*The Straits Times*, 24 January 1996).

## Residential heritage

While conservation schemes have focused mainly on the central area, the aim is also to include private houses and bungalows in outlying areas such as Mountbatten Road as part of the conservation of 'residential heritage' as well as 'secondary conservation areas' such as River Valley, Geylang and Joo Chiat, centres which developed in the twentieth century before the onset of the Pacific War as a result of the outward movement of the population from the city centre. *In toto*, by 1994, conservation schemes include a range of commercial, residential and institutional buildings and involve over 5000 buildings.

## Museums and repositories

The awareness of heritage in other than the built environment has been recognized with the establishment of a National Heritage Board in August 1993 as an autonomous statutory board. Having first been proposed by the 1988 Committee on Heritage, the Board's mission is to explore and present 'the heritage and nationhood of Singaporeans in the context of our ancestral cultures' and 'our links with Southeast Asia, Asia and the world'; to promote public awareness, appreciation and understanding of the arts, culture and heritage by collecting, preserving, interpreting and displaying objects and records; and to help Singapore develop into a regional cultural hub to attract visitors from abroad (*The Straits Times*, 4 November 1993). Sharing similar ideological intents as the earlier bid to preserve monuments and conserve areas, the aim behind the setting up of the Board was to 'make sure that Singaporeans have a deep sense of the past which will provide Singaporeans with the "cultural depth" to see [them] through crises' (*The Straits Times*, 18 March 1992).

The Board seeks to build on the work of existing heritage establishments such as the National Museum, National Archives and Oral History Department with the objective of bringing a 'radical shift' in public perception and interaction with these repositories of heritage. It wants to encourage more public participation, both in visiting museums and contributing towards building up the storehouse of collective memory through donations of memorabilia. For example, the Board promotes school visits to museums and heritage centres and encourages school principals and teachers 'to instill a sense of the past in their students' (*The Straits Times*, 4 September 1993). This is deemed a necessary corrective to what is seen as a lamentable lack of awareness of Singapore's past – particularly 'the struggle for independence and against the communists, the building of a nation state, the values that were taught, the society that was formed and the nation that was built' – among the younger generation (*The Straits Times*, 28 January 1980). More museums are also being added to the heritage network, including the Philatelic Museum converted from the 88-year-old former Methodist Book Room in Coleman Street which opened in August 1995; the Singapore Art Museum which occupies the buildings of the former St Joseph's Institution opened in October 1995; the Asian Civilizations Museum to be sited at the former Tao Nan School in Armenian Street which will house collections from Southeast Asia, East Asia and South and West Asia when opened in mid-1996; a museum displaying vintage fire engines and fire-fighting equipment at the 87-year-old Central Fire Station in Hill Street; as well as the renovation of the existing National Museum as a Singapore History Museum by 1999. In view of the current thinking that museums should reach out not just to art lovers but also the community at large, these repositories are carefully packaged to appeal to as wide an audience as possible. The Singapore Art Museum, for example, includes on its premises a nursery for children, a café, a museum shop, an auditorium, an electronic gallery of digitized images of paintings, as well as special programmes catering to different interests from those of children to corporate bodies (*The Straits Times*, 20 January 1996).

### Debates and dilemmas

In essence, the controversy surrounding conservation in Singapore is little different to the experience of other places. Are sufficient areas being conserved, are the conservation regulations adequate and effective, is building conservation worthwhile while the character of the area changes and traditional ways of life disappear, is conservation serving the interests of locals or tourists? The issue of ethnic balance is perhaps of greater local sensitivity and in reviewing Singapore's conservation programme, this will be considered first.

*Conserving the diversity of colonial and multi-ethnic heritage*

It has been argued that heritage conservation in Singapore will always remain a contentious issue given that 'each generation essentially rediscovers its own past' and places a value on heritage which may be different from past generations (Lee, 1991, p. 4). Furthermore, in a post-colonial society like Singapore, the question of whose heritage warrants conservation is not only complicated by questions as to how far the colonial inheritance should be retained *vis-à-vis* indigenous structures but also different ethnic groups' relative share of the heritage pie. These two questions will be taken up in turn.

Societies emerging from colonialism have to decide how far to divest the landscape of colonial associations by removing its stock of colonial structures and to what extent to accept the colonial legacy as part and parcel of the socio-cultural baggage of the newly-independent state. Western (1985, p. 344), however, notes that in practice, post-colonial societies often 'do not have the capability to rewrite forthwith a new image in their cities' as 'other priorities clamour' and colonial structures are often appropriated for new purposes and re-invested with new meanings. This is precisely the case in Singapore as exemplified by the revitalization of the Civic and Cultural District, referred to in URA documents as the 'colonial hub' of the city. From the government's perspective, not only does the Civic District provide 'an architectural vista of the colonial past' (Lee, 1991, p. 2), it furnishes a suitably impressive setting for staging national celebrations and ceremonies, particularly when plans to mark out 'celebration routes' and 'historic trails' and to accentuate buildings with special lighting have been completed (*URA Annual Report*, 1988/89, p. 17). Hence, for the government, political legitimation does not require wholesale removal of the colonial legacy on the landscape; instead, buildings and built environments inherited from the colonial era can be divested of associations with imperial glory and re-invested with new significance – those of national and civic pride. This is well accepted by most Singaporeans who feel that many colonial buildings have superior architectural and aesthetic qualities which merit them a place in the city scape without conjuring up negative connotations associated with a colonial past (Kong and Yeoh, 1994).

The list of gazetted buildings has been evaluated by a prominent Singapore architect as being 'even-handed [with] a sprinkling of multi-cultural samples of historical buildings' (Tay, 1991, p. 39). This is part of a deliberate strategy to ensure equal representation of the major ethnic groups in the choice of historic monuments and districts. As such, historic districts include the cultural enclaves of the Chinese, Malays and Indians while religious buildings gazetted as national monuments include Chinese temples, Indian temples, Muslim mosques and Christian churches. Instead, rather than sharpen social cleavages along ethnic lines, the government argues that conserving historic places of different ethnic groups in Singapore provides a new 'glue' which could bind a multi-ethnic, multi-cultural society together (Tay, 1991, p. 41). Again, this argument is well accepted by most Singaporeans who feel that the URA's plans to conserve ethnic areas in Singapore were in no way divisive, even if it highlighted differences between ethnic groups. Various reasons were cited for their view. For example, some argued that it was in fact educational for Singaporeans to recognize differences between the ethnic groups. The idea was to exhibit each group's heritage; to complement, not to compete. At the same time, many used the oft-cited slogan 'unity in diversity' to suggest that it was possible to remain distinctive ethnically and yet feel a sense of unity with a larger whole.

*The conservation–redevelopment conflict revisited*

As in any city, there are cases where historic buildings have been lost to redevelopment. The issue in Singapore is whether there is adequate opportunity for the public to influence decisions. The government views conservation as an economically viable and sustainable activity which does not conflict in principle with economic development but serves to realize the 'full potential of an area' (Powell, 1992, p. 41). However, even with the incorporation of urban conservation into economic and urban plans, there are specific instances where buildings of historical and/or architectural significance had to give way to what the government views as a more pragmatic or rational use of land.

For example, Eu Court, a curved corner building with 'landmark qualities' located in the Civic and Cultural District, was torn down in early 1993 to make way for the widening of Hill Street and to alleviate traffic congestion in the area (*Roots*, 1993, p. 3). The case for its demolition was presented as a choice between saving either one of two proximate and equally historically significant buildings, Eu Court and Stamford House; the former was sacrificed for the preservation of the latter because, according to S. Dhanabalan, then Minister for National Development, not only had the latter a 'more outstanding architectural style' but also because it had 'a greater potential to become an active and successful commercial centre' (*Roots*, 1991, p. 5). Eu Court was demolished despite appeals to save it spearheaded by the Singapore Heritage Society, an interest group which champions the values of heritage, which feared that Eu Court was only 'the thin end of a wedge in conservation terms' (*Roots*, 1993, p. 3). Similarly, Crescent Flats in Meyer Road, believed to be the oldest apartment block in Singapore, was razed to make way for condominium development despite letters to the press from the public appealing for its preservation (*Roots*, 1992, p. 7). This conflict reflects a more subtle turn from earlier, more straightforward tensions over whether urban renewal should entail redevelopment or conservation. That the latter is necessary is no longer in question; instead, it is now a matter of which area or building deserves to be conserved, who makes the decision and on what basis. By the 1990s, however, while there are occasional flashpoints hinged on the preservation–demolition of specific structures and buildings, most of the current debate revolves around how conservation should proceed and whether it has been successful as opposed to the actual need for conservation.

**Plate 9.7** Eu Court, demolished in 1993 after restoration to make space for road widening. Photograph courtesy of the URA

*The conservation strategy: material form or intangible spirit?*

A place comprises both the material built environment and the activities and lifestyles of users and inhabitants. Often, conservation is recommended on the grounds of the former, such as the architectural merit, aesthetic value or historical significance of the built environment. This raises questions about the continuance of people's activities and lifestyles. In some places, conservation completely displaces residents and 'alien community interests' take over. These alien community interests may take the form of economic enterprises as often happens in a market economy and this, as Tunbridge (1981, p. 121) has pointed out, almost inevitably involves some trade-off between the 'physical and community fabric'.

In Singapore, urban conservation has entailed meticulous attention paid to the physical fabric and architectural details of gazetted buildings and areas to ensure 'authenticity'. Where private owners are involved in restoration work, stringent URA guidelines intended to produce architectural integrity have to be adhered to so that individual restoration works would not 'compromise . . . the authenticity of the historic district' (*A Manual for Chinatown Conservation Area*, 1988, p. 86). The government's conservation efforts also pay attention to ensuring that the external public built environment retains 'its historic charm'. Accordingly, elements such as street furniture, existing old lamp posts, fire hydrants, 'authentic' signboards and lighting, and 'compatible' materials for five-foot-ways must be 'sensitively selected or designed' (*A Manual for Chinatown Conservation Area*, 1988, p. 47). It is also the government's intention that traditional trades and activities be retained as part of the historical and cultural heritage of the area though new compatible trades may also be introduced. In many already conserved areas, however, it would appear as if new trades and other economic enterprises have taken over existing activities. The government has reiterated that conservation should not entail 'the fossilization of traditional trades and lifestyles that existed before conservation' (Lee, 1991, p. 3). According to Liu Thai Ker, former chief executive officer of the URA: 'There is no earthly justification to say that you must freeze at the point of restoration, because lifestyles have been changing ever since the buildings were built. The URA has therefore left it to market forces to throw up activities in conservation schemes' (quoted in Lee, 1991, p. 3). More succinctly, the then Minister for National Development, S. Dhanabalan, stated: 'Our approach [to conservation] is simple: restore the buildings, and let a new tradition emerge' (quoted in Burton, 1993, p. 37).

As these statements suggest, government believes that urban conservation should be economically viable if not profitable, adding to the economic assets of the country in the same way more conventional landscapes of industrial production do. As put succinctly in a URA newsletter, 'Tanjong Pagar means business' (*Skyline*, January/February 1989, p. 9). In line with such a view, the government has from the outset underscored the crucial role of the private sector in determining the success of conservation projects, as well as stressing that conservation should not be subsidized or become an 'economic burden' to the nation (*Business Times*, 10 September 1991). Thus, other than excluding environmentally pollutive uses *in toto* and proscribing what are deemed incompatible trades from designated core areas (*A Manual for Chinatown Conservation Area*, 1988, p. 52), the URA has left it up to market forces to throw up activities and trades in conservation areas. Instead of retaining existing activities and traditional uses, the URA strongly believes in the 'adaptive re-use' of historic buildings, making them relevant to the needs and uses of modern times. This strategy of 'adaptive re-use' is exemplified in Tanjong Pagar by the transformation of the Jinrikisha Station, which was sold for $2 million and converted into a seafood restaurant. Alternative uses have also been introduced, for example, pubs, restaurants, lounges and offices of a range of businesses from law firms to modelling agencies, in rehabilitated and restored shophouses in Tanjong Pagar and Kreta Ayer. In such localities, conservation has provided a vehicle for the conversion of areas into comparatively high-income consumer service centres, consistent with the island's changing social structure and economic functions but bearing few links to the past.

Even where preserved national monuments are concerned, innovative changes can be made to the functions of gazetted buildings. For instance, tenders were invited to adapt the Old Thong Chai Building, a former Chinese medical institution catering to the poor, 'for shopping and/or institutional uses that are compatible with the character of the building' (*The Straits Times*, 7 July 1993). The same rationale 'to identify key buildings available for cultural re-use' has led to the conversion of the former grounds and buildings of St Joseph's Institution, a premier Catholic boys' school, and the Convent of the Holy Infant Jesus, a religious and educational institution, into a fine arts museum and a commercial and cultural centre respectively.

The tensions of achieving historic yet profitable restoration are thus left to market forces to resolve. This has become a contentious point for some Singaporeans although others appear willing to accept new trades and uses in old buildings. In a recent survey (Kong and Yeoh, 1994), a slight majority of respondents felt that the physical fabric may be conserved, but lifestyles and activities should have the flexibility of changing and that outmoded lifestyles should not be forced on conservation areas. On the other hand, one-third of respondents argued that lifestyles and activities should remain as a legacy to future generations and also because the meaning of place is intimately tied up with the lifestyles and activities such that if the latter disappeared, there was no point in conservation at all. The constant infusion of new activities would lead to the over-commercialization of the place and destroy its spirit. Respondents who subscribed to this view, for example, were perturbed by the fact that in Tanjong Pagar, pubs and restaurants such as J. J. Mohaney, Elvis, Chicago Bar and Restaurant and the Flag and Whistle Pub run on 'alien' concepts and which promote 'western' consumption patterns have eclipsed the traditional family-run Chinese businesses. In their opinion, architecture and aesthetics alone did not capture the past and render it meaningful to Singaporeans; rather restored buildings were 'mere shells' that did not compensate for the loss of the 'original' lifestyle and 'traditional' culture whatever the architectural merits of the restoration.

**Plate 9.8** Elvis Pub in the Tanjong Pagar conservation area

*Conservation for locals or tourists?*

The conservation, management and exploitation of visible heritage in the urban built environment is now a flourishing 'growth industry' in many countries (Hewison, 1987; Hardy, 1988, p. 333; Fowler, 1989, pp. 187–90). In Singapore, while the URA claims that conservation is primarily for Singaporeans and that tourism is secondary (Lee, 1991, p. 1), it is evident that targeting the tourist dollar is a crucial goal of conservation plans and strategies. Conservation projects such as those in Tanjong Pagar and Kreta Ayer specifically aim to provide 'a host of specialized shops, open air cafés and eating places' to create 'the right ambience for tourists and locals alike looking for something different' (*URA Annual Report*, 1984–85, p. 11). Conservation areas are viewed as 'attractions . . . with high tourism appeal' and plans for their development include strategically located hotels – both of the 'boutique' and 'business' variety – 'to capitalize on [the] resurgence of old Singapore' (*URA Press Release*, 16 August 1990).

In the survey noted above (Kong and Yeoh, 1994), the bulk of respondents not only identified the attraction of tourists to Singapore as a prime motivation for urban conservation but felt that conservation benefits tourists more than Singaporeans. Three further studies, the first focused on Kreta Ayer (Yeoh and Kong, 1994), the second on Tanjong Pagar (Yeoh and Lau, 1995) and the third on the Civic and Cultural District (Huang *et al.*, 1995; Teo and Huang, 1995) also reinforce the view that the public, and in particular 'insiders' who have lived and worked in the area prior to conservation, are concerned that the conserved landscape increasingly ministers to the needs of the tourist rather than the local. Chinatown respondents point to the many retail shops and handicraft outlets that specialize in tourist souvenirs and novelty items, the 'tourist prices' of wares, as well as the number of tour buses that visit the area (Yeoh and Lau, 1995). That conserved Chinatown is a landscape made for tourist consumption is particularly evident when dusk approaches and tourists are bussed off: Chinatown residents lament that the place takes on the 'silence of a ghost town without a soul in sight' compared to before when it 'can be said to be a place with no night' (Yeoh and Kong, 1994). Similarly, the study on the Civic and Cultural District also argues that it is 'tourists' perceptions, desires, and concerns' which have guided urban conservation, resulting in the creation of an 'elitist' landscape 'removed from the lived experiences of locals' (Teo and Huang, 1995, p. 593). The conversion of Empress Place, a cluster of buildings which used to house the National Registration and Immigration Offices into a grand museum for exhibitions of artefacts imported or loaned from abroad, for example, led to the 'museumization' of the place for tourists and 'isolated [it] from the daily rhythms of the average Singaporean' (Teo and Huang, 1995, p. 568).

The reworking of local heritage for tourist consumption is taken to the extreme in the case of cultural theme parks which, while capitalizing on an aspect of local culture or history to sell a particular 'theme', have their place firmly planted in 'the world of incentives' as strategies to lengthen the itinerary of visitors to the city (*Incentives & Marketing Asia*, November–December, 1995, p. 7). This is particularly evident in the case of Haw Par Villa, once a pleasure garden of Chinese myths and legends bequeathed by a philanthropist to the people for their enjoyment but now one of a string of commodified leisure pursuits which reinvent tradition for a tourist market (Yeoh and Teo, 1996). While the theme park may appeal to tourists who wish to experience Chinese culture in an environmental bubble, many Singaporeans in a recent survey viewed this as an adulteration of local heritage (Teo and Yeoh, 1997). Despite government rhetoric that conservation safeguards the collective memory of the people and enriches local culture, members of the public perceive urban conservation as being tailored to the tourist gaze and heritage browsing rather than the lifestyles of Singaporeans.

**Conclusion**

From an almost total neglect of heritage in the early years of economic development after gaining independence, Singapore has seen a rapid surge of conservation activities over the last decade. The impact on the city scape has been impressive, as evidenced by national monuments, historic and cultural districts, riverside projects, conserved residential properties and a miscellany of different protected structures and buildings. The need for heritage buildings and conservation areas is now almost undisputed: in the words from *Our Heritage is in Our Hands* (1994, pp. 3, 29), a joint URA and PMB publication, they are 'our history, captured in brick, plaster, wood and stone' and 'to lose these architectural assets would be to erase a living chapter in our history'. These are now the overriding sentiments. Yet, it must be pointed out that much of the conservation initiative is state-driven and state-planned and serves the various ideological intents of the government. The local public, however, has not been completely quiescent and in a maturing democratic country, government policies and actions have increasingly come under the constant scrutiny of public eyes. While few have questioned whether the government should play a predominant role in spearheading urban conservation, some have protested against the 'heavy hand' of the government and the lack of public participation in decision-making on conservation issues (Kong and Yeoh, 1994). The groundswell of public sentiment, however, has yet to coalesce and there is as yet no strong collective voice or sustained public outcry to challenge the government's role in urban conservation. With a public increasingly concerned with the finer things in life and at the same time more censorious of the government, it is likely that heritage and conservation issues will increasingly come under the public gaze in the decade to come.

# 10

## The next lap

After 30 years of rapid growth which has transformed the physical, social and economic environment, some Singaporeans have begun to question whether the emphasis on growth should now be downplayed in preference to improving the quality of life. For Singapore's political leaders, on the other hand, the view is quite unequivocally that there should be no such trade off. Indeed, as the century draws to a close and as Singapore stands on the brink of accepting developed country status, governmental discourse has been peppered with the need to find strategies for further growth and thereby to improve the present standard of living while simultaneously enhancing the quality of life. To help persuade the population of the need to maintain its commitment to economic growth, much use is made of the exercise of constructing visions of what the fruits of this growth may bring in return.

Vision setting commenced in 1984 with *Vision 1999*, in which the goal was to achieve a Swiss standard of living by the year 1999. *Vision 1999* was to be measured by, among other indicators, per capita income. The target was to reach $31 550 by 1999, equal to what the Swiss had achieved in 1984. It was believed that the achievement of such growth would cap Singapore's development into a modern and impressive city.

When *Vision 1999* was first promulgated, Singapore's per capita GNP was $13 599. In little more than half a decade, by 1991, it had risen to $21 870 (*Yearbook of Statistics 1994*). With economic growth in hand, attention has turned to converting this wealth into the development of a 'first class city'. In 1991, the government launched *Living the Next Lap*, a document to guide the city's development, covering all the key areas of life, from housing and education to defence. In 1992, the PAP used it as its election manifesto (Chapter 3). A key component of this vision is the

Revised Concept Plan, a planning blueprint put together mainly by the Urban Redevelopment Authority. Some aspects of the revised plan are already being implemented, while others are still futuristic.

Five years after the launch of *Living the Next Lap*, Singapore's per capita GNP had risen further to $28 820 (*Yearbook of Statistics 1994*). Assuming economic growth of 7% per annum (an undemanding assumption in the light of past performance) for the next three years, *Vision 1999* will be surpassed. Against this background, the mid-1990s saw the articulation of more parts of the Revised Concept Plan into specific plans for the city. In this final chapter, these intentions are reviewed and compared with the ambition of the population.

## A city of the 21st century

The Revised Concept Plan (introduced in Chapter 7) is intended to help Singapore 'make a quantum leap' in the quality of its environment (*Living the Next Lap*, 1991, p. 3). It provides a framework for the physical development of the city in three stages – up to the year 2000, then to 2010 and Year X, thought to be a time in the future in which Singapore's population will reach 4 million (more recently it has been indicated that the target may be raised, possibly up to 5 million). The Revised Concept Plan states an intention to create a developed city for (*a*) business, (*b*) living and (*c*) leisure, and (*d*) one with world class transportation, and (*e*) endowed with nature.

As a city for business, it envisages greater decentralization to four regional centres, to bring jobs closer to homes so as to reduce the need for travel into the city centre. It is anticipated that each centre will serve up to 800 000 people by Year X, which is about 15 times the size of HDB town centres as they exist today. Each centre will become a commercial and cultural hub, with offices, shops, hotels, restaurants and cinemas. About half the floor space in regional centres will be given over to offices, while about 35% will be occupied by retail shops and restaurants. The last 15% will be taken up by hotels and entertainment facilities. These facilities will provide employment opportunities for the population living in existing and new housing estates nearby, and retail and entertainment facilities will serve their needs. The four regional centres planned are Tampines, Woodlands, Jurong East and Seletar (Figure 10.1), and indeed, some progress has already been made in developing Tampines and Jurong East as regional centres.

In addition to the four regional centres, six sub-regional centres about one-third the size of the former are also planned. These will be focused on

**Plate 10.1** Model of Tampines Regional Centre. Photograph courtesy of the URA

MRT stations such as Buona Vista, Bishan and Paya Lebar. About 40% of the space will be taken up by offices, while hotels, entertainment, retail and food outlets will take up the rest (Figure 10.1). Smaller versions of these sub-regional centres are fringe centres, which are centred on MRT stations on the fringes of the city centre such as Newton, Lavendar and Novena. There will be space for one small hotel and some retail and entertainment space, intended to provide a wide range of goods, services and jobs near to where people live.

As part of the decentralization efforts, a new downtown will be established to cater to new and expanding businesses which still require a central location. It is intended that this new downtown, to be centred on Marina South, adjacent to the existing financial and business centre, will take advantage of its waterfront location to create a centre for international business with a distinctive aesthetic atmosphere. Housing, shops, hotels, theatres, concert halls, restaurants and outdoor cafés, green, open spaces and tree-lined boulevards will be integrated within the office district to offer life and activity both day and night.

New types of industrial space are also planned in the form of business parks and new technology corridors, such as an Aviation Park near Seletar Airport and a Medical Park next to the Singapore General Hospital. These parks are intended to house high technology industries as well as provide high quality housing and recreational facilities to attract

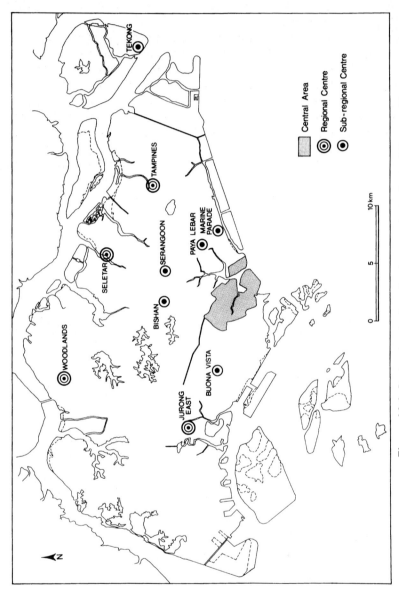

**Figure 10.1** Regional and sub-regional centres in the Revised Concept Plan
*Source: Living the Next Lap* (1991)

talented people. A number of them will also be close to institutions of higher learning and related research facilities and, it is hoped that they will turn into mini Silicon Valleys, encouraged through the fertile exchange of research ideas.

In order to retain a top quality workforce, fitting this entrepreneurial environment, planning will give increasing consideration to the preferences of professional and skilled workers. A greater variety of housing is envisaged. While high-density flats will remain the norm in the public sector, a greater share of private housing is to be provided for occupying a greater range of locations. Whereas previously the state has been reluctant to release coastal land for housing, selected sites have now been identified for waterfront housing, for example, at Simpang, Tanjong Rhu, Kampong Bugis, the Singapore River, and on the island of Buran Darat, off Sentosa Island. As articulated in the Revised Concept Plan (1991, p. 22), 'having a boat near the back yard will no longer be just a dream'. People's access to the water's edge will be enhanced with planned walkways, marinas and waterside recreational facilities. New housing in the central city is also to be allowed in reversal of previous planning policy. For public HDB estates, upgrading, as discussed in Chapter 8, will continue to enable them to share some improved amenity.

**Plate 10.2** Model of proposed Singapore Arts Centre. Photograph courtesy of the Singapore Arts Centre Co Ltd.

Social, cultural and community amenities will be upgraded and increased in number. These include educational institutions (land is being set aside for a third university), medical and health facilities, facilities for the performing arts and more imaginative playspace designed for young people. In the area of medical and health care, more facilities will be provided particularly in view of an ageing population (see Chapter 4), for example, community hospitals and polyclinics. In terms of history, culture and the arts, the Revised Concept Plan (*Living the Next Lap*, 1991, p. 27) contains blueprints for the development of the central city as 'the national stage for the arts'. The Museum Precinct, comprising five museums, is intended to form one focus of activities (see Chapter 9). A new, modern National Library building will be constructed, with the latest in library technology. By the year 2000, a new Singapore Arts Centre will have been completed to house various performing halls with carefully designed acoustic and lighting facilities, while existing theatres such as the Kallang Theatre, Victoria Theatre and Victoria Concert Hall will continue to be upgraded. In addition, regional centres, new towns and sub-regional centres will also have their own smaller versions of arts and cultural facilities.

Leisure and exercise are also priorities under the Revised Concept Plan. For example, cycle tracks to link parks and leisure areas around the island are planned as well as more facilities for other sports, including swimming pools, golf courses, squash and tennis courts, and other spectator sports. Recreational facilities may also take the form of adventure parks and theme gardens, while it is also intended that Singapore's island heritage be better harnessed. Thus, beaches, marinas, lagoons and beach resorts will all be planned. By the year 2010, the plan is to have a scenic coastal road which will allow Singaporeans to enjoy a leisurely drive around the entire island. This will all be made possible with further reclaimed land off the main island, as well as a long island to be reclaimed from the sea, running down most of the length of Singapore's east coast.

A deliberate design intention is to make use of Singapore's natural environment. Development must not be at the expense of the urban or natural environment, and must build on Singapore's reputation as a clean and green city. Under the Green and Blue Plan (Figure 10.2), the idea is to weave together a system of foliage (green) and waterways (blue) to 'heighten the feeling of island living', and 'to create an image of islands within an island . . . the sense of gardens within a garden' (*Living the Next Lap*, 1991, p. 28). The open spaces to be connected will comprise 'nature stations' ('pockets of natural landscape like hills or wooded areas, river banks and the like . . . to help create the image of leaving the busy city far behind'); parks and gardens (such as regional and district parks); sports and recreation grounds (such as golf courses, stadiums, adventure parks

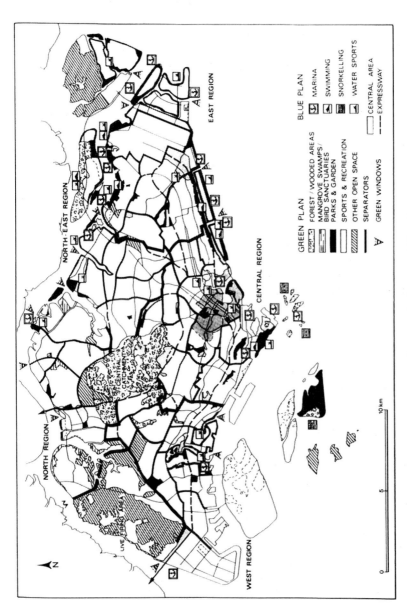

**Figure 10.2** Singapore's Green and Blue Plan
*Source: Living the Next Lap* (1991)

and camp sites); internal greenways and connectors (green linkages connecting major parks and recreational areas); boundary separators (which define neighbourhoods and precincts within a local community); and other open areas (such as military training areas). The intention is also to adapt waterways, including major rivers and canals, for recreational use. In time it may be even possible for people to jog or cycle around Singapore through a network of connectors without having to get onto roads (see Briffett et al., 1996). Within the city centre, the image is of pocket parks and open tree-lined boulevards to serve as 'green lungs' alongside the existing parks such as Fort Canning Hill, Pearl's Hill and York Hill.

Finally, the Revised Concept Plan acknowledges the importance of the transport system: 'If a transport system is inadequate or breaks down, a city can be seriously impaired' (*Living the Next Lap*, 1991, p. 36). A White Paper on Land Transportation, released in 1996, has mapped out what Singapore's 'world class transportation system' might comprise. The projected elements include: the extension of the MRT to cover new housing and regional centres, the development of a new light rail system, an expanded ferry service, pedestrianization of parts of the city, and encouraging the use of bicycles as transport as well as for recreational use. Additionally, one of the key elements of the transport plan is to make Singapore more 'pedestrian-friendly'. This may be achieved by pedestrianizing shopping malls, streets or even entire districts as well as by prioritizing access to public transport.

### Shared visions?

The government's goals for the future hinge on the continued realization of economic growth. Singaporeans' own vision for the future, locally referred to as the 'Singapore Dream' also stresses economic success.

For most Singaporeans, the Singapore Dream comprises aspirations for well-paid employment, home ownership, particularly private home ownership, and ownership of a car. This is largely borne out in a 1996 survey of 418 young Singaporeans aged between 21 and 30. A large proportion (44%) of those surveyed cited a good career as the area of their life of most concern to them. This concern was underscored by the fact that 58% of them thought it was not easy to get a good job with a good income in Singapore at the time of the survey and 69% felt that it would be even more difficult five years hence (*The Straits Times*, 27 June 1996).

Apart from a good career with a good income, the Singapore Dream also includes home ownership. The survey reported that 27% of the respondents were already home owners while 90% of the rest planned to buy a home in the short- to medium-term future. This importance placed on home ownership reflects the success of the government's earlier policy of encouraging home ownership so that Singaporeans may have a stake in the country (see Chapter 8). However, this desire to own one's home now takes on a different complexion from the past. Singaporeans now wish to own private property, whether it is condominiums or houses, a dream cherished by many, particularly the younger generation. As indicated in the results of the survey, 25% of the respondents felt it very important to own private property, while 35% felt it quite important to do so. Only 40% felt it to be unimportant. These sentiments were endorsed by the view of 46% of the respondents that the government should exercise more control on private property prices. Among them, however, there were already those who felt that their dream would be extremely difficult, if not impossible to achieve, and have therefore indicated other types of homes that they would strive to purchase (Table 10.1).

Another component of the 'Singapore Dream' is the desire to afford private forms of transportation. However, according to the survey, this was not as crucial among young Singaporeans as owning private property. Slightly more than half of the respondents felt that it was not important to have a car. About one-third felt it was quite important and only 17% thought it was very important. This augurs better for the government, which is hard pressed to allow more cars on the roads in land-scarce Singapore (see Chapter 6). Further cause for some optimism on the government's part derives from the finding that 88% of the respondents felt that the measures introduced to curb car population on the roads are necessary.

Overall then, the government's vision of a healthy economy and growth that benefits all Singaporeans has much in common with Singaporeans' visions of their own lives in Singapore. The Singapore Dream is increasingly predicated on expectations of good jobs and higher salaries, better

**Table 10.1**  Types of homes desired

| House type | % |
| --- | --- |
| HDB 3–4-room flat | 15 |
| HDB 5-room/maisonette | 15 |
| HUDC flat | 9 |
| Private apartment/condominium | 22 |
| Private house | 8 |

Source: The Straits Times, 27 June 1996

housing, the ability to afford private transportation and generally, a better quality of life. Their attitudes however belie a paradox sometimes termed the 'paradox of affluence' (Wong and Ng, 1993, p. 318). This is evident in the fact that alongside their higher expectations for a good life (*vis-à-vis* the older generation), they also have different attitudes and work values. As Wong and Ng (1993, p. 318) point out, affluence 'may reduce the drive to work and sacrifice for the future' and while absolute deprivation may be eliminated, there is a sense of relative deprivation among those who cannot achieve their Singapore Dream.

### Challenges ahead

As the Singapore government proceeds to put in place its plans for continued economic growth and as it attempts to transform the island into its vision of a world class developed city, domestic, regional and global challenges are ahead. These challenges can be summarized into five areas.

First, the government's vision of continued growth and an improved quality of life in Singapore is subject to external conditions. This is reflected, for example, in National Development Minister Lim Hng Kiang's observation that peace and security in the region are paramount, and instability in four potential trouble spots must be anticipated and avoided, namely, India and Pakistan, China and Taiwan, the Korean Peninsula and the Spratly Islands. In his view, Singapore must be prepared to handle any contingencies that might break out in these regions. The key, he suggested, lies in a good diplomatic service, and a strong defence force that provides deterrence.

A second challenge stems from the fact that, with rising expectations, growing discontent against the government has taken shape in dissatisfaction with the high cost of living. This is true for the younger section of the population as we illustrated earlier, and also for those who perceive inequalities in the spread of wealth and who feel that the indices of a high standard of living are increasingly priced out of their reach. One clear indication of such unhappiness is a recent debate over the rising cost of living. In an exercise in cost review, the government's Department of Statistics had reported that the cost of living had increased by 14% from 1988 to 1993, while incomes had risen by 48% during the same period. It was reported that inflation was low, rising by about 2% a year as shown by the Consumer Price Index (*The Straits Times*, 1 July 1996). Two opposition parties, however, claimed that the cost of living had in fact increased by 76% for the same period as household spending had increased by that proportion. They had further suggested that the Department of Statistics had 'massaged' data to arrive at a low inflation rate (*The Straits Times*, 1 July 1996). Despite backing down from some of their claims, it seems that whatever the statistical evidence presented, some Singaporeans will continue to perceive a growing unfairness in society.

For Singaporeans, this concern about the cost of living expresses itself in various ways. One major example is the concern with rising property prices, particularly private property prices, which have kept such housing further and further out of the reach of young Singaporeans aspiring to own their own private property. Part of the reason for such increases in price is speculation, a serious problem particularly in the Singapore context primarily because of the low risks involved – with limited private housing in Singapore, the demand is almost always there, and speculators only stand to gain. Other reasons for the heightened speculation are the popularity of short-term investment here, and the high gains involved. To curb speculation in the private housing market, the government introduced several measures in mid-1996. These measures were designed to stabilize the property market and prevent price inflation. The measures taken are worth detailing and they indicate how serious an issue this has become:

1. enforcing an 80% financing limit on mortgage loans;
2. restricting Singapore dollar loans to foreigners for the purchase of residential properties in Singapore;
3. restricting permanent residents to one Singapore dollar loan each to purchase a residential property for owner-occupation only;
4. disallowing foreigners who are not permanent residents and non-Singapore companies from obtaining Singapore dollar loans to purchase residential properties;
5. taxing as income the gains from selling properties within three years of their purchase;
6. extending the existing stamp duties on sales of completed properties to cover all sales and sub-sales of uncompleted properties; and
7. imposing an additional stamp duty, payable by the seller, on sales of residential properties within three years of purchase.

It is expected that these measures will have a dampening effect on rising private property prices, representing attempts to deal with potential and actual rising discontent with the government as a result of frustrated aspirations.

A third challenge that leaders must face is a more educated population that wishes its voice to be heard on various issues. The government will need to moderate its view that Singapore, in order to survive as a socially cohesive nation, cannot afford to have opposing voices. As the society matures, an enlarged role for civil society must be accepted. The government must acknowledge that even with a very able line-up, it does not have a monopoly on wisdom and can certainly benefit from ideas, evaluations and feedback from well-informed, concerned citizens. While at present, substantial participation is invited from organized groups only for some policies, for example, through parliamentary select committees on pending legislation, this is insufficient and does not satisfactorily allow for all those with genuine concerns and views and substantial contributions to participate in constructive ways. The present stance that non-political groups should steer clear of making political pronouncements may need to be revisited. An enlarged role for civil society can be positive in giving Singaporeans a greater sense of participation and strengthen emotional bonds between people and country. On the other hand, restricting their role can be damaging to the bonding process and can smack of heavy-handedness and authoritarianism, which will not go down well with the electorate.

As Singapore steps up its drive to encourage regionalization, it raises the question of whether some of the best and brightest people will be lost to other countries. Will living and working elsewhere eventually lead to migration and a brain drain? Will higher incomes in Singapore alone be enough for Singaporeans? Will the perceived stresses of living in Singapore, rising costs of living and curbs on individual freedom push able Singaporeans away? The challenge that the government faces is a question of how to 'tie the emotional hearts of Singaporeans through education and the living experience in Singapore' so that while we may lose people for short periods for economic reasons, 'ultimately, their hearts will still belong to Singapore' (Jumabhoy, 1994, p. 6). The challenge is to develop in Singaporeans a sense of emotional bonds and an appreciation of living in Singapore because it is a harmonious, socially gracious and culturally vibrant society. They would thus return if they have studied and/or worked overseas and defend the country when circumstances require it. It is in this light that the population has been exhorted to place emphasis on 'character, culture, community, courtesy and commitment' (George Yeo, quoted in *The Straits Times*, 15 July 1996), rather than the more materialistic five 'C's that have been said to consume Singaporeans' aspirations – condominium, cash, credit card, car and club membership. In striving to create just such a society, the Prime Minister Goh Chok Tong has outlined his challenge to the nation.

In a speech addressing youth leaders in 1996, Prime Minister Goh Chok Tong outlined his vision for Singapore's socio-cultural development whereby the country is characterized by a civic-conscious and gracious people, and an intellectual, cultivated, compassionate and caring society. It is one in which universities will be throbbing with ideas, and where there is a thriving arts scene.

In part, the Prime Minister is prompted by his view that the country still lags far behind in social graciousness. In fact, he is critical of the behaviour of some Singaporeans, whom he described as belonging to the 'stone age'. For example, they littered, parked their cars anywhere they wanted, vandalized library books, rushed for free used text-books, and stole or damaged public flower displays. In providing an explanation for such behaviour, the Senior Minister Lee Kuan Yew suggested that when people go from living in 'a wooden shed with a zinc roof and a hole in the ground for a toilet' to life in modern air-conditioned apartments, they 'sometimes behave as if they are still using a hole in the ground'. He added: 'In mitigation, all I can say is, we are new rich, behaving crudely' (*The Straits Times*, 22 April 1996).

While there is no serious suggestion that economic growth should be halted, the idea that the 'non-tangible aspects of life' need greater priority is gaining wider currency, as expressed in the Prime Minister's view that there is more to being a successful country than having lots of money. Rather, a successful country is one in which its people are able to appreciate the finer things in life and are concerned for one another and public property. As he articulated explicitly in his dialogue with youth:

> I myself do not regard material wealth as a measure of success. It is more than that, it is the value system of society . . . If Singaporeans are rich but crude, rich but selfish, rich but uncaring, the society cannot hold together for many years because we are going to have internal conflict, tension, and very quickly, the whole place will fall apart (*The Straits Times*, 22 April 1996).

Reminding the people that Singapore had achieved 'advanced developing nation' status, he urged: 'Let us now complement our economic achievements with social, cultural and spiritual development' (*The Straits Times*, 22 April 1996). It is these less tangible qualities that will help provide the social 'glue' that will hold Singaporeans together and anchor them in their homeland.

Careful to emphasize that social, cultural and spiritual development should not be at the expense of economic growth because Singapore cannot afford to be poor again, the Prime Minister argued that it was a conscious choice to achieve economic excellence, and to exhort Singaporeans to work hard and increase productivity. It was of course possible to choose a slower pace of life and easily pay more attention to the social, cultural dimensions of life, although that would be at the expense of material well-being. Instead, his vision was to emphasize the non-tangible aspects of life, while not downplaying the importance of economic development at all. He has therefore thrown a challenge to Singaporeans to become a more gracious and cultivated people while keeping up with the pressures that continued economic development exerts.

What makes a gracious society? Social graces, unlike economic growth or productivity, are difficult to measure. The Prime Minister has suggested two markers. First, he has argued that clean public toilets show how concerned Singaporeans are for public property and the needs of others. Secondly, he has advocated the ability to enjoy good music as a metaphor for the finer things in life. He has encouraged schools to form choirs to teach children to sing and enjoy good music. At a larger level, he argued that the arts are important to Singapore because they make for a more thinking, gracious and sophisticated society.

While putting forward these indicators, the Prime Minister has also asked for suggestions as to what other markers could be used to track improvements in social behaviour. Some suggestions include personal development and the degree of voluntarism in society (*The Straits Times*, 31 March 1996). In terms of personal development, possible indications of a cultivated society may be the number of books people read, or buy, or borrow from the library. In terms of voluntarism, the amount of time and money that Singaporeans contribute to helping the less fortunate would be an indicator of how caring Singaporean society was. It is reported in the 1990 census that 10% of Singaporeans regularly volunteer their time to help those less fortunate, though this is only about two-thirds of the time spent in many developed countries. As Abdullah Tarmugi, Minister for Community Development has pointed out, working towards a gracious society is not only about shedding anti-social behaviour, it is also about promoting positive traits such as voluntarism. Articulating the vision of the younger generation of leaders, he says: 'We want to be affluent, yet caring, civilized and cultivated. Getting what we want and caring for others need not be mutually exclusive goals' (*The Straits Times*, 31 March 1996). Singaporeans, as he pointed out, must not be so preoccupied with the pursuit of material wealth that ugly social behaviour emerges and is condoned and accepted. He encouraged greater altruism and voluntarism as two positive traits that Singaporeans ought to cultivate in order to be a more gracious society. This drive to encourage caring and sharing is reinforced in other social campaigns such as the annual Courtesy Campaign, and the initation in 1996 of a 'small kindness movement', encouraging Singaporeans to perform an act of kindness, no matter how small, to people around them, thus providing the 'direct person-to-person interaction which says "I care"', that the Minister for Community Development had spoken about (*The Straits Times*, 31 March 1996).

The Prime Minister has recognized that to change social behaviour and cultural attitudes and inclinations would take time and sustained effort. He has therefore suggested that sustained effort be directed in the next 15 to 20 years in making Singapore a more gracious society. However, it has also been rightly pointed out by another member of the younger leadership, Minister of Information and the Arts, George Yeo, that the key to developing a keener appreciation of your culture and heritage and a more gracious society lies in imbuing the right values in young children. Only then would graciousness and a true artistic sense emerge from within. As he so pointedly articulated,

> If we are gracious, if we excite interest in the arts purely for economic reasons, if we smile in order to sell a few more trinkets to visiting tourists, then we have not succeeded and that is not really what we want. We want whatever graciousness we have, whatever artistic sense we have, to emanate from within. Otherwise it is all superficial (*The Straits Times*, 16 March 1996).

Indeed, the Information and the Arts Minister touches on an issue that has drawn criticism from Singaporeans. As one commentator argued,

> In reality, does knowing the difference between Bach and Beethoven, or having the skills to tickle both the ivories and the erhu [a Chinese musical instrument], make one the embodiment of consideration, tact and humility – in short, the qualities which add up to graciousness? Even taking the view that the more cultured one becomes, the better behaved one will be – at least in public – is it not more difficult to coat the population with this veneer of civility, than to use fines and campaigns to keep the beast in check (*The Straits Times*, 16 March 1996)?

## Conclusion

The government's vision for the 'next lap' therefore is a multi-faceted one. It is a vision of a country with a strong economy, a world-class city that is efficient and beautiful, a government that is capable and clean, and a people who are gracious and cultivated. It is, to use the Prime Minister's words, 'a near ideal home . . . not just the best house, but the best home for Singaporeans', a place that is much better than what there is now (*The Straits Times*, 5 June 1996). It is a place where the citizens feel a bond to their country and a place where the citizens would not dream of migrating elsewhere.

In seeking to achieve this vision, Goh has adopted a personal stance, suggesting that it is a 'personal target' and asserting his desire to motivate all Singaporeans to work with him to achieve the vision. If the survey of young Singaporeans cited above is anything to go by, the Prime Minister has little convincing to do. Despite the high expectations embodied in the Singapore Dream and the realization that these expectations are difficult to fulfil, there is nevertheless in place a generation of young Singaporeans who feel that Singapore is the best place to make a home, all things considered. There will however remain issues that segments of the population wish to have addressed, such as a more consultative style of government, a greater role for civil society and more attention to non-economic aspects of life, such as conservation of both the built and natural heritage. As Singapore stands poised to enter the next millennium and to be recognized as a developed country, key issues are, to use the state's terms, no longer those of survival but of excellence.

# Bibliography

Aldrich, B. C. (1985) 'Habitat Defence in Southeast Asia', *Southeast Asian Journal of Social Science*, **13**, 1–14.

von Alten, F. (1995) *The Role of Government in the Singapore Economy*, Frankfurt: Peter Lang.

Anantaraman, V. (1990) *Singapore Industrial Relations System*, Singapore: McGraw-Hill.

Ang, J. (1987) 'Editorial', *Awareness*, June, **1**, 1.

Anwar, H. (1996) 'Home Alone is not Lonely – a Personal Experience', in *The Ties that Bind: In Search of the Modern Singapore Family*, pp. 142–67, Singapore, AWARE.

Aoki, A. and Tachiki, D. (1992) 'Overseas Japanese Business Operations: The Emerging Role of Regional Headquarters', *Pacific Business and Industries*, **1**, 28–39.

Arber, S. and Ginn, J. (1991) *Gender and Later Life: A Sociological Analysis of Resources and Constraints*, London: Sage.

Ashworth, G. J. and Turbridge, J. E. (1990) *The Tourist-Historic City*, London: Belhaven Press.

Asian Development Bank (1994) *Key Indicators of Developing Asian and Pacific Countries*, Manila: Asian Development Bank.

Bando, S. (1990) 'The Change in Singapore's Economy and Investment Environment', *Pacific Business and Industries*, **1**, 28–32.

Bankoff, G. and Elston, K. (1994) *Environmental Regulation in Malaysia and Singapore*, Asia Paper 2, University of Western Australia Press in association with Asia Research Centre, Nedlands.

Barlyn, S. (1995) 'It's Singapore!', *Fortune*, 13 November, 68–72.

Batam Industrial Development Authority (BIDA) (1991) *Development Data*, Jakarta: Batam Industrial Development Authority.

Bell, D. *et al.* (1995) *Towards Illiberal Democracy in Pacific Asia*, Basingstoke, Hants: Macmillan Press.

Bellett, J. (1969) 'Singapore's Central Area Retail Pattern in Transition', *Journal of Tropical Geography*, **28**, 1–16.

Bellows, T. J. (1970) *The People's Action Party of Singapore: Emergence of a Dominant Party System*, Yale University, Southeast Asia Studies, Monograph 14.

Benjamin, G. (1988) 'The Unseen Presence: A Theory of the Nation-State and its Mystifications', Working Paper 91, Department of Sociology, National University of Singapore, Singapore.

Birch, D. (1993) 'Staging Crisis: Media and Citizenship', in Rodan, G. (ed.), pp. 72–83, *Singapore Changes Guard*, Melbourne: Longman Cheshire.

Blaut, J. M. (1953) 'The Economic Geography of a One-Acre Farm on Singapore Island: A Study in Applied Micro-geography', *Malayan Journal of Tropical Geography*, **1**, 37–48.

Bloodworth, D. (1986) *The Tiger and the Trojan Horse*, Singapore: Times International Press.

Braddell, T. (1861) *Statistics of the British Possessions in the Straits of Malacca*, Pinang: Pinang Gazette Printing Office.

Brody, E. (1990) *Women in the Middle*, New York: Springer-Verlag.

Briffett, C. (1990) *Master Plan for the Conservation of Nature in Singapore*, Singapore: Nature Society of Singapore.

Briffett, C., *et al.* (1996) 'Of Landscape Corridors, Connectors and Conduits', *Landscape East*, **5**, 20–23.

Briffett, C. and Malone-Lee, L. C. (1992) 'The Case for Environmental Impact Assessments in Singapore', in *Proceedings of the 1992 Convention of the Institution of Engineers*, 28–30 May 1992, National University of Singapore, Singapore, 3–24.

Bristow, R. (1992) *The Origins of the Singapore Land-Use Planning System*, Occasional Paper 32, Department of Planning and Landscape, University of Manchester, Manchester.

Bromley, R. D. F. and Jones, G. A. (1995) 'Conservation in Quito: Policies and Progress in the Historic Centre', *Third World Planning Review*, **17**, 41–59.

Brown, D. (1993) 'The Corporatist Management of Ethnicity in Contemporary Singapore', in Rodan, G. (ed.), pp. 16–33, *Singapore Changes Guard*, Melbourne: Longman Cheshire.

Brown, D. (1994) *The State and Ethnic Politics in Southeast Asia*, London: Routledge.

Buckley, C. B. (1984) *An Anecdotal History of Old Times in Singapore*, Singapore: Oxford University Press.

Burton, S. (1993) 'History with a Bottom Line', *Time*, 12 July, 36–37.

Castells, M. *et al.* (1990) *The Shek Kip Mei Syndrome*, London: Pion.

Castells, M. (1992) 'Four Asian Tigers with a Dragon Head: A Comparative Analysis of the State, Economy, and Society in the Asian Pacific Rim', in Appelbaum, R. and Henderson, J. (eds), pp. 33–70, *States and Development in the Asian Pacific Rim*, Newbury Park: Sage.

Chalmers, I. (1992) 'Loosening state control in Singapore: the emergence of local capital as a political force', *Southeast Asian Journal of Social Science*, **20**, 57–84.

Chan, H. C. (1971) *Singapore: The Politics of Survival*, Singapore: Oxford University Press.

Chan, H. C. (1975) 'Politics in an Administrative State: Where has the Politics Gone?', Occasional Paper 11, Department of Political Science, National University of Singapore, Singapore.

Chan, H. C. (1976) *The Dynamics of One Party Dominance: The PAP at the Grassroot*, Singapore: Singapore University Press.

Chan, H. C. (1987) 'Legislature and Legislators' in Quah, J., Chan, H. C. and Seah, C. M. (eds), pp. 71–91, *Government and Politics in Singapore*, Singapore, Oxford University Press.

Chan, H. C. (1987) 'Political Parties', in Quah, J., Chan, H. C. and Seah, C. M. (eds), pp. 146–72, *Government and Politics of Singapore*, Singapore: Oxford University Press.

Chan, H. C. (1989) 'The PAP and the structuring of the political system', in Sandhu, K. S. and Wheatley, P. (eds), pp. 70–89, *Management of Success: The Moulding of Modern Singapore*, Singapore: Institute of Southeast Asian Studies.

Chan, H. C. (1991) 'Political Developments, 1965–1979' in Chew, E. C. T. and Lee, E. (eds), pp. 157–81, *A History of Singapore*, Singapore: Oxford University Press.

Chan, H. C. and Evers, H.-D. (1978) 'National Identity and Nation Building in Singapore', in Chen, P. and Evers, H.-D. (eds), pp. 117–29, *Studies in ASEAN Sociology: Urban Society and Social Change*, Singapore: Chopmen Enterprises.

Chan, H. H. M. (1995) *The Legal System of Singapore*, Singapore: Butterworths.

Chang, T. C. *et al.* (1996) 'Urban Heritage Tourism: The Global–Local Nexus', *Annals of Tourism Research*, **23**, 284–305.

Chang, Y. C. (1970) 'The Squatter Population of Singapore', *Berita Peranchang*, 1.

Cheah, B. K. (1983) *Red Star over Malaya: Resistance and Social Conflict during and after the Japanese Occupation 1941–46*, Singapore: Singapore University Press.

Chen, T. C. (1974) *Fertility Transition in Singapore*, Singapore: Singapore University Press.

Chen, A. J. and Cheung, P. (1988) *The Elderly in Singapore*, Phase III ASEAN Population Project on Socioeconomic Consequences of the Ageing of Population, Singapore Country Report, Institute of Southeast Asian Studies, Singapore.

Cheng, L. K. (1985) *Social Change and the Chinese in Singapore*, Singapore: Singapore University Press.

Cheng, L. K. (1989) 'Post-Independence Population Planning and Social Development in Singapore', *GeoJournal*, **18**, 163–74.

Cheng, L. K. (1995) *Geographic Analysis of the Singapore Population*, Census of Population 1990 Monograph No. 5, Department of Statistics, Singapore.

Cheng, S. H. (1991) 'Economic Change and Industrialisation', in Chew, E. C. T. and Lee, E. (eds), pp. 182–215, *A History of Singapore*, Singapore: Oxford University Press.

Cheong-Chua, K. H. (1995) 'Urban Land-Use Planning in Singapore: Towards a Tropical City of Excellence', in Ooi, G. L. (ed.), pp. 109–28, *Environment and the City: Sharing Singapore's Experiences and Future Challenges*, Singapore: The Institute of Policy Studies/Times Academic Press.

Cherry, G. E. (1988) *Cities and Plans: The Shaping of Urban Britain in the Nineteen and Twentieth Centuries*, London: Edward Arnold.

Cheung, P. (1989) 'Beyond Demographic Transition: Industrialisation and Population Change in Singapore', *Asia-Pacific Population Journal*, **4**, 35–48.

Chew, E. C. T. (1991a) 'The Founding of a British Settlement' in Chew, E. C. T. and Lee, E. (eds), pp. 36–40, *A History of Singapore*, Singapore: Oxford University Press.

Chew, E. C. T. (1991b) 'The Singapore National Identity: Its Historical Evolution' in Chew, E. C. T. and Lee, E. (eds), pp. 357–68, *A History of Singapore*, Singapore: Oxford University Press.

Chew, S. B. and Chew, R. (1995) 'Immigration and Foreign Labour in Singapore', *ASEAN Economic Bulletin*, **12**(2), 191–200.

Chia, L. S. (1989) 'The Port of Singapore', in Sandhu, K. S. and Wheatley, P. (eds), pp. 314–36, *Management of Success: The Moulding of Modern Singapore*, Singapore: Institute of Southeast Asian Studies.

Chia, L. S. and Chionh, Y. H. (1987) 'Singapore', in Chia, L. S. (ed.), pp. 109–68, *Environmental Management in Southeast Asia*, Faculty of Science, National University of Singapore.

Chia, S. Y. (1989) 'The Character and Progress of Industrialisation in Singapore', in Sandhu, K. S. and Wheatley, P. (eds), pp. 250–79, *Management of Success: The Moulding of Modern Singapore*, Singapore: Institute of Southeast Asian Studies.

Chia, S. Y. and Lee, T. Y. (1992) *Subregional Economic Zones: A New Motive Force in the Asia-Pacific Region.* Paper presented at the 20th Pacific Trade and Development Conference, Washington, D.C., 10–12 September.

Chin, A. (1992) 'Land Transport Policy: Reactive to Proactive', in L. Low and M. H. Toh (eds), pp. 90–113, *Public Policies in Singapore*, Singapore: Times Academic Press.

Chng, M. K. *et al.* (1986) *Technology and Skills in Singapore*, Singapore: Institute of Southeast Asian Studies.

Choe, A. F. C. (1975) 'Urban Renewal', in Yeh, S. H. K. (ed.), pp. 97–116, *Public Housing in Singapore: A Multi-Disciplinary Study*, Singapore: Singapore University Press, for Housing and Development Board.

Chou, C. (1995) *Beyond the Empires: Memories Retold*, Singapore: National Heritage Board.

Chua, B. H. (1985) 'Pragmatism of the People's Action Party Government in Singapore', *Southeast Asian Journal of Social Science*, **13**(2), 29–46.

Chua, B. H. (1989) *The Golden Shoe – Building Singapore's Financial District*, Singapore: Urban Redevelopment Authority.

Chua, B. H. (1991) 'Not Depoliticized but Ideologically Successful: The Public Housing Programme in Singapore', *International Journal of Urban and Regional Research*, **15**(1), 24–41.

Chua, B. H. (1995) *Communitarian Ideology and Democracy in Singapore*, London: Routledge.

Chua, B. H. and Kuo, E. K. Y. (1990) 'The Making of a New Nation: Cultural Construction and National Identity in Singapore', Working Paper 104, Department of Sociology, National University of Singapore, Singapore.

Chua, P. C. (1973) *Planning in Singapore: Selected Aspects and Issues*, Singapore: Chopmen Enterprises.

Clammer, J. (1985) *Singapore: Ideology, Society and Culture*, Singapore: Chopman.

Clammer, J. (1991) *The Sociology of Singapore Religion*, Singapore: Chopman.

Clammer, J. (1993) 'Deconstructing Values: The Establishment of a National Ideology and its Implications for Singapore's Political Future', in Rodan, G. (ed.), pp. 34–51, *Singapore Changes Guard*, Melbourne: Longman Cheshire.

Clark, R. *et al.* (1978) 'Economics of Ageing: A Survey', *Journal of Economic Literature*, **16**, 19–37.

Clutterbuck, R. (1984) *Conflict and Violence in Singapore and Malaysia 1945–1983*, Singapore: Graham Brash.

Coates, A. (1987) *The Commerce in Rubber: The First 250 Years*, Oxford: Oxford University Press.

Colless, B. E. (1969) 'The Ancient History of Singapore', *Journal of Southeast Asian History*, **10**, 1–11.

Corey, K. (1991) 'The role of information technology in the planning and development of Singapore', in S. Brunn and T. Leinbach (eds), pp. 217–31, *Collapsing Space and Time: Geographic Aspects of Communication and Information*, London: Harper Collins Academic.

Corlett, R. (1991) 'Vegetation', in Chia, L. S., Rahman, A. and Tay, D. (eds), pp. 155–84, *The Biophysical Environment of Singapore*, Singapore: Singapore University Press.

Corlett, R. (1992) 'The Changing Urban Vegetation', in Gupta, A. and Pitts, J. (eds), pp. 190–214, *Physical Adjustments in a Changing Landscape: The Singapore Story*, Singapore: Singapore University Press.

Cotton, J. (1993) 'Political Innovation in Singapore: The Presidency, the Leadership and the Party', in Rodan, G. (ed.), pp. 3–15, *Singapore Changes Guard*, Melbourne: Longman Cheshire.

Crawfurd, J. (1828) *Journal of an Embassy from the Governor-General of India to the Courts of Siam and Cochin China, etc.*, London: Henry Colburn.

Daly, M. (1984) 'The Revolution in International Capital Markets: Urban Growth and Australian Cities', *Environmental and Planning A*, **16**, 1003–20.

Daniels, P. and Bobe, J. (1993) 'Extending the Boundary of the City of London? The Development of Canary Wharf?', *Environment and Planning A*, **25**, 539–52.

Demaine, H. (1984) 'Furnivall Reconsidered: Plural Societies in South-East Asia in the Post-Colonial Era', in Clarke, C., Ley, D. and Peach, C. (eds), pp. 25–50, *Geography and Ethnic Pluralism*, London: George Allen & Unwin.

Deyo, F. C. (1981) *Dependent Development and Industrial Order: An Asian Case Study*, New York: Praeger.

Dicken, P. (1992) *Global Shift: The Internationalisation of Economic Activity* (second edition), London: Paul Chapman.

Dicken, P. and Kirkpatrick, C. (1991) 'Services-led Development in ASEAN: Transnational Regional Headquarters in Singapore', *The Pacific Review*, **4**(2), 174–84.

Doshi, T. (1988) *Singapore*, Asia Pacific Energy Series, Resource Systems Institute, East-West Center, Honolulu.

Doshi, T. (1989) *Houston of Asia: The Singapore Petroleum Industry*, Institute of Southeast Asian Studies/East-West Resource Systems Institute, Honolulu.

Drakakis-Smith, D. *et al.* (1993) 'Singapore: Reversing the Demographic Transition to Meet Labour Needs', *Scottish Geographical Magazine*, **109**, 152–63.

Drysdale, J. (1984) *Singapore: Struggle for Success*, Singapore: Times Books International.

Dunlop, S. (1881) *Report on the Census of Singapore, 1881*, Singapore: Government Printing Office.

Economic Committee (1986) 'The Singapore Economy: New Directions', *Report of the Economic Committee*, Singapore: Ministry of Trade and Industry.

Economic Development Board (1988) *Gearing Up for an Advanced Role in the Global Economy*, Singapore: EDB.

Economic Development Board (1992) *Economic Development Board Yearbook 1991–92*, Singapore, EDB.

Economic Development Board (1994a) 'The Disk Drive Industry', *EDB Industry Report*, **1**, 2.

Economic Development Board (1994b) 'The Marine Industry', *EDB Industry Report*, **1**, 5.

Economist Intelligence Unit (1990) 'Singapore', *EIU International Tourism Reports*, **2**, 68–91.

Esmara, H. (1975) 'An Economic Survey of Riau', *Bulletin of Indonesian Economic Studies*, **7**(1), 41–57.

Fainstein, S. (1994) *The City Builders: Property, Politics & Planning in London and New York*, Oxford: Blackwell.

Fowler, P. J. (1987) 'The Contemporary Past', in Wagstaff, J. M. (ed.), pp. 173–91, *Landscape and Culture: Geographical and Archaeological Perspectives*, Oxford: Basil Blackwell.

Fraser, D. (1979) *Power and Authority in the Victorian City*, Oxford: Basil Blackwell.

Fraser, J. M. (compiler) (1948) *The Work of the Singapore Improvement Trust, 1927–1947*, Singapore: Singapore Improvement Trust.

Freedman, M. (1965) 'The Chinese in Southeast Asia: A Long View', *Asian Review*, **2**, 24–38.

Friedmann, J. (1986) 'The World City Hypothesis', *Development and Change*, **17**, 69–83.

Frobel, F. *et al.* (1980) *The New International Division of Labour*, Cambridge: Cambridge University Press.

Fujita, K. and Hill, R. (1995) 'Global Toyotaism and Local Development', *International Journal of Urban and Regional Research*, **19**(1), 7–22.

Fukuda, J. (1995) 'The Riau Islands: Developments in Progress', *Nomura Asia Focus*, April/May, 2–9.

Fukushima, K. and Kwan, C. H. (1995) 'Foreign direct investment and regional industrial restructuring in Asia', in Nomura Research Institute and Institute of Southeast Asian Studies (eds), pp. 3–40, *The New Wave of Foreign Direct Investment in Asia*, Singapore: Institute of Southeast Asian Studies.

Gamer, R. (1972) *The Politics of Urban Development in Singapore*, Ithaca: Cornell University Press.

Gayle, D. J. (1986) *The Small Developing State*, Aldershot: Gower.

Gee, K. K. and Chee, M. L. (1982) 'Deliberate Urbanization: The Singapore Experience', in Sit, V. F. S. and Mera, K. (eds), pp. 95–108, *Urbanization and National Development in Asia*, Hong Kong.

Goh, C. T. (1988) 'Our National Ethic', pp. 12–15, *Speeches: A Bimonthly Selection of Ministerial Speeches*, **12**, 5, Singapore: Ministry of Communications and Information.

Goh, K. S. (1956) *Urban Incomes and Housing: A Report of the Social Survey of Singapore, 1953–54*, Singapore: Department of Social Welfare.

Goh, K. S. (1979) *The Goh Report*, Singapore: Ministry of Education.

Gopinathan, S. (1991) 'Education', in Chew, E. C. T. and Lee, E. (eds), pp. 268–87, *A History of Singapore*, Singapore: Oxford University Press.

Grice, K. and Drakakis-Smith, D. (1985) 'The Role of the State in Shaping Development: Two Decades of Growth in Singapore', *Transactions of Institute of British Geographers*, **10**, 347–59.

Grundy-Warr, C. and Perry, M. (1996) 'Growth Triangles, International Economic Integration and the Singapore-Indonesian Border Zone', in Chiba, T., Fukushima, Y., Rumley, D. and Takagi, A. (eds), pp. 185–211, *Global Geopolitical Change and the Asia-Pacific: A Regional Perspective*, London: Avebury.

Guisinger, S. E. (1985) *Investment Incentives and Performance Requirements: Patterns of International Trade, Production and Investment*, New York: Praeger.

Guisinger, S. E. (1986) 'Do Performance Requirements and Incentives Work?', *World Economy*, **9**(1), 79–97.

Hall, C. M. (1994) *Tourism in the Pacific Rim*, Melbourne: Longman Cheshire.

Hallifax, F. J. (1921) 'Municipal Government' in Makepeace, W., Brooke, G. E. and Braddell, R. S. J. (eds), *One Hundred Years of Singapore*, London: John Murray.

Hardy, D. (1988) 'Historical Geography and Heritage Studies', *Area*, **20**, 333–38.

Harris, N. (1986) *The End of the Third World: Newly Industrialising Countries and the Decline of Ideology*, Harmondsworth, Middlesex: Penguin.

Hassan, R. (1977) *Families in Flats*, Singapore: Singapore University Press.

Henderson, J. (1989) *The Globalisation of High Technology Production*, London: Routledge.

Henderson, J. (1993) 'The Role of the State in the Economic Transformation of East Asia', in Dixon, C. and Drakakis-Smith, D. (eds), pp. 85–114, *Economic and Social Development in Pacific Asia*, London: Routledge.

Henderson, J. and Appelbaum, R. (1992) 'Situating the State in the East Asian Development Process', in Appelbaum, R. and Henderson, J. (eds), pp. 1–26, *States and Development in the Asian Pacific Rim*, Newbury Park: Sage.

Hewison, R. (1987) *The Heritage Industry: Britain in a Climate of Decline*, London: Methuen.

Hill, M. and Lian, K. F. (1995) *The Politics of Nation Building and Citizenship in Singapore*, London: Routledge.

Hill, S. (1991) 'Why Quality Circles Failed but Total Quality Management Might Succeed', *British Journal of Industrial Relations*, 294, **4**, 541–68.

Hilton, M. and Manning, S. (1995) 'Conversion of Coastal Habitats in Singapore: Indicators of Unsustainable Development', *Environmental Conservation*, **22**(4), 307–22.

Hirst, P. and Thompson, G. (1996) *Globalization in Question: the International Economy and the Possibilities of Governance*, Cambridge: Polity Press.

Ho, L. Y. (1993/94) 'Layers of Meaning: A Study of Historic Monuments in Singapore', Academic Exercise, Department of Geography, National University of Singapore, Singapore.

Hodder, B. W. (1953) 'Racial Groupings in Singapore', *Malayan Journal of Tropical Geography*, **1**, 25–36.

Holland, E. and Watson, P. (1982) 'Singapore's Area Licence Scheme: Results and Lessons', in Taylor, J. and Williams, D. (eds), pp. 279–300, *Urban Planning Practice in Developing Countries*, Oxford: Pergamon Press.

Huang, S. *et al.* (1995) 'Conserving the Civic and Cultural District: State Policies and Public Opinion', in Yeoh, B. S. A. and Kong, L. (eds), (1995), pp. 24–45, *Portraits of Places: History, Community and Identity in Singapore*, Singapore: Times Editions.

Huff, W. G. (1994) *The Economic Growth of Singapore*, Cambridge: Cambridge University Press.

Hughes, H. (1969) 'Conclusions', in Hughes, H. and You, P.-S. (eds), pp. 177–210, *Foreign Investment and Industrialisation in Singapore*, Canberra: Australian National University.

Hughes, H. (1993) 'An External View', in Low, L., Toh, M. H., Soon, T. W., Tan, K. Y. and Hughes, H. (eds), pp. 1–26, *Challenge and Response, Thirty Years of the Economic Development Board*, Singapore: Times Academic Press.

Hui, J. (1995) 'Environmental Policy and Green Planning', in Ooi, G. L. (ed.), pp. 13–46, *Environment and the City: Sharing Singapore's Experiences and Future Challenges*, Singapore: The Institute of Policy Studies/ Times Academic Press.

Humphrey, J. (1982) 'The Urbanisation of Singapore's Rural Landscape', in MacAndrews, C. and Chia, L. S. (eds), pp. 334–66, *Too Rapid Rural Development: Perceptions and Perspectives from Southeast Asia*, Ohio: Ohio University Press.

International Institute for Management Development/World Economic Forum (IIMD/WEF) 1993. *World Competitiveness 1993*, Davos, Switzerland: World Economic Forum.

Johnstone, B. (1995) 'Culture Clash in Cyberspace', *New Scientist*, 25 March, 38–41.

Jones, D. M. and Brown, D. (1994) 'Singapore and the Myth of the Liberalizing Middle Class', *The Pacific Review*, **7**, 79–87.

Jones, D. M. *et al.* (1995) 'Toward a Model of Illiberal Democracy', in Bell, D., Brown, D., Jayasuriya, K. and Jones, D. M. (eds), pp. 163–67, *Towards Illiberal Democracy in Pacific Asia*, Basingstoke, Hants: Macmillan Press.

Josey, A. (1974) *Lee Kuan Yew: The Struggle for Survival*, Sydney: Angus and Robertson.

Jumabhoy, R. (1994) 'Taking on Wings', *Singapore 1994*, Ministry of Information and the Arts, Singapore, 1–7.

Kamil, Y. *et al.* (1991) 'A Malaysian Perspective', in Lee, R. Y. (ed.), pp. 37–74, *Growth Triangle: The Johor-Singapore-Riau Experience*, Singapore, Institute of Southeast Asian Studies.

Kanai, T. (1993) 'Singapore's New Focus on Regional Business Expansion', *NRI Quarterly*, **2**(3), 18–41.

Kaye, B. (1960) *Upper Nankin Street Singapore: A Sociological Study of Chinese Households Living in a Densely Populated Area*, Singapore: University of Malaya Press.

Keeling, D. (1995) 'Transport and the World City Paradigm', in Knox, P. and Taylor, P. (eds), pp. 115–31, *World Cities in a World System*, Cambridge: Cambridge University Press.

Khublall, N. (1991) *Law of Real Property and Conveyancing*, Singapore: Longman.

Khublall, N. and Yuen, B. (1991) *Development Control and Planning Law in Singapore*, Singapore: Longman.

Kian, K. C. (1988) 'Urban Renewal Planning for City-States: A Case Study of Singapore', PhD Thesis, Department of Urban Design and Planning, University of Washington.

King, A. D. (1985) 'Colonial Cities: Global Pivots of Change', in Ross, R. and Telkamp, G. J. (eds), pp. 7–32, *Colonial Cities: Essays on Urbanism in a Colonial Context*, Dordrecht: Martinus Nijhoff.

Kivell, P. (1993) *Land and the City: Patterns and Processes of Urban Change*, London: Routledge.

Koe, L. C. C. and Aziz, M. A. (1995) 'Environmental Protection Programmes', in Ooi, G. L. (ed.), pp. 200–220, *Environment and the City:*

*Sharing Singapore's Experiences and Future Challenges*, Singapore: The Institute of Policy Studies/Times Academic Press.

Koh, K. L. (1995) 'The Garden City and Beyond: The Legal Framework', in Ooi, G. L. (ed.), pp. 148–70, *Environment and the City: Sharing Singapore's Experiences and Future Challenges*, Singapore: The Institute of Policy Studies/Times Academic Press.

Kong, L. (1993) 'Ideological Hegemony and the Political Symbolism of Religious Buildings in Singapore', *Environment and Planning D: Society and Space*, **11**, 23–45.

Kong, L. (1994) '"Environment" as Social Concern: Democratizing Public Arenas in Singapore?', *Sojourn*, **9**(2), 277–87.

Kong, L. and Yeoh, B. S. A. (1992) 'The Practical Uses of Nature in Urban Singapore', *Commentary*, **10**, 36–44.

Kong, L. and Yeoh, B. S. A. (1994) 'Urban Conservation in Singapore: A Survey of State Policies and Popular Attitudes', *Urban Studies*, **31**, 247–65.

Kong, L. and Yeoh, B. S. A. (1996) 'Social Constructions of Nature in Urban Singapore', *Southeast Asian Studies*, **34**(2), 402–23.

Kumar, S. and Siddique, S. (1994) 'Beyond Economic Reality: New Thoughts on the Growth Triangle', pp. 47–56, *Southeast Asian Affairs 1994*, Singapore: Institute of Southeast Asian Studies.

Kuo, E. (1976) 'A Sociolinguistic Profile', in Hassan, R. (ed.), pp. 134–48, *Singapore: Society in Transition*, Kuala Lumpur: Oxford University Press.

Kuo, E. (1992) 'Confucianism as Political Discourse in Singapore: The Case of an Incomplete Revitalisation Movement', Working Paper 113, Department of Sociology, National University of Singapore, Singapore.

Kwok, K. W. (1993) 'The Problem of "Tradition" in Contemporary Singapore', in Mahizhnan, A. (ed.), pp. 1–24, *Heritage and Contemporary Values*, Singapore: Times Academic Press.

Kwok, K. W. (1996) 'Singapore: Consolidating the New Political Economy', pp. 291–308, *Southeast Asian Affairs 1995*, Singapore: Institute of Southeast Asian Studies.

Lai, A. E. (1995) *Meanings of Multiethnicity: A Case Study of Ethnicity and Ethnic Relations in Singapore*, Kuala Lumpur: Oxford University Press.

Langdale, J. (1985) 'Electronic funds transfer and the internationalisation of banking and finance', *Geoforum*, **16**, 1–13.

Lau, A. (1992) 'The National Past and the Writing of the History of Singapore', in Ban, K. C., Pakir, A. and Tong, C. K. (eds), pp. 46–68, *Imagining Singapore*, Singapore: Times Academic Press.

Lau, K. E. (1994) *Singapore Census of Population 1990: Transport and Geographical Distribution*, Statistical Release 5, Department of Statistics, Singapore.

Lau, T. L. (1992/93) 'Environmental Issues: Singapore Students' Awareness', Academic Exercise, Department of Geography, National University of Singapore, Singapore.

Lebra, J. and Paulson, J. (1980) *Chinese Women in Southeast Asia*, Singapore: Times Books International.

Lee, E. (1989) 'The Colonial Legacy' in Sandhu, K. S. and Wheatley, P. (eds), pp. 3–50, *Management of Success: The Moulding of Modern Singapore*, Singapore: Institute of Southeast Asian Studies.

Lee, E. (1990) *Historic Buildings of Singapore*, Singapore: Preservation of Monuments Board.

Lee, H. L. (1989) 'The National Identity: A Direction and Identity for Singapore', pp. 26–38, *Speeches: A Bimonthly Selection of Ministerial Speeches*, **13**, 1, Singapore: Ministry of Communications and Information.

Lee, H. T. (1991) 'The Conservation Dilemma', *Mirror*, **27**(15), 1–4.

Lee, S. K. (1995) 'Concept of the Garden City', in Ooi, G. L. (ed.), pp. 129–47, *Environment and the City: Sharing Singapore's Experiences and Future Challenges*, Singapore: The Institute of Policy Studies/Times Academic Press.

Lee, S. K. and Chua, S. E. (1992) *More Than A Garden City*, Singapore: Park and Recreation Department.

Lee, S. Y. (1978) 'Business Elites in Singapore', in Chen, P. S. J. and Evers, H. (eds), pp. 38–60, *Studies in ASEAN Sociology: Urban Society and Social Change*, Singapore: Chopman Publishers.

Lee, T. Y. (1991) *Growth Triangle: The Johor-Singapore-Riau Experience*, Singapore: Institute of Southeast Asian Studies.

Lim, C. Y. (1989) 'Social Welfare', in Sandhu, K. S. and Wheatley, P. (eds), pp. 171–200, *Management of Success: The Moulding of Modern Singapore*, Singapore: Institute of Southeast Asian Studies.

Lim, C. Y. and Associates (1988) *Policy Options for Singapore*, Singapore: McGraw-Hill.

Lim, H. S. (1991) 'Features of Japanese Direct Investment and Japanese-Style Management in Singapore', in Yamashita, S. (ed.), pp. 85–117, *Transfer of Japanese Technology and Management to the ASEAN Countries*, Tokyo: University of Tokyo Press.

Lim, I. (1993) 'Clarke Quay: Singapore's First Riverside Festival Village', *Changi*, October, 21–24.

Lim, K. S. (1992) *Vanishing Birds of Singapore*, Singapore: The Nature Society.

Lim, L. and Pang, E. F. (1984) 'Labour Strategies and the High-Tech Challenge', *Euro-Asia Business Review*, **3**(2), 27–31.

Lim, L. Y. *et al.* (1994) *State of the Residential Property Market in Singapore*. Singapore: School of Building & Estate Management, National University of Singapore.

Lim, W. S. W. (1975) *Equity and Urban Environment in the Third World with Special Reference to ASEAN Countries and Singapore*, Singapore: DP Consultant Service.

Lo, T. L. and Quah, E. (1995) 'Management of Non-Hazardous Solid Waste', in Ooi, G. L. (ed.), pp. 221–43, *Environment and the City: Sharing Singapore's Experiences and Future Challenges*, Singapore: The Institute of Policy Studies/Times Academic Press.

Low, L. (1991) *The Political Economy of Privatisation in Singapore*, Singapore, McGraw-Hill.

Low, L. (1993) 'The Economic Development Board', in Low, L., Toh, M. H., Soon, T. W., Tan, K. Y. and Hughes, H. (eds), pp. 61–120, *Challenge and Response Thirty Years of the Economic Development Board*, Singapore: Times Academic Press.

Low, L. and Toh, M. H. (1989) 'The Elected Presidency as a Safeguard for Official Reserves: What is at Stake?', Occasional Paper 1, Times Academic Press/Institute of Policy Studies, Singapore.

Low, L. *et al.* (1993) *Challenge and Response Thirty Years of the Economic Development Board*, Singapore: Times Academic Press.

Malaysian Institute of Economic Research (MIER) (1989) *Johor Economic Plan 1990–2005, Final Report*, Kuala Lumpur: Malaysian Institute of Economic Research.

Marshall, J. in collaboration with Wood, P. *et al.* (1988) *Services and Uneven Development*, Oxford: Oxford University Press.

McGee, T. G. (1972) 'Beach-Heads and Enclaves: The Urban Debate and the Urbanization Process in South-East Asia since 1945', in Yeung, Y. M. and Lo, C. P. (eds), pp. 60–75, *Changing South-East Asian Cities: Readings in Urbanization*, Singapore: Oxford University Press.

Mekani, K. and Stengal, H. G. (1995) 'The Role of NGOs and Near NGOs', in Ooi, G. L. (ed.), pp. 282–303, *Environment and the City: Sharing Singapore's Experiences and Future Challenges*, Singapore: The Institute of Policy Studies/Times Academic Press.

Milton-Smith, J. (1986) 'Japanese Management Overseas: International Business Strategy and the Case of Singapore', in Clegg, S. R., Dunphy, D. C. and Redding, S. G. (eds), pp. 395–412, *The Enterprise and its Management in East Asia*, Centre of Asian Studies, Occasional Papers and Monographs 69, University of Hong Kong, Hong Kong.

Ministry of Finance (1986) *Report of the Property Market Consultative Committee*, Singapore: Ministry of Finance.

Ministry of Finance (1987) *Report of the Public Sector Divestment Committee*, Singapore: Ministry of Finance.

Ministry of Health (1984) *Report of the Committee on the Problems of the Aged*, Singapore: Ministry of Health.

Ministry of Home Affairs (1989) *Report of the Advisory Council on the Aged*, Singapore: Ministry of Home Affairs.

Ministry of National Development (1988) *Town Councils: Participating in Progress*, Singapore: Ministry of National Development.

Ministry of National Development (1989) 'Master plan for agrotech industry', *Productivity Digest*, January, 1–4.

Ministry of Trade and Industry (1991) *Strategic Economic Plan – Towards a Developed Nation*, Singapore: Ministry of Trade and Industry.

Ministry of Trade and Industry (1993) *Report of the Cost Review Committee*, Singapore: Ministry of Trade and Industry.

Mumford, L. (1961) *The City in History: Its Origins, Its Transformations, and Its Prospects*, London: Penguin Books.

National Computer Board (1992) *A Vision of an Intelligent Island: the IT2000 Report*, Singapore: National Computer Board.

Neville, W. (1992) 'Agribusiness in Singapore: A Capital-Intensive Service', *Journal of Rural Studies*, **8**(3), 241–55.

Neville, W. (1993) 'The Impact of Economic Development on Land Functions in Singapore', *Geoforum*, **42**, 143–64.

Ng, C. Y. and Sudo, S. (1991) *Development Trends in the AsiaPacific*, Singapore: Institute of Southeast Asian Studies.

Ng, G. H. (1992) 'Service Directions for Voluntary Welfare Organisations Serving the Elderly', in Yap, M. T. (ed.), *Social Services*, Singapore: Times Academic Press.

Ng, S. K. (1993/94) 'Environmental Consciousness among Women in Singapore', Academic Exercise, Department of Geography, National University of Singapore, Singapore.

Ong, J. H. (1989) 'Community Security', in Sandhu, K. S. and Wheatley, P. (eds), pp. 250–79, *Management of Success: The Moulding of Modern Singapore*, Singapore: Institute of Southeast Asian Studies.

Ong, T. C. (1990) Opening Speech delivered at the People's Action Party Women's Wing Seminar on 'Family and Core Values', 1 July 1990, PUB Auditorium, Singapore.

Ong, T. C. (1992) *Kim Keat and Beyond*, Singapore: Singapore National Printers.

Ooi, G. L. (1990) *Town Councils in Singapore: Self-determination for Public Housing Estates*, Occasional Paper No. 4, Institute of Policy Studies, Singapore.

Ooi, G. L. (1993) 'The Housing and Development Board's Ethnic Integration Policy', in Ooi, G. L., Siddique, S. and Soh, K. C. (eds), pp. 4–24, *The Management of Ethnic Relations in Public Housing Estates*, Singapore: Times Academic Press/The Institute of Policy Studies.

Ooi, G. L. (1995) 'Environmental Management in Singapore', in Taylor, M. (ed.), pp. 129–50, *Environmental Change: Industry, Power and Policy*, Aldershot: Avebury.

Organisation of Economic Cooperation and Development (OECD) (1992) *International Direct Investment: Policies and Trends in the 1980s*, Paris: OECD.

Pannell, Kerr and Forster (1986) *Tourism Development in Singapore*, Singapore: Singapore Tourism Promotion Board.

Parks and Trees Act (1985) *The Statutes of the Republic of Singapore*, Revised Edition, Singapore: Government Printer.

Parsonage, J. (1992) 'Southeast Asia's "Growth Triangle": A Subregional Response to a Global Transformation', *International Journal of Urban and Regional Research*, **16**(2), 307–17.

Pearson, H. F. (1982) 'Lt. Jackson's Plan of Singapore', in Sheppard, M. (ed.), pp. 150–54, *Singapore – 150 years*, Singapore: Times Books International.

Perry, M. (1991) 'The Singapore Growth Triangle: State, Capital and Labour at a New Frontier in the World Economy', *Singapore Journal of Tropical Geography*, **12**(2), 138–51.

Perry, M. (1992) 'Promoting Corporate Control in Singapore', *Regional Studies*, **26**(3), 289–94.

Perry, M. (1994) 'Anatomy of the Singapore International Commodity Exchange', *Singapore Journal of Tropical Geography*, **15**(1), 25–40.

Perry, M. (1995) 'New Corporate Structures, Regional Offices and Singapore's New Economic Directions', *Singapore Journal of Tropical Geography*, **16**(2), 181–97.

Phang, A. B. L. (1990) *The Development of Singapore Law: Historical and Socio-Legal Perspectives*, Singapore: Butterworths.

Phang, S. Y. (1992) *Housing Markets and Urban Transportation: Economic Theory, Econometrics and Policy Analysis for Singapore*, Singapore: McGraw-Hill.

Planning Act (1990) *The Statutes of the Republic of Singapore*, Revised Edition, Singapore: Government Printer.

Powell, R. (1992) 'Urban Renewal and Conservation in a Rapidly Developing Country', *Singapore Institute of Architects Journal*, November/December, 37–41.

PRCAICPHD (Proceedings and Report of the Commission Appointed to Inquire into the Cause of the Present Housing Difficulties in Singapore) (1918), Singapore: Government Printing Office.

Preservation of Monuments Act (1985) *The Statutes of the Republic of Singapore*, Revised Edition, Singapore: Government Printer.

Pugh, C. (1989) 'The Political Economy of Public Housing', in Sandhu, K. S. and Wheatley, P. (eds), pp. 833–59, *Management of Success: The Moulding of Modern Singapore*, Singapore: Institute of Southeast Asian Studies.

Quah, J. (1988) 'Controlled Democracy, Political Stability and PAP Predominance: Government in Singapore', in Langford, J. W. and Brownsey, K. L. (eds), pp. 125–69, *The Changing Shape of Government in the Asia Pacific Region*, Halifax: The Institute for Research on Public Policy.

Quah, J. (1990) *In Search of Singapore's National Values*, Singapore: Times Academic Press/Institute of Policy Studies.

Quah, J. (1994) 'The Political Consequences of Rapid Economic Development in Singapore', in Jong, S. J. (ed.), pp. 397–417, *Development in the Asia Pacific: a Public Policy Perspective*, Berlin: Walter de Gruyter.

Rao, V. V. B. (1990) 'Income Distribution in Singapore: Trends and Issues', *The Singapore Economic Review*, 25(1), 143–60.

Regnier, P. (1991) *Singapore: City-State in Southeast Asia*, London: Hurst & Company.

Rice, R. (1989) 'Riau and Jami: Rapid Growth in Dualistic Natural Resource-Intensive Economies', in Hill, H. (ed.), pp. 125–50, *Unity and Diversity: Regional Economic Development in Indonesia Since 1970*, Singapore: Oxford University Press.

Rigg, J. (1991) *Southeast Asia: A Region in Transition*, London: Unwin Hyman.

Rodan, G. (1985) 'Industrialisation and the Singapore State in the Context of the New International Division of Labour', in Higgott, R. and Robinson, R. (eds), pp. 172–94, *Southeast Asia: Essays in the Political Economy of Structural Change*, London: Routledge.

Rodan, G. (1989) *The Political Economy of Singapore's Industrialisation*, London: MacMillan.

Rodan, G. (1992) 'Singapore's Leadership in Transition: Erosion or Refinement of Authoritarian Rule?', *Bulletin of Concerned Asian Scholars*, **24**, 3–17.

Rodan, G. (1993a) 'Preserving the One-party State in Contemporary Singapore', in Hewison, K., Robinson, R. and Rodan, G. (eds), pp. 77–108, *Southeast Asia in the 1990s: Authoritarianism and Democracy*, Sydney: Allen & Unwin.

Rodan, G. (1993b) 'Reconstructing Divisions of Labour: Singapore's New Regional Emphasis', in Higgott, R., Leaver, R. and Ravenhill, J. (eds), pp. 223–49, *Pacific Economic Relations in the 1990s*, Sydney: Allen & Unwin.

Rodan, G. (1996) 'Class Transformations and Political Tensions in Singapore's Development', in Robinson, R. and Goodman, D. (eds), pp. 19–45, *The New Rich in Asia: Mobile Phones, MacDonalds and Middle Class Revolution*, London: Routledge.

Rodgers, R. and Wong, J. (1996) 'Human Factors in the Transfer of the Japanese Manufacturing System to Singapore', *International Journal of Human Resource Management*, **7**(2), 455–88.

Rodrigue, J. P. (1994) 'Transportation and Territorial Development in the Singapore Extended Metropolitan Region', *Singapore Journal of Tropical Geography*, **15**(1), 138–51.

Roff, W. (1964) 'The Malayo-Muslim World of Singapore at the Close of the Nineteenth Century', *Journal of Asian Studies*, **24**, 76–90.

Rose, D. and Chicoine, N. (1991) 'Access to School Daycare Services: Class, Family, Ethnicity and Space in Montreal's Old and New Inner City', *Geoforum*, **22**(2), 185–201.

Rowe, J. (1965) *Primary Commodities and International Trade*, Cambridge: Cambridge University Press.

Salaff, J. W. (1988) *State and Family in Singapore: Restructuring an Industrial Society*, Ithaca: Cornell University Press.

Sandhu, K. S. (1970) 'Some Aspects of Indian Settlement in Singapore, 1819–1969', *Journal of Southeast Asian History*, **10**, 193–201.

Sassen, S. (1991) *The Global City: New York, London, Tokyo*, Princeton NJ: Princeton University Press.

Savage, V. R. (1991) 'Singapore's Garden City: Reality, Symbol, Ideal', *Solidarity: Special Issue on Architecture and Development in Southeast Asia*, 131–32, 67–75.

Savage, V. R. (1992a), 'Landscape Change: From Kampung to Global City', in Gupta, A. and Pitts, J. (eds), pp. 5–29, *The Physical Environment of Singapore: Adjustments in a Changing Environment*, Singapore: Singapore University Press.

Savage, V. R. (1992b) 'Human-Environmental Relations: Singapore's Environmental Ideology', in Ban, K. C., Pakir, A. and Tong, C. K. (eds), pp. 187–217, *Imagining Singapore*, Singapore: Times Academic Press.

Savage, V. R. and Kong, L. (1993) 'Urban Constraints, Political Imperatives: Environmental "Design" in Singapore', *Landscape and Urban Planning*, **25**, 37–52.

Saw, S. H. (1964) 'The Changing Population Structure of Singapore During 1824–1962', *Malayan Economic Review*, **9**, 90–101.

Saw, S. H. (1969) 'Population Trends in Singapore, 1819–1967', *Journal of Southeast Asian History*, **10**, 36–49.

Saw, S. H. (1980) *Population Control for Zero Growth in Singapore*, Singapore: Oxford University Press.

Scherschel, P. (1991) 'The EDB's Mission for the 1990s', *Singapore Business*, **15**(8), 22–30.

Scott, A. (1987) 'The Semiconductor Industry in Southeast Asia: Organisation, Location and the International Division of Labour', *Regional Studies*, **21**(2), 143–60.

Seah, C. M. (1987) 'Parapolitical Institutions', in Quah, J., Chan, H. C. and Seah, C. M. (eds), pp. 173–94. *Government and Politics of Singapore*, Singapore: Oxford University Press.

Seow, F. (1994) 'To Catch a Tartar: A Dissident in Lee Kuan Yew's Prison', Monograph 42, Yale University Southeast Asia Studies, New Haven, Connecticut.

Shantakumar, G. (1991) 'Workshop Summary', in Yap, M. T. (ed.), pp. 169–71, *Social Services*, Singapore: Times Academic Press.

Sharma, B. and Lan, L. L. (1994) 'Labour Market Flexibilities as HRM Strategies: The Example of Singapore', *Journal of Asian Business*, **10**(1), 61–77.

Sheppard, M. (ed.) (1982), *Singapore – 150 years*, Singapore: Times Books International.

Sieh Lee, M. L. (1988) 'Malaysian Workers in Singapore', *The Singapore Economic Review*, **33**(1), 101–11.

Sim, L. L. and Yu, L. B. (1992) *Private Housing in Singapore*, Singapore: SNP Publishers.

Simon, D. (1984) 'Third World Colonial Cities in Context: Conceptual and Theoretical Approaches with Particular Reference to Africa', *Progress in Human Geography*, **8**, 493–514.

Simpson, W. J. (1907), *Report on the Sanitary Condition of Singapore*, London: Waterlow and Sons.

Singapore Municipality (1923) *Administrative Report of the Singapore Municipality*, Singapore: Government Printing Office.

Singapore Tourist Promotion Board (1995) *Annual Report on Tourism Statistics*, Singapore: STPB.

Soon, T. W. (1993) 'Education and Human Resource Development', in Low, L., Toh, M. H., Soon, T. W., Tan, K. Y. and Hughes, H. (eds), pp. 235–70, *Challenge and Response Thirty Years of the Economic Development Board*, Singapore: Times Academic Press.

Spencer, A. and Chia, L. S. (1985) 'National Policy Towards Cars: Singapore', *Transport Review*, **5**(4), 301–23.

Statham, P. (1989) *The Origins of Australia's Capital Cities*, Cambridge: Cambridge University Press.

Sullivan, G. *et al.* (1992) 'Labour Migration and Policy Formation in a Newly Industrialized Country: A Case Study of Illegal Thai Workers in Singapore', *ASEAN Economic Bulletin*, **9**(1), 66–84.

Sundaram, J. K. (1986) *A Question of Class: Capital, the State and Uneven Development in Malaya*, Singapore: Oxford University Press.

Tai, C. L. (1988) *Housing Policy and High-Rise Living: A Study of Singapore's Public Housing*, Singapore: Chopmen.

Tan, C. H. (1995) *Venturing Overseas: Singapore's External Wing*, Singapore: McGraw-Hill.

Tan, J. H. (1972) 'Urbanization Planning and National Development in Singapore', Paper Presented at the SEADAG Urban Development Seminar on 'Planning for Urbanization within National Development Planning Southeast Asia', 4–7 January 1972, Local Government Center, University of the Philippines, Manila.

Tan, K. Y. (1995) 'Economic Development and the State: Lessons from Singapore', in Fitzgerald, R. (ed.), pp. 55–75, *The State and Economic Development*, London: Frank Cass.

Tan, N. (1991) 'Health and Welfare' in Chew, E. C. T. and Lee, E. (eds), pp. 339–56, *A History of Singapore*, Singapore: Oxford University Press.

Tang, M. and Thant, M. (1994) 'Growth Triangles: Conceptual and Operational Considerations', in Thant, M., Tang, M. and Kakazu, H. (eds), pp. 1–29, *Growth Triangles in Asia*, Hong Kong: Oxford University Press.

Tay Kheng Soon (1991) 'Heritage Conservation: Political and Social Implications: The Case of Singapore', *Singapore Institute of Architects Journal*, March/April, 37–41.

Taylor, M. and Neville, W. (1980) 'The Malleability of Managerial Attitudes: The Case of Singapore's Plastics and Electronics Manufacturers', *Singapore Journal of Tropical Geography*, **1**(1), 55–56.

Teh, C. W. (1975) 'Public Housing in Singapore: An Overview' in Yeh, S. H. K. (ed.), pp. 1–21, *Public Housing in Singapore*, Singapore: Singapore University Press.

Teo, P. (1994a) 'The National Policy on Elderly People in Singapore', *Ageing and Society*, **14**, 405–27.

Teo, P. (1994b) 'Assessing Socio-Cultural Impacts: The Case of Singapore', *Tourism Management*, **15**, 126–36.

Teo, P. and Huang, S. (1995) 'Tourism and Heritage Conservation in Singapore', *Annals of Tourism Research*, **22**, 589–615.

Teo, P. and Yeoh, B. S. A. (1997) 'Remaking Local Heritage for Tourism: Haw Par Villa in Singapore', *Annals of Tourism Research*.

Teo, S. E. (1986) 'New Towns Planning and Development in Singapore', *Third World Planning Review*, **8**, 252–71.

Teo, S. E. (1992) 'Planning Principles in Pre- and Post-Independence Singapore', *Town Planning Review*, **63**(2), 163–85.

Teo, S. E. and Kong, L. (1997) 'Interpreting "Quality" in the 1990s: Public Housing in Singapore', *Urban Studies*.

Teo, S. E. and Savage, V. R. (1991) 'Singapore Landscape: A Historical Overview of Housing Image' in Chew, E. C. T. and Lee, E. (eds), pp. 312–38, *A History of Singapore*, Singapore: Oxford University Press.

Thant, M. *et al.* (1994) *Growth Triangles in Asia*, Hong Kong: Oxford University Press.

Thio, E. (1969) *British Policy in the Malay Peninsula 1880–1910*, Singapore: University of Malaya Press.

Thio, E. (1991) 'The Syonan years. 1942–1945', in Chew, E. C. T. and Lee, E. (eds), pp. 95–114, *A History of Singapore*, Singapore: Oxford University Press.

Thoo, M. L. (1982/83) 'Hawkers in Old Chinatown', Academic Exercise, Department of Geography, National University of Singapore, Singapore.

Todaro, M. (1979) 'Urbanization in Developing Nations: Trends, Prospects and Policies', *Journal of Geography*, **79**, 164–74.

Toh, M. H. and Low, L. (1993) 'Local Enterprise and Investment', in Low, L. *et al.* (eds), pp. 193–234, *Challenge and Response Thirty Years of the Economic Development Board*, Singapore: Times Academic Press.

Tongzon, J. and Ganesalingam, S. (1994) 'An Evaluation of ASEAN Port Performance and Efficiency', *Asian Economic Journal*, **8**(3), 317–30.

Tunbridge, J. E. (1981) 'Conservation Trusts as Geographic Agents: Their Impact upon Landscape, Townscape and Land Use', *Transactions Institute of British Geographers*, **6**, 103–25.

Tunbridge, J. E. (1984) 'Whose Heritage to Conserve? Cross-Cultural Reflections upon Political Dominance and Urban Heritage Conservation', *Canadian Geographer*, **28**, 171–80.

Turnbull, C. M. (1972) *The Straits Settlements 1826–67: Indian Presidency to Crown Colony*, Singapore: Oxford University Press.

Turnbull, C. M. (1977) *A History of Singapore, 1819–1975*, Kuala Lumpur: Oxford University Press.

Turnbull, C. M. (1989) *A History of Singapore 1819–1988*, second edition, Singapore: Oxford University Press.

Tan, C. H. (1995) *Strategic Policies and Business in Singapore*, Singapore: McGraw-Hill.

Thynne, I. (1989) 'The Administrative State in Transition', in Thynne, I. and Ariff, M. (eds), pp. 19–58, *Privatisation: Singapore's Experience in Perspective*, Singapore: Longman.

Turner, I. (1994) *The Singapore Red Data Book: Threatened Plants and Animals of Singapore*, Singapore: Nature Society of Singapore.

UNCTAD (1994) *World Investment Report*, New York: United Nations.

UNCTAD (1995) *World Investment Report*, New York: United Nations.

UNCTC (1991) *World Investment Report*, New York: United Nations.

UNCTC (1992) *World Investment Report*, New York: United Nations.

United Nations Industrial Survey Mission (UNISM) (1961) *A Proposed Industrialization Programme for the State of Singapore*, United Nations Programme of Technical Assistance, New York.

Valencia, M. (1991) *Malaysia and the Law of the Sea: The Foreign Policy Issues, the Options and their Implications*, Kuala Lumpur: Institute of Strategic and International Studies.

Vatikiotis, M. (1991) 'Search for a Hinterland', *Far Eastern Economic Review*, 3 January, 34–37.

Varaprasad, N. (1989) 'Providing Mobility and Accessibility', in Sandhu, K. S. and Wheatley, P. (eds), pp. 420–35, *Management of Success: The Moulding of Modern Singapore*, Singapore: Institute of Southeast Asian Studies.

Vickridge, I. (1992) 'The Metabolism of Singapore: The Disposal of Wastes', in Gupta, A. and Pitts, J. (eds), pp. 389–416, *The Singapore Story: Physical Adjustments in a Changing Landscape*, Singapore: Singapore University Press.

Warren, J. F. (1986) *Rickshaw Coolie: A People's History of Singapore (1880–1941)*, Singapore: Oxford University Press.

Wee, Y. C. (ed.) (1990) 'Singapore? In Harmony with Nature', *Proceedings of the International Conference on Tropical Biodiversity 'In Harmony with Nature'*, 12–16 June 1990, Kuala Lumpur, 528–33.

Wee, Y. C. (ed.) (1992) *Proposed Golf Course at Lower Pierce Reservoir: An Environment Impact Assessment*, Singapore: Nature Society of Singapore.

Wilkinson, B. (1986) 'Human Resources in Singapore's Second Industrial Revolution', *Industrial Relations Journal*, **17**(2), 99–114.

Wilkinson, B. (1994) *Labour and Industry in the Asia-Pacific: Lessons from the Newly-Industrialized Countries*, Berlin: de Gruyter.

Wong, A. K. and Yeh, S. H. K. (1985) *Housing a Nation: 25 Years of Public Housing in Singapore*, Singapore: Maruzen Asia.

Wong, J. and Wong, A. (1989) 'Confucian Values as a Social Framework for Singapore's Economic Development', in Conference on Confucianism and Economic Development in East Asia, Conference Series 13, Taipei: Chung-Hua Institution for Economic Research.

Wong, K. C. *et al.* (1984) *Report of the Tourism Task Force*, Singapore: Ministry of Trade and Industry.

Wong, K. S. (1988) 'What is a Community?', p. 47, *Speeches*, **12**(3), Singapore: Ministry of Communications and Information.

Wong, L. K. (1991a) 'The Strategic Significance of Singapore in Modern History' in Chew, E. C. T. and Lee, E. (eds), pp. 41–65, *A History of Singapore*, Singapore: Oxford University Press.

Wong, L. K. (1991b) 'Commercial Growth Before the Second World War' in Chew, E. C. T. and Lee, E. (eds), pp. 17–35, *A History of Singapore*, Singapore: Oxford University Press.

Wong, P. K. (1995) 'Competing in the Global Electronics Industry: A Comparative Study of the Innovation Networks of Singapore and Taiwan', *Journal of Industry Studies*, **2**(2), 35–61.

Wong, P. K. and Ng, C. Y. (1993) 'Singapore: Coping with a Maturing Economy', *Southeast Asian Affairs 1993*, 313–24.

Wong, P. P. (1992) 'The Newly Reclaimed Land', in Gupta, A. and Pitts, J. (eds), pp. 243–258, *The Singapore Story: Physical Adjustments in a Changing Landscape*, Singapore: Singapore University Press.

World Resources Institute (1986) *World Resources 1995–96*, World Resources Institute, New York.

Wurtzburg, C. E. (1954) *Raffles of the Eastern Isles*, London: Hodder and Stoughton.

Yap, M. T. (1989) 'The Demographic Base', in Sandhu, K. S. and Wheatley, P. (eds), pp. 455–76, *Management of Success: The Moulding of Modern Singapore*, Singapore: Institute of Southeast Asian Studies.

Yeh, S. H. K. (1972) *Homes for the People: A Study of Tenants' Views on Public Housing in Singapore*, Singapore: Housing and Development Board.

Yeh, S. H. K. (1989) 'The Idea of the Garden City', in K. S. Sandhu and P. Wheatley (eds), pp. 813–32, *The Management of Success: The Moulding of Modern Singapore*, Singapore: Institute of Southeast Asian Studies.

Yen, C.-H. (1986) *A Social History of the Chinese in Singapore and Malaya 1800–1911*, Singapore: Oxford University Press.

Yeo, G. (1989) 'Importance of Heritage and Identity', pp. 47–49, *Speeches: A Bimonthly Selection of Ministerial Speeches*, **13**(1), Singapore: Ministry of Communications and Information.

Yeo, K. W. and Lau, A. (1991) 'From Colonialism to Independence, 1945–1965', in Chew, E. C. T. and Lee, E. (eds), pp. 117–53, *A History of Singapore*, Singapore: Oxford University Press.

Yeoh, B. S. A. (1991) 'Municipal Sanitary Surveillance, Asian Resistance and the Control of the Urban Environment in Colonial Singapore', *University of Oxford School of Geography Research Papers*, **47**, 1–53.

Yeoh, B. S. A. (1996) *Contesting Space: Power Relations and the Urban Built Environment in Colonial Singapore*, Kuala Lumpur: Oxford University Press.

Yeoh, B. S. A. and Kong, L. (1994) 'Reading Landscape Meanings: State Constructions and Lived Experiences in Singapore's Chinatown', *Habitat International*, **18**(4), 17–35.

Yeoh, B. S. A. and Kong, L. (1995) 'Place-Making: Collective Representations of Social Life and the Built Environment in Tiong Bahru', in Yeoh, B. S. A. and Kong, L. (eds), pp. 88–115, *Portraits of Places: History, Community and Identity in Singapore*, Singapore: Times Editions.

Yeoh, B. S. A. and Lau, W. P. (1995) 'Historic District, Contemporary Meanings: Urban Conservation and the Creation and Consumption of Landscape Spectacle in Tanjong Pagar', in Yeoh, B. S. A. and Kong, L. (eds), pp. 46–67, *Portraits of Places: History, Community and Identity in Singapore*, Singapore: Times Editions.

Yeoh, B. S. A. and Tan, B. H. (1995) 'The Politics of Space: Changing Discourses on Chinese Burial Grounds in Post-war Singapore', *Journal of Historical Geography*, **21**(2), 184–201.

Yeoh, B. S. A. and Teo, P. (1996) 'From Tiger Balm Gardens to Dragon World: Philanthropy and Profit in the Making of Singapore's First Cultural Theme Park', *Geografiska Annaler* , **78B**(1), 27–42.

Yeung, W.-C. H. (1994) 'Hong Kong Firms in the ASEAN Region: Transnational Corporations and Foreign Direct Investment', *Environment and Planning A*, **26**, 1931–56.

# Index